LEADERS for AMERICA's SCHOOLS

The Report and Papers
of the
National Commission
on Excellence
in Educational Administration

Edited by

DANIEL E. GRIFFITHS

Chairman of the National Commission on
Excellence in Educational Administration

ROBERT T. STOUT

Professor, Arizona State University and
Director of Studies for the National Commission
on Excellence in Educational Administration

PATRICK B. FORSYTH

Executive Director, The University Council for
Educational Administration

McCutchan Publishing Corporation
P.O. Box 774
Berkeley, California 94701

ISBN 0–8211–0616–3

Library of Congress Catalog Card Number 88–60449

.Contents

Contents

Contributors to this Volume

C.M. Achilles, University of Tennessee
Peter Abrams, Northern Illinois University
Terry A. Astuto, University of Virginia
Roland S. Barth, Principals' Center at the Harvard Graduate
    School
James R. Bliss, Rutgers University
William L. Boyd, The Pennsylvania State University
Judith Chapman, Monash University, Australia
David L. Clark, University of Virginia
Virginia Collier, University of Texas
Bruce S. Cooper, Fordham University
Nolan Estes, University of Texas
Chester E. Finn, Peabody College of Vanderbilt University
Patrick B. Forsyth, University Council for Educational
    Administration
William Foster, University of San Diego
Frederick Frank, Northern Illinois University
Richard P. Gousha, Indiana University
Thomas B. Greenfield, Ontario Institute for Studies in
    Education, Canada
William D. Greenfield, Portland State University
Daniel E. Griffiths, New York University
Willis D. Hawley, Peabody College of Vanderbilt University
Barbara Jackson, Fordham University
Alan H. Jones, Indiana University
Frederick D. Levan, Arizona State University
Peter L. LoPresti, Indiana University
Muriel Mackett, Northern Illinois University
Martha M. McCarthy, Indiana University
R.J.S. "Mac" Macpherson, University of New England,
    Australia
Michael Murphy, University of Utah
M. Scott Norton, Arizona State University

Jeri Nowakowski, Northern Illinois University
John B. Peper, Jefferson County Public Schools
Kent D. Peterson, Peabody College of Vanderbilt University
Nancy Pitner, consultant
Paul A. Pohland, The University of New Mexico
Susan Sclafani, University of Texas
Charol Shakeshaft, Hofstra University
Robert T. Stout, Arizona State University
Leonard A. Valverde, University of Texas
Kevin A. Wilson, University of Saskatchewan, Canada

Members of the Commission

Daniel E. Griffiths
  Chairman of the National
  Commission,
  and New York University
Richard L. Andrews, Professor
  University of Washington
Roland Barth, Co-director
  The Principals' Center at
  Harvard
Bill Clinton, Governor
  State of Arkansas
Alonzo Crim, Superintendent
  Altanta Public Schools
Luvern L. Cunningham, Professor
  The Ohio State University
William Dill, President
  Babson College
Robin Farquhar, President
  University of Winnipeg
Barbara L. Jackson, Professor
  Fordham University
Judith Lanier, Dean
  Michigan State University
Martha M. McCarthy, Professor
  Indiana University
Eleanor McMahon,
  Commissioner of Higher
  Education
  State of Rhode Island
Edna May Merson, President
  National Association of
  Elementary School Principals

Richard D. Miller, Executive Director
  American Association of
  School Administrators
Cecil Miskel, Dean
  University of Utah
Robert O'Reilly, President
  National Conference of Professors
  of Educational Administration
Thomas Payzant, Superintendent
  San Diego Public Schools
Nathan Quinones, Chancellor
  New York City Board of
  Education
W. Ann Reynolds, Chancellor
  California State University
Richard A. Rossmiller, Professor
  University of Wisconsin-Madison
John C. Sawhill, Managing Director
  McKinsey & Company
Albert Shanker, President
  American Federation of Teachers
Thomas A. Shannon, Executive
  Director
  National School Boards
  Association
Paula Silver, Professor
  University of Illinois
Robert St. Clair, President
  National Association of
  Secondary School Principals
Max Weiner, Dean
  Fordham University

Donald J. Willower, Professor
  The Pennsylvania State
  University

ix

Staff of the Commission

Robert T. Stout, Director of Studies,
and Arizona State University

Patrick B. Forsyth, Staff Coordinator
and the University Council for
Educational Administration

Joyce K. McGuinness
Special Assistant to the
Commission, and
New York University

Terence A. Weninger
Special Assistant to the
Commission, and
Arizona State University

Acknowledgments

If ever a national project was a cooperative enterprise, the National Commission on Excellence in Educational Administration was it. From the moment of its conception, people and institutions have worked together to provide the resources of time, talent, and money to make the work of the Commission possible.

The need for a Commission was first realized by Professors Michael Murphy, University of Utah, and Richard Rossmiller, University of Wisconsin, Madison. The idea was picked up enthusiastically by the University Council for Educational Administration (UCEA) Executive Committee and the member deans. The UCEA undertook to sponsor and support the Commission. Its director, Patrick Forsyth, has been a tower of strength.

Financial support for the Commission came from:

The Danforth Foundation

The Ford Foundation

The John D. and Catherine T. MacArthur Foundation

University Council for Educational Administration

Association of Colleges and Schools of Education in State Universities and Land Grant Colleges and Affiliated Private Universities

New York University

Arizona State University

The three Commission meetings were subsidized by the Johnson and the Spring Hill Foundations.

The regional meetings were hosted by:

Arizona State University

University of Oregon

Georgia State University

University of Houston

Texas A & M

The Ohio State University

New York Alliance for the Public Schools

The expenses incurred by Commission members attending regional meetings were paid by their organizations or institutions.

A special vote of thanks is due to those who wrote papers to stimulate the thinking of the Commissioners. The paper writers worked without honoraria, as did everyone associated with the Commission.

Many individuals deserve special thanks for their work: Terence Weninger, Arizona State University, must rank high on anyone's list for his diligence and skill in handling the logistics of the Commission; Professor Robert Stout, Arizona State University, contributed greatly to the analysis of a vast amount of data and the general work of the Commission; Ann Lewis, for her work as writer and editor; Joyce McGuinness, New York University; for coordinating the Commission meetings; Professor James Bliss, Rutgers University, for the supply and demand study; Professors Norman Boyan and Laurence Iannaccone, University of California, Santa Barbara, and Professor Charles Achilles, University of Tennessee, for participation in a two-day brainstorming session to kick off the Commission's work; Professor Scott Norton, Arizona State University, for his continuing advice and contributions; and to Melissa Metos for her technical assistance.

The Commission profited from a close association with the National Governors' Conference, which resulted in an exchange of information and mutual participation in meetings.

The Commission could not have functioned without the UCEA office staff: Rita Gnap, Kathleen Groth, Carmen Gomez, and Lynnette Harrell.

And finally, we must thank the almost 1300 people who participated in meetings, wrote papers, critiqued drafts of reports, and gave advice.

Daniel E. Griffiths, Chairman
18 March 1987

Preface

For almost four years, the American public has been listening to various segments of society call for changes in the education system, from preschool to postgraduate study. The proposals began as major modifications of standards for students, then turned to developing a new capacity for accomplishment through restructuring the teaching profession. From these proposals it became obvious that the needed agenda was not merely change, but a revolution in the way schools are organized, in the quality of those who teach, in the expectations for every child who enters the education system, and in the regard given education by all of society.

These things are necessary for the survival of not only the education establishment, but America's way of life and governance, which are buffeted by global economic competition and other forces over which our country has little control. The ability of the United States to continue to strengthen its institutions and provide adequately for its people will depend upon the wise, vigorous investment made in them.

This volume is divided into two sections. The first consists of the recommendations of the National Commission on Excellence in Educational Administration; this section includes notes that document the positions taken. The second section contains the papers that provided the background for the staff and Commission's work.

A revolution in education requires competent, skilled, and visionary leadership. This is the issue addressed in the report by the National Commission on Excellence in Educational Administration. The report adds to the spiral of reform-minded attention directed at students, teachers, college faculty, and school board members, but focuses on those whose professional competence influences all others — the superintendents and principals who lead the schools. Although this report addresses the roles of principals and superintendents, its recommendations apply to other school administrators as well. Revolutions occur because of, not in spite of, leadership.

The twenty-seven-member Commission, composed of leaders within and outside the education profession, was asked by the University Council for Educational Administration to examine the quality of educational leadership in America. The members of the Commission gathered periodically to review and direct the work of the staff. Information and advice were sought from over 1,250 people, primarily during six regional seminars. The day-long seminars were attended by legislators, chief state school officers, school board members, and practicing school teachers, administrators, professors, and graduate students. To broaden its scope, scholarly and creative papers were commissioned from a worldwide group of provocative thinkers. The staff, drawing upon these resources, produced the drafts of this report that eventually led to this vision of what schools must become, how schools will be led, and what policymakers should contribute to preparing and supporting school leadership.

The Commission also learned how much improvement is needed in educational administration. Although important exceptions to the following can be found, research reveals troubling aspects throughout the field, including:

- lack of a definition of good educational leadership
- lack of leader recruitment programs in the schools
- lack of collaboration between school districts and universities
- the discouraging lack of minorities and women in the field
- lack of systematic professional development for school administrators
- lack of quality candidates for preparation programs
- lack of preparation programs relevant to the job demands of school administrators
- lack of sequence, modern content, and clinical experience in preparation programs
- lack of licensure systems that promote excellence
- lack of a national sense of cooperation in preparing school leaders

The sum of the recommendations contained in Section I of this volume will alter dramatically the structure of schools, including the relationship between teachers and administrators, the preparation of educational administrators, and, subsequently, their licensure and their work. Section I aspires to nothing less than the restructuring of a national understanding of the requirements for future educational leadership.

Following the report of the Commission is a section called "Notes," which contains numerous citations intended to support generalizations accepted by the Commission as well as to support its recommendations. The documentation draws on the work of established, knowledgeable scholars and of practitioners.

The second section of this book contains papers commissioned from scholars in the United States, Australia, Canada, and Germany. The original idea was that these papers would present to the Commissioners new ideas and alternatives to current American practice. In large part, this goal was achieved. The papers address the present critique of educational administration, theory and research in educational administration, practice, preparation programs, and international perspectives. No effort was made to present all-inclusive viewpoints or balanced coverage of people and topics. An effort *was* made, however, to present viewpoints that might lead the Commissioners to question deeply held attitudes, opinions, and ideologies. Many of the Commission's recommendations vary markedly from present thought and practice, which suggests the papers may have had the desired effect.

No doubt, some will view these proposals as radical while others will see them as part of a continuum of change already occurring. However seen, they are intended as calls for action. The Commission appeals for an understanding of the seriousness of changes being asked of schools and their leaders. Policymakers and influentials throughout the country are asked for resolve and great urgency in meeting the task of reform in educational administration.

D.E.G.

R.T.S.

P.B.F.

SECTION I

Leaders for America's Schools: The Report of the National Commission on Excellence in Educational Administration

1

A Vision of School Leadership

It is 7:15 A.M. when Lee Jones, the principal of Jefferson School, pulls into the school parking lot, but many cars are there already. The Early Bird activity bus has just unloaded a group of youngsters who head for different parts of the building.

Jones catches up with those bound for Jefferson School's Technology Center, which houses the computers equipped with modems. The students have come early to send queries to a history class in Paris, France. They want help on their research project about the underground resistance in France during World War II. The principal chats with the students as they walk down the hallway and asks to read their project report when it is finished. The French teacher might be able to use it. Leaving coat and briefcase at the office, Jones begins the early rounds of the school. In the Adult Center a primary grade team is consulting with a parent about her son's diagnostic test scores in reading. Before the conference is over, the team and parent will have worked out the child's study plan for school and home and determined how they will communicate about it over the next few weeks. Making coffee in the kitchen area at the Adult Center are a master teacher and student teacher getting ready for a breakfast meeting with a chemist from a nearby laboratory. The chemist, following Jones's speech at a meeting of the local Chemical Society about the goals of Jefferson's science curriculum, has offered to teach a unit on scientific methods to older students.

Documentation for recommendations, general background, and relevant data are found in the notes following this section.

3

In the preschool wing Jones checks with the director of the community-run day-care program about the helper project. The student council has enlisted students to help an hour a day with activities for the little children. The principal and director talk about how to evaluate the experience for young and older students.

Before school begins, Jones has looked in on a retired public accountant tutoring a young Early Bird having trouble with math, and has chatted with a group of adults finishing up a project from their communications class before they head off for work. The class has developed a videotape of the oldest members of their families discussing school in the old days. The tape, to be shown on the school's cable TV system, is their final exam. Jones has also greeted the students as they arrived and confirmed the day's activities.

Jones's morning obligations include:

Reading a report on the evaluation of a program for slower learners at the school and making a list of possible improvements in the program;
Reviewing the objectives of a new literature/writing unit developed by the school language arts team and some faculty of the nearby university;
Attending the first large group lecture of the team and making notes to discuss later with the master teacher;
Scheduling a budget expert to talk with the parents' council and the teachers of the school before they begin planning next year's school budget.

Just before lunch Jones meets with a master teacher and two student teachers who have developed a unit on civic responsibility, the history project that brought the students in early to use the telecommunications system. They discuss resources they might request from their university team.

Based on student complaints that the program for individualized learning in history contains redundant software units, Jones speaks with a master teacher about forming a teacher-student committee to review the integration of video cassettes and computer-programmed instruction. They agree that the committee should examine history's software library for overlap and scope and report necessary changes to the history faculty.

After lunch the principal meets with the ten master teachers (one from each learning area) about how they plan to give their annual assessment report to the school community. They discuss what graphics to ask the central office to develop, how to describe new instructional goals, and when to schedule reports from students on their projects.

It is early afternoon, and Jefferson's administrative intern from State University presents her recommendations for disciplinary action on two students. Jones and the intern also review together a master teacher's evaluation of a student teacher whom they will observe the next day.

Jones places a few phone calls—to parents of the students who are to work off their discipline with a service project at school, to the school council president about plans for the upcoming report card day for the school. Then Jones begins another stint of management-by-walking-around as the students board buses, meets with a teacher to find out how the new literature lecture is tying into writing projects, and meets with the union representative in the building to discuss the awards luncheon for two teachers who have just received national board certification.

But before leaving the building, Jones jots down items from today that will prompt action tomorrow. The teacher who has taken the lead on the new reading program can be assisted by a willing parent; another teacher should be congratulated on his approach to a child having problems; the professional-development center needs to be asked for a computer search on evaluating peer teaching for the day-care director; and a requisition needs to be prepared ordering another phone for the teachers' lounge.

Jones's last act is to prepare notes for a case study on the program for slower learners. Jones is to present the case to other principals at their weekly conference.

The lights will stay on long after Jones leaves. The day-care center is open for several more hours; the Technology Center is waiting for a class of parents and students; and the after-school program, run jointly by the school, recreation, and health departments, has been planned to meet the needs of students and community members through its classes and activities.

Preparing leaders for the schools American society needs is a challenge. While no composite profile can cover all the priorities or describe every nuance of school administration, a day with the principal of Jefferson School illustrates the direction of changes already taking place. Schools must

Demonstrate that they are learning communities. Standards are high and understood by both students and staff. Resources are available to all in the community who need them. The school serves as a partner with the universities in preparing teachers and administrators, and the school staff is caught up in constant professional self-renewal.

Foster collegiality. Teachers and administrators plan, implement, evaluate, and learn together. The administrator becomes a leader and facilitator, matches needs with resources, is aware of when to intervene and when not to, and constantly prepares for the specific needs of the students and staff.

Individualize instruction. Individualization requires appropriate assessment and proper instructional grouping based on sound educational reasons rather than architectural or bureaucratic ones. It also requires the use of resources outside the school to help children with problems that impede learning, sufficient and varied classroom resources, and an investment in teachers that ensures that individualized instruction succeeds.

Encourage involvement. A good school will belong to many constituencies because they will have roles in setting its standards, reviewing its progress, and shaping its programs. Educational professionals will respect parents as a child's first and most important teachers and support them as essential partners in their learning process. Neighbors, business leaders, retired people, and others will be drawn into the learning community. A school administrator must not only create this climate of involvement but also be an advocate for children within the community, acquiring the resources to meet needs.

Recently the public schools' capacity to educate children and young people with diverse needs has been severely questioned. But even if improvements bring education performance up to traditional standards, that would not be sufficient. American society needs an unprecedented level of intellectual leadership. To provide the quality of learning that is demanded, educational leadership must show great resourcefulness and creativity in devising new structures that make full use of teaching talent. There won't be enough excellent teachers; those currently working must be used wisely.

The evolution of reforms over the past years has progressed from cosmetic changes in course requirements to radical restructuring of the school environment. The new roles envisioned for teachers in reports of both the Holmes Group and the Carnegie Forum Task Force on Teaching as a Profession draw education into a broader field of management research from which it has been isolated for too long. At the same time, these reports identify the unique setting of the school workplace, envisioning how teachers could respond to greater autonomy and professionalism. Yet reforms cannot be successful without strong, well-reasoned leadership from principals and superintendents.

The Commission endorses this view of school-based change, fully aware of the awesome and exciting differences this would mean in the responsibilities of school administrators and in the skills they would need. The school community, for example, should have the authority to develop programs; control budgets; hire, promote, and retain staff; and select materials. One result of these changes, of course, would be smaller central-office staffs.

And the superintendency, while retaining its statutory functions, would also change.

As Kelly Jackson, superintendent of education, dresses for the day, the telecommunications system is displaying the morning news. Noting that a report on science education will be released in Washington later in the day, Jackson begins to formulate comments. Reporters are certain to want the superintendent's reactions.

The first stop of the morning is at City Hall to drop off written comments about a proposed new-parent program at the community hospital. Because of concern that the plan provides for no follow-up, Jackson wants it to include a referral service to school programs for parents. The city human services director agrees, and they develop a joint statement for the upcoming city council meeting.

By mid-morning, Jackson has talked with a newspaper reporter and agreed to a television interview about the status of science education in the district's schools. The interview will be based on a report of science achievement scores and the report of a community task force on integrating laboratory techniques into primary grades. Jackson then chairs a small meeting of principals working with the State University team on management skills.

Before leaving to speak to the Business–School Partnership League about the district's long-term plan for achieving excellence, Jackson checks with the district business manager on items for an upcoming school board meeting and makes a note that the facilities planning report has omitted a mandatory public hearing.

The afternoon begins with a call to the school board chairperson on the positive reaction to the luncheon speech. Jackson next mediates a disagreement over supplemental reading materials used in one of the schools. Jackson has read the report from the school faculty, the central-office staff analysis, and a report from the School Librarians' Association that critiqued the materials. The meeting produces a decision; the materials are too advanced and are better used at the next grade level.

Jackson then reviews the applications of finalists for the principal's position at a new high school. The application files contain reports from the assessment center, educational records, observations, written assignments given the applicants, interviews, and reports from a peer-review committee. Also, Jackson's administrative intern has checked the research on qualities desirable in a principal assigned to a newly opened school. The recommendation to the board of education will be well documented.

The superintendent takes a few minutes for exercise in the staff fitness room before going to teach an advanced course on curriculum and instruction at State University.

This description of a day in the life of Kelly Jackson does not demonstrate the whole story of the emerging role of the superintendent of education, but it does lead to several generalizations. Superintendents of education must lead in many ways.

They must symbolize education in the community. Through their public statements they must express, project, and embody the purpose and character of public education.

They must be able academicians with the ability to recognize excellence in teaching, learning, and research. They must know where and when to intervene to strengthen academic structures, choose able principals, and support their search for talented teachers. They must know how to gather data and also how to analyze and use it.

They must exercise the wisest kind of political behavior by resolving the conflicting demands of many constituents and, in turn, gaining their support for education.

They must be highly competent managers who demonstrate their skill in selecting staff, planning for the future, building the budget, and constructing and maintaining the school plant.

Beyond these broad categories of leadership, superintendents act as executive officers of boards of education, deal with the media, administer the union contract (which superintendents have had a responsibility to negotiate), collaborate with all other youth-serving organizations in the community, work well with experts, and are skilled group leaders, speakers, and writers. They must provide the vision that inspires all those touched by the community of learning to do their best.

Today's few superintendents and principals who attain the skill and leadership outlined in the preceding scenarios do so against considerable odds. The preparation is not available, and the concepts of how schools must be organized and led are not widely held.

Implementing the Commission's recommendations will enable quality leadership to flourish.

2

What Public Schools Should Do

The Commission's vision for the public schools requires changes in the way schools actually operate so that teachers will play significant roles in helping to formulate and implement educational policies affecting the instructional program, teachers will have more discretion over classroom decisions, and individual schools will have more control over curricular, personnel, and budget matters within district-wide policy. School districts are urged to broaden the scope of their educational activities, participate in recruitment and preparation of administrators, invest financially in the professional development of administrators, and employ women and ethnic minorities as principals and superintendents.

School boards, superintendents, and principals should develop a specific plan to implement these recommendations. Each has a unique and important role to play: school boards in governance and generating public and financial support for change, and superintendents, principals, and other administrators in providing instructional leadership. Working together, they can bring these recommendations into fruition. The public schools and students they serve will be the beneficiaries.

The Public Schools Should Share Responsibility with Universities and Professional Organizations for the Preparation of Administrators

While the univesities should take major responsibility for preparing educational administrators, public schools and professional organizations offer opportunities and unique perspectives for preparation. Both should be used in joint programs with universities to supervise clinical experiences, to provide faculty for campus classrooms, and to participate in field research. Just as superintendents and principals can be used professionally on university campuses, professors of educational administration could be used in elementary and secondary schools. They might substitute for a regular principal on leave or serve as long-term consultants to the central administration. Professors of educational administration need to keep their own administrative skills up to date and stay attuned to administrative practice.

School Districts Should Design, Operate, and Monitor Professional Development Programs for Administrators

While the state should subsidize the professional development programs for administrators (and teachers), local school districts should develop and monitor such programs. In a later recommendation the Commission calls for individual programs designed to meet the needs of each administrator, perhaps as annual growth plans.

The Public Schools Should Have Programs to Recruit Quality Administrators from Among Their Teachers

There is a large pool of educators with administrator certificates, but schools in the future will need quality leadership that can respond positively to more-sophisticated preparation and job responsibilities. Regrettably, the record is discouraging. Ninety-four career choices are available to those taking the Graduate Record Examination. Prospective school administrators rank fourth from the bottom on their GRE scores; only home economics, physical education, and social work candidates score lower. As the teaching force declines in numbers as well as quality, and more highly motivated teachers opt for career ladder advancements rather than administrative posts, school districts will need to make vigorous efforts to recruit qualified candidates for administration. Assessment centers may be useful in identifying and developing skills of potential school leaders and practicing administrators.

School Districts Should Have Policies That Specifically Identify Promising Candidates for Principalships and Superintendencies Among Women and Ethnic Minorities

In spite of research demonstrating that women make good administrators, the percentage of women principals has declined, and the number of women superintendents has increased only from 1.7 percent to 3 percent since 1970. These conditions prevail despite federal and foundation-supported attempts to encourage women into administration. Yet the pool of potential administrators among women is growing. Currently, about one-half of the graduate students in educational administration are women.

Blacks and Hispanics are underrepresented dramatically in administrative posts, reflecting the declining percentage of blacks entering higher education and the continued low incidence of Hispanic enrollments. Because of the high cost of a college education today and a shrinking student aid program, fewer minorities are choosing education, preferring careers with higher entering salaries.

Through vigorous policies that give recruitment of women and minorities into administrative posts a high priority, superintendents and school boards can affect the entire school system, including students considering career choices.

Practicing Administrators Have an Obligation to Analyze Their Work and Contribute Actively to the Development of Its Clinical Knowledge Base

Practitioners must contribute to the knowledge base in educational administration, capitalizing on the insights they gain from administration. Practitioners are particularly useful in determining new areas for research or areas where research efforts need to be supplemented.

School Districts Should Invite Leadership from All Parts of the Community

All superintendents and principals should, as many now do, reach out to the community and enlist those with leadership ability to aid the schools. A dimension of the superintendent's role is to advocate and sell education, always mobilizing community support.

Secondary Schools Should Encourage Talented Students to Become Teachers and Educational Leaders

If the nation's schools are to have the excellent teachers and administrators they will need in the future, they must be willing to compete for the most competent students from a shrinking cohort of young people. Counselors should have current information about the profession; award and scholarship programs should be used to stimulate interest in education.

3

What Professional Organizations Should Do

The major professional organizations for school administrators have barely begun to tap their potential to improve the profession. Their members—superintendents, central-office personnel, and principals—represent the best constituency to analyze the changes needed in the preparation of administrators and to seek those changes actively. These organizations could have an especially important role in several areas.

The Profession Should Recruit Intellectually Superior and Capable Individuals to Administrator Preparation Programs

Given the number of individuals holding teaching positions, the pool of potential school administrators is quite large. There has been no systematic attempt, however, to recruit the ablest from this pool. The process has been largely one of self-selection. Professional organizations should identify outstanding candidates for school administration and encourage them, through scholarship programs, to undertake preparation. The organizations could also have as a special goal the identification of women and members of minorities who should be enlisted into administrator preparation.

The Profession Should Become Involved Substantively in the Preparation of Educational Administrators, Especially in Planning, Implementing, and Assessing Programs

University programs need the expertise of practicing school administrators to develop the best and most relevant learning experiences. Representatives from professional organizations should be included on both a short-term and long-term basis on university committees that design, deliver, and evaluate administrator preparation programs.

Likewise, the professional associations should select highly qualified members to serve on such committees and provide them with the necessary support to make their contributions as useful as possible.

A National Policy Board on Educational Administration Should Be Established

The board would include representatives from those national organizations with interests in educational administration. The board would have several functions including the following: (1) monitor the implementation of the Commission's recommendations, (2) conduct periodic national reviews of preparation programs for educational administrators and professors, (3) encourage the development of high-quality programs for the preparation of educational administrators, (4) produce white papers on critical national policy issues in education, (5) hold forums for discussions of issues in educational administration, and (6) generally ensure good communication among interest groups about policy concerns.

An early agenda item would be the consideration of the establishment of a national academy or board of professional school administration. Currently there is no forum to recognize those school administrators whose performance and contributions to the profession exceed all standards. The national academy would fill this void and accept for membership candidates who have provided evidence of sustained exemplary performance, who have shared their ideas through presentations and publications, and who have succeeded in rigorous examination. The academy is similar in purpose to the Carnegie Task Force's suggestion for a National Board for Professional Teaching Standards. Certification by the academy would be voluntary. The academy would have direct and beneficial effects on state licensure standards and administrator preparation programs.

4

What Universities Should Do

When Lee Jones was recruited as a potential administrator, the school district also provided support for further study. Given a sabbatical with partial continuing salary, Jones entered the program at State University in a cadre of thirty full-time students. The school district was willing to make such an investment in Jones because of demonstrated leadership as a teacher, good communication skills, and an excellent academic background.

With an undergraduate degree in arts and sciences and a master's degree in teaching, Jones was ready to begin preparation for school leadership. Jones's cohort started with required coursework focused on the study of administration, advanced curriculum design and management, and administrative skills development. Coursework for the cohort took place throughout the campus: in public administration, in business, in arts and sciences, and in education. Because of a particular interest in multicultural education, Jones took some anthropology courses. All members of the cohort completed the required administrative core subjects including law, finance, personnel, facilities planning, and politics of education. In order to develop a historical and cultural perspective of educational administration, the cohort studied the development of educational administration as a profession and the functioning of the educational systems in America and in other countries.

In addition to their coursework, the cohort in school administration was immediately introduced to the skills center and a planned sequence of short-term field experiences carefully supervised by the administration faculty and a group of exceptional practitioners serving the university as clinical professors. Guided and independent practice in the skills center helped students become convincing public speakers and develop other skills important to public-service administrators.

The next sequence in Jones's studies involved the application of administrative studies and research findings to school problems. The cohort first focused on research findings and clinical study within the university setting, using such techniques as meta-analysis and simulation. Later, groups of students working with clinical and research professors engaged in problem-solving activities in actual school environments.

The next part of Jones's preparation was supervised practice, consisting of short- and long-term internships under the direction of research faculty and practitioners who were clinical faculty members at State University.

Singling out a specific type of school setting to specialize in, one with a multicultural student body, Jones entered the final phase of graduate preparation, demonstrating competence. Under the supervision of clinical professors, Jones served as a principal intern, sharing experiences and observations with fellow students and the professors. Evaluation of Jones's progress was based on the practical application of knowledge and skills and a group field-study project in addition to traditional measures of competence and demonstrated abilities at the university's administrative skills center.

Currently, university preparation for educational administration is the same as for researchers and professors. It consists of a traditional university degree program of coursework, periodic examinations, and a thesis. As in other service professions, however, school administrators need more than mastery of a body of knowledge. Their performance depends on the ability to determine the needs of those they serve and to meet those needs with practical skills rooted in an appropriate knowledge base. These unique responsibilities of school administrators lead us to suggest that their university preparation should differ from that of researchers because it must emhasize the application of knowledge and skills in clinical rather than academic situations.

Complex demands on educational leaders require that preparation programs be designed around five strands:

1. The study of administration
2. The study of the technical core of educational administration and the acquisition of vital administrative skills
3. The application of research findings and methods to problems
4. Supervised practice
5. Demonstration of competence

Preparation for professional practice as we envision it rests on some assumptions that thus far have not been characteristic of school administrator preparation. It is assumed that because of its importance, preparation is preservice; that is, no one is allowed to practice before he or she is prepared. Logically, preparation is a sequenced and mentored path from theory to practice. It is also assumed that students will progress through the preparation program as a cohort. The nature of professional work, complicated analyses, and problem solving requires that students learn to value their colleagues and become accustomed to seeking and giving advice and working closely with other professionals. Students in a cohort learn the importance of colleagueship and other professional values. A further assumption is that preparation is accomplished in blocks of full-time study. Preparation to serve in occupations key to our society's health should not be taken lightly. People who choose to serve in critical occupations make personal sacrifices to ensure their preparation and competence and to demonstrate their commitment to serving society as trusted professionals. Although full-time preparation is generally superior, some universities have developed alternatives to full-time preparation that may accomplish many of the same goals. Last, it is assumed that professional preparation is a joint responsibility of the university and the profession. Universities respond to the changing nature of professional work; practitioners take active roles in the mentoring and inducting of new practitioners. To ensure the relevance of preparation, the development of new knowledge, and the improvement of professional practice, the university and the profession work closely to plan, design, and deliver professional preparation.[1]

The Commission's recommendations for universities are directed at different levels: professors, deans, presidents.

TO PROFESSORS

Administrator Preparation Programs Should Be Like Those in Professional Schools that Emphasize Theoretical and Clinical Knowledge, Applied Research, and Supervised Practice

The Commission argues that the logic of professional preparation, which introduces students to theory and research and then gradually guides them into the world of practice, is well-suited for the important work of school administration. The necessarily close working relationship between the university and the world of practice will benefit the quality of research and the quality of administrator preparation. In addition, public interests are served because administrators have studied school administration in the university and have had as mentors a team of research and clinical professors prior to independent practice.

---

[1] Griffiths' paper, "The Preparation of Educational Administrators," in this volume, contains one approach to a program that meets the Commission's guidelines. There could, of course, be others.

The Position of Educational Administration Program Chairperson Should Be One of Leadership with Responsibility for Program Development and Renewal

Too often, program leadership is regarded as temporary and a duty rather than as a challenge. This should change immediately. The creation of a dynamic, effective setting for the study of schools and the preparation of school administrators is not a chance happening. Scholars who reluctantly serve as chairpersons are unlikely to create an exciting setting. Election by peers does not guarantee strong leadership. Program chairpersons should be committed to constantly improving programs, to linking administrator preparation to the best resources on the campus and in the field, and to supporting only high-quality research.

Professors Should Collaborate with Administrators on Reforming Curricula for Administrator Preparation

Administrator preparation programs must undertake the major reforms indicated in this report, and the impetus to do so will have to come from the current faculty. Faculty efforts, however, must be in concert with the best of professional practice if they are to have the necessary relevance and currency.

The Faculty of Administrator Preparation Programs Should Have Varied Academic Backgrounds and Experience

The program faculty should reflect balanced diversity. In addition to traditional specialties such as organizational studies and school finance, a department should have clinical professors, some of whom are professional, practicing administrators. Also, a department will need faculty who can recruit students, evaluate them, develop mentor programs, and supervise internships.

Professional Development Should Be Included in the Performance Reviews of Professors

Changes in preparation programs, a maturing research capacity, and requirements for knowledge relevant to administrative practice make the professional development of professors of educational administration particularly crucial. The development plan should be formalized so that its importance is evident and so that planning can be done to fund aspects of the plan that require external resources.

TO DEANS

Universities Should Fund and Staff Administrator Preparation Programs at a Level that Makes Excellence Possible

In many universities the resources of administrator preparation programs have been reduced to a point where an adequate program is not possible. Almost 40 percent of the departments report a reduction in the number of faculty lines in educational administration during the past ten years, with two faculty members lost for every member added. Many programs no longer employ graduate and research assistants; few have adequate support staff and equipment.

If the programs shift to a clinical approach for the training of administrators, as strongly recommended by the Commission, they will need more resources. It is ludicrous for universities to expect improvement and development of relevant, rigorous clinical preparation without adequate funding.

The Reward Structure for Professors Should Be Changed to Recognize Curriculum Reform, Instructional Innovation, and Other Activities in Addition to Traditional Scholarship

The excellent programs of preparation envisioned by the Commission rely on more than traditional scholarship. Professors must be actively involved in working for school improvements, designing and evaluating school-based research, and recruiting and monitoring highly qualified candidates for school administration.

The Commission acknowledges that consulting with school districts is a legitimate activity of professors. However, this should be considered a part of the assignments of the professors, subject to peer review and university coordination and regulation, with compensation plans developed that are fair to all parties.

Universities Should Provide Scholarships and Other Incentives to Recruit Able Students, Particularly Those from Ethnic Minority Groups

Working with school districts and professional organizations, universities need to identify and recruit highly capable individuals to enter teaching and school administration. Recruitment should begin with information and incentives to high school students.

The desired recruits should demonstrate high intellectual capacity, leadership potential, and the communication skills so necessary for education careers. Universities should use screening and selection procedures that complement other kinds of assessments to identify talented students. They should arrange for subsidized internships, scholarships, and work experience through public and private sponsors to support those recruited for the profession.

TO PRESIDENTS AND ACADEMIC VICE-PRESIDENTS

Universities Unable to Accept the Spirit of Excellence Described in this Report Should Cease Preparing Administrators

There are 505 institutions offering courses in school administration in the United States, but less than 200 have the resources and commitment to provide the excellence called for by the Commission.

The years ahead will be dominated by changes in school demographics, teaching technologies, and the roles of educators. These changes will require school leaders comfortable with creativity, experimentation, and rigorous standards for their programs. Such persons cannot be prepared by mediocre programs in academically weak institutions.

The preparation programs must have intellectual vigor, high standards of practice, and a challenging faculty who are themselves active scholars, valued consultants, and exciting mentors. Departments of educational administration must be vibrant intellectual communities. Unfortunately, surveys indicate that a large percentage of current faculty members consider their programs to be of high quality and see no need for major changes.

Universities must require periodic review by outside experts to evaluate the effectiveness of administrator preparation programs.

The Commission believes a quality program requires a minimum of five full-time faculty members (the median number of educational administration faculty in all administrator preparation programs is 3.9), first-rate instructional materials, sophisticated technologies, and a cohort of highly qualified full-time students.

Because it is concerned about the great number of individuals being prepared and licensed in programs with inadequate resources and little commitment to quality, the Commission recommends that the campuses prepare fewer—better. Like other professional programs, an excellent one in educational administration will have fewer students and require greater university support. Only institutions willing to support such excellence should continue to prepare school leaders.

University leadership needs to join with that of state governors, as expressed in their report, *Time for Results*, "to focus resources and energies on a limited number of excellent administrator preparation programs."

5

What State Policymakers Should Do

Although the schooling of future generations is, in the lofty rhetoric of public discourse, touted as the nation's most critical responsibility, it is difficult to think of another profession in which screening is so poorly executed. Current licensure procedures do a great disservice because they purport to designate individuals particularly suited by character, intelligence, and skill to administer schools; but that claim is indefensible. This is the major issue that state policymakers need to address, but not the only one.

Each State Should Have an Administrative Licensure Board to Establish Standards, Examine Candidates, Issue Licenses, and Have the Authority to Revoke Licenses

The Commission agrees with the Holmes Group and The Carnegie Forum on Education and the Economy that educators must be given more authority and responsibility for teaching and learning. Part of that empowerment requires that administrators take collective responsibility for setting and enforcing standards of admission to the profession as well as for continuing practice. Where they do not already exist, the Commission recommends that each state establish a school administrator licensure board composed of administrators, professors of educational administration, and school board members. The authority of the board would include establishment of standards for licensure, the thorough examination of candidates, the adoption and enforcement of a code of ethics, and the granting and revoking of licenses, based on established procedures.

Licensure Should Depend on the Completion of a State-Approved Program, Demonstration of Knowledge and Skills, Evidence of Performance, Recommendation by the Professional Preparation Program, Adherence to a Professional Code of Ethics and, for Principals, Teaching Experience

The licensure procedure must ensure quality in school leadership. The Commission recommends that applicants for licensure be limited to persons who have completed a state-approved program, passed rigorous written and oral examinations, and shown competence in either simulated or actual work settings.

Although teaching experience should be a prerequisite for the position of principal, it may not be necessary for the superintendency in very large cities. In that case the teaching requirement might be waived in lieu of skills gained from experience in other appropriate settings. All other superintendents should have had teaching experience.

The standards should be written to reflect the skills, knowledge, and attitudes considered desirable for educational administrators, not the numbers of courses taken. Merely accumulating course credits should not be a "back door" entrance to school administration.

The assessments should ascertain that a candidate has good communications skills as well as pedagogy, management, and leadership skills. As a long-term goal, state boards of licensure could cooperate on the development of a common testing program for all states, although authority over licensure should reside with each state licensure board.

Licenses for Educational Administrators Should Have Two Tiers: Entry-Level and Fully Licensed Status

The entry-level license would be granted after completion of a state-approved program, but prior to professional practice. A school administrator would become fully licensed only after documenting successful performance in a full-time administrative position for at least three years.

Temporary or Emergency Licensure Should Not Be Granted

Studies by the Commission and others indicate there are two to three times as many people currently holding school administrator licenses as there are positions. Rather than increase the pool, the objective of state policymakers should be to limit it to only the fully qualified.

A License Should Be Issued for a Specified Time Period. Renewal of the License Should Depend on Successful Performance and Continuing Professional Development

Professional knowledge and skills become dated. This is especially true in education now that sophisticated research techniques are making a major contribution to the field. A few states have attempted to keep education leaders up to date, but the Commission generally is unimpressed with the quality and scope of these programs. Moreover, these programs often are disassociated from professional control and preservice preparation; they lack sequence and continuity.

The Commission recommends that school administration licenses require renewal, to be granted on the basis of successful performance and continuing professional development under the quality control of the state licensure board.

Licenses Should Be Portable from State to State

The Commission makes this recommendation because school boards must have the freedom to recruit exceptional administrators from all regions of the United States.

School Administrators Should Be Able to Transfer Retirement Benefits from State to State

Currently retirement benefits are not portable, which further limits the pool of school administrator candidates available to school districts. The Commission recognizes the difficulties in developing and administering plans to allow portable benefits, but points out this could be a worthwhile undertaking of professional organizations working with states.

States Should Supplement the Cost of Financing Professional Development Programs for Educational Administrators

High-quality programs of professional development for school administrators will be costly, but they are a needed investment. Just as most states have line-item appropriations for teachers' professional development, all states should set aside funding for the continuing education of school administrators. State leadership could enlist the support and involvement of the private sector in helping school administrators keep abreast of the latest knowledge and practices in management and service delivery. Further, the state board of professional school administrator licensure should be responsible for the monitoring and quality control of professional development.

Each State Should Develop Policies for the Recruitment and Placement of Minorities and Women in Administrative Positions

State and federal programs of equal opportunity and affirmative action are not working in educational administration. For example, only 3 percent of the superintendents in the country are female, and the number of female principals has declined in recent years. Yet half of the graduate students in educational administration are female. State policies should vigorously encourage the hiring of qualified females for administrative positions.

The ethnic minority problem is different. There are too few ethnic minority students in higher education, a problem that begins with early education programs that are inadequate for the needs of minorities. States need to address these larger societal problems, then follow up with career counseling, scholarship aid for needy students, and affirmative-action policies to ensure that larger numbers of ethnic minorities will be encouraged to choose educational administration as a career.

6

What Federal Policymakers Should Do

The Commission believes that the federal government should undertake or expand efforts that will produce more capable leadership for the nation's schools. This is a matter of national concern; one that requires national attention and federal support.

The Federal Government Should Continue to Provide Significant Funding for Research in Educational Administration

Educational administration needs an expanding knowledge base developed by competent researchers and incorporating contributions from leadership in other countries and from other professions. The federal government should increase its investment in research applicable to school administration. Further, it should be the catalyst for encouraging public schools, professional organizations, and universities to pool their efforts to improve the profession. The federal government should fund research that helps educational administration draw from the best practices and knowledge of management in the private sector and in relevant professions. Above all, emphasis should be given to support research on the unique role of the education administrator.

The Federal Government Should Fund a Graduate Fellowship Program in Educational Administration for Ethnic Minorities

Federal programs can be both substantive and symbolic. Such a fellowship program not only would benefit individuals and school administration in general but would stimulate state and local efforts to make ethnic minority participation in educational administration a priority.

7

What the Private Sector Should Do

Concurrent with the education-reform proposals of the past few years has been a resurgence of interest by the private sector, especially foundations and business and industry, in public education. Indeed, many forward-looking reform recommendations have come from panels that included representatives of major corporations in this country. The interest is recognizably self-serving; only a much better-educated population will have the skills necessary for this country to compete globally.

One by-product of this renewed involvement has been the realization of how much the private sector can help education. This is less a matter of material contribution, more one of expertise and political leverage. The field of school administration would benefit greatly from continued and increased involvement with the private sector. Likewise, schools have knowledge about new populations and effective practices that the private sector would find useful.

Business, Industry, and the Public Schools Should Exchange Specialized Personnel to Provide Each Other with Relevant, Useful Information

Education personnel have experience in working with a great diversity of populations, those who are entering or will enter the workforce. And business and industry have developed sophisticated and elaborate training programs for their personnel that incorporate contemporary technology. The two sectors should exchange appropriate information and personnel.

Foundations Should Support Research-and-Development Programs Focused on the Clinical Phases of Preparation

Research that addresses the knowledge, skills, attitudes, and values to be gained through clinical experience needs funding sources that allow it to be creative and sustained. This is one of the great contributions foundations make to the education field that generally is unavailable from public sources.

Businesses and Industries Should Provide Technical Assistance to Education Agencies in the Development of Optimum Uses of Technology

The rate of technological change is so rapid that public-sector institutions have difficulty keeping pace. They do not have the expertise nor the funding needed. The private sector, on the other hand, can make this kind of investment and, in many instances, is creating the technology that education should be using. Partnerships focused on this issue alone would contribute greatly, not only to the knowledge base in school administration, but to the effective application of technology by school administrators.

Foundations, Businesses, and Industries Should Provide Fellowships for Ethnic Minorities to Pursue Preparation for School Administration

The Commission believes that the private sector must accept the challenge to increase the number of minorities in educational administration. As noted before, minority representation in higher education is dismally low. The Commission would not want the improvement of school administration through full-time programs of study to discourage even more ethnic minorities from entering the profession.

The private sector must join the public sector in enabling ethnic minorities to participate as fully as others in a renewed, substantively improved field of educational administration.

Business, Industry, and Education Leaders Should Participate Jointly in Management-Training Programs

The demand for greater autonomy in schools springs not from the education sector, but from evolving management practices. Educational administration would not be playing "catch up" if it had been learning, along with the business sector, about successful new organizational practices. Further, joint training arrangements would provide the business sector with more information about school-related issues and possibly stimulate greater collaboration between public school administration and private resources.

Conclusion

This report has presumed much by the wide sweep of its recommendations. Although the focus of the report has been to assert ways in which the preparation of school administrators must be improved, of necessity related themes have been addressed. Preparation of educational administrators cannot be isolated from their identification, recruitment, licensure, employment, and continued professionalization. Nor can it be separated from either the major changes in responsibility of future leaders or the new structures of the schools they will lead. All the parts are linked. The absence of change in one will inhibit change in the others. But a beginning must be made.

Although the proposals call for high levels of expenditure of will and resolve, they are not expensive in monetary terms. The cost of these reforms is insignificant—just a tiny percentage of what is spent in this country on all phases of public schooling. As an investment, the reforms will have tremendous returns.

The proposals have been addressed to policymakers and influentials in a number of segments of the education scene. They have the capacity to do what is asked. They can be persuaded that doing so is right. Unless all of them accept the challenges presented here, the reforms advocated in the major reports, already sparking public debate and commitments, may become a revolution that dies for lack of leadership, taking with it the confidence of the American public and the will of the American society to support an education system that can assure it of a viable future.

Notes

Preface

The national reports of particular interest to the National Commission on Excellence in Educational Administration are:

A nation prepared: Teachers for the 21st century. (1986). New York: Carnegie Forum on Education and the Economy.

Tomorrow's teachers: A report of the Holmes Group. (1986). East Lansing: The Holmes Group, Inc.

Time for results: The governors' 1991 report on education. (1986). Washington, D.C.: National Governors' Association Center for Policy Research and Analysis.

School boards. (1986). Washington, D.C.: The Institute for Educational Leadership.

The Commission is addressing problems drawn from:

Achilles, C. (1984). Forecast: Stormy weather ahead in educational administration. *Issues in Education* 2: 127–35.

Barth, R. (1986). On sheep and goats and school reform. *Phi Delta Kappan* 68: 293–96. Also, this volume, Chapter 15.

Foster, W. (1988). Educational administration: A critical appraisal. This volume, Chapter 9.

Greenfield, T.B. (1988). The decline and fall of science in educational administration. This volume, Chapter 13.

Griffiths, D.E. (1979). Intellectual turmoil in educational administration. *Educational Administration Quarterly* 25(3): 43–65.

Peterson, K.D., and Finn, C.E., Jr. (1985). Principals, superintendents, and the administrator's art. *The Public Interest* 79: 42–62. Also, this volume, Chapter 11.

31

Shakeshaft, C. (1988). Women in educational administration: Implications for train-
ing. This volume, Chapter 29.
Cornett, L. (1985). Rethinking the selection and preparation of school principals.
Paper presented to the National Governors' Association Task Force on School
Leadership and Management, Little Rock.

Perhaps the most complete and scholarly critique of preparation programs is:
Pitner, N. (1987). School administrator preparation: The state of the art. This
volume, Chapter 28.

1. A Vision of Educational Leadership

The following is a list of the background documents and information that figured
into the thinking of the Commission. The societal changes described in the following
note are drawn from:
Kanter, R.M. (1983). *The change masters.* New York: Simon and Schuster.
Education Vital Signs. (1985). Compiled by the editors of *The American School Board
Journal* and *The Executive Educator.*
Griffiths, D.E. (1975). The collapse of consensus. *New York University Education
Quarterly* 7(1): 1–7.
Graubard, S.R. (1980). The end of consensus? [Summer issue]. *Daedalus, The Journal
of the American Academy of Arts and Sciences.*

An array of social, political, technological, and demographic changes makes it
more difficult than ever before for educational leaders to achieve their goal of quality
education for all. Discussions at the regional seminars concentrated on the following
changes:

1. Widespread use of birth control has decreased the number of children and
   changed the proportions of age groups in society, leading to a decline in public
   support for education.
2. The women's movement has sharply reduced education's best source of able
   teachers, with women being placed in positions of leadership in government,
   business, and the professions.
3. Political parties have been weakened through splintering and the multiplica-
   tion of special interest groups, making it difficult, if not impossible, to govern.
4. More than half of all wives are employed outside the home.
5. Over half of all families have two wage earners.
6. The median amount of schooling for all wage earners has moved past one year
   of college.
7. Almost two-thirds of all households have no children.
8. Approximately 20 percent of all families are headed by women with no
   husband present. The annual income for these families is less than one-half
   that of families headed by married couples.
9. Ethnic minorities constitute the majority of school enrollments in twenty-
   three of the twenty-five largest cities.
10. The demand for new teachers exceeds the supply.

An excellent discussion of the role of the principal and an incisive analysis of the concept of the instructional leader is found in:
Greenfield, W.D. (1986). Moral, social, and technical dimensions of the principalship. [Summer issue]. *Peabody Journal of Education.*

The discussion of changes in the division of authority in schools and society draws on:
Chapman, J. (1988). A new conception of the principalship: Decentralization, devolution, and the administration of Australian schools. This volume, Chapter 31.
Murphy, M.J. (1988). Alternatives for educational administration: Lessons from abroad. This volume, Chapter 32.
Soutar, D.H. (1982). An overview of management development in mining and other industries. Paper presented at the American Institute of Mining, Metallurgical, and Petroleum Engineers, Dallas, Texas.
Yankelovich, D., and Immerwahr, J. (1984, January/February). Putting the work ethic to work. *Society*, 58–76.

Descriptions of how principals function and conclusions about the work of principals and superintendents may be found in:
Griffiths, D.E. (1987). Administrative theory. In N. Boyan (Ed.). *The handbook of research on educational administration.* Chicago: Longman, Inc.
Griffiths, D.E. (1966). *The school superintendent.* New York: Center for Applied Research in Education.
Clark, D., and Astuto, T. (1988). Paradoxical choice options in organizations. This volume, Chapter 12.
Hoyle, J.R.; English, F.W.; and Steffy, B.E. (1985). *Skills for successful school leaders.* Arlington, Va.: American Association of School Administrators.
NAESP. (1984). *Standards for quality elementary schools.* Arlington, Va.: National Association of Elementary School Principals.
NAESP. (1986). *Proficiencies for principals.* Arlington, Va.: National Association of Elementary School Principals.

References to school boards and superintendents are detailed in:
School boards. (1986). Washington, D.C.: The Institute for Educational Leadership.

Ideas for restructuring schools and the roles of teachers and administrators are found in:
Time for results: The governors' 1991 report on education. Section devoted to the work of the Task Force on Leadership and Management.
Tomorrow's teachers: A report of the Holmes Group. (1986). East Lansing: The Holmes Group, Inc.
A nation prepared: Teachers for the 21st century. (1986). New York: Carnegie Forum on Education and the Economy.
Patterson, J.L.; Purkey, S.C.; and Parlier, J.V. (1986). *Productive school systems for a nonrational world.* Washington, D.C.: Association for Supervision and Curriculum Development.

Crim, Shanker, and Greene. (1986, December). On the education of a teacher. *Innovator* 18(3).
Shanker, A. (1987, January 18). Management creates sense of purpose. *Where We Stand, New York Times.*

The Edmonton School District in Alberta, Canada, has, very probably, gone farther with school-site administration than other districts in North America. The school budget is determined jointly by teachers, administrators, community people, and students. Decisions are made regarding the number of teachers needed in the school as well as how much should be spent for supplies and equipment. In 1986–87 an experiment was conducted in which local decisions were made concerning how much consultant time will be purchased from central administration.

What Public Schools Should Do
Ideas on the role of public schools in the preparation of school administrators are found in:
Peterson, K.D., and Finn, C.E., Jr. (1985). Principals, superintendents, and the administrator's art. *The Public Interest* 79: 42–62. Also, this volume, Chapter 11.

Recruitment of administrators was discussed in:
Goodlad, J.L. (1984). *A place called school: Prospects for the future.* New York: McGraw-Hill.
Frasher and Frasher reviewed seven studies in which the performance of men and women school administrators were compared. They found either no sex differences or women received higher ratings.
Frasher, J.M., and Frasher, R.S. (1979). Educational administration: A feminine profession. *Educational Administration Quarterly* 15(2): 1–13.

Representation of blacks in school administration is discussed in:
Jackson, B.L. (1988). Education from a black perspective with implications for administrator preparation programs. This volume, Chapter 23.

The factors that should be taken into account in the selection of administrators are discussed in:
Miskel, C. (1983). The practicing administrator: Dilemmas, knowledge, and strategies for improving leadership. In W.N. Hird (Ed.), *The practicing administrator: Dilemmas and strategies*, pp. 1–21.

The importance of assessment is discussed in:
NASSB Bulletin 70 (486): 1–58.

A good example of a program designed to introduce ethnic minority secondary school students to careers in education is the Mentor in Education program. For information write to:
> Barbara Probst
> New York Alliance for the Public Schools
> 32 Washington Place
> New York City, New York 10003

What Universities Should Do

The main sources of criticisms of the study and practice of educational administration and the preparation of educational administrators are:

Achilles, C. (1984). Forecast: Stormy weather ahead in educational administration. *Issues in Education* 2: 127–135.

Foster, W. (1988). Educational administration: A critical appraisal. This volume, Chapter 9.

Greenfield, T.B. (1988). The decline and fall of science in educational administration. This volume, Chapter 13.

Griffiths, D.E. (1979). Intellectual turmoil in educational administration. *Educational Administration Quarterly* 25(3): 43–65.

Peterson, K.D., and Finn, C.E., Jr. (1985). Principals, superintendents, and the administrator's art. *The Public Interest* 79: 42–62. Also, this volume, Chapter 11.

Shakeshaft, C. (1988). Women in educational administration: Implications for training. This volume, Chapter 29.

Cornett, L. (1985). Rethinking the selection and preparation of school principals. Paper presented to the National Governors' Association Task Force on School Leadership and Management, Little Rock.

Discussions of alternatives to current approaches to preparing educational administrators are found in:

Pohland, P.A. (1988). The return of the Mayflower: British alternatives to American Practice. This volume, Chapter 33.

Murphy, M. (1988). Alternatives for educational administration: Lessons from abroad. This volume, Chapter 32.

Other articles on the preparation of educational administrators include:

Daniel E. Griffiths. (1988). The professorship revisited. This volume, Chapter 21.

Hawley, W.D. (1988). Universities and the improvement of school management. This volume, Chapter 10.

Mackett, M.; Frank, F.; Abrams, P.; and Nowakowski, J. Computers and educational excellence: Policy implications for educational administration. This volume, Chapter 19.

Valverde, L.A.; Estes, J.; Collier, V.; and Selafani, S. An exemplary preparation program: The cooperative superintendency program of the University of Texas. This volume, Chapter 30.

Blodgett, B. (1986). Casing the world economy. *TWA Ambassador*, March: 41–45.

Cooper, B.S., and Boyd, W.L. (1987). The evolution of training for school administrators. In J. Murphy and P. Hallinger, Eds. *Approaches to administrative training in education*. Albany, N.Y.: SUNY Press.

A paper with a suggested program and comprehensive bibliography is:

Achilles, C.M. (1988). Unlocking some mysteries of administration and administrator preparation: A reflective prospect. This volume, Chapter 8.

How the preparation program should reflect the research on gender difference is discussed in:

Shakeshaft, C. (1988). Women in educational administration: Implications for training. This volume, Chapter 29.

The perspective on the education of blacks for educational administration is given
by:
Jackson, B.L. (1988). Education from the black perspective with implications for
administrator preparation programs. This volume, Chapter 23.

The generalizations concerning the test scores of people entering teaching and
educational administration were drawn from three sources:
Combined SAT scores for college-bound high school seniors by intended field of
study. (1986). *A nation prepared: Teachers for the 21st century*. New York: Carnegie
Forum on Education and the Economy.
Griffiths, D.E., et al. (1986). *Teacher education in Massachusetts: The public sector*. Boston:
Board of Regents for Higher Education.
Guide to the use of the Graduate Record Exam. (1985). Princeton: Educational Testing
Service, 23.

A survey of certain UCEA doctoral programs is reported in:
Norton, M.S., and Levan, F.D. (1987). Doctoral studies of students in educational
administration programs in UCEA member institutions. *Educational Considerations*,
14: 21–24.

Professional doctorates are discussed in:
Eells, W.C. (1963). *Degrees in higher education*. Washington, D.C.: The Center for
Applied Research in Education, pp. 45–52.

Ideas for the professional model of preparation were drawn from:
Schein, E.H. (1972). *Professional education*. New York: McGraw-Hill.

New theories of administration and organization are presented in:
Burrell, G., and Morgan, G. (1979). Sociological paradigms and organizational
analysis. London: Heinemann.
Griffiths, D.E. (1987). Administrative theory. In N. Boyan (Ed.), *The handbook of
research on educational administration*. Chicago: Longman, Inc.

An example of the kind of research emerging from new theoretical approaches is:
MacPherson, R.J.S. (1987). Talking up and justifying organisation: the creation and
control of knowledge about being organised. *Studies in educational administration*.
Armidale, NSW, Australia: Commonwealth Council for Educational Administration. Also, this volume, Chapter 14.
Peterson's guide to graduate study. (1986). Book 1 lists 505 institutions offering graduate
courses in educational administration. They are distributed as follows:
216—offer only master's degrees
484—offer the master's plus other degrees
173—offer doctorates (three offer only the doctorate: Claremont, Gonzaga, and
International Graduate School)

21—offer only the certificate of advanced study or educational specialist certificate.

The discussion of supply and demand for educational administrators is drawn from:
Bliss, J.R. Public school administrators in the United States: Analysis of supply and demand. This volume, Chapter 16.

One of the few papers on the clinical education of school administrators in existence is:
Peper, J.B. Clinical education for school superintendents and principals: The missing link. This volume, Chapter 27.

What State Policymakers Should Do

During the information-gathering phase of the Commission's work, little enthusiasm was generated for this topic even though issuing licenses to people who meet certain standards is an important state function. In fact, the licensing programs enacted by states and implemented by colleges and universities were thought to constitute a national scandal. School administration licenses guarantee little except that the individual has collected graduate coursework over a period of years. Although the schooling of future generations is, in the current rhetoric of public discourse, touted as our nation's most critical responsibility, it is difficult to think of another profession in which screening is so poorly executed.
Gousha, R.; LoPresti, P.L.; and Jones, A.H. Report on first annual survey of certification and employment standards for educational administrators. This volume, Chapter 17.
Bliss, J.R. Public school administrators in the United States: Analysis of supply and demand. This volume, Chapter 16.

Commission members and the staff heard much criticism of professional development programs. Both content and process were said to be inadequate to the needs of contemporary and future administrators. Among the most serious criticisms were that the principles of adult learning were violated routinely, programs were discontinuous, fragmented, and of low quality; they required participants to be passive and were unconnected to the issues administrators were engaged in resolving. In addition, content was criticized as impractical, not reflective of best practices, and, often enough, simply erroneous. Two papers of interest are:
Roland, Barth. (1986). On sheep and goats and school reform. *Phi Delta Kappan* 68; 293–96. Also, this volume, Chapter 15.
Many good models of professional development exist in the United States. Mentoring is occurring within and across school districts. The Peer Assisted Leadership (PAL) program of the Far West Laboratory for Educational Research and Development is one example.
State and university-sponsored academies for principals and superintendents exist in more than one-half the states. The professional associations sponsor many excellent programs including academies, conferences, and assessment centers.

The principles of adult education that should guide professional development are well defined. School administrators want their learning experiences to be of high quality. They expect to be consulted about content and about the manner in which it is presented. They are active learners who learn from each other and from many other sources. They expect to learn both technical skills and broader conceptions and applications. They expect that programs will be efficiently presented in a well-integrated manner. Participants also expect that they will be given ample opportunity to practice skills and to receive clear, specific feedback on their performance. Finally, participants expect to see a connection between experiences and both their own long-range needs and the long-range plans of their employers.

Roland Barth. (1985, April). Principal centered professional development. Presented at the annual meeting of the American Educational Research Association. Chicago, IL.

SECTION II

Critique of Educational Administration

The authors of the papers in this section offer critiques of current administrative practice and of current preparation for practice. In each paper, alternative, and presumably better, preparation programs are discussed. The authors generate alternatives from different conceptual considerations of educational administration.

The paper by C.M. Achilles is an elaborated description of necessary changes in preparation. The conceptual base of the paper is in the notion of "profession": "Programs must accommodate the notion of *profession*." He distinguishes preparation for craftsmen, technicians, academicians, and professionals, each of which has different responses to questions of content, preparation modalities, and the purposes for which preparation is offered. From this framework, Achilles derives a preparation program for educational administrators tailored to professionals' subsequent practice in educational organizations.

William Foster's work rests on the argument that positivist theory in educational administration has outlived its usefulness. A new paradigm must be used (he favors critical theory) to investigate administrative work and to ground the preparation of administrators. In Foster's view administrative work is moral work, and future administrators of education must attend to questions of equity and democracy. Consequently, administrator preparation programs that are justified in terms of the assumptions of positivist administrative theory are, in fact, unjustifiable. Given the required new directions of social science theory and administrative work, these programs must be altered. Foster's major reform would be that "Programs in educational administration must begin to identify themselves as major avenues for the moral and intellectual education of aspiring administrators." In a parallel way Foster calls for the reformation of administrative work as a moral and human enterprise, with particular attention given to the work of principals.

Willis Hawley's criticisms come from a different conceptual perspective. His argument is that current reforms in teaching must be accompanied by a different view of educational administration. He argues that "the quality of administrative support and organizational structures teachers experience define the upward boundaries of teacher effectiveness." Consequently, his proposals for reform in administrative work address what he believes are the components of good teaching: instructional leadership, problem solving, evaluation, and the like.

Hawley's criticisms of university programs to prepare administrators range widely. Among them are that university faculty are only marginally more knowledgeable than the students, that faculty are not research oriented, that the Ph.D. and Ed.D. are indistinguishable and a "schizophrenic mix of doctoral study in the disciplines and practice-oriented application," that faculty have too many students, and that the profession lacks self-esteem. Hawley then challenges university programs to alter in ways that will foster the preparation of administrators. Many of his recommendations parallel those of the Commission, including his recommendations to state policymakers. Hawley's recommendations are straightforward and feasible within current political contexts.

Kent Peterson and Chester Finn begin their critique from the same point as Hawley: the centrality of the principal as instructional leader. Current preparation programs, they argue, simply do not teach the right things in the right ways. Two overall problems must be overcome: the lack of high standards of quality and the failure to develop a uniquely professional degree program. With high standards and a unique professional degree program, the right content can be offered. Such content will include that proposed by the American Association of School Administrators in 1982 and matters of educational values.

Peterson and Finn also discuss necessary changes in licensure and employment practices. Arguing that reform is necesssary in education, they ask on what should the fulcrum of reform stand. Their answer is that "administrators make a serviceable fulcrum and the universities that train them supply a promising if today somewhat shaky place on which to stand."

Although each author in this section rests criticisms on somewhat different conceptual grounds, they are virtually unanimous in their suggestions for reform. Standards must be raised, content must be changed to reflect the professional needs of administrators of educational organizations, values and ethics must be attended to, collaboration must be accomplished, and university faculty themselves must take an aggressive stand toward self-reform.

8

Unlocking Some Mysteries of Administration and Administrator Preparation: A Reflective Prospect

C.M. Achilles

> He has considerable gifts. He possesses two out of the three qualities necessary for the ideal detective. He has the power of observation and that of deduction. He is only wanting in knowledge, and that may come in time.
>
> Sherlock Holmes, "The Sign of Four"

Like the young French detective whom Holmes is admiring—albeit with faint praise—many of our best administrators and administrator preparation "programs" have two out of three elements necessary for the ideal. Lesser ones may, like the Ancient Mariner, "stoppeth one of three." In fact, some critics have asserted that administrator preparation programs are not really programs at all (Achilles, 1985, 1984a,b; Hawley, 1988; Peterson and Finn, 1985; Pitner, 1982; and numerous other sources).[1] I propose in this paper that administration has at least three elements: the why, the what, and the how. The complete administrator knows *what* to do, *how* to do it, and most important of all, *why* an action is appropriate. A complete preparation

---

[1] In addition to the list of references is a list of additional readings that highlight key elements of this paper.

41

program will address all three elements. But administration should be reaching that maturity where all three program elements are the rule, not the exception, and the construct for the preparation programs will admit new elements as they emerge.

Apologia

Administration's amorphousness and diversity constitute both its vulnerable underbelly and its strength and appeal. Whereas several national reports have explicitly focused public attention on concerns for education, criticisms of administration, although widespread, have been less direct and concentrated. Until now. The issues, however, still seem unsettled and uncrystallized. Is the *real* problem administrator preparation? Preservice training? In-service training? Program *content* or *structure*? Administration in general? Administrators? Higher education? All of the above? One task, it seems, is to define clearly some problems at the heart of the issue.

There has been no paucity of attention to educational administration. Since 1980 several comprehensive compilations describing problems in administration have illuminated issues and needs and have offered solutions. Two issues of *Educational Administration Quarterly* address this topic (Hoy, 1982a; Fogarty, 1983) and Pitner (1982) prepared a state-of-the-art paper for the Center for Educational Policy and Management (CEPM). The Fogarty, Hoy, and Pitner pieces provide scholarly, often polite, insight and background; other pieces have been less reverent in their criticisms. In an issue of *The Public Interest*, Peterson and Finn (1985) identified and discussed numerous problems in educational administration, especially those related to higher education. Among their litany of concerns were quality, preparation, certification, lack of rigor, selection, "Mickey Mouse" programs, lack of standards, poorly planned and designed programs, etc., etc. In *Issues in Education* II (Achilles, 1984b) projected increasing concern for the pool of potential administrators as the quality of the teaching force declines if we continue to limit entry into administration to those who have teaching experience. Papers presented at the National Conference of Professors of Educational Administration (NCPEA) and the American Educational Research Association (AERA) have reported research and offered solutions (for example, Cooper, 1984; Miklos, 1984; Reed, 1984). Cornett (1983) described the preparation and selection of school principals; Baltzell and Dentler (1983) studied the selection of American school principals. But when have scholarly papers had much influence without political clout, attendant reward structures, or widespread public indignation?

Recommendation E, "Leadership and Federal Support," of *A Nation At Risk* addresses leadership in American schools. This recommendation of the National Commission on Excellence in Education (1983) says, in part:

"Principals and superintendents must play a crucial leadership role in developing school and community support for the reforms we propose, and school boards must provide them with the professional development and other support required to carry out their leadership role effectively. . . . school boards must consciously develop leadership skills at the school and district levels if the reforms we propose are to be achieved" (p. 32). The commission notes that the federal government must provide "student financial assistance and research and graduate training" to help attain this leadership goal.

Cornett's (1983) report for the Southern Regional Education Board (SREB) calls for improving preparation programs through research, theory, practicality, knowledge, and some clear cooperation. "Colleges need to develop programs solidly grounded in theory, but which also include some practicality. Internships, offered in full cooperation with school districts, are one solution. An additional approach might be a program that includes some of the knowledge-based work which is best taught in the university setting and more practical courses which would be taught by practicing administrators" (p.14).

Goodlad (1984), The National Commission on Excellence in Education (1983), and Baltzell and Dentler (1983), among others, have arrived at similar conclusions regarding preparation for principalship in American schools. Goodlad covers much ground—recruitment, full-time study, cooperative approaches, and planned programs at major universities:

> Two rarely practiced procedures . . . are basic to correcting the sloppiness and upgrading both the status of the principalship and the quality of those that aspire to it. First, there should be a continuous district-wide effort to identify employees with leadership potential. Second, the district must be willing to make an investment designed to pay off in the future. . . . Once identified as promising, potential candidates should be . . . scheduled for paid two-year study leaves, to be taken at *major universities offering a carefully planned program.* [Pp. 306–307. Emphasis added]

These statements of need and concern demonstrate the melange of problems confronting administration. The picture gets no clearer as we move from administrators to administrator preparation.

Although persons in educational administration speak about preparation programs, the notation of "program" is very tenuous. These programs often are not programs at all, but in deference to tradition, I shall continue to use the designation "program." Institutions of higher education offer programs at three degree levels (master's, specialist or advanced study, and doctoral) and may provide certification courses distinct from degrees. (In some states it has been possible to become certified as an administrator without completing an advanced degree program.) Institutions may have both Ph.D. and Ed.D. programs, often with little of substance to distinguish between them. With all of the options available, there should be a discrete program and degree available for each niche in bureaucracy! Alas, such is not the case (Silver and Spuck, 1978; Pitner, 1982); programs at all three levels are very similar. One is likely to find beginning students in advanced classes or advanced students in beginning classes and students taking courses haphazardly, seemingly at random. Program content and sequence are not clearly differentiated.

Future administrators tend to self-select into preparation programs; there is little attempt to recruit selectively or to screen vigorously for the programs. Seldom are persons denied admission to or "successful" exit from administrator preparation programs. Candidates usually take a collection of courses. These courses are *not*

— taken in any particular sequence,
— differentiated for differing degree levels or levels of administration,
— designed within some unifying and conceptual framework,
— developed according to theory (or change theory, or almost any other theory) and especially according to adult learning theory,
— closely aligned with desired outcomes, or coordinated with the work administrators do—or should do, or
— evaluated rigorously, either singly or for their contribution to a total program.

The programs are often parochial (Pitner, 1982, p. 14), designed for the "drop-in" student, disjointed, lacking in rigor. And higher education contributes mightily to the problems by reserving its fiscal support for a few students who aspire to research or to the professorate—for those who wish to teach or study about administration rather than to practice administration. This stratagem *discourages* full-time preservice study.

Pitner (1982) has reviewed the practice of school administration—that is, what administrators really do. Although programs offer many courses on such topics as finance and politics of education, principals spend much time on the job with discipline, extracurricular activities, service, pupil control, organizational maintenance, and noninstructional matters. Interestingly, the literature, critics, and practitioners all indicate that education needs principals who deal with instructional leadership and change and are adept at school-site management. These contradictions between course work and practice should be given serious attention since current research suggests that student outcomes seem related to administrator behaviors that are *not* commonly identified through observational studies in schools *or* taught in preparation programs (for example, Brookover et al., 1982; Clark, Lotto, and McCarthy, 1980; Clark, Lotto, and Astuto, 1984; Edmonds, 1979; Firestone and Wilson, 1985; High, 1984; Keedy, 1983; Purkey and Degen, 1985; Purkey and Smith, 1983; Rutherford, 1985; Shoemaker and Fraser, 1981).

Preparation programs tend to be traditional. They may include some behavioral science courses and "how-to" courses. Some include something from the humanities, but few have either originated or maintained the humanities emphasis (Achilles, 1981; Farquhar, 1970; Miklos, 1983). Further supporting the contention that preparation programs are haphazard is Farquhar's statement (cited in Pitner, 1982, p. 13) that "by 1974 students in many institutions were free to build or negotiate almost their entire program."

Fortunately, however, the disparaging of preparation programs is not limited to practitioners in education. Although many successful administrators indicate that their preparation programs were of little or no value, so do those in other practices and professions, including medicine, law, and business (Pitner, 1982, pp. 18–20). There has been little research on the outcomes of preparation programs. Indeed, there is little research on the processes and outcomes of higher education. This unfortunate situation hinders program development and any attempts to differentiate programs by quality.

In spite of these and many other criticisms of administration and preparation programs, there are rays of hope. Increasing knowledge in related areas can directly influence administrator preparation programs. Yet for any changes to have impact, the move forward must be unified and cooperative. Improvements cannot move apace without evaluation and without strenuous, rigorous attention to *program concerns* (contents, structure, evaluation) and to *personnel concerns* (recruitment, selection, retention).

Numerous writers have identified processes, approaches, and research that could be used to improve specific elements of educational administration. Rather than emphasize one deficiency or avenue to excellence, the remainder of this paper is purposely eclectic. It seeks (1) to draw together several themes identifying problems that need to be addressed and (2) to offer suggestions for improvements.

Administration: Some Assumptions

The *practice* of administration is an *applied* field. Much as a medical doctor strives to effect a cure by employing armamentaria derived from such disciplines as biology, zoology, anatomy, physics, and psychology, so an administrator strives to orchestrate resources into goal achievement by employing a blend of strategies (processes) from such disciplines as anthropology, psychology, sociology, and economics. The *study* of administration *may* be a discipline. (A discipline has its own body of knowledge and accepted methods of inquiry. There is certainly room for debate on administration's "fit" on these criteria.) Some have considered administration a profession, for it shares much with those fields considered the "true" professions: medicine, law, theology, dentistry. (As mentioned before, isn't it strange that practitioners in all these fields seem to denigrate their preparation programs? [Pitner, 1982, pp. 18–20]). Administration deals with people, people concerns, and people problems. In addition, there is currently a move toward ethical practice.[2]

Some have debated whether administration is an art or a science. Recently there has been serious consideration that administration has many elements of a craft (Achilles, 1985a; Blumberg, 1984; Miklos, 1984). (Would a cynic suggest craftiness?) Other recent studies (such as High, 1984; Keedy, 1983) suggest that "successful" administrators have an expertness or recognized expertise that helps them gain influence with subordinates and activate the norm of reciprocity that helps in achieving group goals.

To the question, "Are administrators born or made?" I would answer, "Yes!" Not everyone is suited to the professional practice of administration, and those who are, are suited in varying degrees. This notion gives credence to the importance of recruitment, selection, and training in preparing administrators.

If administration is a blend of art, science, and craft, persons can profit from preparation programs that include all these elements: scholarship (research, study), instruction and training, and practice. The combination of the nature–nurture dichotomy and function of training suggests that if an apt person receives the requisite preparation and training, then he or she should become an admirable professional practitioner. (Strange idea, isn't it? I first encountered it in the writings of a humanist describing how to get "professional" public servants—administrators, if you will—for the Republic. See Cicero, M.T., *Pro Licinio Archias*.)

And finally, there are two pragmatic and instrumental considerations for improving administrator preparation programs: (1) the time is right for some serious changes, and (2) there is enough blame to go around so that rather than try to assess the relative faults of any group, it is time to pull in unison toward some desired goals. Thus we need to set goals, chart courses of action, get the show on the road, review our results, and continue to make program refinements.

I have generated my assumptions about administration from common or "craft" knowledge, from a synthesis of available information, and from contemplation. In very abbreviated form these guiding assumptions are:

---

[2] UCEA's Career Development Seminars have addressed ethics, as has the NCPEA's Humanities and Values Continuing Interest Group. Note also Farquhar (1979); Immegart, G.L., and J.M. Burroughs, eds. (1970), *Ethics and the School Administrator*; Kimbrough, R.B. (1985), *Ethics: A Course of Study for Educational Leaders*, AASA; and attention to ethics and philosophy in such texts as, for example, Graff, O.B., et al. (1966), *Philosophic Theory and Practice in Educational Administration*.

1. All is not well in administration's "River City."
2. Administration, if not a "true" profession, is at least an emerging and "bound" profession.
3. Administration, if not a "true" discipline, is at least emerging with a body of knowledge, methods of inquiry, and a reluctant willingness to evaluate its own practice.
4. Administration is an *applied* field, blending art, science, and craft. Preparation programs must reflect this admixture.
5. Administrators are both born and made; persons carefully recruited and selected can improve through appropriate preparation. (It seems unnecessary to dwell on the fact that constantly changing conditions will require administrators to engage in continuous study, personal and professional growth, and renewal.)
6. Preparation programs for administrators are important and have the potential to "make a difference." Carefully planned programs are superior to the rather happenstance approach found today.
7. Scholarly study of administration is important for improvement. This includes the serious study of administrator selection and preparation, and of the alignment of preparation with what administrators do, and what they should do.
8. Little progress can be made without planned cooperation among many groups. Divisiveness will be dysfunctional; territoriality should be diminished and judicious experimentation and evaluation encouraged.

These are the major assumptions at the base of my suggestions. A few other assumptions are more elusive; they may better be considered assertions, since they are less well supported than are the assumptions. They emerge throughout the following suggestions for improvement.

Suggestions for Improvement

This section presents some suggestions to remedy identified problems or to reduce needs in the preparation of educational administrators. For convenience, suggestions are categorized by major groups that have a stake in the process: higher education, state education agencies, school systems, associations, federal government, and education in general. Some suggestions involve several groups working cooperatively.

Higher Education

Higher education is in position to lead in the change. Pitner (1982, p. 47) cites J.C. March in noting that universities should do what they do best: "Universities do as good a job as anyone at most aspects of management training. They do better at providing the basic knowledge. . . . The univer-

Table 8–1

A Suggested Model to Guide Development of Preparation Programs

Level Activity	I	II	III	IV
Purpose	Understanding. Conceptual control.	Skill building. Expanded knowledge base.	Transfer of skill and knowledge. Synthesis.	Application of skills and knowledge. Relationships.
Relation to Change	Awareness/interest; initiation. Dissemination.	Trial/evaluation; implementation. Demonstration.	Use/adoption; incorporation. Diffusion.	Institutionalization and renewal.
Method(s)	Lecture, reading. Some question-and-answer (Q and A). Didactic, one-way communication.	Demonstration. Group work. Discussion. Critique. Q and A. Two-way communication. Case studies; case record.	Practice with feedback. Simulation; role play. Involvement. Q and A. Coaching; counseling. Development of "action plan."	Practice with feedback. Synthesis and application. Counseling. Consulting. Self-motivation. Analysis of practice.

Communication Is Primarily . . .	One-way. Leader to class or group.	Two-way, but leader directed.	Two-way. Interactive and equal.	See III.
Mode(s)	Classes. Large group. Individual.	Labs, seminars. Small group. Individual.	Small group; mostly one-on-one. Individual.	Pairs, teams, coaching. Individual work.
Possible Assessment Strategies	Paper-pencil tests. Memory. Rote.	Oral and written test processes. Demonstration of skill.	Observe and critique. "Paragraph analyses." Demonstrate/discuss.	Discuss/refine. Informal processes. Elaborate design.
Examples of Courses, Experiences, etc.	History/theory of administration. Theory of leadership. Decision/game theory. Communication theory.	Parent conferencing. Scheduling. Communication skills. Decision simulations.	Prepare a schedule. Problem solving. Write policy/reports.	

(Programs should progress in a generally sequential manner from Level I to Level IV.)

sity has a special domain of competence. The domain of intellect. What the university does best . . . is to develop new knowledge. . . ."

Higher education can and should engage in research, theory development, intellectual development, and delivery of training. But this requires structure and organization. Higher education should first clean up its own act—lead by leading—and get *on* with it while there is still a modicum of respect left for the field. Some suggestions follow:

1. Align the content and processes of administrator preparation programs with what administrators *do*, and with what theory says that they *should do*. (Base these efforts on some current study of administration.) Reduce the gap between the theory and practice through field efforts.

2. Build and offer programs that are *programs*. The programs should address three concerns: why, what, and how; they should be based on research, theory, and practice; they should include general knowledge (humanities), behavioral sciences, and field or practical experiences. (Figure 8–1 portrays some of these considerations. Exact relationships among the elements need to be determined. See suggestions 3, 4, and 5 following and Achilles, 1985.)

   Programs must accommodate the notion of *profession*. To do this we may need to borrow some elements or processes from preparation programs in other professions until we develop some evaluation-research basis for our own programs and until we develop a true educational model. Programs must be *planned* and *sequential*. They must move from didactic processes for conceptual understanding (using usual academic processes of lecture, readings, and the like) to skill building (using demonstrations, visitations, simulations, and role playing) to the transfer of skill (coaching, guided practice, and independent practice). Until better approaches become available, I would suggest that preparation programs be structured within a model such as that in Table 8–1. Examples (using familiar designations) of the differences in levels (I, II, III, IV) are shown at the bottom of Table 8–1. Level IV is generally composed of repeated reflective practice and professional development. It may represent in-service.

   Follow the professional model and have *cohorts* of students going through preparation experiences together. Start a group through the program at one or at most two times each year. Carefully note which courses or course sequences will be service courses open to nonmajors and persons from other fields. (This approach will ease scheduling demands and free some staff for practice, intern supervision, and "residency" study.) Grouping students in a cohort— the class of '91,

KEY QUESTIONS			
How	What	Why	Training
Craftsman Practice	Trail/Error	N/A	Apprenticeship
Technician Training	Theory Base	N/A	Schooling Apprenticeship
Academician N/A or Vicarious observation	Research	Study Analysis	Schooling Study
Professional Practice	Training	Study Reflection	All of Above

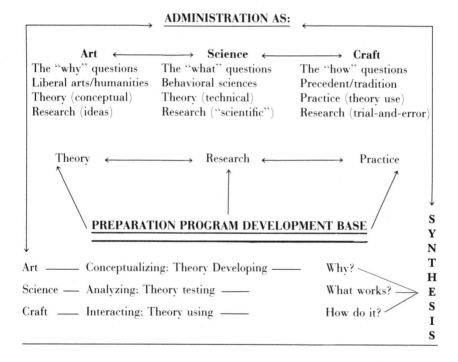

Figure 8–1
Some Key Issues in the Development of Administrator Preparation Programs

From Achilles, 1985. Thanks to P. Silver for adding to these considerations.

for example—will also build camaraderie and a support system for the students. (See also suggestion 9.) Avoid drop-in, part-time programs.

3. Create a structure and process to coordinate the study of administrator preparation programs. *Activate this.* It need not be expensive. It might be done through UCEA and a program center, but it should include non-UCEA institutions. The center's staff will plan, coordinate, and orchestrate the study and will suggest evaluation designs for comparability. Staff will collect information and disseminate ideas for program improvements. This new structure will be a rallying point or central focus for program improvement efforts. Its use will be voluntary. It will *not* be an expensive monolith. This center will be important, for as Greenfield (1985) has said, "The study of administrator preparation programs, processes, and associated outcomes has proceeded in a theoretical vacuum and has focused primarily on technical knowledge and skill associated with the school administrator's role" (p. 99).

4. Differentiate programs for different degree levels and different administrative responsibilities. Programs for new administrators (for discussion, consider those interested in the principalship) would include content and skills for the vice-principalship or for the principal of a small school (generally elementary), because these are usually entry-level opportunities. The field experiences for this entry-level group would lead to induction and socialization into the profession.

    Expanded bases for preparation programs (art, science, craft/theory, research, practice) will allow—no, require—program differentiation. Differentiation will allow each person to pursue some discipline or skill area to mastery or proficiency. This activates the principal-as-expert as a primary way to obtain influence with teachers and makes room for more "why" (art) and "how" (craft) in preparation programs.

    Administration might consider a degree similar to the MBA for the advanced practitioner. An advanced practitioner might have a master's degree as the entry degree and the MSA (Master in School Administration) as the advanced degree, or the specialist, or certificate of advanced study. But these advanced practitioner degrees would have clear differences in program and skill requirements from the entry degree.

5. Experiment with and evaluate program processes and outcomes. What is better, taking into account cost, outcome, acceptance by the field and higher education, and so on: (1) a cadre of higher-education-based "clinical professors" who guide students' field experiences, (2) a cadre of local-school-based "practitioner mentors"

who exemplify practice and will guide new administrators (much like a cooperating teacher), (3) a combination of 1 and 2, or (4) some other procedure? Results of program experimentation should be sent to the center (see suggestion 3) for compilation, comparison to other results, and dissemination.

6. Find appropriate cooperative settings for field problems, internships, practice, and visitations. Identify practitioners who will work within the preparation programs as exemplars. Provide continuing rewards and training opportunities for this exemplary group. These exemplars will be field supervisors for level III experiences (see Table 8–1).

7. Involve others in recruitment as one way to reduce the ubiquitous self-selection process. Local school systems should identify potential leaders and provide some resources for persons to attend advanced programs (district commitment). Those chosen should expect to devote effort to some full-time study in a carefully planned program (individual commitment). Use advanced screening steps between recruitment and final selection. One such device could be assessment center methodology.

8. Have strict departmental control recommendations, both for certification and employment. *Departmental* recommendations should be reserved for only those who successfully complete a *planned program* in administration. The departmental recommendation or endorsement would be a statement of departmental assurance regarding each graduate's program completion, including field work and internships. This seemingly simple step is deceptively complex. It will require each department to make a statement regarding what it believes about quality preparation programs and what it will accept before issuing a recommendation. Since certification typically is in the hands of another agency (the state), departments may need to develop a program framework like that depicted in Table 8–2 to fulfill obligations to those already enrolled. Only through evaluation and demonstrably superior results will departments be able to convince others of the benefits of planned programs.

   Until departments of educational administration have defensibly outstanding preparation programs and ways to differentiate those who have completed the rigorous, planned programs from those who have met only minimum standards, external groups and agencies will continue to set program and certification requirements. External control undermines professionalism. But how many departments have well-defined, well-evaluated, well-conceptualized programs that they would offer as "ideals" when they discuss requirements and certification?

9. Insist on some full-time residential study in planned programs. Residency *can* be important if faculties and students use the oppor-

Table 8–2
Model Showing Differentiations in Program Quality and Design

	Certification	Various Degree Levels
Minimum Program	Courses to meet minimums as required by certifying agency.	Certificate plus. . . . (Plan to abandon this option as soon as possible.)
Departmental Endorsement (Ideal)	*Planned* program. Some residency. Field experience. Targeted writing activity.	*Planned* program. Extended residency. Guided and extended field activities. Detailed writing experience. Pre- and post-assessments. Demonstrated areas of expertness.

Service courses offered as needed to nonmajors; workshops for skill building; in-service for renewal and updating.

tunity wisely. Use residency time for projects or experiences other than courses. Note Hodgkinson's (1976) comments. "One of the most significant of recent findings in higher education has to do with the importance of a student being in a residential atmosphere. It's quite clear that such an atmosphere is critical in helping people develop in terms of self-reliance, initiative, and basic maturity" (p. 4).

Full-time study has been tied to cooperative involvement in recruitment by several writers and researchers. Greenfield (1985) noted:

> Districts could identify and select the most promising individuals from this group for participation in a formal training program at the university level, with the district or the State bearing the full cost of participation at the individual's normal salary level, perhaps with an additional dislocation and tuition allowance. The objective would be to facilitate *full-time* participation in a formal training program. Successful completion of the formal training would qualify the individual for permanent or provisional certification as an administrator, and the individual would then be eligible for administrative appointment. [P. 112]

10. Jointly plan, emphasize, and conduct diverse activities as part of the planned program of study. Such activities might be field problems, participation in conferences or workshops or principals' academies, or noncredit experiences. Experiences should be considered part of the formal program and be treated as such (with standards, products, credits) . They would be planned and conducted cooperatively with other agencies.

11. Keep some departmental funding to support full-time study by aspir-

ing practitioners of administration rather than dispense all support to those who plan to be researchers or professors. The informed and excellent *practice* of administration is extremely important, if only because practitioners constitute the largest client group for our preparation programs. Also reserve some departmental resources to build, support, and reward a cadre of field supervisors.

12. Just as departmental recommendation or certification is important as one indication of the quality of an individual, so are some assurances of departmental program quality. A rigorous, self-monitored process for endorsing preparation programs needs to be explored.

   A particular preparation program might be approved by several groups, including associations, the NCATE, and the UCEA. Some attempt at reciprocity should be initiated with state certifying groups based on the departmental approval process. Program or departmental endorsement is similar to personal recommendations at another level.

My suggestions are not all directed to higher education. However, as the major actor in the administrator preparation, higher education must make some important changes in order to keep its leadership role. Many efforts need to be *cooperative*—truly cooperative—if changes are to be successful. Because some cooperative actions have been included in suggestions for higher education (such as numbers 6–10), the suggestions for other groups and agencies are somewhat less detailed.

State Education Agencies (SEAs)

State education agencies are pivotal because education is really a state function. These agencies make and implement important education policy, doing so with a statewide perspective. In carrying out their responsibilities, SEAs often require research, demonstration or pilot projects, evaluations, literature reviews and summaries, and specialized training—activities that higher education should (1) be able to do well and (2) incorporate into ongoing preparation efforts. Opportunities to cooperate are legion. State education agencies could do the following to strengthen administrator preparation efforts:

1. Provide support and assistance in improving certification for administrative positions. Set stringent standards and certify only those persons recommended by accredited institutions of higher education. (See suggestion 8 in the section on higher education.) Move toward approval of well-designed preparation programs and certification based on successful completion of such programs. Recognize, through reciprocity, graduates of programs certified in other states. (See recommendation 12 in the section on higher education.)

2. Work with preparation programs to provide field problems, research and evaluation opportunities, and internships for full-time students of administration. Reserve some funds, to be distributed competitively, for preparation programs that will use advanced students to work on specific statewide education problems as part of their planned programs.

3. Cooperate with preparation programs in many ways. Identify exemplary programs and schools for visitations by prospective administrators. Encourage internships in state-supported projects. Allow state education agency staff to be mentors or field supervisors for full-time students in high-quality and planned preparation programs.

4. Involve higher education in some aspects of state-supported in-service training (such as principals' academies). Encourage higher education to build into their planned programs some provision for incorporating principals' academies as part of the total preparation program.

5. Advise higher education personnel of ways that the state will measure and reward excellence in educational administration, and work cooperatively with program planners so that they may incorporate appropriate changes in preparation programs. This should be done statewide and also nationally through the center or clearinghouse. (See recommendation 3 in the section on higher education.)

6. Encourage the use of diverse preparation models in the state. Evaluate the results of new, but conceptually sound, preparation programs and help improve preparation programs through experimentation and evaluation. Make certification standards strict, but flexible enough to encourage continuous program improvement and development.

7. Discourage the proliferation of administrator preparation programs within the state. The field of education, and educational administration in particular, already grants more graduate degrees than any other field (Peterson and Finn, 1985). Part-time, haphazard collections of courses do not allow participants to learn the three elements necessary in a profession—the how, the what, and the why.

8. The "quick fix" in teaching and in administration is short-sighted (Ohanian, 1985). Cookbook approaches do not substitute for knowledge of administration as a profession. Do not encourage shallow, "how to" courses or experiences that cheapen the concept of administration as a profession. Insist on comprehensive, well-designed pre-service and in-service training; do not sanction efforts that do not meet rigorous standards. The SEAs can help control proliferation through the certification of *programs* and by refusing to certify persons who do not graduate from approved programs. It will not suffice to make strenuous adjustment in university training programs if certification

routes are open to people who avoid rigorous programs. This will simply subvert the process.

One cooperative effort to improve educational administration might join higher education and the state education agency in each state as major partners, and involve other stakeholders in educational administration. Each state should carefully assess its requirements for high-quality preparation programs.

State and higher-education personnel should, through self-study or evaluation, determine what must be done to bring various administrator preparation programs up to a high standard of quality (perhaps by adopting recommendations of the National Commission on Excellence in Educational Administration [1987]). The groups should then determine the costs of raising the quality of the programs and of maintaining a high level of quality. These steps will help state decision makers determine just how many high-quality programs the state needs and can afford. The hard step will be deciding how to reduce the number of programs so that those remaining will exemplify the highest standards. Mediocre programs must be discouraged. States should not dilute the mandate for quality by supporting mediocre programs, and the profession should take steps to raise its own standards.[3]

School Systems

School systems are the largest employers of educational administrators. They should be full and active participants in the preparation of administrators and in the improvement of educational administration. Some ways they could do this follow.

1. Recognize the central position of local administrators in school improvement and pupil gains (see, for example, Berman and Pauly, 1975; Clark et al., 1980 and 1984; Edmonds, 1979; and Firestone and Wilson, 1985) by paying serious attention to administrator preparation and selection.
2. Actively recruit top-quality candidates for training in administration. Help develop a high-quality personnel pool from which the best will be selected for advanced programs.
3. Develop in-district mechanisms for identifying potential administrators and for supporting their training (Baltzell and Dentler, 1983). Encourage local educators to attend only the best programs.

---

[3] Dale Mann, Teachers College, Columbia University, brought out these points during a recent conversation. The ideas as presented here will need refinement, but this brief suggestion identifies both the need and the problem.

4. Sponsor in-district (or district-wide) professional development for administrators and prospective administrators. Within-district administrator in-service training is the logical outgrowth of school-based in-service training for teachers. Within-district programs allow administrators, working with carefully selected consultants who can bridge the theory–practice chasm, to use local district problems as the basis for common professional-development experiences.

5. Evaluate administrators carefully and use these results as part of the larger issue of evaluating administrator preparation programs.

6. Provide mentors or field supervisors to work with university-based preparation programs. Support internships at challenging sites and use internship activities to help solve the real-world administrative problems of the district.

7. Participate in conceptually sound preparation programs that offer benefits to the district. Encourage new higher-education–local district preparation models (such as the Paired Administrator Training Model suggested by Achilles and Hughes [1972]). Imaginative preparation programs can provide full-time study combined with in-district experiences. Note the suggested model in Table 8–3, where "A" is an administrative trainee and "B" is an experienced practicing administrator. A carefully planned program will offer both members of the "paired team" cooperative and complementary experiences of full-time and part-time study, planned field activities, and guided practice. The model is based on academic quarters; it can be adjusted for semester programs.

Table 8–3

Suggested Model for Improving Preparation Programs by Incorporating Planned Field Experiences, Full-time Study, Combined Preservice (A) and In-service (B) Opportunities, and Numerous Other Benefits

	Summer	School opening	Fall	Winter*	Spring**	School closing	Summer
On Campus	A,B	A,B	A	A,(B)	(B)		Various
In District			B	A,B	A [B]	A,B	Options
Time Sequence	Summer	School opening	Fall	Winter*	Spring**	School closing	Summer

*Cooperative field problem.   **Practicum or internship (Guided practice).
A = Administrative trainee; B = Experienced administrator ( ) = optional; [ ] = as a field supervisor.

Source: Archilles and Hughes, 1972.

Professional Groups and Associations

Many professional groups and associations have a considerable stake in administration and administrator preparation. All engage in educating and training administrators in various ways, from disseminating information through newsletters and journals to holding conferences and sophisticated, usually single-purpose, seminars, workshops, and academies. These efforts, responses to the perceived needs of practitioners, are responsible and time-honored roles for professional associations. Associations can help improve educational administration in the following ways.

1. Take more active roles in encouraging improved preparation programs in higher education.

2. Support internal "policing" of the profession by helping to set standards for preparation and professional practice. Seek a role in recognizing or endorsing sound preparation efforts that address the why, what, and how elements of the profession of administration.

3. Offer, for higher education personnel engaged in administrator preparation, specialized workshops or programs (perhaps at conventions) on state-of-the-art professional applications in actual practice. This will bring the best of practice from throughout the nation to the attention of professors, who have much to learn from the study of practice. Possibly they will incorporate the best elements into their courses.

4. Periodically poll members for their perceptions and assessments of preparation programs. Make these results known to program planners through such things as inserts or mailers included in regular mailings to members. Support or encourage forums or workshops wherein practitioners and program planners can study, discuss, and improve program designs. Encourage scholarly study of preparation programs.

5. Develop structured induction activities for new practitioners according to administrative roles—supervisor, elementary school principal, and the like.

6. Help members, especially building-level administrators, become adept at planning and leading staff-development efforts. Problem-oriented faculty meetings and building-level in-service programs are important components of school leadership. As personnel evaluation becomes more important, so will the need to help staff build individualized professional development plans to remediate deficiencies.

7. Encourage involvement from graduate students, especially from those in full-time study, through planned programs and incentives. (For example, reduce member fees and waive convention registrations.)

8. Build a structure of advanced recognition for practitioners based, perhaps, on tests of cognitive knowledge and proof of exemplary practice. (For example, borrowing from medicine, one designation might be "Fellow in the National Academy of Secondary School Principals.")

Federal Government

The federal government has become more of a partner in education. The National Commission on Excellence in Education, however, spoke only briefly on the federal role in administration and leadership in education. Because of the national needs and interests, the federal government should consider some major involvement, mostly in research and training.

1. Support several diverse training models for administrators and *insist* on thorough evaluation of these models (Similar to the EPDA efforts of the late 1960s and early 1970s). Focus on preparation programs for practicing administrators.
2. Provide support for the study of important topics such as ways to attract and retain top people for administration and the influence or impact of administration on school outcomes.
3. Since the increased centralization of federal research and development (R&D) funding, opportunities for paid graduate student involvement at nearby campuses have diminished (note education's parochialism as discussed by Pitner, 1982, and Peterson and Finn, 1985). This could be offset by a federal voucher plan for a specified number of full-time study leaves for prospective or in-service administrators. The number of positions for these vouchers could be allocated to states by a formula, perhaps based on the number of school-age children in the state.
4. Coordinate efforts for recognition of strong preparation programs, for certification by *program* completion, and for reciprocity of certification if major program standards are met. Reciprocity and recognition need to be national in scope.
5. Provide modest support for a clearinghouse or center (see recommendation 3 in the section on higher education) that is within the established structure of administrator preparation.

Educational administration is not separate from education in general. Some recommendations for educational administration are applicable to the field of education.

1. Important new ideas need to get quickly into the hands of both professors and practitioners. Cooperative links among local, state, federal, association, and higher-education groups will accelerate the use of knowledge by educational administrators. Consideration needs

to be given to constructing some process to do this. Any process should be within the existing framework, not something added on.
2. Improvement must be measured. Changes must be based on some theoretic construct specific to education. Educators should give serious attention to developing an "education model" in the theoretic and systems sense.

For years education has tried, often vainly and uncritically, to respond to, emulate, or adopt other models. By following the medical model, education moved toward professionalism through internships, through diagnosing (the illness) and prescribing (the remedy), and through analysis of problems to attempt to understand the nature of the malady eroding education. In responding to the business model, education rushed into such things as accountability, management, viewing pupils as "products," behavioral objectives, and zero-based budgeting. Response to the planning model provided education with PPBS, PERT, Gantt charts, and systems analysis. The scientific model required experimental design, control groups, and randomness.

Each model has contributed to progress in education. Each has also caused problems because of Procrustean attempts to fit education into some model designed for another social institution. Education is concerned with the application of concepts from many fields (such as learning theory, motivation, change, and communications) and requires its own model. An education model certainly will borrow heavily from other models, but it will address education issues as its first priority. This model will need to include (1) the *art* aspect (liberal arts including philosophy, history, and fine arts) to guide us with the *why* questions, (2) the *science* aspect (research, behavioral science) to guide us with the *what* questions, and (3) *craft knowledge* (Blumberg, 1984) or conventional wisdom (tradition, trial and error, case study) to guide us with the *how* questions.

An education model will help us both to plan for the future and to assess current practice. In fact, there may be several education models; the model for academe may differ from the model for public schools. Such models should influence administrator preparation. But how do we know? Where are the models? This is one area for serious inquiry by the profession itself.

There are many places to start the improvement efforts. Although it may be wise to move on several fronts simultaneously, the three areas of recruitment, selection, and training are closely enough related to be subsumed into the larger framework of administrator preparation. The suggestions for higher education independently address key considerations. These independent issues add up to plans for expanded and improved preparation programs. Greenfield (1985) summarizes it well. "The formal training program . . . would probably require two years of full-time participation by prospective administrators, and while this is a marked departure from current practice, it is proposed that the graduate of such a program would be more likely than is presently the case to be well grounded (expert) in the technical, conceptual, and social knowledge and skills required for effectively administering a school. The interventions suggested above are testable and informed by theory. . . "(p. 113).

After a fairly thorough review of literature (see the section of additional readings), and based on considerable experience and a general "feeling" for a field of educational administration (tacit knowledge, a la Polanyi?), I would conclude that the time has come for serious and widespread attention to educational administration. It seems *so* obvious, yet "there is nothing more deceptive than an obvious fact" (S. Holmes, "The Boscombe Valley Mystery"). I can only wonder: If it is so obvious, why haven't we acted sooner? In spite of Holmes' droll warning, I'm convinced that now is the time for new viewpoints, new models, and new structures in educational administration. All involved in this very large enterprise need to build from a sturdy tripod: *why, what, and how!*

References

Achilles, C.M. (1981). *Quo vadis? (quo vaduisti vadesque?): Some approaches to the use of humanities in leadership preparation programs.* Paper given at the American Educational Research Association, Los Angeles, ERIC: ED 202–166.

Achilles, C.M. (1984a, August). *A proposal for excellence in educational administration.* Paper given at the National Conference of Professors of Educational Administration, Orono, Maine. ERIC: ED 246557; EA 017028.

Achilles, C.M. (1984b, Fall). Forecast: Stormy weather ahead for educational administration. *Issues in Education* II (2): 127–35.

Achilles, C.M. (1985, August). *Building principal preparation programs on theory, practice and research.* Paper given at the annual meeting of the National Conference of Professors of Educational Administration, Mississippi State University, Starkville, Miss.

Achilles, C.M., and Hughes, L.W. (1972, July). The paired administrator team concept: A promising administrator training model. *Planning and Changing* 3(2): 45–50.

Baltzell, D.C., and Dentler, R.A. (1983). *Selecting American school principals: A sourcebook for educators.* Washington, D.C.: ABT Associates for National Institute of Education, 1–65.

Berman, P., and Pauly, E. (1975). *Federal programs supporting educational change, vol. II: Factors affecting change agent projects.* Santa Monica, Calif.: Rand Corp.

Blumberg, A. (1984, Fall). The craft of school administration and some other rambling thoughts. *Educational Administration Quarterly* 20(4): 24–40.

Brookover, Wilbur B., et al. (1982). *Creating effective schools.* Holmes Beach, Florida: Learning Publications, Inc.

Clark, D.L.; Lotto, L.S.; and Astuto, T.A. (1984, Summer). Effective schools and school improvement: An appraisal of some recent trends. *Educational Administration Quarterly* 20(3): 41–68.

Clark, D.L.; Lotto, L.S.; and McCarthy, M.M. (1980, March). Factors associated with success in urban elementary schools. *Phi Delta Kappan* 61(7): 455–60.

Cooper, L. (1984). *Improving professional practice: Cooperative professional development*. Paper given at the National Conference of Professors of Educational Administration, Orono, Maine.

Cornett, L.M. (1983). *The preparation and selection of school principals*. Atlanta, Georgia: The Southern Regional Education Board.

Edmonds, Ronald. (1979, October). Effective schools for the urban poor. *Educational Leadership* 37(1): 15–24.

Farquhar, R.H. (1970). *The humanities in preparing educational administrators*. Eugene: ERIC-CEPM, University of Oregon.

Farquhar, R.H. (1979, March). *Preparing administrators for ethical practice*. (Draft). Paper given at the University Council on Educational Administration Career Development Seminar on "Ethics in Administration." (See also *Alberta Journal of Educational Research*, 27(2), June 1981: 192–204.)

Firestone, W.A., and Wilson, B.L. (1985, Spring). Using bureaucratic and cultural linkages to improve instruction: The principal's contribution. *Educational Administration Quarterly* 21(2): 17–30.

Fogarty, B.M. (ed.) (1983, Summer). Educational administration 1959–1981: A profession in evolution. Special Issue of *Educational Administration Quarterly* 19(3).

Goodlad, John I. (1984). *A place called school: Prospects for the future*. New York: McGraw-Hill.

Greenfield, W.D., Jr. (1985, Fall). The moral socialization of school administrators: Informal role learning outcomes. *Educational Administration Quarterly* 21(4): 99–120.

Hawley, W.D. (1988). Universities and the improvement of school management. (Chapter 10, this volume.)

High, R.M. (1984, August). Influence-gaining behaviors of principals in schools of varying levels of instructional effectiveness. Unpublished doctoral dissertation, University of Tennessee, Knoxville. *DAI*, 45, 10. p. 3040, A84.

Hodgkinson, H.L. (1976, April). Why education R & D? National Institute of Education reprint from *American Education*.

Hoy, W.K. (Ed.) (1982a, Summer). Special issue on research and thought in educational administration. *Educational Administration Quarterly* 18.

Hoy, W.K. (Ed.) (1982b, Summer). Recent developments in theory and research in educational administration. *Educational Administration Quarterly* 18: 1–11.

Keedy, J.L. (1983). Norm setting as a component of principal effectiveness. Unpublished doctoral dissertation, University of Tennessee, Knoxville. *DAI*, 43, 9. p. 2846, A83.

Miklos, E. (1983, Summer). Evolution in administration preparation programs. *Educational Administration Quarterly* 19(3): 153–78.

Miklos, E. (1984). *The pursuit of excellence in educational administration*. Paper given at the annual meeting of the National Council of Professors of Educational Administration, Orono, Maine.

National Commission on Excellence in Education. (1983). *A nation at risk: The imperative for educational reform.* Washington, D.C.: Department of Education.

National Commission on Excellence in Educational Administration (1987, March). Leaders for America's schools. Tempe, Ariz.: University Council on Educational Administration.

Ohanian, S. (1985, June). On stir-and-serve recipes for teaching. *Phi Delta Kappan* 66(10): 696–701.

Peterson K.D., and Finn, C.E. Jr. (1985, Spring). Principals, superintendents, and the administrator's art. *The Public Interest* 79: 42–62.

Pitner, N. (1982, February). *Training the school administrator: The state of the art.* Eugene: CEPM. University of Oregon. (Chapter 28, this volume.)

Purkey, S.C., and Degen, S. (1985, Spring). Beyond effective schools to good schools: Some first steps. *R & D Perspectives.* Eugene: CEPM. University of Oregon.

Purkey, S.C., and Smith, M.S. (1983). Effective schools: A review. *Elementary School Journal* 83: 427–52.

Reed, Rodney J. (1984, April). *The institute for school administrators: A successful model for professional and personal growth.* Paper given at the American Educational Research Association meeting, New Orleans.

Rutherford, W.L. (1985, September). School principals as effective leaders. *Phi Delta Kappan* 67(1): 31–34.

Shoemaker, J., and Fraser, H. (1981, November). What principals can do: Some implications from studies of effective schooling. *Phi Delta Kappan* 63(3): 178–82.

Silver, P.F., and Spuck, D.W. (Eds.) (1978). *Preparatory programs for educational administrators in the United States.* Columbus: Ohio State University, University Council for Educational Administration.

Additional Readings

Achilles, C.M. (1987). A vision of better schools. In W. Greenfield (Ed.), *Instructional leadership: Concepts, issues, and controversies,* pp. 13–17. Boston, Mass.: Allyn and Bacon.

Achilles, C.M., and Keedy, J. (1983/84). Principal norm setting as a component of effective schools. *National Forum of Educational Administration and Supervision* 1(1): 58–68. Also ED 227–545.

Achilles, C.M., and Norman, D. (1974, Fall), Communication and change in education. *Planning and Changing* 5(3): 138–42.

Achilles, C.M.; Young, R.; and High, R. (1985, April). *Tracking the implementation of three years of effective schooling elements in project SHAL, St. Louis MO, (1981–1984).* Paper given at the annual meeting of the American Educational Research Association, Chicago.

Achilles, C.M.; Young, R.; Leonard, J.; Codianni, A.; and High, R., (1983, April). The change process in real life: Tracking implementation of effective schooling elements in Project SHAL, St. Louis. Paper given at the annual meeting of the American Educational Research Association, Montreal. ERIC: ED 231039.

Achilles, C.M.; Young, R.; Leonard, J.; and High, R. (1983). Development and use of a replication and evaluation model to track the implementation of effective schools elements in an inner-city setting: Project SHAL, St. Louis, MO, *Resources in Education,* ED 227–546.

Adler, M. (1982). *The paideia proposal*. New York: Macmillan & Co.

Beck, Robert E. (1981). *Career patterns. The liberal arts major in bell system management.* Speech to the Association of American Colleges. Reprinted in Project QUILL series by AAC.

Boyan, N.A. (1981, February). Follow the leader: Commentary on research in educational administration. *Educational Researcher* 10(2): 6–13, 21.

Bridges, E.M. (1982, Summer). Research on the school administrator: The state of the art, 1967–1980. *Educational Administration Quarterly* 18(3): 12–33.

Brookover, Wilbur B.; Beady, C.; Flood, P.; Schweitzer, J., and Wisenbaker, J. (1979). *School social systems and student achievement: Schools can make a difference.* New York: Praeger.

Charters, W., and Jones, J. (1973). On the risk of appraising non-events in program evaluation. *Educational Researcher* 2(11): 5–7.

Colton, David L. (1985, Spring). Vision. *National Forum* LXV(2): 33–35.

Corbett, H.D. (1982, November). Principals' contributions to maintaining change. *Phi Delta Kappan* 64(3): 190–92.

Croghan, J., and Lake D.G. (1984, November). Strategic considerations for improving the principalship. Occasional Papers in Educational Policy Analysis, No. 411. Southern Regional Council for Educational Improvement, Research Triangle Park, North Carolina.

Crowson, R.L., and Morris, Van Cleve. (1985, Fall). Administrative control in large-city school systems: An investigation in Chicago. *Educational Administration Quarterly* 21(4): 51–70.

Cuban, L. (1983, June). Effective schools: A friendly but cautionary note. *Phi Delta Kappan* 64(10): 695–96.

Culbertson, J. (1983, Summer). Leadership horizons in educational administration. *Educational Administration Quarterly* 19(3): 273–96

Donmoyer, R. (1985, Spring). Cognitive anthropology and research on effective principals. *Educational Administration Quarterly* 21(2): 31–58.

Duke, D.L., and Stiggins, R.J. (1985, Fall). Evaluating the performance of principals: A descriptive study. *Educational Administration Quarterly* 21(4): 71–98.

Erickson, D.A. (1979, March). Research on educational administration: The state of the art. *Educational Researcher* 8(3): 9–14.

Federal Reserve Bank of Philadelphia. (1975). Which school resources help learning? Efficiency and equity in Philadelphia public schools. *Business Review.* Prepared by A.A. Summers and B.L. Wolfe.

Finn, C.E., Jr. (1984, April). Toward strategic independence: Nine commandments for enhancing school effectiveness. *Phi Delta Kappan* 65(8): 518–24.

French, J.R., and Raven, B. (1959). The bases of social power. In D. Cartwright (Ed.), *Studies in Social Power*, pp. 150–67. Ann Arbor: Research Center for Group Dynamics, Institute for Social Research, University of Michigan.

Goldhammer, K. (1983, Summer). Evolution in the profession. *Educational Administration Quarterly* 19(3): 249–72.

Goodlad, John I. (1979, January). Can our schools get better? *Phi Delta Kappan* 60(5): 342–47.

Griesemer, J.L, and Butler, C. (1983). *Education under study*. Chelmsford, Mass.: North East Regional Exchange, pp. 1–62.

Griffiths, D.E. (1983, Summer). Evolution in research and theory: A study of prominent researchers. *Educational Administration Quarterly* 19(3): 201–22.

Hall, G., and Loucks, S. (1977). A developmental model for determining whether the treatment is actually implemented. *AERA Journal* 14(3).

Hange, J. (1985). *Forum on teacher education: Reflections on current issues*. Proceedings Report. Charleston, WV: Appalachia Educational Laboratory.

Hersh, R.H. (1982, Fall). What makes schools, teachers more effective? *Catalyst for Change* 12(1): 4–8.

High, R.M., and Achilles, C.M. (1986, Spring). An analysis of influence-gaining behaviors of principals in schools of varying levels of instructional effectiveness. *Educational Administration Quarterly* 22(1): 111–19.

Hoyle, J.R. (1982). *Guidelines for the preparation of school administrators*. Arlington, Virginia: AASA.

Hoyle, J.R. (1985, Winter). Programs in educational administration and the AASA preparation guidelines. *Educational Administration Quarterly* 21(1): 71–93. Also *AASA Guidelines*, Hoyle, 1982.

Joyce, B.R., and Showers, B. (1982, October). The coaching of teaching. *Educational Leadership 40(1)*: 4–10.

Katz, R.L. (1974, Sept–Oct). Skills of an effective administrator. *Harvard Business Review* 52(2): 90–102.

Kirst, M.W. (1983, Winter). Effective schools: Political environment and educational policy. *Planning and Changing* 14(4): 234–44.

Mackenzie, D. (1983, April). Research for school improvement: An appraisal of some recent trends. *Educational Researcher* 12(4): 5–16.

Mannasse, Lorri. (1984, February). Principals as leaders of high performing systems. *Educational Leadership* 41(5): 42–46.

Martinko, M.J.,and Gardner, W.L. (1983). Executive summary. *The behavior of high performing educational managers: An observational study*. Tallahassee: Dept. of Management, College of Business, Florida State University.

Mazzarella, Jo Ann. (1985, Winter). The effective high school principal: Sketches for a portrait. *R&D Perspectives*. Eugene: CEPM, University of Oregon.

National Association of Secondary School Principals. (1984). *The effective principal: A research summary*. Reston, Virginia: NASSP.

Peters, T.J., and Waterman, R.H. (1982). *In Search of Excellence*. New York: Harper and Row.

Peterson, K.D. (1986). Obstacles to learning from experience and principal training. *Urban Review* 17(3): 189–200.

Renihan, P. (1985, Fall). Organization theory and the logic of the dichotomy. *Educational Administration Quarterly* 21(4): 121–34.

Rowan, B. (1984, Summer). Shamanistic rituals in effective schools. *Issues in Education* II(1): 76–87.

Rowan B.; Bossert, S.T.; and Dwyer, C.D. (1983, April). Research on effective schools: A cautionary note. *Educational Researcher* 12(4): 24–31.

Russell, J.S.; White, T.E.; and Maurer, S.D. (1985). *Effective and ineffective behaviors of secondary school principals linked with school effectiveness*. Paper given at the American Educational Research Association meeting, Chicago.

Schlechty, P., and Vance, V. (1981, October). Do academically able teachers leave education? The North Carolina case. *Phi Delta Kappan* 63(2): 106–12.

Shoun, S.; Lintz, N.; and Achilles, C. (1981, Winter). As is the principal. . . . *Catalyst for Change* 10(2): 14–18.

Showers, B. (1985, April). Teachers coaching teachers. *Educational Leadership* 42: 43–48.

Sirotnik, Kenneth A. (1985, Spring). School effectiveness: A bandwagon in search of a tune. *Educational Administration Quarterly* 21(2): 135–40.

Spady, W. (1984, October). Exchanging lessons with corporate America: Report of an interview. *Thrust* 14(2): 18–22.

Strother, D.B. (1983, December). Practical applications of research: The many roles of the effective principal. *Phi Delta Kappan* 65(4): 291–94.

Sykes, G. (1983, October). Contradictions, ironies, and promises unfulfilled: A contemporary account of the status of teaching. *Phi Delta Kappan* 65(2): 87–93.

Unikel, B.W., and Bailey, M.A. (1986, May). A place where principals can learn. *Principal* 65(5): 37–39.

Vance, V., and Schlechty, P. (1982, September). The distribution of academic ability in the teaching force: Policy implications. *Phi Delta Kappan* 64(1): 22–27.

9

Educational Administration: A Critical Appraisal*

William Foster

Educational Administration as a Profession

As a profession, educational administration, which includes the various positions associated with school management, such as principals and superintendents, has been an occupation of responsibility and trust, one to which many in the teaching profession have aspired. As a profession, the position of educational administrator has been to improve, control, and manage, to whatever extent practical, the conduct of formal schooling. And as a profession, the practice of educational administration is intricately linked with the practice of schooling in the United States.

In their role as leaders educational administrators have a dual and sometimes contradictory mission: to preserve tradition and to be agents of change. They must ensure that schooling preserves and communicates the values of society, while at the same time they must see that schools are on the forefront of educational, social, and technological change. This mission is not

* I would like to thank both Dr. Joseph Rost, of the University of San Diego, and Dr. Virgil Blanke, of The Ohio State University, for the detailed suggestions made for, and which I have incorporated in, this paper. Joe Rost helped me to identify issues and recommendations that were more to the point of what I needed to say; Virgil reminded me that I had neglected issues of major importance.

easy; achieving both aspects of it is perhaps impossible. But this is what we ask of our administrators, and it is in sympathy with this difficult task that I present the following comments.

Basically and primarily, educational administration must find its mission and its purpose in the purpose of schooling generally. And this is no easy task: while we can look at corporations and industry and fairly specifically locate their purpose—in developing a better product or in producing a profit—specifying purpose is much more of a problem with schools. Indeed, the question of what schools are all about is one with a historical pedigree and no quick answer. Yet it must be asserted with some force that educational administration must derive its position and principles from more general assumptions about the nature of education in our society; otherwise, we are left to administer institutions about which we know little and expect less.

Essentially, and with apologies to the great number of thinkers who have expressed this in more complex terms, the role of American educational institutions can be conceived in either instrumentalist or developmental terms. An instrumentalist position would see the schools as instruments for preparing individuals for their future jobs, for developing an efficient and effective economy, and for ensuring a qualified and willing labor force. On the other hand, a developmental position would see the schools as primarily concerned with the individual as a member of the polity; education serves to liberate the individual from ignorance, to provide the individual with aspirations and dreams, to give the individual an image of a complete and wholesome society, and thereby to assure the preservation of a just and democratic state. Both positions, indeed, have merit, yet each are quite distinct in their basic assumptions about what schools are all about, and each carries different implications for the profession of educational administration.

Perhaps most of what we currently see and read about in education could be characterized as instrumentalist. Certainly the effective schools movement falls into this category, for here the concern is largely related to how schools can be effective in preparing future workers to compete in a local, national, and world economy. The legitimation for much of this movement is that effective schools will produce students who will be able to contibute to an effective labor force. The report entitled *A Nation At Risk* (National Commission on Excellence in Education, 1983), with its hyperbolic metaphors of war and battle, is perhaps the epitome of this kind of thinking. The idea here seems to be that the nation is at risk because we are not producing youngsters who will be able to compete effectively in the world economic markets of the future. Whatever the appeals of this notion, it represents an instrumentalist perspective of education.

A developmental perspective is held by both amateur and professional philosophers of education. In their view schooling serves to develop a populace actively involved with current political and social issues. This presupposes a literate and skilled populace; yet the major function of education goes much beyond providing so-called minimal competencies. Indeed, as Michael S. Katz (1982) has put it, the development of a "critical literacy" is imperative. Critical literacy, for Katz, is "the capacity and inclination to think critically and act on the basis of informed judgment" (p. 194). Critical literacy is consistent with what the educational philosopher Kenneth Strike calls the central purpose of schooling: "*the democratic distribution of rationality*" (1982, p. 12), meaning that schools in a democratic and liberal society serve to ensure that *all* citizens are actively engaged in acquiring those skills that will enable them to act rationally and to make critical decisions.

This approach to education stresses the rights of citizens in a democracy to participate in the decision-making process and to critically evaluate those issues and opportunities important to their welfare. In adopting this approach, a purely instrumentalist position is rejected. It is not enough, in other words, to suggest the purpose of schools is to provide useful skills that will enable individuals to earn a living, or to suggest the purpose of schools lies in securing minimal competencies that lead to functional literacy in our society. While schools may do both, the achievement of either carries no guarantee that individuals will not uncritically accept state oppression, powerlessness, or the unchangeable circumstances of their existence. Only with a critical spirit, inculcated through a developmental process, will the individual have the ability to assess and consider public policy and private opportunity.

This is where the recent excellence movement in education fails. In reviewing the excellence movement, Lasch (1985) observes that the reform of education through the excellence slogan really rests on two distinct issues, one having to do with jobs, the other with citizenship. The first makes a crucial link between schooling and the economy, promoting schools for their training potential and because of our apparent need to catch up to other world economies. In this view schooling is only instrumental to the achievement of future economic supremacy. This is the dominant consideration of the excellence-in-education movement. The other issue connected with this movement is that schooling is in itself a public good because of its intimate connection to an informed and politically active citizenry, with politics seen here in its classical sense as the common search for the virtuous and just state. This minority view of education sees excellence as residing in the achievement of equity. Education is viewed here not as training in technical skills for the sake of the national economy but as imparting knowledge of the arts and the sciences for the sake of the individual and the polity. This essentially means helping students become critically literate. Lasch's thoughts are appropriate here:

Since a revival of education has to go hand in hand with a transformation of work and citizenship, those who still believe in general education can no longer afford to ignore larger social questions. Nor can they remain neutral in struggles to democratize our political and industrial life. Education is a political question, not just because many organized interests have a stake in the existing educational system, but because it cannot survive at all, except as a shadow of itself, a collective ritual, in an uncongenial political environment. And the technological society that surrounds us, even though it is not overtly repressive, even though indeed it insists again and again on the importance of education, is about as uncongenial as an environment can get. [1985, p. 11]

This is the context within which educational administration must work. If the idea of administration is linked to the purpose of schools, then administration itself can be considered in either instrumental or critical terms. The history of the field suggests that the instrumental model is prevalent; this model views administration as a science of control whose function lies primarily in managing an organization in the most efficient manner. Administrators are trained within a functionalist paradigm, assuming that goals are unproblematic and given that the school operates in much the same manner as a machine—a little administrative oil will guarantee smooth running. The guiding principles of a critical approach to administration, on the other hand, would be those of reflective inquiry and democratic participation. Rather than see administration as the rational control of organizations, a critical administration would be concerned with the empowerment of organizational members through the use of alternative strategies of management. The contrast between these two ways of thinking about administration will be more fully explored in the next section.

The Administrative Art: Current Issues

Organizational and administrative theory in Western societies is undergoing a quiet revolution. Traditionally, the theory of organizations has been guided by what might be labeled a rational-bureaucratic model and the theory of administration by what might be called a neo-scientific model. Each of these has come under increasing attack, an attack that will be briefly described here in order to support an argument that educational administration needs to be rethought.

The dominant way of considering organizations has been to think of them as rational, almost mechanistic structures that operate in a bureaucratic fashion (Benson, 1977; Burrell and Morgan, 1979). In this view the organization takes on a life of its own, independent of the individuals that compose it, and it is considered a goal-seeking entity attempting to maximize its chances for survival. The systems approach to organizations, with its attendant organismic metaphors, is perhaps the most sophisticated and popular example of this genre. Here, the organization is considered a system composed of subsystems, each of which operates to help fulfill organizational goals. When the subsystems mesh together, the effect is organizational success. Such an approach is a functionalist one in that each part of the organization has a particular function and the organization itself has specific and set functions in society.

This conceptualization of organizations can be extended to administration. Administrators, in this view, are expected to be rational, goal-seeking individuals guided by the scientific method. Taylor's (1947) view of "scientific management" provided the groundwork for this type of thinking: through "scientific" measurement of workers' abilities and task needs, the administrator could formulate the most efficient method of conducting business. Callahan's (1962) classic treatise on the "cult of efficiency" documents how pervasive this concept was in educational administration, and how much educational administrators hoped to emulate their business-world brethren. The idea that science and research would provide the one best way of administering schools has been a concept of much significance to educational administration; it has of course grown in sophistication and technology since Taylor, but the germ of the idea remains the same. For example, Hoy and Miskel, authors of a widely used and respected text in educational administration, write that "When theory is based on systems that are logical, rational, explicit, and quantitative, practice will be similarly rational" (1982, p. 28). Similar views are found in virtually all major texts on educational administration.

Thus, in both organizational and administrative theory the dominant approach has been to attempt to scientize both organizations and administration, to remove the domain of values from consideration, and to develop a predictable, efficient method, all in the hope of rationalizing practice.

The revolution in organizational and administrative theory has been to expose this type of thinking for the mythology it is (Benson, 1983). It is not that these views are incorrect; rather, like functionalist approaches generally, they represent only partial truths disguised as an entire cosmology. Three alternative perspectives on organizations and administration express the current dissatisfaction with orthodox theory in these areas.

The first occurs within the traditional framework but represents an effort to provide a less formalistic and more relevant description of organizations and their administration. Weick's (1976) view of organizations, particularly school organizations, as being "loosely coupled" systems is one example. He sees the organization not so much as a rational, goal-achieving system than as a set of loosely coupled units where rationality may be as much a post-hoc explanation of what occurred at it may be a method for goal achievement. March and Olsen's (1976) concepts of "organized anarchies" and "garbage can decision making" are other examples. Applied originally to universities but later adopted by others for many types of organizations, these concepts point to the anarchic nature of organizations wherein different interest groups pursue their own agendas, solutions are looking for problems to solve, and there is no one grand master plan for running the organization. Rather, the organization is largely a process wherein events happen. A particular outcome may be as much a product of chance circumstances as it is of planning.

The second departure from orthodox theory is that represented by the phenomenological school. In educational administration, T.B. Greenfield is its most articulate spokesman. Organizations, for the phenomenologists, are not objective, concrete structures; rather, they are consensual realities, constructed through the members' collective agreements. Organizations, Greenfield tells us, are "inside people and are defined completely by them as they work out ideas in their heads through their actions in the practical world" (1983, p.1). Organizations do not act; people act. And because it is people who act, and in their actions create organizations, the individuals' subjective values are crucial to any understanding of organizational theory and administrative theory. Rather than basing administrative theory on a model of natural science, as his more traditional colleagues might, Greenfield suggests (1982, p. 7) that history and law might be appropriate disciplines for training administrators, for these fields consider the scope of human events and the pathos that accompanies them.

A third challenge mounted to orthodox conceptions of organization and administration consists of a series of related arguments loosely grouped under the term " critical theory." This approach attacks the assumptions on which both standard organizational and administrative theory are based, notably the idea of value neutrality and the presumption of science. Critical theory would claim that all of the social sciences, including those that deal with organization and administration, are value embedded, and that the real issue is in analyzing whose values are being furthered by these sciences. Critical theory, further, unabashedly endorses such values as liberation and equity, and sees the role of the social sciences not just in defining more appropriate control systems for running organizations but, more importantly, in self-reflective activity designed to recognize systems of domination, and, in so doing, to increase the possibility for a truly democratic regime. Like phenomenology, critical theory would consider organizations social constructions rather than objectively given. However, it would go on to say that such constructions become historically located and thus result in the unequal distribution of power and opportunity within society. A critical administrative theory is therefore an attempt to create a dialectic and a dialogue about administration, about schools, and about society.

The current status of both organizational and administrative theory, then, is somewhat in disarray. This is true in business, public, and educational administration. In the business world such highly popular works as Peters and Waterman's *In Search of Excellence* (1982) reject the traditional business-school model of the rational organization in favor of a more symbolic and cultural approach, and lesser known works, such as Culbert and McDonough's (1985) text on radicalized management, call for the rethinking of traditional management practices. In organizational theory Frost (1980) and Benson (1977), among others, have called for a newer and more radical approach. In public administration Bellone (1980) and others have called for a "new" public administration that takes values seriously.

The summary result of these various new perspectives on organization and administration has been the equivalent of a "paradigm shift," a fundamental shift in the way the organizational and administrative world is viewed. As Clark, a professor of education, succinctly puts it:

> Slowly, but inexorably, our understanding of organizations and organizing will be illuminated by new perspectives. Cumulatively, these perspectives will define and refine an alternative paradigm that will become the progenitor of numerous competing theories and structures. . . . The traditional paradigm will atrophy along with its derivative schema because it differs too markedly from the logic-in-use in organizations. [1985, p. 77]

That a paradigm shift is occurring in both administrative and organizational theory, and social science more generally, is fairly well established. But the force of this paradigm shift does not lie so much in the rejection of positivistic research methodology and functionalist thought, nor so much in the legitimacy of alternative perspectives, but more in the establishment of a *moral context* for the social sciences generally. This essentially means that the purpose and role of the social sciences in addressing the valuative and moral dimensions of human life will take the forefront. It is this that will constitute the basic dimensions of the new paradigm. The distinguished economist Albert Hirschman, in a presentation on morality and the social sciences, sums up this position most eloquently:

> It is . . . possible to visualize down the road a kind of social science that would be very different from the one most of us have been practicing: a moral-social science where moral considerations are not repressed or kept apart but are systematically commingled with analytic argument without guilt feelings over any lack of integration; where the transition from preaching to proving and back again is performed frequently and with ease; and where moral considerations need no longer be smuggled in surreptitiously nor expressed unconsciously but are displayed openly and disarmingly. [1983, p. 31]

This type of "moral-social science" is the foundation of a new paradigm and will inform new ways of looking at educational administration.

The Challenge of Administration

One of the notable failures of educational administrative theory has been its inability to come up with a theory of administration that has a truly educational rather than business character. If administrative theory, however, is seen in moral terms and with a goal of critical literacy, there is more of a possibility of developing an administrative theory geared to the needs of schools particularly. Such a development, however, will have to overcome what I consider to be two dominant types of challenges to the field: challenges of equity and challenges of democracy.

Challenges of equity have to do with how administrators, and administrative theory itself, can deal with the educational disenfranchisement of various groups in our society, and with how critical literacy can be democratically distributed without regard to social classifications. A number of studies have shown that many of the major problems associated with the education of working and under classes are located in the interaction between school and student. Student dropouts, for example, are typically blamed for lack of ability or lack of motivation, but, as Papagiannis and his colleagues show (1983), school failure "is a socially organized 'accomplishment' involving both teachers and students in the culturally sanctioned allocation of social roles" (p. 371), and dropping out is for many youngsters a particularly *rational* response to the circumstances of school.

In a related study, Anyon (1981) examined schools in various settings: working-class, middle-class, professional, and executive-elite areas. She reports that school knowledge in the working-class school "was not so much bodies of ideas or connected generalizations, as fragmented *facts* and *bahaviors* . . ." (p. 119), while in the affluent, professional setting, such knowledge was "more abundant, difficult, analytical, and conceptual . . . [with] frequent attempts to engage the children in inquiry and in solving problems conceived by themselves" (p. 124). Ogbu, an anthropologist, studied black children in Stockton, California. Ogbu concluded that the black minority, and certain other minority groups, could be accurately labeled "castelike" because "(1) they have been incorporated into the society rather involuntarily and permanently, (2) they face a job and status ceiling, and (3) they tend to formulate their economic and social problems in terms of collective institutional discrimination, which they perceive as more than temporary" (1982, p. 299). Because of this, such minority groups develop what Ogbu terms survival strategies, which sometimes include a rejection of schooling and those "special services" provided to them by schools. Time spent in schools, in other words, was for some of these youths counterproductive because the time invested would not lead to the same reward level a white youngster would receive for the same investment.

Should these issues, which carry a stark and naked reality about schooling, be of any administrative concern, or should they grace only the pages of academic journals and the blackboards of sociology classes? The answer, if we accept the reformulation of administration as a moral science with an interest in critical literacy, is clear. The studies, and the issues and problems they surface, are a real and everyday concern to administrators and need recognition within a science of educational administration. What they point to, indeed, is the very great need for a science of administration to come to terms with the current distribution of wealth, knowledge, and power in our society and to begin to develop a number of alternative proposals designed to increase these for all of us. Further, we find that little attention is paid to other issues of equity, particularly our concern for peace and for the establishment of human dignity in all societies. A science of administration must make such moral issues a primary focus in order to at least communicate to our youngsters the urgency of world problems.

Challenges of democracy pose another concern. Dewey, the great American philosopher, showed us that for the student schooling is not preparation for life, it *is* life. The paradox of administration and of teaching has been this very question: How does one run a public institution with some semblance of order and control and still develop an environment within which democracy can flourish? The challenge can be met by administrators who remain aware of two principles: (1) a democracy such as ours is a collection of interest groups, coalitions, and politics, and (2) a leader's role is to empower followers. These aphorisms mean, first, that a democratically run school or school system is neither anarchic nor necessarily a "town hall." Rather, it means that particpation and voice are fundamental and that decision making becomes shared to a much greater degree than current practice seems to allow. The perennial conflicts would be resolved, as they often are today, through coalition-building, political activity, and informed choice, rather than through technical planning and systematic procedures. The result is more messy, and perhaps not as well managed, but is nevertheless an appropriate one. As it stands today, there is an unfortunate gap in status, responsibility, and control among students, parents, teachers, and administrators. The need of individuals to participate in student life and working life is one that cannot be denied and can be satisfied only through closing this gap by encouraging teacher, student, parent, and community participation in all aspects of the school administration. The current tendency to increasingly bureaucratize the school through state mandates and legislation, to standardize schooling through required textbooks and tests, and to otherwise deprofessionalize teaching is unfortunate and suggests that community determination of the educational program will remain only a dream.

A second point to consider is the administrator's role as a school leader. Burns, the Pulitzer Prize winning author and historian, makes a distinction between transactional and transformational leadership (1978), a distinction that has completely reformed leadership studies. Transactional leadership refers to those exchanges made between leaders and followers in order to meet the needs of both; transformational leadership, however, is when the leader is able to transform and change, to elevate, followers' needs, wants, and motives. It is giving to followers, rather than taking from them; it is, in Bennis's words (1984), empowering followers by showing them the possibilities and raising their consciousness; that is, by giving them power. This, indeed, is what an effective school leader does: the leader communicates with teachers, parents, and students; shows them the possible; and provides them with more efficacy and control. The leader's job is not to regulate but to elevate. To give followers power is to give them voice and the ability to participate effectively in governance. Leadership such as this and the democratic administration of schools go hand in hand.

Reforming the Profession

Given the discussion that has been presented to this point, what can be done to reform the profession of educational administration to ensure that the future cadre of administrators is concerned not only with the effective and efficient management of schools but also with issues of equity and democracy? In their review of administrative preparation programs, Peterson and Finn (1985) offer the following assessment:

> Even the most cursory look at conventional graduate programs in educational administration uncovers the reason why . . . major lacunae exist in so many of them. The required courses in such programs—closely tracking those spelled out in state certification requirements—commonly emphasize building management rather than instructional leadership, paying far closer attention to such subjects as school law and school finance (sometimes even to such minutiae as 'facilities and transportation' or 'scheduling') than to understanding what makes good teaching, what constitutes an outstanding history textbook, or how to determine whether a youngster is learning up to the level of his ability. [P. 49]

Their indictment is accurate, but what they identify as some of the alternative skills are really the result of education in critical literacy—the ability to identify and critique a subject or area—rather than in techniques whose components have been readily identified and can be easily taught. Preparation programs need to consider more readily the current developments in the field of organizational theory, administrative theory, and leadership. To this end this section will offer some recommendations for training administrators and for their roles as administrators.

Training Educational Administrators

1. Programs in educational administration must begin to identify themselves as major avenues for the moral and intellectual education of aspiring
administrators. National, state, and other agencies concerned with the
training and education of administrators should encourage such programs to
develop and apply more consistently concepts dealing with moral, ethical,
political, and equity issues in both coursework and program development.
Such programs should be encouraged to investigate new and different
paradigms for the training and education of administrators, concentrating on
the idea of administrative science as a specifically moral science.

2. In light of the above recommendation, rediscover the university as an
arena for debating ideas and for advancing scholarship. Identify those skills
needed to help maintain schools (such as scheduling, plant management,
and contract negotiation) but which require training rather than education,
and let school systems assume responsibility for training administrators in
those skills. Let university programs be devoted to the continuing education
of administrators in such areas as administrative theory; political theory;
leadership; the United States Constitution and the laws of United States; the
history, sociology, and psychology of education; and the nature of a participatory democracy.

3. Allow and even encourage innovative and experimental programs in
the training of educational administrators. The paradigm shift and the
presence of alternative perspectives in administrative theory suggest that the
time is right for allowing administrator preparation programs to reconsider
their standard coursework and to try out different training models.

4. Encourage institutions of higher learning to incorporate concepts from
the disciplines of history, law, and politics within their coursework in order to
refresh administrators' familiarity with the principles of a representative
democracy, with the constitutional demands placed on them, and with the
history of a free nation.

5. Redesign the host of competencies, objectives, and other specified
criteria for administrators adopted by the credentialing agencies in a number
of states. These requirements currently have a chilling effect on innovation
and experimentation in administrator preparation programs. While such
state controls may have their place in regulating the quality of entry into and
exit from the profession, they need to be more sensitive to the idea of the
administrator as a school leader and less concerned with the idea of an
administrator as a building or plant manager. Such competencies must
address the idea of the administrator as a champion of values, as a proponent
of change, as a messenger of participation.

The Role of Educational Administrators

1. Renew the role of the principal. Long considered a school manager, the principal might more adequately be considered a school leader. As a leader, the principal would be more concerned with instructional development and the development of community. The principal's role is currently too occupied with paperwork; it would profit from redefinition, with appropriate support from the central office. Consider the value of teachers' electing school leaders every three to four years. De-emphasize the idea of instructional control to the extent that it means close supervision of teachers by the principal for the purpose of measuring time-on-task or other methodological interventions. Consider the principal to be responsible for long-term assistance and development, consonant with the conception that teachers, as trained professionals, should be allowed to make decisions in their classrooms.

2. Create a long-term internship track within schools, along the line of an "assistant school leader." Individuals interested in administration would first, outside a university program, be nominated and accepted for this track and would then (1) understudy the principal and (2) assume responsibility for attendance, budget, and other reporting functions. The expectation would be that these individuals would gain through experience a basic knowledge of the technical requirements of administration as well as a knowledge of school leadership; these skills would be important for both teachers and future principals.

3. Reduce the number of people involved in any one educational unit by either creating schools within schools or establishing physically separate units. The personal administration of schools required to implement these suggestions is stymied by large, unwieldy institutions that require the expansion of bureaucratic structures simply to get something done.

4. Support more strongly the idea of principals' centers or leadership institutes, which would give administrators the opportunity to refresh their knowledge and to make contact with their peers. Such centers should be designed to acquaint principals and other administrators with the latest developments in school-based research, political theory, leadership theory, and other areas of significance to the occupation.

5. Revamp in-service education in school districts. Allow principals and teachers to be more heavily involved in running such programs, and make such programs site specific. Include in such programs means to develop critical inquiry skills. Too often such in-service education programs provide general and inappropriate topics selected because of their currency or the presenter but which do not address adequately the needs of the teachers, students, or administrators. Training in designing relevant programs should be encouraged.

Conclusion

The administration of a formal network of schools designed to educate youngsters of a nation of more than two hundred and thirty million people is no easy task. Yet this task is fundamental to the continued existence of a nation founded on constitutional principles and committted to basic human ideals. It is imperative that the practice of administration itself be rededicated to those ideals. Longer training periods in essentially the same old concepts will not suffice; neither will attempts to "tighten up" the field through more stringent state requirements. James March once commented that "changing education by changing educational administration is like changing the course of the Mississipi by spitting into the Allegheny" (1978, p. 219). Perhaps he had in mind piecemeal reforms rather than the reformation in thinking proposed here.

References

Anyon, J. (1981). Elementary schooling and distinctions of social class. *Interchange* 12(2-3): 118–32.

Bellone, C.J. (Ed.) (1980). *Organization theory and the new public administration*. Boston: Allyn and Bacon.

Bennis, W. (1984). Transformative power and leadership. In T.J. Sergiovanni and J.E. Corbally (Eds.), *Leadership and organizational culture*. Urbana: University of Illinois Press.

Benson, J.K. (1977). Innovation and crisis in organizational analysis. In J.K. Benson (Ed.), *Organizational analysis: Critique and innovation*. Beverly Hills, Calif.: Sage.

Benson, J.K. (1983). Paradigms and praxis in organizational analysis. In L.L. Cummings and B.M. Staw (Eds.), *Research in organizational behavior*, Vol. 6. Greenwich, Conn.: JAI Press.

Burns, J.M. (1978). *Leadership*. New York: Harper & Row.

Burrell, G., and Morgan, G. (1979). *Sociological paradigms and organisational analysis*. Exeter, NH: Heinemann.

Callahan, R. (1962). *Education and the cult of efficiency*. Chicago: University of Chicago Press.

Clark, D. (1985). Emerging paradigms in organizational theory and research. In Y.S. Lincoln (Ed.), *Organizational theory and inquiry: The paradigm revolution*. Beverly Hills, Calif.: Sage.

Culbert, S.A., and McDonough, J.J. (1985). *Radical management: Power politics and the pursuit of trust*. New York: The Free Press.

Frost, P. (1980). Toward a radical framework for practicing organization science. *Academy of Management Review* 5(4): 501–07.

Greenfield, T.B. (1982). Against group mind: an anarchistic theory of organization. *McGill Journal of Education* 17(1): 3–11.

Greenfield, T.B. (1983). Environment as subjective reality. Paper presented at the Annual Meeting of the American Educational Research Association, Montreal.

Hirschman, A.O. (1983). Morality and the social sciences: A durable tension. In N. Haan, R.N. Bellah, P. Rabinow, and W.M. Sullivan (Eds.), *Social science as moral inquiry*. New York: Columbia University Press.

Hoy, W.K., and Miskel, C.G. (1982). *Educational administration: Theory, research and practice*. 2d ed. New York: Random House.

Katz, M.S. (1982). Critical literacy: A conception of education as a moral right and a social ideal. In R.B. Everhart (Ed.), *The public school monopoly: A critical analysis of education and the state in American society*. San Francisco: Pacific Institute for Public Policy Research.

Lasch, C. (1985). "Excellence" in education: Old refrain or new departure? *Issues in Education* 3 (1): 1–12.

March, J.G. (1978). American public school administration: A short analysis. *School Review* 86(2): 217–50.

March, J.G., and Olsen, J.P. (1976). *Ambiguity and choice in organization*. Bergen, Norway: Universitetsforlaget.

National Commission on Excellence in Education (1983). *A nation at risk: The imperative for educational reform*. Washington, D.C.: U.S. Department of Education.

Ogbu, J. (1982). Cultural discontinuities and schooling. *Anthropology and Education Quarterly* 13(4): 290–307.

Papagiannis, G.J.; Bickel, R.N.; and Fuller, R.H. (1983). The social creation of school dropouts: Accomplishing the reproduction of an underclass. *Youth and Society* 14(3): 363–92.

Peters, T.J., and Waterman, R.H. (1982). *In search of excellence*. New York: Harper & Row.

Peterson, K.D., and Finn, C.E., Jr. (1985). Principals, superintendents, and the administrator's art.*The Public Interest* 79: 42–62.

Strike, K.A. (1982). *Educational policy and the just society*. Urbana: University of Illinois Press.

Taylor, F.W. (1947). *Scientific management*. New York: Harper Bros.

Weick, K. (1976). Educational organizations as loosely coupled systems. *Administrative Science Quarterly* 21(1): 1–19.

10

Universities and the Improvement of School Management: Roles for the States*

Willis D. Hawley

Introduction

There are many reasons to believe that the current school improvement movement is different and more promising than were its predecessors. The most significant difference is the recognition of the centrality of teaching to the process of learning. Happily, political action and research have come together to make clear what many parents knew but few scholars and policymakers apparently believed—schools can be only as good as the teachers who staff them.

This recognition should be matched—though it is not by most of the national reports and many state plans—by the apppreciation that the quality of administrative support and organizational structure teachers experience define the upward boundaries of teacher effectiveness. That is, high-quality instruction depends significantly on district- and school-level resources,

---

* These proposals, in slightly different form, were made to the annual meeting of the Council of Chief State School Officers, Sun Valley, Idaho, July 27, 1984.

working conditions, opportunities for professional development, and incentives over which school administrators have very great influence. Thus, while good teaching results in school effectiveness, effective leadership is probably the single most important determinant of good teaching.

I shall do three things in this short paper: (1) identify what universities should do to improve school management; (2) suggest why too many universities could not do most of these things, even if they wanted to; and (3) outline some things that might be done, especially by states, to improve the education of school administrators.

What Universities Should Do to Help Improve School Management

Universities could take at least ten significant steps to enhance the effectiveness of school managers:

1. Focus on developing the skills necessary for *instructional* leadership. Those skills are known and they can be taught. They are not being taught systematically in most places.

2. Develop in their students capabilities for analysis, problem solving, evaluation, and communication.

3. Model what is being taught through instruction, evaluation, and interpersonal relations. This might be facilitated by adding "clinical professors" to the faculty—active but part-time professionals who are continuing members of the faculty. This approach is common practice in medical schools.

4. Upgrade the rigor of the curriculum. For example, the curriculum should be broader in its theoretical reach, be stronger in its focus on the use of information, and place more emphasis on effective writing. The substance of courses should reflect current research on exemplary practices.

5. Reach out to other disciplines and professions. Business schools are often seen as appropriate collaborators in the training of school managers. Collaboration, however, is less rewarding and more difficult to do than it seems. The curriculum in school administration could draw on the research and literature from other university departments including English, philosophy, economics, sociology, and history in ways that directly complement professional studies.

6. Change the format for doctoral studies. Most programs are a schizophrenic mix of doctoral study in the disciplines and practice-oriented application. The distinction between the Ed.D. and Ph.D. has been lost, and there is a need to revitalize the Ed.D. We need to strive for a *professional* curriculum based on agreements about basic knowledge

and abilities and about rigorous written and performance tests of what people know and whether they can do the things embodied in the curriculum.

7. Upgrade standards for admission and exit. Many institutions have no effective screens. More doctoral degrees are awarded in educational administration than in any other field.

8. Insist that the faculty members responsible for advanced training be involved in systematic inquiry or, at least, in using research to develop training materials, educational practices, or educationally useful products.

9. Develop collaborative research and development projects including training activities with state and local agencies that consciously integrate the research, instruction, and "service" roles of the university. Some examples of this include staff development, the introduction of new curricula, and the use of computers to improve management.

10. Loosen the tie between the delivery of instruction and the provision of service on the one hand and credit-generating courses and degree programs on the other hand. Here again, the role of the university should be collaborative and should focus on capacity building within state and local agencies. These efforts need not—should not—focus solely on the development of narrow "practical" skills.

These ten proposals, if implemented, would result in increasing the ability of universities to enhance the competence of school managers by improving the instructional programs, fostering meaningful involvement in related research and development activities and promoting collaboration with state and local educational agencies. Many other things could be done, but these ten seem to have the highest priority and, for the most part, involve nonincremental changes in the way universities foster more effective educational administration.

Can Universities Significantly Increase Their Contributions to Effective School Management?

It is one thing to talk about what universities *should* do to improve educational administration; it is another to identify what they are *able* to do. While it is unpleasant to acknowledge this, given current resources, capabilities, processes, and dispositions, most universities are having little effect on school management and are not likely to be of much help in the foreseeable future. Bluntly, most programs for training school administrators range in quality from embarrassing to disastrous. The problems are many:

1. Most faculty are only marginally more knowledgeable than their students.
2. Few persons teaching on doctoral programs are now or ever have been involved in research and are not qualified to supervise research. Thus, very little good research is being conducted by faculty and students. In turn, students often consider research to be esoteric and trivial.
3. Admission standards are weak and performance criteria ill-defined. For these reasons, and because most students are part time, expectations for how much should be learned are usually not high.
4. Professors of educational administration often bear much heavier teaching and advising loads than do doctoral professors in other fields. Frequently, doctoral programs in school administration are money makers used to support the work that universities consider more important. Other disciplines often have little interest in working with education students, and faculty in other departments of the university are often unwilling to work with schools of education, even to the point of adjusting course offerings to the schedule of part-time students.
5. Uncertainty of purpose and lack of self-esteem among the education administration professoriate contribute to and are fostered by low status not only within universities but within schools of education.
6. There is virtually no investment in targeted and systematic professional upgrading of college faculty. This is a particularly important problem in fields that change rapidly and serve individuals who are themselves involved in the change process.
7. Linkages to practitioners are typically weak and are more often based on personal relationships than on the identification of interdependent but distinct capabilities.

In short, we have a great need to improve the quality of educational administration faculty and program within universities. Without improvements, we will continue to have a near-obsolescent capacity. One can readily argue that universities, in schools of education and in other units, have considerable potential for supporting efforts to improve school management. This potential, however, is but a distant vision for all too many universities educating school leaders, and there are no mechanisms for revitalization.

Improving Universities' Capacities for Improving School Administration—Carrots and Sticks

A number of things can be done to induce and support changes in the capacity of universities in order to improve school management. Some of these things are within the capability of universities, but few universities seem to have such ambitions. The problem is so great that it will require forces and resources external to universities to bring about needed changes. Exhorting universities to do better in and of itself will only sustain the status quo. State governments need to encourage universities to help improve school administration, and to do so they can use the following "carrots and sticks."

1. Support efforts to strengthen the education administration professoriate. As in other fields, this involves providing opportunities for professional development. For example, states could provide to individuals, on a competitive basis, vouchers for full-time study usable at both public and private institutions.

2. Reduce the number of institutions offering advanced programs in educational administration. It is not clear how best to do this, and there is no effective accrediting agency. Some possible ways to reduce the number of institutions are:

   a. Insist on higher admission requirements for graduate programs receiving state support.

   b. Eliminate salary credits for degrees above the master's. This would change educators' (consumers') incentives to pursue advanced training so that more weight is put on the perceived value of the program in enhancing professional competence than on the ease by which the degree or credit could be obtained. This would introduce more genuine market conditions and would encourage change.

   c. Assist in the development of performance tests that could be used to counsel students, certify programs, and authorize expenditures of vouchers.

3. On an experimental basis, support the development of a national written test of analytical, writing, and management skills and professional knowledge akin to the National Bar Exam but focused on problem solvng.

4. Develop ways of systematically evaluating administrators' performance and rewarding excellence in school administration.

5. Put money into staff development targeted to the needs of principals and middle-level staff and do this through a voucher plan in which both public and private universities and school systems could participate.

6. Encourage state universities to devote more energy to the needs of school systems by altering funding formulas to allow in-service, on-site staff development. Why must a professor teach a conventional credit class in conventional ways to be involved in teaching?

7. Do not allow principal or administrator academies to grant credit or degrees. Collaboration, not unfair competition, should be the goal. There is absolutely no reason to believe that state agencies can, over

time, perform educational functions related to advanced study as well as could the best universities. Indeed, the opposite is true. Moreover, weaker university programs would probably accept such credits for degrees in order to attract students.

8. Support collaborative reasearch and development between schools and universities on a competitive basis.

9. Consider assisting in the development of better in-service training materials. We are still in the jug and mug mode of instruction. Computers, video disks, cable television, two-way satellite communication, and the like, open new possibilities, but material development is too expensive for individual programs. It would be sensible for the federal government to do this, but the promise here is not substantial.

Conclusion

In closing I have five final comments on the future needs of and directions for improvement in educational administration. First, we are not likely to achieve significant and lasting changes in American education without substantial improvements in the quality of school management. As our expectations for schools increase, so will the challenges to educational managers grow. In addition, disproportional numbers of school administrators will retire in the next few years. The opportunity for improving school management, however, now exceeds our grasp.

Second, the solution to the problem is not to make university professors more like practitioners. Indeed, the opposite is true. The solution is to build on the unique role of universities in the development and dissemination of knowledge so that collaboration between universities and schools can be based on a genuine interdependence that strengthens both research and practice. It seems important to maintain the tension between practicality on the one hand and theory and ideas on the other.

Third, as we think about the contributions universities can make to improving school management, we should not limit our reach to schools of education. Universities have a broad range of resources that most would-be and practicing school administrators never encounter. Moreover, some of the problems in schools of education can be traced to discriminatory funding policies and university-wide practices that make it difficult for low-status professional programs to play their appropriate roles.

Fourth, both public and private universities that can make contributions should be nurtured. Of the dozen best educational administration programs, half are in private universities. Moreover, precisely because they must be more market oriented, private uiversities may be more innovative and entrepreneurial. Don't make their lives more difficult. Competition among service providers is a good thing.

Finally, in the pursuit of efforts to improve the contributions universities can make to school management, it seems important that states resist the temptation to solve the problem by relying too heavily on the containment and reduction of inadequacy and on other essentially regulatory policies. Such policies will lead to some improvements, but they limit ambition. In schools of education these regulatory policies lead to discriminatory funding policies and university-wide practices that make it difficult for low-status professional programs to play their appropriate roles. Do not alter capacity—the need is to engender new commitments and capabilities and to provide conditions and incentives that energize. We are involved, after all, in a noble quest, and its drama is a tool we underutilize when we rely on regulation and ignore developmental strategies.

11

Principals, Superintendents, and the Administrator's Art

Kent D. Peterson and Chester E. Finn, Jr.

School critic Emily Feistritzer may have erred when she asserted in mid 1984 that "nothing in American education is in greater need of reform than the way we educate and certify classroom teachers. Perhaps she overlooked principals and superintendents, a much smaller cadre of men and women who wield even greater authority over the nation's public schools and whose own education and certification are ordinarily erratic, oftentimes mediocre, and in some cases even dysfunctional.

Practically never does one encounter a good school with a bad principal or a high-achieving school system with a low performance superintendent. Ample research into the characteristics of particularly effective schools confirms the conclusions of common sense: The caliber of institutional leadership powerfully influences the quality of education. Yet at a time when the nation is deeply concerned about the performance of its schools, and near-to-obsessed with the credentials and careers of those who teach in them, scant attention has been paid to the preparation and qualifications of those who lead them.

Reprinted with permission from *The Public Interest* No. 79 (Spring 1985): 42–62. © 1985 by National Affairs, Inc.

This is curious for many reasons, not least because a relatively modest investment of intellectual and political energy in this domain could yield hefty returns. There are 2.3 million teachers, but school principals and superintendents together number fewer than 100,000 individuals. And whereas most teachers enjoy the dual protections of tenure and union membership, most principals do not, nor are the latter invariably bound to uniform salary schedules. Moreover, the next few years will witness a big turnover in their ranks. Upwards of 50 percent of all current principals hired in the 1960s and 1970s expect to retire or change jobs by 1990. Hence this is a profession vulnerable to policy changes as well as one where such changes need to occur quickly if they are to influence the quality of American school leadership for the remainder of the century.

Another new development makes this an opportune time to scrutinize the preparation and selection of education's middle managers. Traditionally, the principalship was the surest route out of the classroom and upward through the profession for the teacher who sought greater status, more influence, and a larger salary. Superintendents, in turn, have usually come from the ranks of former principals, often with several stops en route through the staff bureaucracies of school system central offices. The education profession has been a single pyramid with a large number of teachers at the bottom and a small number of administrators at the top. Now, however, we are seeing the development of "career ladders" for teachers in a few states (such as Texas and Tennessee) and communities (such as Charlotte-Mecklenburg, North Carolina) and are apt to see many more of these. Opportunities will thereby become available for talented and ambitious instructors to become "master teachers," "mentor teachers," "supervising teachers," and the like, with attendant increases in prestige and remuneration. Under these conditions the teaching occupation will become more like the college professoriate, conferring added status, responsibility, and pay on individuals who continue in the core role. And, just as being a full professor is more attractive to many academics than serving as dean or provost, teachers may find that remaining in the classroom is more rewarding than working at an office job. Moreover, as teaching gains some of the attributes of a true profession, the status and authority of the principal will change, and in time so will the position of the school superintendent. Hence it is none too soon to examine the means by which people are trained, certified, and chosen for these key positions.

Licensing and the Universities

Today, essentially all principals and superintendents are former teachers—the traditional structure of the profession here well butressed by the requirement in nearly every state that one must have taught a minimum of three years before becoming eligible for an administrator's license. This means that most principals and superintendents got their undergraduate education in teacher's colleges. It also means that one almost never finds a retired military officer, former bank manager, or ex-college dean heading a public school system. Lateral entry into administration, common enough in business and other sectors, is practically unheard in public education— though private schools sometimes choose former professors, quondam deans, clergymen, even the occasional business executive, to lead them.

State licensure is everywhere a precondition to the principalship, and usually to the superintendency. (In a few jurisdictions, the superintendent is popularly elected rather than appointed by the school board.) Apart from teaching experience, licensure requirements vary considerably, from a handful of designated courses in school administration and school law to the possession of a master's degree from an "approved program" of graduate study. But whether few or many, these requirements are nearly always stated in terms of paper credentials supplied by colleges of education—transcripts and credit hours that must parallel those on a list maintained by the certification bureau of the state education department. License seekers rarely have to pass any sort of test or examination analogous to a bar exam or to medicine's "national boards," nor does the education profession enforce any substantial standards for those seeking administrative certification. One gains entry into the association of principals and superintendents simply by paying dues to them; attainment of that august station depends wholly on getting licensed by the state and hired by a school system, not on demonstrating knowledge or proficiency to one's professional peers.

In practice, earning a master's degree in education, usually in school administration, is the most common way of satisfying state licensure requirements. Fewer than 5 percent of all principals lack such degrees, which are awarded in large numbers by many universities. One third of *all* American master's degrees conferred in 1980–81 were in the field of education, and these included 9,300 in administration *per se* and thousands more in related subfields. (In the same year, the nation's universities handed out 2,000 master's degrees in hospital and health care administration, 6,700 in public administration, 33,800 in business administration.)

In the higher elevations of graduate study, the field of education also looms large, accounting for almost one quarter of earned doctorates. At this level, administration is the largest education subspecialty, numbering 1,600 degrees in 1980–81, about half as many as were earned in either the physical sciences or the social sciences.

Unlike most professional fields, however, educational administration displays no clear line of demarcation between the master's degree and the doctorate. Holding an Ed.D. or Ph.D. is a means of acquiring extra status and perhaps a better job, especially if one aspires to be superintendent of schools in a good district or, perhaps, a high school principal in one of the "lighthouse" systems such as New Trier, Greenwich, or Brookline. But in no state is it necessary to have the terminal degree in order to obtain an administrator's license.

The curious thing about such a license is that even where it is nominally necessary to possess a master's degree, one is rarely obliged to pass through a coherent program of professional training at a single university. The master's degree that is needed to become certified as a school administrator need not necessarily be a degree *in* school administration; in many states, any master's degree will do, if one has also accumulated the mandatory transcript entries, no matter how piecemeal the process of accumulation.

This arrangement naturally makes life easier for the aspiring school administrator, typically a part-time graduate student who takes a course or two each semester, often at night or on weekends, and another set of courses during summer vacation, all the while holding down a full-time job in the school system. Most universities allow students to transfer credit for courses taken elsewhere (including those taken many years earlier). Hence the institution that awards the degree may actually have been the source of a small fraction of the transcript credits that the degree holder presents to the state certification bureau.

This pattern is even more common at the doctoral level, where only by happenstance will an individual receive his terminal degree from the same institution where he earned his master's degree. Moreover, one can get by in some states without presenting a completed degree at all, so long as one's transcript contains an accumulation of courses with the correct titles. It is therefore possible to acquire one's graduate training in a congeries of institutions over a lengthy period, piling up course credits without the discipline of a formal program in school administration and without receiving the benefit of consistent supervision or feedback from the faculty of any single university. Many institutions of higher education will cheerfully cooperate; about 265 of them run administrator training programs recognized by the National Council for Accreditation of Teacher Education; dozens more offer degrees and many others supply isolated courses that may be counted toward licensure requirements. Thus academic preparation for school leadership is more apt to resemble a slow but lengthy wade along a shallow and meandering stream of unrelated course offerings than the total immersion in a deep pool that is the standard preparation for careers in law, medicine, and academe.

Still, graduate schools of education do function as gatekeepers to the precincts of school administration, controlling access and defining participation by furnishing the requisite courses and transcript entries with which a would-be administrator attains formal eligibility for such a position. Their norms, their standards, their educational requirements, and their professional expectations are more influential than any other single set of factors and will continue to be so long as states recognize their transcripts as the primary credentials, a situation the colleges of education understandably hope to preserve.

How did the universities acquire this hegemony over eligibility for positions of school leadership? In essence, they imitated the traditional professions, entry into which is, to all intents and purposes, restricted to the graduates of university-based "preservice training" programs beyond the baccalaureate—programs that undertake to supply a body of distinctive knowledge and set of prescribed skills, the acquisition of which is then tested through examinations given jointly by the state and the profession or through completion of an elaborate supervised internship. (Until recently, residents of some states could bypass law school and "read law" with a veteran attorney in preparation for the bar examination, but now—so far as we know—the university-conferred law degree is required in all jurisdictions. The M.D. degree is required of entrants into medicine, save for immigrants who may instead pass what amounts to an equivalency test. Only rarely does anyone become a professor without an earned doctorate in his discipline.)

The Evolution of Administration

University-based programs in educational administration developed later than those of the other professions, though Harvard established one for a time in the late nineteenth century. Paul Hanus proposed it and, reports Arthur Powell, President Eliot "strongly endorsed the idea to 'aim distinctly at training superintendents'," for he sensed that they "needed to be regarded as experts qualified to assume 'full charge of the intellectual and moral management of the schools'." This program fell into desuetude in the twenties, because President Lowell "doubted the legitimacy of school administration as a proper field of study." But in the meantime the idea of doctoral level study in education had begun to gain legitimacy at Columbia's Teachers College, starting with the appointment of Dean James E. Russell in 1898.

Though administration did not reappear as a distinct subspecialty until later, its legitimacy was fairly well established on many campuses by the 1920s and 1930s, as principles of "scientific management" began to be applied to the schools. This development portended specialized—and university-based—training for the managers. And as possession of a college degree became a standard requirement for teachers—replacing the old "normal school" pattern—it was entirely predictable that persons engaged to supervise teachers and administer schools would be expected to have more advanced training than their subordinates. By the 1940s, educational administration was an accepted field of graduate education on many campuses, and these programs burgeoned as the postwar baby boom led to a massive expansion of school enrollments and to the need for many more principals and other specialized administrators. By the 1960s, hundreds of colleges and universities had programs in educational administration, and most of these endure today.

Other industrial nations have tended to follow the American pattern. Canada and Australia opened their first graduate programs in educational administration in the late 1950s. In Europe, where formerly the person in charge of a school was likely to be either a "head teacher" or a civil servant, today one finds under development new programs for the training of school leaders, formalizing their preparation through a sequence including university study, on-the-job training, and government licensure.

Though the elements of this mix have for some time been the norm for public schooling throughout the United States, the sequence differs sharply from the patterns by which administrators are prepared and chosen for the institutional units of other professions. In law offices, hospitals, and universities themselves, middle-level managers and unit leaders either are selected informally from within the ranks of the professions, according to demonstrated competence and peer judgements, or else individuals are specially trained as managers outside the professions of those whose work they will direct. The managing partner of a law firm is simply a lawyer; the dean of a college is a professor. A hospital administrator, on the other hand, is rarely a physician nowadays, and although the director of student activities on a university campus may possess a degree in higher education, he is not likely to be a trained scholar or practicing teacher. Nursing, social work, and public administration more closely resemble education insofar as line professionals seeking to scale the organizational hierarchy are apt to return to the university for additional formal training in administration. Yet the public school remains one of the few domains in which leadership positions are actually restricted to people who, years after entering the field as line professionals, go back to graduate school for further education in order to meet an additional set of state licensure requirements.

No doubt this sequence serves the interests of the graduate schools of education and in some ways those of the occupation. It probably yields a form of natural selection, reducing competition for available administrative jobs, simplifying the tasks of the license-givers (since the state does not make real competency judgments about individuals, any clerk can see whether one's paper credentials conform to the formal requirements), and sparing the profession the awkwardness and bother of peer evaluations. But does it make for better schools? Is there a valid relationship between what individuals do in universities in order to become licensed as educational administrators and the actual knowledge, skills, and competencies that they need in order to be effective unit managers and system leaders in the public schools? If not, sizable sums of time and money are being squandered, some by the individuals who endure this routine, more by the society that underwrites the bulk of their training. (Of the 3,663 master's degrees in educational administration awarded in the southeastern states in 1979–80, only 557 came from private universities. The rest were financed predominantly by the taxpayer.)

"Mickey Mouse" Programs?

An overall assessment of the quality and utility of these programs is not easy to make. It is possible that one factor contributing to the strong educational showing of private schools is their freedom to hire whomever they like to direct them. But nowhere in the United States is there a significant population of public school principals and superintendents who did not follow the familiar pattern of graduate education and state certification. Because of the requirement that administrators be experienced teachers—a surprising number turn out to have been coaches—it is impossible to disentangle the effects of their formal training as administrators from the consequences of this severe limitation on the pool of potential candidates. Still, two kinds of evidence suggest that the training-and-certification sequence leaves something to be desired. Survey after survey of practicing school administrators reveals that most judge their university training to have been easy, boring, and only intermittently useful to them in their work. As with teacher education, one frequently hears such phrases as "Mickey Mouse" used to characterize large portions of what was encountered in graduate school. Second, as the public's concern about school quality has mounted, and as the centrality of the principal's role as instructional leader has won wider appreciation, a number of states, school systems, professional associations, even foreign countries have made elaborate arrangements to retrain previously certified administrators who are already on the job. These typically take the form of summer institutes or extended workshops at which school principals are carefully shown such fundamental techniques as how to evaluate teachers, how to interpret research findings, how to construct a coherent curriculum, and how to diagnose the institutional problems that yield low student achievement test scores. These programs are occasionally offered by universities, and university-based experts are commonly engaged to teach in them, but most of them operate outside the framework of graduate training required for state certification, seemingly because such graduate training does not reliably furnish skills and knowledge of this kind.

Even the most cursory look at conventional graduate programs in educational administration uncovers the reason why these major lacunae exist in so many of them. The required courses in such programs—closely tracking those spelled out in state certification requirements—commonly emphasize building management rather than instructional leadership, paying far closer attention to such subjects as school law and school finance (sometimes even to such minutae as "facilities and transportation" or "scheduling") than to understanding what makes good teaching, what constitutes an outstanding history textbook, or how to determine whether a youngster is learning up to the level of his ability.

The courses that future school administrators take in graduate school, as Berkeley education professor James Guthrie and two associates concluded after careful examination of programs approved by California's credentialing commission, "give great attention to human relations and public relations courses and skills." Though such techniques may be worth possessing, "the knowledge and skills needed to become an effective educational leader and school manager are generally not those provided" by the administrative credentialing programs on the forty-four state campuses that offer them. Certainly these programs are remote from the kinds of study that might prepare one to assume "the intellectual and moral management of the schools," as Charles W. Eliot phrased these responsibilities many years ago.

Yet even as its content emphasizes operational tasks, the shape of the conventional graduate program hews close to the traditional model of the arts and science discipline. To earn a master's degree in educational administration, a student takes a set of required courses and electives generally taught in conventional classrooms through a familiar blend of lecture and discussion. Rarely does such a degree program require any systematic internship or supervised work in schools.

The arts and science model continues through the doctoral program, in which the student takes additional courses and seminars and then embarks upon a written dissertation, sometimes after passing a comprehensive or qualifying examination. Some programs that lead to the Doctor of Education Degree—ostensibly a "professional" rather than a "research" credential—allow students to substitute an administrative project for the dissertation. But those that yield a Ph.D. in educational administration virtually always follow the procedures for a conventional Ph.D., which is to say they are constructed as if their graduates were destined for roles as university scholars rather than as school administrators.

Absent Standards

Whereas law, medicine, and college teaching have over the years evolved their own distinctive models of graduate education, tailored—more or less successfully—to the specialized knowledge and peculiar skills required for effective performance in their professional roles, school administration has done nothing of the sort. Few programs have emulated graduate schools of business administration, public administration, or even hospital administration, many of which employ case method, supervised internships, and field projects as well as conventional classroom teaching and research. With rare exceptions, a graduate program in educational administration resembles an arts and science program more closely than anything else and has very little about it that implies the nature of the tasks awaiting its alumni.

The formal structure of the program would not matter so much if the courses initiated their students into a well-ordered body of important knowledge and imparted a set of analytic techniques that must precede mature independent work in the field, as is generally the case with the academic disciplines. Nor would structure matter hugely if the nominal checkpoints of the program—admission, satisfactory progress through it, and completion—were associated with rigorous standards of intellectual performance and individual growth. But because this profession has never reached internal agreement on any particular body of knowledge or set of skills that all its members should possess, because there is no universal competency test akin to the bar examination, and because most graduate programs in educational administration are easy to enter, hard to flunk out of, and not very difficult to complete so long as one has stamina, it is tough to justify the ersatz arts and science structure.

Like teacher education, most programs in school administration have what Dan Lortie terms "eased entry." If entrance requirements exist at all, they are not very competitive and most applicants are accepted, this in marked contrast to the situation facing prospective matriculants to most law and medical schools. In California, Guthrie found fewer than one applicant in thirty is refused admission. A handful of institutions—the University of Wisconsin comes to mind—stipulate and enforce threshold standards of grades, Graduate Record Examination scores, and the like; others, however, only go through the motions of requiring transcripts and test results, sometimes quietly assuring applicants that these will not really count in the admission process.

Eased entry downgrades the status of the student in the eyes of the populace, diminishes the value of his eventual degree, and decreases the likelihood that the green recruit will deem himself among the specially chosen bearers of a rare and valued professional heritage. This would not be a serious problem if the graduate program later weeded out the less able or diligent students via tough courses with stringent requirements and substantial intellectual demands. Yet more than 80 percent of those admitted to the California programs eventually receive their administrator's certificate, and we know of no state in which the pattern is markedly different. This is not too surprising, inasmuch as programs in school administration seldom have exacting intellectual standards in their course work; the courses themselves are often textbook-bound; they rarely have specific prerequisites and infrequently function as part of a continuum of knowledge and skills that become more sophisticated as one progresses. The part-time character of the programs dims the sense of group identity and the chance for strong professional socialization that would come from sustained interaction with exceptional peers and mentors, thereby accentuating the shallowness of the experience. Worse, eased entry and its corollaries deny these programs the ability to perform the central role of a professional school as David Riesman and Christopher Jencks depicted it in 1968: "not primarily to teach a narrowly defined set of skills of the kind measured by examinations, but to define a set of general criteria that recruits to the profession ought to meet and to screen out those who do not measure up."

Research Degrees?

The culminating experience of the educational administration doctorate (and sometimes the master's degree) at most universities is the dissertation. Though it may take the future school superintendent years to complete, the result is often poor in quality and rarely contributes materially to the enlargement of human knowledge. Its ordinary destination is the library shelf and microfilm reel, where it lingers unread forever.

This throwback to a centuries-old model of doctoral-level education obliges the future principal or superintendent to dedicate a hefty portion of his professional training to the completion of a task that has little relevance to his future responsibilities. Though educational leaders should certainly be knowledgeable readers and frequent users of research findings in their work, few if any of them will ever engage in formal research.

The point of a doctoral dissertation, after all, is to compel the mature graduate student to think originally and independently about a significant research issue, advances in which will augment the aggregate knowledge of his chosen field, while honing his skills as a scholar and demonstrating his readiness to enter the academic guild. This makes sense when preparing for a life of scholarship. But in school administration, one is called upon primarily to be an effective leader of a complex organization that serves a distinctive clientele, not to build scholarly knowledge. Though most universities cling to the dissertation requirement for education doctorates, perhaps deeming it a more manageable form of quality control than anything so tricky as professional competency testing, we are not alone in thinking it ill-suited to the education of school leaders. In 1978, Teachers College president Lawrence A. Cremin urged an end to this "mimicking of the Ph.D. program in the traditional academic areas" and its replacement by "ample opportunity . . . for individual and collaborative scholarship and performance that can be subjected to systematic review and appraisal."

Partly because of the amount of time and energy given over to the emulation of traditional scholarship, the preparation of school administrators generally lacks something that might be immeasurably more valuable to the practitioner, namely a well-organized and closely supervised clinical or apprenticeship experience. Getting a Ph.D. in history entails acting like a historian, just as completing a medical education requires much time spent in preceptorships, internships, residencies, and other understudy relationships with experienced doctors in clinical settings. Similarly, legal education is rarely complete without summers in law firms, year-long clerkships, or the multiyear apprenticeship that the neophyte associate serves at the elbow of a senior partner. Yet few educational administrators-in-training are encouraged, much less required, to undergo a rigorous supervised clinical experience of any sort.

That they may hold down full-time jobs in school systems is beside the point. During an authentic apprenticeship, the fledgling professional tests his developing skills under the careful scrutiny of a tested veteran from whom he receives regular feedback; he measures the fit between theory and practice; and he gauges the usefulness of the research-based knowledge he has been acquiring against the demands of the job itself. The apprentice tries his own hand in situations where he has the support of expert practitioners who are also available to give advice and to save the client from egregious blunders. Furthermore, such clinical experiences can solidify the collegial bonds between novice and master.

In education, however, many a new principal is "handed the keys" and given full responsibility for a building, even a cluster of buildings, without ever having engaged in the practice of school administration under the watchful eye and with the supporting hand of a seasoned professional. With luck, the bureaucratic structure of a school system will ensure that the new principal was once an assistant principal and that the superintendent previously held staff positions in the central office. But only by happenstance do those subordinate administrative roles include good supervision or an understudy relationship with an outstanding leader. Indeed, if one was the assistant principal in charge of discipline, or the assistant superintendent for facilities and equipment—common roles for assistants today—one might never have helped direct the central educational activities of the institution or observed much of the daily work of teachers. A tiny fraction of the nation's 15,000 local school systems consciously "grow their own" future leaders by placing promising candidates in intern-like settings and by supplying special training opportunities. The states, the professional organizations, and the universities tolerate this; they may even welcome it; but they also tolerate, if not welcome, the many school systems that make no effort whatsoever to ready their people for leadership roles.

Though there are many inadequacies in the sequence by which men and women are prepared and selected for management positions in American public schools, they are not necessarily all the fault of universities. Supervised internships, for example, would surely be a good thing in education as in law and medicine; but law schools generally abjure responsibility for such clinical experiences (save for hothouse versions like moot court) and leave these to the profession at large. In the preparation of doctors, on the other hand, one can scarcely discern where the medical school's responsibility stops and that of the hospital begins. The problem with school administration is that neither the university nor the profession nor—outside a handful of well-run school systems—the employer routinely shoulders these obligations.

University-based preparation programs ought therefore to be viewed in context. But they are the linchpin in the whole mechanism, the primary filter in the preparation and selection pipeline. That is why it is unconscionable that so few of these programs actually equip administrators for their later responsibilities; so few act as effective gatekeepers for the profession by screening candidates at the point of entry; so few reliably build occupational commitment, collegiality, or professional norms by setting high standards and enforcing them through rigorous scrutiny by peers and mentors. Too many have exit requirements that are slack and unrelated to the work of the profession. What is more, these are often inefficient requirements, the kind that squander much time and effort in burdensome activities bearing only a hazy relationship to the institutional and occupational demands that their graduates will face.

Training Real Leaders

What might a better program look like? Any thorough response must begin by specifying the knowledge and skills that all educational administrators should possess before assuming responsibility for the leadership of schools or school systems. This is the stuff of endless debate and some legitimate controversy; one cannot assume that the optimal preparation for the principalship of a remote primary school in North Dakota is identical to the training desirable for the Los Angeles superintendent. Still, most of what a good school administrator needs to know and be able to do is self-evident. It is neither arcane nor arguable. One commendable version was offered by the American Association of School Administrators (AASA) in 1982, spanning seven major areas of knowledge and skills: school climate and how to improve it, political theory and how to apply it, the curriculum and how to construct it, "instructional management systems" and how to run them, staff members and how to evaluate them, school resources and how to allocate them, educational research and how to utilize it. Under each of these headings, the AASA suggests, administrators need a mix of empirical and theoretical knowledge and they need a feel for how to put their knowledge and skills into operation within the school organizatiion so as to increase its effectiveness.

To such a list we might add the development of a well-defined educational philosophy or ideology (as well as understanding of rival philosophies) so that the school leader has solid values and clear beliefs by which to make the many decisions that cannot be handled with knowledge and expertise alone. The issue is not, however, whether this list or that list is superior. It is, rather, that today *no* set of competencies, experiences, and knowledge is commonly accepted as the core of any well-designed program of graduate study for future school administrators, such that imparting these becomes the key criterion for having one's training program approved, and acquiring them becomes the main precondition for getting licensed to run a school or school system. Far from being embedded in the curriculum of the nation's hundreds of colleges of education and in the licensure requirements of the fifty states, even the bland suggestions of the AASA are objects of obloquy and apathy. It is ironic but true that on some university campuses, those purporting to prepare men and women to lead nation's schools to higher achievement in the years ahead have no clear notions about what essential knowledge constitutes high achievement among their own students.

But infusing real quality into the preparation of school administrators will take more than consensus about what they ought to learn. A good program would have stringent entry requirements, high standards of performance during coursework and other training experiences, and opportunities for candid, precise feedback to students about their performance. (Another contemporary irony is that future administrators whose schools will be judged by test scores refined to several decimal places are often taught by professors who pride themselves on being "nonjudgmental.") Coursework should naturally span the best current research and theory in the field, and faculty members should expect students to acquire—and to demonstrate that they now possess—both the requisite knowledge and the skills by which that knowledge can be analyzed, synthesized, and applied. There should be a well-designed apprenticeship in which the fledgling administrator works closely with proven school leaders in actual administrative tasks and receives timely and critical assessments of his performance. Finally, those who will become line administrators have little need of a dissertation; instead, they should carry out a major project that draws upon their store of knowledge and skills, that relates theory to practice, that obliges them to use research findings in the execution of a series of leadership tasks that challenge their abilities to reason, analyze, synthesize, and later appraise their own performance, and that constrains them to write clearly and cogently about the experience.

Such projects could vary a great deal. The prospective high school principal might devote the better part of a year to leading a team of teachers who are reworking the humanities curriculum, to overhauling the guidance and counseling system within the school, or to planning and running a model summer program for the most talented eleventh-grade chemistry students in that part of the state. The aspiring elementary school principal could organize and carry out a series of intensive workshops for language arts teachers, develop and lead a mini-school for slow learners, or devise a comprehensive system for monitoring individual pupil achievement vis-à-vis the school's curricular objectives. The future superintendent of schools will ordinarily take on a larger project; he may develop a new magnet school or, if population trends are running the other way, plan and effect the consolidation of two schools into one. He could organize and run a statewide principals' academy designed to train present administrators in central leadership skills and organizational knowledge. He might take charge of the first year of his school system's new master teacher program and seek to overcome attitudinal and bureaucratic hurdles in the path to its success. Whatever the content of the major project, it should represent a significant piece of work on a real leadership problem, the solution to which entails analysis of research findings, aggregation of pertinent knowledge, the application of suitable theories, actual performance in a sustained administrative role, and the retrospective written analysis of how effective the performance was and why. Though such a project calls for the exercise of considerable autonomous authority, the advanced graduate student will also need ready access both to the counsel of expert administrators within the school system and to university faculty who can make sure that his knowledge is sound, his theories suitable, and his final analysis rigorous.

Who Regulates Administrators?

School administration is a profession in considerable need of quality control, and the universities that train its members ought to supply more of that. But quality control across an entire profession goes well beyond standards for graduate programs. It is concerned with all aspects of occupational recruitment, formal and informal training, licensure or certification, selection for employment, on-the-job supervision and evaluation, the development of clear performance criteria and mutually enforced norms of professional ethics, regular means of recognizing superior performance, and orderly procedures for dealing with incompetents.

Responsibility for such quality control as there is in educational administration today is divided among four separate and sometimes fractious bodies: the university, which bestows credits and degrees; the state, which confers certification; the employer (usually a local school system), which hires, pays, and promotes the individual principal or superintendent; and the organizations and associations of the profession as a whole, a profession that today has few norms for its membership but that could wield considerable influence over the standards and expectations of the other three bodies.

In such fields as law and medicine, the profession is the dominant force: The graduate schools, the states, and in most instances the individual employers honor its norms and codes, accept its definition of what must be learned and how this should be demonstrated, and frequently regard its leaders and spokesmen as their own. In education, however, we find segmented responsibility for quality control; no single actor has the lead role, and the profession is probably the weakest and most amorphous of the four.

The formal structures are present, to be sure. There are licensure requirements, ostensibly based on demonstrated prior achievement, and they are even-handedly (that is, bureaucractically rather than politically) applied. Colleges of education must ordinarily have their training programs approved by the state and, in many instances, accredited by a national professional body. Employers may hire only duly-licensed individuals, and these men and women ordinarily join professional associations that publish journals, hold conferences, supply "in-service" training, and keep their members informed about pertinent developments. Oftentimes, there are close relationships among key figures in the associations, the dominant professors in the university training programs, the state officials who set licensure requirements, and the more influential school administrators around the country.

All these structures are in place, and they may well yield a bare minimum of quality control, enough to keep the system credible and to preserve sufficient public confidence and professional reassurance to enable organizational operations to continue, even in the face of widespread disenchantment with the actual performance of the schools.

In reality, however, the quality control is minimal indeed, and no one is clearly responsible for elevating it. In the argot of social science, there is a lot of "satisficing" where there ought to be "optimizing." None of the major actors makes waves; none springs surprises; none imposes heavy demands on the others. Real quality control of the kind that would yield smarter, wiser, and more effective school leaders on a consistent basis is simply not in place.

It may be thought that the standards of this profession today are as slack as the rewards are meager and that present entry norms are where they need to be if the supply of available school administrators is going to equal the demand. Yet the compensation level is far from pitiful. School superintendent salaries averaged $52,483 in 1984. (The recently fired Chicago superintendent earned $120,000 a year.) Principals earn less, averaging $34,000 to $40,000, depending on the size and level of school, but their pay is sufficiently greater than that of teachers to induce a steady flow of educators into graduate programs that provide administrators' certificates. In California, where rapid population growth is producing a genuine shortage of qualified teachers, the administrator training programs are turning out credentialed graduates in such large numbers that the state could replace all its school managers every five years. "Clearly," Guthrie concludes, "supply far exceeds demand."

Thus conditions are right for a marked elevation of the standards for entry into the ranks of school administrators and for retention and promotion within those ranks. What can the university do to help catalyze that process? It can start by delimiting its domain of responsiblity and then imposing rigorous standards within that domain—standards that must naturally apply to its faculty as well as its students, to its own curricular and pedagogical practices as well as to what it expects of persons who endure them.

The university's stock in trade is knowledge. As James March puts it, "The advantage of university training in the training of administrators is primarily in the intellectual domain. It is in providing the research basis for intelligence, and in teaching the intellectual skills of management." These skills involve thinking, reasoning, analyzing, and evaluating, all of which can be imparted through a well-planned sequence of courses, internships, and independent study. The content will vary somewhat from one campus to the next but would certainly include more of the elements recommended by Guthrie and his Berkeley colleagues: "theories of teaching, curriculum strategies, program evaluation, cost effectiveness analysis, management information systems, quantitative decision making techniques, computer use, and planning techniques," courses of study commonly found in good business management programs.

Yet no graduate school can supply all the learning and skills needed by expert educational leaders, for some of these come only with practice and some are better acquired in other settings.

The universities can choose to concentrate all their energies on intellectual and cognitive matters, or they can begin with that base and join with school systems and experienced professionals in constructing internship, midcareer refresher programs, and other more practical educational components atop that base. But without a solid base in theory, in research, in knowledge, and in the application of analytic thinking to concrete management problems, the university has little to offer the prospective school administrator.

This means that universities must also look to the composition and caliber of their own faculties. The study of educational administration has never been a field that attracted large numbers of the nation's ablest scholars. Nonetheless, it is a legitimate field of inquiry, it does possess a body of knowledge, and today it is practically begging for more and better research utilizing the methods of numerous specialties. Like so many "applied" fields, educational administration is not a unique discipline so much as an area of inquiry organized around a set of problems, issues, and institutions and drawing on the insights and techniques of many disciplines. Yet many a professor of educational administration is not an active scholar in any field or discipline; many are expractitioners who earned doctorates along the way but spend little time on research, are not especially comfortable with theory, and are better known for their fund of war stories than for their ability to develop cognitive skills in students or to impart research-based knowledge about the instructional and organizational features of the school and school system. Departments and programs in educational administration commonly suffer from the low campus status associated with colleges of education in general; but their difficulty in recruiting first-rate scholars is compounded by their ambivalence about whether their primary tasks are intellectual or clinical. By clearly defining the role of the university as a supplier of formal knowledge, some of this uncertainty should dissipate.

Suggesting that the university's proper role is intellectual rather than clinical does not mean that its faculty should operate entirely in the domain of theory. The underlying paradox, as Nathan Glazer noted in 1974, is that while schools of education (like other schools of what he termed the "minor professions") habitually mix practitioners with discipline-based scholars in faculties whose task is to train future practitioners, the usual way such faculties elevate their status and reputation is by distancing themselves from the life and work of the practitioner. What American graduate schools of education most urgently lack, Oxford's Harry Judge concluded after visiting ten of them a few years ago, are "scholars with a commitment to improving practice based on research."

If standards for school administration are not sharply raised, and if the training-and-certification sequence is not rapidly overhauled in accord with these higher standards, we will miss a rare opportunity to transform a large fraction of the nation's school leadership for many years to come. The combination of school enrollments that are again rising, a high rate of retirements during the next few years among veteran principals and other administrators, keen popular interest in the quality of elementary and secondary schooling, and the unprecedented amount of attention being given to education by governors, legislators, business leaders, and other influential laymen leads to an authentic chance to make bold changes.

Should Administrators Have Been Teachers?

Besides the alterations in university training programs that we have sketched, other reforms warrant consideration. Though there is every reason to demand that a school leader know good and bad teaching when he sees it, we know no good reason to require principals and superintendents themselves to have taught school for years. Alongside career ladders for teachers should probably be erected new occupational structures for school leaders, some starting young in the schools, others entering laterally after successful careers as managers or leaders in other fields.

If the teaching requirement were erased, the pool of potential school administrators would instantly swell by millions of people, and at least some of these would be men and women of great leadership potential and solid track records, individuals who have already run substantial units and systems whithin the private sector, the military, perhaps higher education itself.

Would the teachers in a school allow themselves to be led by one who had not come up through the ranks? We think so, provided two conditions are met. The teachers must themselves have access to "career ladders" on which they can climb to positions of greater status, responsibility, and pay without moving into administration; and the administrators must of course become knowledgeable about pedagogy and insightful about classroom practice so that they can provide substantial assistance to teachers in their schools. This will undoubtedly require some first-hand knowledge and practical experience, but a flexible and motivated leader can pick these up in a few months of intense experience, direct observation, and the study of videotaped examples. Though this approach may not yield an emotional "feel" for the rhythms of the school year, it is also true that having taught for a long time, even having been a superb teacher, does not necessarily equip one for leadership, nor for appraising and counseling less experienced teachers. Learning about teaching *by* teaching can be a very parochial experience, and it is a far cry from supervising other teachers. Outstanding surgeons do not necessarily turn into skillful medical directors, nor do superb scholars always make good deans.

The primary responsibility for changing professional entry norms rests with the states, which need radically to revise their requirements for licensure and certification, replacing classroom experience and paper credentials with clear proof of actual knowledge and skill and—for senior or advanced certificates—demonstrated prowess in leadership positions.

Employers of school administrators, in turn, should insist on much more than possession of a state license. Just as admission to the bar does not instantly make one a good bet for a client needing an attorney with wide-ranging experience in libel law, winning state cetification as a school administrator is just one step along the path to major responsibilities for building and systemwide leadership. Yet today only a handful of school systems engage in sophisticated searches for the ablest and best-qualified principals and superintendent to be found. Fewer still have clear criteria and procedures by which to cope with once-satisfactory administrators who lose the spark, fall into bad habits, or otherwise falter.

The professional association, too, should cease thinking of themselves primarily as membership organizations and should develop norms, standards, ethical codes, and substantive prescriptions by which universities, states, and local employers can appraise their own practices. There have been flickers of such responsible behavior among several of the better groups, including the AASA curricular recommendations and the skill assessment centers run by the National Association of Secondary School Principals. For the most part, however, these organizations have more of the outward trappings of professional associations—conventions, member services, publications—than the norm-setting infrastructure by which a true profession governs itself.

It may well be that piecemeal reform is simply inadequate to the task of overhauling the training, licensure, and professional standards of school administrators. It may also be that the profession lacks the fortitude or the perspective for a thoroughgoing, self-induced overhaul. Perhaps governors, business leaders, and blue ribbon commissions will need to bring school administration under the kind of intense scrutiny that they have applied to school teaching. Maybe one state needs to burst from the pack with a radically different model of training, licensure, selection, evaluation, and recruitment into this field. Perhaps the universities need a modern-day Flexner to map their route through a systematic—and systemwide—reformulation of the precepts and practices of administrator training.

Certainly the stakes are high. The educational status quo, though comfortable, is unsatisfactory. An immense amount of leverage can be exerted on the schools through their principals and superintendents. Give me a place to stand, Archimedes said, and I will move the earth. American public schools are nearly as inertial as the planet itself, but their administrators make a serviceable fulcrum and the universities that train them supply a promising if today somewhat shaky place on which to stand.

SECTION III

Theory and Research in Educational Administration

The papers in this section present both themes and challenges, and the challenges are directed to both scholars of administration and those who administer. The themes and the challenges are provocative and represent new ways of thinking about an old question: What is of significance for an organization in administrators' actions?

A theme surely welcome to readers of this volume is that administrative actions have real consequences for organizations. This assertion, while apparently simple, leads obviously to a set of subquestions about the actions and their consequences and about such matters as shared responsibility, accountability, and management by committee. Each of the authors asserts that the responsibility for an organization devolves to a few people rather than many, that is, to administrators. As T.B. Greenfield says, "Administration is about power and powerful people." After discussing a series of choices that administrators face, David Clark and Terry Astuto conclude, "Administrators can opt for a consistent strategy of choice. . . ." Macpherson says, "This first section of this paper describes how administrators gain control over aspects of social reality and the moral and organization knowledge deemed to be policy." Thus, in answer to an often-asked question, "Is anyone in charge here?" the authors of these papers answer "Yes, and it is the administrator."

The thing of which an administrator is in charge is treated similarly in the papers. Rejecting such notions as "organization as bureaucracy" or "organization as machine" or "organization as decision system," the authors discuss "organization as culture." Clark and Astuto discuss the multiple causes of action and consequences in organizations. Macpherson writes about "how organizing people and developing organizations can be inter- peted as a form of cultural action." Greenfield argues that organizations are filled with such cultural phenomena as human beliefs, passions, habits, frailties, and noble aims. As cultures, organizations are distinguished by the influence they have on beliefs, by their complexity, by the multiple relation- ships among persons and events, by how they change, and by the ways an administrator must think about them. Extending this metaphor, the authors analyze educational administration as administration of a particular culture, the primary activity of which is education, ultimately a moral activity. Clark and Astuto explore paradoxical choice options in the context of decisions about schooling. Greenfield and Macpherson discuss the particular content of decisions about education.

The authors also describe the tools of administrators in organizations as cultures. Talk, cultural capital, cultural knowledge, power, choice among paradoxical choices, ethics and values, construction and reconstruction of social reality, and strategic choice are all tools with which the administrator must become familiar and adept. These tools differ markedly from the tools that have been linked to other metaphors describing organization.

Finally, a common theme in the papers is that administrators work in multiple arenas and at multiple levels with multiple and shifting agendas. Macpherson states the issue directly: "[the administrators] I researched were found to have three major operational selves (labeled System Man, Structure Man, and Political Man) and a fourth deeper self: Reflective Man." An administrator views an organization as an arena of complex actions and consequences, in which success requires adopting multiple analytic and action perspectives.

The authors also present challenges. The major challenge is to scholars in educational administration. Boldly put, the challenge is to recognize that positivist, value-free science is neither useful for understanding nor possible. A new set of theories must be created that expressly allow for values both as variables of significance in organizations and as influences over the questions researchers ask and the way the questions are framed. As Clark and Astuto argue, "Breakthroughs in understanding will occur by challenging old models of research and organizational theory. . . ." Macpherson and Green- field are more insistent. Macpherson argues that the positivist perspective has "tended to perpetuate and justify a bureaucratic rationality" and as such has been unable to explain much of what actually happens in organizations. Greenfield's paper is a full attack on what he argues to be the legacy of Herbert Simon's work. Greenfield argues that administrative science has not helped to understand or control organizations, that the substantive (content) issues of education have been ignored, that the focus has been wrong, and that it has ignored the value-laden characteristics of choice making.

This challenge is followed by a second: that new phenomena must be studied using methods not generally in favor during the last thirty years. By implication, the results of such study are unlikely to contribute to "grand theory" but rather to context-bound explanations.

The final challenge to scholars is to begin to prepare administrators in new ways. As Greenfield argues, "We must seek new models for administrative training—ones that acknowledge responsiblity, right judgment, and reflection as legitimately and inevitably part of administrative action."

The authors also present challenges to administrators. Clark and Astuto challenge them to understand and act on a series of conflicts not resolvable by compromise. An administrator must choose between actual, not apparent, paradoxes. Such paradoxes present "designated leaders and other organizational participants with strategic choices, not a compromise of trade-off or accommodation."

As a group, the authors also challenge the administrator to confront the value premises of action. Administrators are powerful people who make decisions that alter the lives of others. Critical decisions in organizations are based not on facts but on pieces of evidence that are made to be "facts" by administrators who can control social meaning in the organization. Some evidence becomes fact and some does not. Administrators speak for themselves, facts do not; however, administrators wish to convince others that their decisions are based on facts.

In addition, administrators are challenged to both produce knowledge about organizations and the craft of administration and reflect critically on their own actions. Administrators are challenged to think and write about what they do and why they do it for the purposes of extending knowledge and, more critical, considering the moral consequences of their actions. As Macpherson states, "[educational administrators] need to examine their administrative habitus and the ideologies served by their practices."

The papers in this section are bold in their challenges to conventional thought about theory. While each paper broaches a different set of questions, there is consistency among them in that their questions are worth asking and the new frameworks for answering these questions are available to both scholars and practitioners.

12

Paradoxical Choice Options in Organizations

David L. Clark and Terry A. Astuto

Foreword: Thoughts from Fifty and Twenty-five Years Ago

We still give much lip service to the forgotten individual, but the whole complex of thought, except when our immediate personal concerns are involved, relates to the cooperative and social aspects of life. We are so engrossed constantly with the problems of organization that we neglect the unit of organization and are quite unaware of our neglect. It almost seems to be our purpose to forget the individual except as he compels consideration. (Chester I. Barnard, an address to the Fifth Summer Conference Course in Industrial Relations, Graduate College, Princeton University, September 20, 1935. Printed for private distribution in 1935. Published in Barnard, *Organization and Management*, 1956, p. 4.)

Many of our attempts to control behaviour, far from representing selective adaptations, are in direct violation of human nature. They consist in trying to make people behave as we wish without concern for natural law. . . . When we fail to achieve the results we desire, we tend to seek the cause everywhere but where it usually lies: in our choice of inappropriate methods of control. . . . When people respond to managerial decisions in undesired ways, the normal response is to blame them. It is *their* stupidity, or *their* uncooperativeness, or *their* laziness which is seized on as the explanation of what happened, not management's failure to select appropriate means of control. [Douglas McGregor, *The Human Side of Enterprise*, 1960, pp. 9–10]

Let us consider some solid advice for the aspiring administrator:

> The buck stops here.
>
> Look before you leap.

Now suppose this advice is false, that a set of counteraphorisms describes the truth of administration:

> The buck never stops in an organization.
>
> Leap for sure; look if you have time.

Does either set have any claim as an aphorism? Does either set fit better with the experiences of practitioners?

Paradoxes of Practice
Buck Stopping and Passing

"Buck stopping" is dignified in organizational theory by the term "accountability." Presidents from Truman through Carter to Reagan have popularized it in the political arena by claming responsibility for disasters as diverse as the failure of the rescue mission in Iran and death of the marines in Beirut. Fortunately, for the politicians as well as for less prominent leaders and employees, no one, except for reasons of general political preference, believes these assertions, although they are pleased that the blame can be placed somewhere, at least symbolically. The complexities of causality in organizations are such that linear causality focusing on an individual is the exception, not the rule. Why did SAT scores decline? Why are they now rising? Has supply-side economics worked? Will the national debt lead us to destruction? Is the superintendent of schools responsible for irregularities in an elementary school or embezzlement by a trusted subordinate? Did Head Start succeed? Whom should we credit or blame? In the real world of organizations and people the answers to such questions are assertions and counterassertions, not statements of fact.

Can a stronger case be made for the claim that the buck never stops in an organization? Probably, because complex organizations are characterized by conditions of multiple causality, and the stories of organizational life are both retrospective and idiosyncratic. Recall the last time an error in a school or college was reported to you. Chances are the storyteller was a hero; villains do not tell stories. Organizational stories are about other people responsible for incidents that turn out badly. A good counteraphorism for organizational consideration might be "the buck stops there."

Looking and Leaping

Support for goal-based planning is in the folklore of our society. Parents introduce children to the notion that to succeed in life they must have personal goals to pursue. Goal-based planning is rooted axiomatically in the definition of organizations as goal-attaining entities. The single most likely action of a newly elected chief executive officer is to appoint a goals task force or commission. A whole technology has been built around looking before leaping, that is, management by objectives, program planning and budgeting systems, zero-based budgeting.

However, another body of literature has given rise to a new aphorism. Peters and Waterman observed that "learning and progress accrue only when there is *something* to learn from, and the something, the stuff of learning and progress, is any completed action" (1982, p. 134). In education, the school improvement literature supports the argument that innovative schools learn from their trials (and errors) and thus become better at innovating. The remarkable success of the alternative schools movement in the 1970s was due, at least in some measure, to the fact that they were ill-defined solutions that fit a host of problems; individual schools and school systems could make of them what they would. What did alternative schools do for education? They broke a negative amplifying cycle in urban schools and gave people in urban schools the sense that they could accomplish something. Educational organizations are not ineffective because they are unstable organizations, rife with trials. Rather, ineffective schools have become frozen in their mediocrity and failure. Look before you leap is sensible advice for an administrator. But equally sensible advice is do something; create some movement and change in the organization; leap, and look if you have time.

What is the source of these nonaphoristic maxims? We think they derive from the ambiguous knowledge base in administrative and organizational studies. In this paper we will explore two propositions about that knowledge base:

1. The paradoxical aphorisms of practice are, indeed, rooted in conflictual bodies of theory and empirical research that students of organizations treat as independent and parallel.
2. The paradoxes of practice are actual, not apparent, and present designated leaders and other organizational participants with strategic choices, not with a compromise or a trade-off or an accommodation.

Paradoxes of Theory and Research

We will argue that organizational theory and organizational studies have given rise to seven paradoxes of organizing. Each paradox consists of two paired elements, supported by a body of research and theory, that are vying continuously for primacy in every institutional setting:

1. *Activity* (multiple trials and innovation) vs. *stability* (substantiality in

the job setting; a focus on the technical core of the organization's activity)

2. *Distinction* (organizational identity defined and sustained through organizational culture and sense-making) vs. *intention* (organizational identity defined and sustained through systematic, organization-level goal setting)

3. *Variability* (divergent behavior, the search for alternative value premises and solutions, adjustment to individual social enactment processes) vs. *regularity* (clarity of the job roles, rules, policies, and procedures; reliability of response across people and over time)

4. *Efficacy* (reinforcement of the individual's sense of personal competency and organizational contribution) vs. *accountability* (systematic efforts to ensure individual and group productivity)

5. *Facilitation* (seeking preferences, building problem-solving capacity, supporting change efforts) vs. *intervention* (ordering preferences, solving problems, mobilizing resources)

6. *Empowerment* (increasing personal autonomy in preference, choice, and judgment) vs. *control* (retention of critical preference, choice, and judgment activities at the apex of the organization)

7. *Disaggregation* (loose coupling, piecemeal change, emphasis on individuals and primary workgroups) vs. *holism* (tight coupling, comprehensive reform, centralization, and structural integrity)

We will next note briefly, by example and reference, evidence often given to support each element of the seven paradoxes.

Activity vs. Stability

The efficacy of organizational activity is justified by organizational theorists on the grounds of organizational learning. Weick, for example, states: "Meaning is retrospective and only elapsed experience is available for meaningful interpretation. The practical implication of this is that an organization would be in a better position to improve . . . if the elapsed experience were filled with action rather than inaction" (1979, p. 245).

Studies of the change process add another dimension of support for a high level of organizational activity. Regardless of the substantive learning that occurs in trials of innovations, organizations that experiment learn the process of innovation itself; organizations that innovate become better at innovation.

Peters and Waterman (1982) popularized the phrase, "a bias for action," as one of the key characteristics of their survey of excellent companies. Their homelier argument for activity—"do it, fix it, try it" (p. 132)—emphasized not only organizational learning and innovation but a way to combat a negative cycle in an organization or to make headway on a problem that seems to be defying solution. They report that "an analysis of Amoco, recently revitalized to become the top U.S. domestic oil finder, suggests just one success factor: *Amoco simply drills more wells*" (p. 141).

But, there is another side to this issue. The basic structural design of organizations is intended to provide substantiality to the job setting. Formalization, specialization, standardization, and the hierarchy itself are designed to focus attention on the technical core of the organization's activity, to assure durability as divisive forces impact on that core, and to provide organizational occupants with a continuing sense of the central activity, if not the mission, of the organization.

The popular appeal of an intensive focus on the technical core activity of an organization is exemplified in education by the periodic fascination with a return to the basics. The research of the late 1970s and early 1980s on instructionally effective schools purported to document the importance to pupil success of focusing on the basics in urban elementary schools. The interpretation of the classroom teaching research on engaged learning time has given rise to state and federal educational policy directives pushing schools and school systems toward greater stability in the technical core, emphasizing the three R's or the new basics (including science and computer science).

Is the choice between activity and stability exclusive? No, even the most innovative organization protects its technical core; even the most conservative organization experiences self-induced change. Is the conflict in the choice comprehensive, that is, is it represented in every choice option? No, like most organizational elements the choice option of activity and stability is variably coupled. A school superintendent may opt for stability in morning bus routes or internal systems of fiscal management, which does not necessarily conflict with the activities being pursued by other individuals or groups in the system. Is the choice conflictual? Oh, yes! Choice options arise regularly (though infrequently) to challenge the organization's substantiality. Choice options arise regularly (and frequently) that stifle new ideas at near their point of germination, well before they have the opportunity to challenge substantiality. Some organizations, and individuals within them, find ways to support the stability of the organization; other individuals support choice options that foster activity. And there are winners and losers in this conflict, so that eventually an organization can be characterized, at a point in time, as high or low active, high or low stable? As in all aspects of organizing, the conflict is continual. As soon as a choice is made to foster activity, proponents of stability arise to argue, "this place is infected with faddism"; as a choice emphasizes stability, activity-oriented members complain, "every new idea is killed around here before it gets started."

This, then, is the first of the seven strategic choice options that confront administrators in their daily organizational lives.

Distinction vs. Intention

Schein (1985, p. 23) defined culture as the pattern of learned underlying assumptions a group holds about an organization. The various definitions of culture offered in the literature emphasize, in one way or another, that culture is: (1) the product of individual and group sensemaking; (2) which results in shared meanings about the organization; (3) that are relatively stable, bridge organizational members and units, and include assertions about "how we do things here" and "how we do in comparison to other organizations."

Key authors in the field assert that cultures may be functional or dysfunctional for various organizational purposes and challenges and they may be strong or weak. Strong cultures can be created deliberately and are related to organizational effectiveness (Schein, 1985, p. 17).

We have used the term "distinction" to include the literature of organizational culture and to denote the various ways in which the purpose and commitment of the organization are discovered in (1) shared sensemaking that derives from retrospective interpretation of "what is going on around here," (2) a seach for preferences based on what has worked in the past or is working in the present, and (3) a sense of retrospective rationality based on the meanings individuals assign to their workplace. Under such conditions the leader (and other group members) would discover the organization's intentions by reinforcing their strongest elements that exist around individuals, programs, or small groups.

Intentionality, that is, goal-based planning and operating, is a truism of administrative practice. Organizations are frequently defined as goal-attaining entities. An entire technology of administration is built around acceptance of the notion that "you can't get there if you don't know where you are going." The acceptance of the role of goals in organizational literature is reflected in current texts on organizational studies, such as Daft (1986): "Goals represent the reason for an orgnization's existence. An organization is a goal-attainment device. Without some purpose, there is no need for the organization. Goals summarize and articulate that purpose" (p. 93), and "Understanding organizational goals is the first step toward understanding organizational effectiveness. . . . Goals were defined earlier as the desired future state of the organization. *Organizational effectiveness* is the degree to which an organization realizes its goal" (pp. 101–02).

Three assumptions are implicit in these statements: (1) intent precedes action; (2) goals are prospective; and (3) the role of goals in the organization is axiomatic—the very definition of an organization depends on goal definition and its effect on goal attainment.

Are the concepts of distinction and intentionality conflictual or complementary, or merely parallel? Again, we argue that they are markedly different views of what is important in organizations and to organizational effectiveness. The dichotomy of assumptions about how an organization defines itself is clear:

Intentionality	*Distinction*
1. Intent precedes action.	1a. Intention is discovered in action.
2. Goals are prospective states to be achieved.	2a. Distinction is the retrospective interpretation of what works.

An organizational culturist would be appalled by the prospect of installing a management-by-objectives (MBO) system to define or regularize organizational culture. An MBO specialist would count culture management as a mystical (and probably mythical) tool of organizational engineering . These choice options provoke arguments. They proceed from different views of what works in organizations.

Variability vs. Regularity

Research on organizational innovation and change processes cites the need for safe havens and toleration of idiosyncratic behavior by organizational inventors and change agents. March and Olsen argued for a technology of foolishness to offset the technology of regularity and make "the individuals within an organization more playful by encouraging the attitudes and skills of inconsistency" (1976, p. 81). Variability supports the encouragement of product champions and entreprenuers who often require either exemption from organizational rules or exceptional institutional reinforcement, or both. Variability allows the fostering of primary work groups that are exhibiting productivity or give the promise of productivity.

March and Olsen contended that "strict insistence on purpose," consistency, and nationality limits our ability to find new purposes (1976, p. 77). Variability, in contrast, may uncover useful, alternative value premises. Since it can be argued that organizations frequently identify goals retrospectively, variability provides the opportunity to explore new directions and potential objectives. Planfulness promotes regularity; playfulness promotes variability. As March and Olsen (1976) state, "Playfulness is the deliberate, temporary relaxation of rules in order to explore the possibilities of alternative rules. When we are playful, we challenge the necessity of consistency" (p. 77).

Variability allows for organizational forgetfulness, a necessary feature of renewal: "Retained information is sacred in most organizations, ... and this means that routines, standard operating procedures, and grooved thinking . . . work against the organization being able to discredit its past knowledge. . . .

The thick layering of routines in most organizations, coupled with the fact that departures from routine increase vulnerability, mean that discrediting is rare" (Weick, 1979, p. 5). Forgetfulness and doubt enhance the organization's ability to rethink past enactments and increase quality. The process of forgetfulness results in the possibility of an organization unfreezing itself—a necessary precondition of many forms of organizational change.

Yet no one need fear an underemphasis on regularity in organizations. The bureaucratic organizational form has provided an essential structure that assumes regularity and reliability through written rules, policies, job descriptions, and standard operating procedures. The training, experience, and socialization of administrators reinforce the desirability of regularity, routine, and predictability. All of the traditional organizational literature supports the notion that it is necessary for individuals to know what the responsibilities are of their positions, how they are expected to perform, and how they will be evaluated. Regularity is a *sine qua non* of the bureaucracy that works.

In the literature of education, the research on instructionally effective schools is the most convincing recent argument that regularity results in high organizational productivity. That literature not only emphasizes the necessity of an orderly, structured environment in instructionally effective schools and classrooms but combines that characteristic with the necessity for clearly communicated performance expectations for teachers and students. There are multiple reasons to support the description frequently proffered that such schools are bureaucracies that work.

We need not continue to pretend that we are considering the question of conflict and complementarity anew with each strategic pair. By now it is evident that we believe that an administrator confronting a choice option in each area is presented with a dilemma sustained by the knowledge base in the field. The empirical and theoretical arguments for regularity are convincing. So are those for variability. Each choice option that fosters one denies, or at best tolerates, the other.

Efficacy vs. Accountability

Good schools and school systems are portrayed in the organizational literature as populated by confident people who exhibit both personal and institutional efficacy. Employees believe they can successfully complete their own work tasks, are important to the organization, and can influence what happens in the organization. This sense of efficacy translates into pride and commitment to the organization: "There is emotional and value commitment between person and organization; people feel that they 'belong' to a meaningful entity and can realize cherished values by their contributions" (Kanter, 1983, p. 149).

The relationship between efficacy and effectiveness is argued on three grounds:

1. Shared expectations for success reduce the sense of risk that impedes organizational innovation.
2. A shared sense of personal efficacy translates into a belief that the organization is effective and supports the establishment and maintenance of a strong, positive organizational culture.
3. A personal sense of efficacy allows individuals to assume greater reponsibility for their own work and reduces the burden of close supervision.

Of course, there is another side to this coin: Accountability is a cornerstone of bureaucratic functioning. Public schools in particular are being subjected currently to a revival of interest in holding them accountable for the money they spend and the outcomes they produce. State legislatures and local boards of education are instituting policies that require the attainment of specified standards for progress across grades and schools and allow for interdistrict and interstate comparison of educational attainment. Almost all state legislatures are considering some form of merit pay for teachers. An interest in accountability represents a general commitment of the American people to the importance of individual and institutional competition and responsiveness. And the literature and technology of organizational studies are testimony that accountability is integral to traditional organizational theory.

Again, let us revisit the issue of the conflictual nature of the two strategic choice options. This time we will employ a more extensive example based on personnel evaluation. In a review of research on evaluation systems, Fuller and colleagues (1982) noted that evaluation systems can serve both efficacy and accountability—a clear challenge to the contention that these concepts are in conflict: "Evaluation activity has traditionally controlled behaviors of subordinate actors to ensure compliance with central goals. Evaluation processes may also influence individual efficacy of both actors . . . when the subordinate actor perceives that evaluation of his/her program is soundly based" (pp. 23–24). Evaluation was defined as soundly based if the subordinate thought that the evaluated performance was affected by his or her own effort as a performer.

However, a separate body of evidence indicates that one tends to assess favorably one's own performance:

In a recent psychological study when a random sample of male adults was asked to rank themselves on "the ability to get along with others," *all* subjects, 100 percent, put themselves in the top half of the population. Sixty percent rated themselves in the top 10 percent of the population, and a full 5 percent ever so humbly thought they were in the top 1 percent of the population. In a parallel finding, 70 percent rated themselves in the top quartile in leadership; only 2 percent felt they were below average as leaders. Finally, in an area in which self-deception should be hard for most males, at least, 60 percent said they were in the top quartile of athletic ability; only 6 percent said they were below average. [Peters and Waterman, 1982, pp. 56–57]

In summarizing research from business and industry, Lawler (1981) noted that individuals tend to overrate their own performance and underestimate the performance of others, which becomes a source of dissatisfaction with the evaluation system and the job.

This is the rub. If people are consistently underevaluated, they can make sense of that experience only by denying the validity of the evaluation on some grounds such as the criteria, the process, or the skill of the evaluator. To the extent that an evaluation system distinguishes clearly among employees on the basis of each (that is, to the extent that it serves the option of accountability), it will fail to serve to increase individual efficacy. An evaluation system can be devised to support efficacy. Under such a system, everyone should be above average and most of those rated should be in the top quartile of the population. This system will, of course, fail to meet the criterion of accountability. These options are in conflict.

Facilitation vs. Intervention

Facilitation and intervention highlight the role of the organizational leader in the choice between the two options. A facilitative approach to organizational leadership is rooted in two assumptions: (1) problem solving and innovation are best handled closest to the point of effective action; and (2) in most organizations, most of the time, preferences are problematic and the technology to attain preferred ends is unclear (Cohen, March, and Olsen, 1972). The choice of facilitation trades the design of a solution to a problem for the opportunity to encourage multiple designs and solutions at a variety of organizational levels.

Support of facilitation can be found in: (1) Ouchi's contemporary description of quality control circles, that is "the objective of the Q-C Circle is to permit every employee to be a planner and an engineer as well as a worker" (1982, p. 228): (b) the traditional literature of organizational theory that advises moving decisions to the point of action; and (c) March and Olsen's view of the leadership role: "Managers who make decisions might well view that function somewhat less a process of deduction or a process of political negotiation, and somewhat more as a process of gently upsetting preconceptions of what the organization is doing" (March and Olsen, 1976, p. 80).

Support for facilitation might also be rooted in a Theory Y view of organizational participants or Eric Hoffer's description of his laboring colleagues—"the people I work and live with are lumpy with talents" (1967, p. 33).

Facilitation presumes that an organization is populated by skilled, committed people, and a directive, interventionist management stance squanders the available human resources. Solutions, ideas, and potential new futures are believed to exist in abundant supply in the expertise, activities, and ingenuity of organizational members. Facilitation requires managers to act in ways that mobilize strengths, increase the capacities of individuals to enhance organizational effectiveness, and entertain alternative, plausible futures.

However, a facilitative posture toward leadership and management simply does not fit the predominant image of the effective, decisive, assertive executive in control of the organization and its destiny. It does not fit the image of the leader as a problem solver.

Intervention *is* the modal assumption of what top management is all about—not mindless autocracy or heavy-handed centralization, but participative management and strategic planning at or near the apex of the organization. Administrators establish goals, operationalize their attainment (that is, design interventions or a plan of implementation), monitor operations, and evaluate outcomes precisely because they assume that in most organizations, most of the time, preferences are well defined and the technology to attain them is clear. The literature on the change process in educational organizations assumes that solutions exist that fit the problems of schools and classrooms. The difficulty lies not in identifying or devising solutions but in the processes of adoption, implementation, and institutionalization among recalcitrant employees. Enlightened leaders involve followers in planning for implementation and loosen the hyperrational elements of monitoring and evaluating the change process, but the process of intervention is still the basic approach to organizational reform.

Advocates of an interventionist strategy root their support for the necessity of the approach in (1) the importance of the planning process—at least at the macrolevel, (2) the difficulty of effecting change at the operational level, and (3) the evaluation of the effectiveness of solutions in meeting organizational problems. None of these processes (planning, change, or evaluation), it is argued, can be forfeited by a responsible administration.

The compromise that has been worked out to accommodate the inherent conflict in these strategies is human resources management. Advocates of a facilitative strategy would argue that this compromise errs in the direction of the traditional view of the leader as designer. Advocates of an interventionist strategy would argue that participative management provides for necessary involvement without unnecessary loss of control.

Empowerment vs. Control

None of the choices illustrates more clearly the paradoxical nature of the options than the conflict between empowerment and control, since empowerment involves the diffusion of control. Kanter (1983) defined empowerment as making organizational power tools more widely accessible to organizational participants. These power tools are "Supplies of three 'basic commodities' that can be invested in action: *information* (data, technical knowledge, political intelligence, expertise); *resources* (funds, material, space, time); and *support* (endorsement, backing, approval, legitimacy)" (Kanter, 1983, p. 159). The result of using these tools is to increase personal autonomy in decisions of preference, choice, and judgment.

Kanter (1983) noted that as control is relaxed, innovative responses by workgroups and individuals will increase. Empowerment encourages innovation everywhere in the organization. Initiative for action and freedom of choice are moved away from the organization's managerial center.

We have now reached a point in the discussion where the interrelationship of particular choice options is evident. Empowerment should increase activity by multiplying the points at which action can be initiated; it requires variability because traditional mechanisms of control in organizations are regularized; it should support personal and organizational efficacy because more power is available to more people; and empowerment reinforces facilitation by assuming that innovation occurs throughout the organization.

But observers, including Kanter, are disturbed by the consequences of trading off control; for example:

> Unlimited circulation of power in an organization without focus would mean that no one would ever get anything done beyond a small range of actions that people can carry out by themselves.
>
> Besides, the very idea of infinite power circulation sounds to some of us like a system out of control, unguided, in which anybody can start nearly anything. (And probably finish almost nothing.) Thus, the last key to successful middle-management innovation is to see how power gets pulled out of circulation and focused long enough to permit project completion. But here we find an organizational dilemma. Some of the conditions are contrary to the circulating conditions, almost by definition. [Kanter, 1983, pp. 171–72]

Arguments in favor of retaining control are reflected in the positive language associated with such retention—quality control, decisive leadership, a sense of direction, in control of one's self or one's job, quality assurance, calling the signals, a commmanding presence, maintaining order. Even empowerment tools are often legitimated by reference to the language of control—for example, "Quality Control Circles." Control interacts with other choice options in a synergistic fashion. A focus on the organization's technical core can be assured by centralized control. Control demands regularity, fosters accountability, and creates the necessary conditions for centralized intervention.

The standard view of control in organizations was expressed by Daft: "A basic assumption underlying theory is the need for managers to control the organization" (1986, p. 28). The debatable issues follow, but do not challenge, that assumption: Shall the control be tight or loose? What should be the control mechanisms? According to traditional organizational studies, the answers to these questions are determined by organizational characteristics; for example, organizations of large size, routine technology, infrequent innovation, and certain environment are likely to reflect tight control through a centralized, bureaucratic structure employing rational, analytic decision-making processes. Loose control is associated with uncertain environments, nonroutine technology, small size, frequent innovation, and trial-and-error decision making.

Control is usually described at two levels. Organizational control involves top management in goal setting, monitoring, evaluation, and feedback. Employee control involves some form of output or productivity record and/or direct observation of employees on the job. The necessity for responsible managers to engage in control activities at both levels is a theorem derivative from the axiom of management control.

There seems little need to argue the conflictual nature of these strategies for organizing. Both Kanter and Daft seek a golden mean between the two. We suspect that a better description is to note that individuals foster one and tolerate the other and that the election of one or the other influences markedly the nature of the organization.

Disaggregation vs. Holism

In the general literature of organization, disaggragation has come to mean the looseness of coupling among units, people, processes, and functions within an organization and between the organization and its external environment.

Weick (1982) contended that schools and school districts are loosely coupled systems and that this loose coupledness has some distinct advantages for organizational effectiveness. In a loosely coupled organization, Weick (1982, pp. 674–75) noted, individual units can (1) preserve novelty so that they are reservoirs of flexibility, (2) adapt more quickly to conflicting demands, (3) improvise more effectively, and (4) respond swiftly enough to seal off some small problems before they become large problems.

In the literature of organizational change, disaggregation appears in the advocacy of supporting change efforts by individuals and subunits, focusing on the invention of alternative, often competing, solutions, and avoiding comprehensive, hyperrational designs for change. Fullan noted evidence that "leadership commitment to a particular version of change is negatively related to ability to implement it" (1982, p. 82). Despite efforts to systematize planned change throughout the organization, cumulating evidence indicates that innovation is crushed by efforts to make it comprehensive, rational, and faithful to the design of a particular solution (Berman, 1981).

The counterpoint is obvious. In classical bureaucratic theory, disaggregation is an organizational pathology. The pressure on managers, embedded in bureaucratic theory and the problem-solving paradigm, is to ferret out and tighten loose coupling to achieve effectiveness through control, intervention, accountability, and regularity. Modifications in tight coupling and planned-change strategies are introduced to account for contingencies that arise in practice, for example, engaging in participatory decision making and management to tap into ideas in the grass roots of the organization; modifying the organization's stance on the specifics of innovations (adaptive implementation); decentralizing responsibility for particular management functions; engaging in trials of innovations in subunits before attempting organization-wide diffusion.

Peters and Waterman (1982) commented on disaggregation and holism thusly: "Simultaneous loose-tight properties . . . is in essence the coexistence of firm central direction and maximum individual autonomy. . . . Organizations that live by the loose-tight principle are on the one hand rigidly controlled, yet at the same time allow (indeed, insist on) autonomy, entrepreneurship, and innovation from the rank and file" (p. 318). If that were within the realm of possibility, it would simplify the training of administrators and the practice of administration. In fact, the conflict is obvious and has emerged most recently in the contentious debate in the literature about loose coupling (for example, Lutz, 1982). To fail to recognize the distinction between the choice options is to dull administrators and organizational members to the consequences of the choice. As Weick warned: "Administrators must be attentive to the 'glue' that holds loosely coupled systems together because such forms are just barely systems. In fact, this borderline condition is their strength, in the sense that it allows local adjustment and storage of novel remedies. It is also their point of vulnerability, because such systems can quickly dissolve into anarchy" (1982, p. 675). We are contending that administrators deal with seven basic organizational choice options that are conflictual. The conflict is qualified by the fact that it is neither exclusive nor comprehensive. However, more important, the conflict is unmitigated because the sum effect of the strategic choices over time determines the organization's essential character.

Resolution of the Paradoxes

These seven paradoxes confront designated leaders and other organizational participants with strategic choices. They cannot be resolved by compromise or accommodation. Arguing, for example, that an organization can function by emphasizing rigid control and insisting on innovation (Peters and Waterman, 1982, p. 318) is to try to solve the paradox by creating an anomaly. We will attempt to defend the proposition that leaders in effective organizations adopt strategies that result in a consistent pattern of choice options across the seven paired elements. The contemporary literature on effective organizations supports the position that any such strategic pattern would include activity, distinction, variability, efficacy, facilitation, empowerment, and disaggregation.

An obvious counterargument raises doubts about the feasibility of electing this pattern of choice options. Will not it lead to a disorganized anarchy in which no one knows what they are doing or why? Would the glue that holds together an organization dissolve? We think not for three reasons:

1. The routine of polity
2. The infrequency of strategic choice options
3. The wisdom of people

The Routine of Polity

Organizations are powerful behavior settings—so powerful, in fact, that they continue to function uninterruptedly with interim leadership, feckless leaders, cheats and tyrants, in good times and bad, and then come back for more. The heritage of bureaucracy provides an assumed and expected hierarchy of authority with policies, procedures, and job expectations that guard constantly against disintegration into anarchy. The limits of "foolish" behavior that are contemplated within organizational settings are narrow. The boardroom, the classroom, the office, the hallway, the laboratory, and the library impose behavioral limits for most people, most of the time, that require few recorded rules or policies. The organizational leader who feels that she or he needs to reinforce the regularity of an organizational behavior setting has to be wholly unfamiliar with studies of the change process in organizations. Except in rare periods of extreme crisis, it is difficult to imagine the need to cool down the intensity of change-oriented behavior. To the contrary, the leader can anticipate that she or he will be confronted daily with individuals seeking to simplify, not complicate, their organizational interpretations. Those efforts at sense making will emphasize stable rules and relationships. Over time, organizational members will begin to agree on interpretations of roles and rules that, for all practical purposes, eliminate the consideration of alternative choices of behavior.

The sameness of everyday existence is protected and cherished by organizational participants even in the most innovative of organizational settings, just as it is in nonorganizational settings such as leisure-time activities, family activities, social clubs, and churches. The organizational structure and the tendency to simplify and systematize daily tasks are reinforced by our societal commitment to regularity through problem solving, goal setting, and rational decision-making models. Finally, the broader cultural environment reinforces the dailiness of existence in organizations and protects both the organizations and their participants from excessive stimulation.

The Infrequency of Strategic Choice Options

The opportunity for strategic choice arises infrequently and irregularly in organizations. First, choice options seldom occur. Most of the opportunities to exercise choice involve the reiteration of preexisting organizational decisions. By failing to disrupt the flow of routine decision making, the administrator acts by oversight to affirm standard procedures. Other choices demonstrate the loose coupling of the paradoxes: that is, in many instances a choice maintains the integrity of one element with little consequence for its conflictual counterpart. Examples are insistence on legitimate fiscal accounting systems in the daily management of funds or accounts, the maintenance of reliability in the execution of transportation routes for students, direct intervention in classroom governance when the physical or psychological safety of children is at stake, and maintenance of a stable and safe physical environment in a building.

Second, when the choice options do occur, the administrator often cannot exercise the option. Only a few opportunities arise in which (a) the conflict in the strategic choice is apparent and (b) the leader has the tools and the timely occasion to exercise a choice, such as when a faculty member proposes an irregular curricular option for a trial period; a work group (maybe even a department) has a chance to edit a prestigeful journal or establish a research center; an individual or group is producing in exceptional ways that fall outside the organization's conventional criteria for success. Our contention is that such choice options occur by chance, very rarely, and even by the administrator's design, seldom.

Third, when choice options do occur, and when the administrator is in a position to exercise choice, that choice likely will not be public; it normally will occur between two or three persons. If the choice supports some form of irregularity, the individuals involved are unlikely to report it to a broader audience.

Finally, in the few instances in which the choice option arises, the leader is in a position to actually make a choice, and it is public, the action is likely to be misinterpreted by many organizational members. So, for example, the school superintendent who supports four school principals who have proposed an alternative curricular structure is as likely or more likely to be viewed as an advocate of the particular structure, or as a critic of the standard structure, or as a Machiavellian intervener or controller.

A leader attempting to influence an organization by the strategic choice pattern she or he pursues will be hard pressed to do so even if the actual choices are consistent across issues, individuals, and time. Minimal inconsistency will bewilder other organizational participants.

The Wisdom of People

Finally, administrators who consistenly make unilateral choices in support of activity, distinction, variability, efficacy, facilitation, empowerment, and disaggregation do not run the risk that people will run wild in the organization. We rest our case on the wisdom of people.

Those who fear the process of moving from a centralized autocracy that assumes accountability, exercises control, ensures stability and regularity, and designs interventions and intentions are those who fear the efficacy of people. People in a humane organization will protect their opportunities for self-actualization by resisting the negative confusion and formlessness of anarchy; they will exhibit self-control. Such an organization, in the final analysis, will be wiser, more effective, and more humane than that which could be invented and implemented by most contemporary designated leaders.

Summary and Conclusions

The central arguments of this paper are as follows:

— Administrators, in and outside education, are offered conflictual and confusing guidance about their roles. The genesis of that guidance is in administration's ambiguous knowledge base.
— The conflicts (or paradoxes) add up to distinctly different strategies of organizing. Current literature on effective organizations argues that such organizations are characterized by activity, distinction, variability, efficacy, facilitation, empowerment, and disaggregation.
— Administrators can opt for a consistent strategy of choice reflecting these emphases without serious concern about organizational disruption or anarchy.

We contend that the practice of administration, the education of administrators, and research on the processes of administration are at a troublesome impasse because of a reluctance to confront and deal with the conflicts inherent in our knowledge base:

1. *Practice*—Administrators are afflicted daily with such advice as mix and match tight and loose coupling, emphasize initiating structure and consideration, and be accountable for teacher performance and enhance the job environment for teachers. The signals are so contradictory that the introspective practitioner says "they don't understand my job" or, worse yet, attempts to follow the advice and nullifies potential gains in practice with countermoves that offset the gain.

2. *Education*—Graduate and in-service programs for administrators reflect the confusion of practice. It is little wonder that courses in school finance and school law are considered by administrators to be more useful than courses in organizational theory, personnel administration, or leadership. The courses in specialized content areas provide unambiguous guidelines to practice. The course dealing with the general functions of the administrator as leader reflects the dichotomy of the knowledge base.

3. *Research*—It is impossible to resolve the paradoxes of practice by examining the knowledge base because administration's conflictual nature is barely recognized in the research. The conclusion by Bass (1981) in *Stogdill's Handbook of Leadership* is disturbing and, we think, symptomatic of the impasse represented by the unwarranted compromise of basic strategic conflicts in the field. "It is one thing to say we know nothing because we do not obtain consistent results. . . . Yet, it may be that to achieve consistency of results requires accounting for a complexity of variables. . . . What are needed are better measurement, a broader appreciation of which situational variables are more important . . . and . . . larger samples" (p. 617).

We doubt that. Breakthroughs will occur by challenging old models of research and organizational theory, not by more of the same. And one of the oldest ways of thinking about organizing that needs to be challenged is the assertion that "it's not an either–or proposition." It probably is.

References

Barnard, C.I. (1956). *Organization and management.*Cambridge, Mass.: Harvard University Press.

Bass, B.M. (1981). *Stogdill's handbook of leadership.* New York: The Free Press.

Berman, P. (1981). Educational change: an implementation paradigm. In R. Lehming and M. Kane (Eds.), *Improving schools: Using what we know.* Beverly Hills, Calif.: Sage Publishing.

Cohen, M.D.; March, J.D.; and Olsen, J.P. (1972). A garbage can model of organizational choice. *Administrative Science Quarterly* 17: 1–25.

Daft, R.L. (1986). *Organization theory and design.* St. Paul. Minn: West Publishing Company.

Fullan, M. (1982). *The meaning of educational change*. New York: Teachers College Press.

Fuller, B.; Wood, K; Rapoport, T.; and Dornbusch, S.M. (1982) The organizational context of efficacy. *Review of Educational Research* 52(1): 7–30.

Hoffer, E. (1967). *The ordeal of change*. New York: Harper and Row.

Kanter, R.M. (1983). *The change masters*. New York: Simon and Schuster.

Lawler, III, E.E.(1981). *Pay and organization development*. New York: McGraw-Hill, Inc.

Lutz, F. W. (1982). Tightening up loose coupling in organizations of higher education. *Administrative Science Quarterly* 27: 653–69.

March, J.G., and Olsen, J.P. (1976). *Ambiguity and choice in organizations*. Bergen, Norway: Universitetsforlaget.

McGregor, D. (1960). *The human side of enterprise*. New York: McGraw-Hill.

Ouchi, W.G. (1982). *Theory Z*. New York: Avon Books.

Peters, T.J. and Waterman, R.H. (1982). *In search of excellence*. New York: Warner Books.

Schein, E.H. (1985). *Organizational culture and leadership*. San Francisco: Jossey-Bass.

Weick. K.E. (1979). *The social psychology of organizing*. Reading, Mass.: Addison-Wesley.

Weick, K.E. (1982). Administering education in loosely coupled schools. *Phi Delta Kappan* 63 (10): 673–76.

Additional Readings

Deal, T., and Kennedy, A. (1983). Culture: a new look through old lenses. Paper presented at the annual meeting of the American Educational Research Association, Montreal.

Dornbusch, S.M., and Scott, W.R. (1975). *Evaluation and the exercise of authority*. San Francisco: Jossey-Bass.

Edmonds, R. (1979). Effective schools for the urban poor. *Educational Leadership*. 37 (1): 15–24.

Morgan G. (1983). *Beyond method*. Beverly Hills, Calif.: Sage Publications.

Pfeffer, J. (1982). *Organizations and organization theory*. Marshfield, Mass.: Pitman Publishing.

13

The Decline and Fall of
Science in Educational
Administration

Thomas B. Greenfield

The study of educational administration is cast in a narrow mould. Its appeal stems from a science of administration whose experts claim that an objective view of the social world enables them to conduct value-free inquiry. They claim to possess knowledge that enables them to control organizations and to improve them. But such large claims appear increasingly unsound, for the science that justifies them rests on methods and assumptions that dismiss the central realities of administration as irrelevant. Those realities are values in human action. If administrative science deals with them at all, it does so only in a weakened or spuriously objective form. For this reason, scholars in educational administration are now called to consider whether their way forward is still to be defined, as it has been for a generation or more, by a single path called "the way of science." The alternative path would seek to understand administrative realities within a broader conception of science—a conception recognizing that values bespeak the human condition

Reprinted with permission from *Interchange*, vol. 17, no. 2 (1986). © 1986 *Interchange*.

and serve as springs to action both in everyday life and in administration. But values are subjective realities, and people bind them inextricably to the facts in their worlds. Thus, an adequate new science may no longer be content to split facts from values, and deal only with the facts.

Promoters of the science of administration claim to have found a rational basis for human decision-making and a value-free technology for increasing the effectiveness and efficiency of organizations. Within a critical perspective, I will examine the basis of those claims and their mobilization on behalf of what Halpin (1970) called the "New Movement" in educational administration. My aim is, first, to describe the intellectual and ideological development of this once revolutionary movement. Second, I will examine the consequences and offer a critique of the scientific approach to understanding the problems of administration. Third, I will suggest an alternative to New Movement science in educational administration. And finally, I will speak about the problems of administrative studies in education today and suggest how those who are concerned to improve such studies might approach them in the future.

The Rise of Science in Administration

Self-conscious science entered administrative studies through the work of Herbert Simon. Published in 1945, *Administrative Behavior*[1] constituted a wholly new approach to the understanding and study of administration. His thinking transformed the field. Simon offered a totally new conception of the nature of administration, and, more importantly, a new set of rules for inquiry into administrative realities. From that time forward, his vision, his *Weltanschauung* of the world of administration, has dominated the field.

What Simon offered was a method of value-free inquiry into decision-making and administrative rationality. This method severely limited what could be considered as "administration" or "administrative decision-making," but its great advantage was that it brought the force of science to buttress any claims that might be made about the nature of administration or about the best means for improving organizations and life within them. Thus, the unfortunate consequence of Simon's work has been to shift attention from questions about the nature of administration to an obsessive concern for the methods of inquiry into it.

Simon's critique of older knowledge in administration was that it offered

---

[1] I will refer to the 1957 edition and use the valuable perspective that Simon's "Introduction to the Second Edition" provides on his work. The year 1957 also marks the beginning of "New Movement" science in educational administration.

little more than practitioners' prescriptive judgements on their experience. Simon's vision called for a knowledge of administrative realities founded on and validated by the power, objectivity, and utility of science. This transformation in administrative thought is perhaps worthy of being called a "Revolution," for it stands for the belief that only the methods of science can yield reliable insights into the realities of administration.

With the publication of Simon's seminal work in 1945, the methods of positivistic science were established as the only ones by which scholars might gain reliable knoweldge of administrative realities. Following this bias, scholars of contemporary thought in administration, like March (1965, pp. x –xii), have classified as "old" any knowledge created before 1950. This presentist bias stems from the ahistorical outlook of positivism and is seen in March's designation of his own and Simon's work as "adult" and "most fashionable." But for March and other advocates of the science of administration, what most powerfully distinguishes old knowledge from new—and useless knowledge from useful—is that new and reliable knowledge can stand only on a foundation of empirical science.

Simon's achievement was to overthrow the past wisdom of the field—a wisdom that derived from the experience, observation, and reflection of writers who were administrators, not scientists. The practitioner-scholars, such as Taylor, Urwick, and Fayol, regarded their knowledge as scientific. But their wisdom was expressed as "principles," and the truth of what they claimed rested more upon insight and assertion than upon science. Noting that the principles of administration occurred only in pairs, Simon (1957, p. 20) damned them as nothing more than mutually contradictory proverbs. Such knowledge suffered, he said, from "superficiality, oversimplication, lack of realism" (p. 38). To correct these errors, Simon set out to build a theory of administration on scientific knowledge, and his lasting contribution was to convince both scholars and practitioners that he had realized his vision. What is striking is how easily he appeared to have won the battle.

The work of Chester Barnard (1938), another of the scholar-practitioners, stands in dramatic contrast to Simon's. Barnard was essentially a moralist, and for him the heart of administration lay in the leader's creation of cooperative effort and commitment to institutional purpose among members of an organzation. Yet Barnard was apparently dazzled by Simon's claim to have science on his side. He wrote a preface to *Administrative Behavior* in which he acknowledged Simon's "important contribution" as "a set of tools . . . suitable for describing an organization and the way an administrative organization works" (Simon, 1957, p. xli). But he also expressed confidence that these tools would simply confirm his belief in the abstract "principles of general organization" and the importance of experience (such as his own) in understanding administration. In fact, Simon's science undermined the interpretation of experience as a means for understanding organizations, and it deflected attention from the moral questions about purpose and commitment highlighted by Barnard.

Unlike the scholar-practitioners, Simon did not attempt to provide a prescription for administrative action. Instead, he made minimal assumptions about the nature of administration and narrowed the limits of inquiry. Simon set out to build a "vocabulary of administrative theory," a vocabulary that would say nothing that could not be expressed in "operational definitions" (1957, pp. xlvi, 37). Such theory and its vocabulary would then be open to validation according to the norms of truth recognized by positivistic science. Simon's starting point for a scientific theory of administration was a single proposition: "Decision-making is the heart of administration." From this vantage point, he set out to explore "the logic and psychology of human choice" (1957, p. xlvi). The flaw in this definition is not so much its narrowness, for choice is certainly a fundamental and unavoidable dynamic in the making of organizational and administrative realities. Rather, the weakness stems from Simon's own choice to explore only the *factual basis of choice* and to ignore value and sentiment as springs of human action. Because science could not speak to the "ethical content" of decisions, Simon eliminated values from his putative science of administration. Thereafter he was content with his struggle to predict and control decisions purely from their "factual content":

> The question of whether decisions can be correct and incorrect resolves itself, then, into the question of whether ethical terms like "ought," "good," and "preferable" have a purely empirical meaning. It is a fundamental premise of this study that ethical terms are not completely reducible to factual terms. . . . Factual propositions cannot be derived from ethical ones by any process of reasoning, nor can ethical propositions be compared directly with the facts—since they assert "oughts" rather than the facts. . . . Since decisions involve valuations of this kind, they too cannot be objectively described as correct or incorrect. [Simon, 1957, p. 38]

Simon's great contribution was his recognition that making decisions is the essence of administration. In a way not found in previous studies, he saw that decisions are taken by human beings, not by boxes drawn on an organization chart. He knew that "principles" founded on such abstractions would be impotent.

> To many persons, organization means something that is drawn on charts or recorded in elaborate manuals of job descriptions, to be duly noted and filed. Even when it is discussed by some of its most perceptive students—for example, Colonel Urwick—it takes on more the aspect of a series of orderly cubicles contrived according to an abstract architectural logic, than of a house designed to be inhabited by human beings. [Simon, 1957, p. xvi]

Simon's great failure was his own decision to focus exclusively on the factual basis of decisions and to regard as irrelevant all the other forces that shaped them, but which his science could not predict or control. And so the science of administration defined by Simon retreated in the face of the intractable powers and imponderable choices that make up the realities of life.

Simon and Positivism in Administrative Science

Since positivism dominates Simon's conception of science, it seems fair to use "science" in this discussion to mean positivistic inquiry. As Phillips (1983), Eisener (1983), and Culbertson (1983)suggest, positivism is both a philosophy of empiricism and a set of rules for determining what constitutes truth. The force of the assumptions of this method of inquiry dispenses with any knowledge not based upon objective and empirical observation. Such inquiry must therefore deny the world of value. It must abjure as proper subjects for scientific study all of what Halpin (1958, p. xii) called "social philosophy" and all questions pertaining to "right human conduct." The positivist argument is, however, a powerful one. It reduces all internal states, all perceptions, feelings, and values to epiphenomena, to an unspeakable affect, to an externality that, as Hodgkinson (1983, p. 43) points out, "one can only rebut . . . by referring to one's own phenomenological and, there-fore, unverifiable experience . . . and by taking a position outside the limits of positivist discourse."

There is, of course, a broader conception of science in which the scientist is not only an observer but also an interpreter of reality. This view acknowl-edges that human interest and its possible biases are inextricably interwoven in what we call scientific truth (Bauman, 1978; Giddens, 1976; Rabinow and Sullivan, 1979; Toulmin, 1983). Such broader conceptions of science should, I believe, be accommodated within the study of educational administration, and, indeed, they are beginning to be expressed there—at least by the minority voices in the field who are advocates of alternative approaches. Fortunately these can now be found in the increasingly comprehensive and powerful statements of scholars such as Hodgkinson (1978b; 1983), Bates (1983a; 1985), Foster (1985), Gronn (1983; 1985; 1986), and Lakomski (1984; 1985a,b,c).

Simon's conception of administration as decision-making and his dedica-tion to the belief that the methods of posivistic science could be used to understand and improve the rationality of administrators' decisions have powerfully shaped the modern field of study. From these theoretical points of departure, he constructed a model of rationality—the limited, sufficing rationality of "administrative man" who makes only decisions that are "good enough." Simon's administrative man "satisfied," as opposed to omniscient "economic man" who maximized and made the best possible decisions. Simon's view of administration thus retained the assumptions of the economic model, but modified them to accommodate a less than perfect rationality. What is perhaps not so readily apparent is that he also retained the assumptions so dear to systems theorists—that administration is a function in a productive system and that this function is open to manipulation in the same way as other independent and objective conditions. For Simon, administration was simply an element or function in a productive system; as such, it could be regarded as operating in precisely the same manner as all other technical variables of a productive system.

The Failure of Adminstrative Science

My aim here is not so much to demonstrate the failure of administrative science in education, for I have been over that ground many times—too many times—before (Greenfield, 1975, 1978, 1980; 1985a; 1985b). Over the last decade or more, the continuing "turmoil" in the field has been well chronicled elsewhere (Griffiths, 1979). And the implications of the furor have been drawn so fully and so clearly that only the obtuse or the uninformed could claim to be unaware of them (Gronn, 1983; 1985a). I have argued that administrative science has failed in education, but I believe its failure is equally apparent in the other sub-fields of administration as well. The difference in the sub-fields is perhaps best seen in the contrast between the journals, *Administrative Science Quarterly* and *Educational Administration Quarterly*. The former recognizes the Revolution may be in trouble, and its articles reflect a radically expanded view of administrative theory and empirical inquiry; the latter denies, or seems to, that there are any problems in the unfolding of the Revolution.[2] The predominating opinion in that journal continues to recommend more and larger doses of science largely in the form of improved methodologies, but still within the restrictive notions of theory and method that have pervaded the field since Simon blazed the revolutionary path.

The revolutionary goals that Modern Organization Theory promised generally for administration were echoed in Halpin's New Movement in educational administration (Greenfield, 1985b). Although the ideology of these movements still reigns supreme as a kind of Doctrine of the Revolution

---

[2] Perhaps seeing language itself as the problem, the editors of *EAQ* recently announced a prohibition on first person pronouns. Ironically they chose to begin their battle against the subjectivism of the world in a text dealing with *ethnographic intent*. So they extirpated "I," "me," and "my" from Wolcott (1985), whose text thereby suffered a sea-change.

of Science in Administration, this Revolution, in my view, has failed; it has been unable to answer why the science that Simon stipulated to solve administrative problems has notably failed to do so.

Mainstream thought in educational administration stands, though perhaps now with a weakened conviction, on Simon's restrictive definition of administrative realities, embracing, a fortiori, his view of appropriate inquiry. For the most part, modern administrative theorists have heeded Simon's argument that the science of administration can be concerned only with means, not ends. The spirit of positivism, which is now pervasive, discourages historical inquiry, and so puts to flight any notion that scholars of administration should know their intellectual origins and the assumptions on which their field rests. But placed in the history of ideas, the belief that administration is (or can be) a science appears as a phenomenon of the mid-twentieth century. As we near the end of the century, this belief is beginning to appear as a misplaced faith. It is also becoming clear why it is an enormous error to conceive of adminstration as a science rather than as a moral act or as a political event.

Because positivistic science cannot derive a value from a fact or even recognize values as real, we have a science of administration which can deal only with facts and which does so by eliminating from its consideration all human passion, weakness, strength, conviction, hope, will, pity, frailty, altruism, courage, vice, and virtue. Simon led the science of administration down a narrow road which in its own impotence is inward-looking, self-deluding, self-defeating, and unnecessarily boring. These shortcomings are created by the blinkered view of choice and administrative action afforded by a narrowly empiricist science which lets us see but a pale and reduced reflection of the human will to achieve a purpose, to mobilize resources, to influence others—to do all that people in fact do as they make choices and strive to transform their values into realities.

The current overwhelming acceptance of positivistic science in administration has led theory and research to emphasize the epiphenomena of reality rather than the phenomenological force of that reality itself. This approach yields "hard," but often impotent, irrelevant, or misleading data that are the only reality recognized by the hyhpothetico-deductive models favored in such science. In this science, only that which is quantifiable and calculable is real, for that is the only kind of reality consistent with the limited rationality that finds its ultimate expression in the linear workings of computers. What is lost in such approaches is human intention, value, commitment—human passion and potential. What is lost is human will and choice, the sheer power of people pursuing their purposes, a pursuit that brings what some may call good and others evil. Hodgkinson (1978b, p. 18) has shown, moreover, that administrative science has led us to focus upon the personality traits of administrators—upon the mere characteristics of administrators rather than upon their character. In consequence, the empirical study of administrators has eluded their *moral* dimensions and virtually all that lends significance to what they do.

If this selective focusing is noticed in contemporary critiques of research, it appears only in Haller and Knapp's (1985) terms. Their response to the futility of research on the superficial characteristics of administrators is not to look more deeply, but to remove entirely the individual as a focus in administrative research. For them, a focus on the individual confuses "the *questions* that are studied with the *subjects* . . . of the studies." They recommend examining only the organizational production functions that administrators oversee. This position highlights the ultimate concern of adminstrative science—the effectiveness and efficiency of the organization, which is, of course, conceived as an entity independent of human will, purpose, and values.

What Simon Omitted: Right, Responsibility, Reflection

Simon's aim and hope were sweeping and daring: to enhance organizational efficiency and effectiveness by ensuring that administrators chose— within the limits of the rationality open to them—the best possible means to achieve a given end. But to fulfill the promise of the new science of productive rationality, administrative man had to disappear as a value-bearer and willful and unpredictable chioce-maker. Thus Simon's administrative man emerged in a devalued, dehumanized, and technologized form.

> Once the system of values which is to govern an administrative choice has been specified, there is one and only one "best" decision and this decision is determined by the organizational values and situation, and not by the personal motives of the member of the organization who makes the decision. Within the area of discretion, once an individual has decided, on the basis of his personal motives, to recognize the organizational objectives, his further behavior is determined not by personal motives, but by the demands of efficiency. [Simon, 1957, p. 204]

So, if this view defines the limits of a science of administrative decision-making, it must be noted that some vital questions of administration lie beyond them. All that governs the choice of the values for the system are beyond it, as is the question of what objective reality could exist to keep the personal motives, character, or ideology of individual members from impinging upon the choices they make in pursuing the values of the organization.

The horror of Simon's neutered science appears only with the realization that it conforms, almost perfectly, to the view that administrators seem to want to have of themselves: that they are instruments of an objective, selfless, rationality. Administrative science, as Simon conceived it, has done much to establish the belief that de-valued, but rational decision-making is desirable, attainable, and scientifically verifiable. This belief relieves the anxiety of decision-making and removes the administrator's sense of responsibility for his decisions. Scott and Hart (1979, pp. 46–47) show how a de-valued rationality can help administrators deal with practical problems, but only at the price of desensitizing them to the values that must be engaged in making a difficult decision:

> The management of organizations is a practical and mundane effort. Implicit within the pragmatic rule is a warning against philosophizing. . . . Organizations are run by managers who must make decisions about goals, policies, and strategies of action that influence human values and behavior, both within and outside the organization. . . . The vice president for personnel of a large company that must lay off five hundred employees is certainly not encouraged to consider the impact of this action on their lives. Instead, consideration is given to the health of the company.

A commitment to science in organizational affairs is not simply a commitment to rationality; it is, rather, a commitment to a restricted framework of rationality. Such a framework, called science, eases the sense of responsibility for powerful actors in organizational and administrative settings. It denies both responsibility and personal choice in the making of everyday decisions and in the making of decisions in the powerful world of organized reality. Such science takes sides in conflicts about the rightness of organizational purpose and about appropriate means for achieving them, but it denies it takes sides and claims to look dispassionately at such reality. As Hodgkinson (1978b, p.163) says, "Obedience or compliance can be construed as a way of abdicating responsibility." In our society with its reverence for science and technique, obedience to a truncated concept of rationality has become a cover for the powerful administrator: science and rationality provide the ultimately persuasive and irrefutable excuse for the abdication of personal choice and responsibility.

To choose and to acknowledge responsibility for one's choice is often a risky way of living. It may require standing with those who are defined as heretics by a powerful and possibly vengeful authority. The safe course for administration is suggested by Szasz's rueful observation:

> The Platonic maxim that "It is better to suffer wrong than to commit it" is fine for those to whom life is a spectator sport; the players, however, need something that gives them a little more protection in the clinches. [Szasz, 1976, p.33]

The moral dilemma of the administrator whose best judgement leads him to stand on the wrong side of authority was noted nearly fifteen centuries ago by Boethius, "the last of the Romans." A scholar turned administrator, he tried to serve both the emperor and—as it turned out—the wrong pope. His reward for acting according to conscience was death at the hands of his master, Theodoric the Ostrogoth. The emperor, however, first placed

Boethius under house arrest and thereby gave him time to reflect on his actions and to write *The Consolation of Philosophy*. There he makes the case that philosophy is the only consolation for a miscalculated risk. In his meditation, the figure of Philosophy appears to Boethius (1969, p. 53) and points out the high price of choosing to serve truth rather than sovereign power.

If you desire
To look on truth
And follow the path
With unswerving course
Rid yourself
Of joy and fear,
Put hope to flight,
And banish grief.
The mind is clouded
And bound in chains
Where these hold sway.

In organizational politics and administrative affairs, the acknowledgement of clearly chosen values can be dangerous. But as Boethius's life makes clear, acknowledgement enables us—both leaders and followers—to reflect upon our values. And in thinking about our lives, we may come to recognize that our decisions represent something beyond the decisions themselves; they bespeak a value and perhaps a commitment. As Hodgkinson (1978b, p. 172) points out, such commitment:

is, of course, subject to critique from other philosophical positions, but all that the proponents of these contending positions can do is to seek to persuade their audience by reason and rhetoric and all the powers at their disposal that they have the better values. In the end the act of choice is individual; and if free and conscious, then moral.

The Infusion of Science into Educational Administration

Science emerged in public administration in 1945 with Simon's work and has dominated all parts of the field since then. The spirit of positivism spread to educational administration in the 1950s in a form Halpin (1970) called the "New Movement." This revolution began with a small band of social scientists who set out to redeem the older studies through science (Halpin, 1958; Campbell and Lipham, 1960). Halpin (1970, p. 161) describes the shock of the scholar-practitioners when advocates of the new science-based administration confronted them with the news that their knowlege was "atheoretical and sloppy." He also reports that the reception the practitioners gave this news was "less than cordial." But, by 1957, the New Movement scientists were in command, and they announced to a seminar held at the Midwest Administration Center of the University of Chicago the arrival of the scientific millennium in educational administration.

From that point onwards there began a remarkably rapid transformation of the theory, research, and graduate instruction in educational administration. Deaf to critical voices who warned against the founding of inquiry on a flawed and narrow foundation, scientists of the New Movement did not waver in their conviction. They justified their new understanding of administration with the claim that it brought research into line with the requirements of science and of rationality itself (Culbertson, 1983). Seeing the strategic advantage of having Science on their side, practitioners soon began to endorse New Movement assumptions and ideology. Under the banner, "Administrative Theory as a Guide to Action," the Midwest Administration Center of the University of Chicago sponsored a second conference on theory, one that brought together social scientists and practitioners in the special mix that now marks so much of scholarly and professional endeavour in the field. Although Campbell warned the Conference that the millennium was not yet at hand, and though he cautioned that "scientific knowledge offers maps, not prescriptions," he also discouraged stragglers from the way by expressing the view that "social science is principally the description of an intelligent, rational person in action" (Campbell and Lipham, 1960, pp. 175–76).

Halpin, however, was later torn by doubts concerning his role in promulgating a science that promised to enable the administrator to "make wiser decisions" (Halpin, 1966, p. 285). He acknowleged that the ringing title of the conference invited administrators to believe in theory as a guide for action, when in fact there was "no theory worthy of the name available to report" (Halpin, 1970, p. 157). But scholars and practitioners of the time were prepared to testify that the emperor called Science had clothes. Indeed, Marland, one of the superintendents at the 1959 conference (Campbell and Lipham, 1960, p. 34), told how practitioners awaited with interest the "science of administration" and how they "listen[ed] attentively to the counsel of social scientists."[3] Marland compares the science-supported administrator to the bush pilot who

> now finds himself in the pilot's chair of a monstrous flying machine of untold power and dimensions. The social scientist tells us that there are buttons to push, levers to adjust, gauges to watch, beacons to reckon, and codes to decipher. He tells us that one cannot fly this craft by the seat of the pants, but that certain buttons and levers, when actuated, produce specific and predictable results in the performance and the posture of the craft. [Campbell and Lipham, 1960, p. 24]

---

[3] The attitude of the time is seen in Marland's deferential reference to "scientist Halpin" (Campbell and Lipham, 1960, p. 34).

What has been called "modern organization theory" (Haire, 1959; March, 1965) was created in close parallel with Halpin's "New Movement" in educational administration. Both may be seen as movements reflecting Simon's pioneering attempt to establish the study of organizations and administration on an objective scientific basis. Both began with a conscious break from previous studies that were viewed as mired in "social philosophy" (Halpin, 1958, p. xii). Both advocated that science, cast in an objective, positivistic mould, could save the field from the philosophers, moralists, and other subjectivists. Together they represented the deliberate founding of a new science of organization which aimed to establish the experimental verification of "hypoythetico-deductive theory"—abstract, mathematically expressed theory that was held by its proponents to be the highest form of scientific knowledge. That there was no such theory of this kind in existence did not seem to deter advocates from seeking it, indeed, from launching research into organizations to test it. Such theory, it was held, would produce control over organizations in the same way that it permitted control over the physical world. The aim of the New Movement in educational administration was to generate such theory about schools, to place it in the hands of administrators, and to train them in its use. And so began the effort to train educational administrators in the science of organizations.

Convinced by a similar logic, Haller and Knapp (1985, p. 161) have more recently urged researchers not to focus on administrators, but rather to study relationships within organizations. They define educational administration as "the study of the patterned relationships . . . with particular attention to the effects of those relationships on the transmission of subject matter to learners." The image of organizations assumed here is that of a productive unit staffed by human beings who are subsidiary to the unit and largely independent of it. In this conception, it is relationships and structures that are important, not people themselves.

The scientific view of educational administration continues to recommend systems theory, a conception which sees the organization as a productive unit striving under conditions of limited rationality to increase its output to a constraining environment. This view also continues to see the failure of science-based theories of administration as remediable by better and more powerful methodology. Such opinion thus reflects Simon's empiricism and his hope for improving the effectiveness and efficiency of the organization through rational decision-making. In these circumstances, it is not surprising to find that discussion of the failure of science-based theory and research soon reduces to technical issues—skewed distributions, outliers, Tukey's test, and box and whisker plots.[4]

---

[4] Among the many who call for better technique to shore up the sagging science of

The Consequences of the New Science of Organizations

Despite the promise that the science of organization and administration was to be objective, quantitative, and value-free, the *images* of organization found in the theory-based research of the New Movement carry important values and philosophical assumptions. Taking these values and assumptions into consideration, four consequences of the movement should be noted.

The Growing Belief in Administration as Science

The New Movement gave social validation to the belief that an objective science for guiding organizations had been been invented. With this belief widely accepted, so too was the idea that administrators should be trained in the science through programs of study in universities. Oftentimes, these programs have been state-mandated and tied to certification. Such programs teach the science of organization to administrators in the conviction it will enable them to do what they are supposed to do: direct organizations to achieve their goals in the most effective and efficient manner open to them. In this connection, the dominating metaphors of the science of administration are worth noting. Belief in the rationality of decision-making is prime among them, though this notion is closely tied to the systems concept that the organization is "real" and exists in a natural balance with its environment. In the systems view, to study an organization scientifically means to study an aspect of natural reality—a reality that can be explored objectively and explained in the law-like, universal languages of mathematics and logic. Individuals disappear—and with them human agency, responsibility, and morality—and natural forces take over the conduct of human affairs. And so we have the language of abstraction—so common in the literature—that, for example, speaks of "accommodating the organization to the reality demands of the environment and transforming the external situation" (Boyd and Crewson, 1981, p. 331).

To establish this science, it was necessary, as Hodgkinson pointed out, to commit the biological fallacy of endowing the organization with an ontological reality. The organization is conceived not only as real, but as more important than the people within it:

> and worse; the organization is not only reified, but deified. And the agent is not personally or morally responsible for the acts which are under the authority or *authorship* of the collectivity. . . . And outwardly benevolent organizations can become latent collective forces for evil. [Hodgkinson, 1978, p. 173]

---

administration, see Willower (1979; 1980), Hoy (1982), Fields (1985), and Haller and Knapp (1985). Implicitly they defend the assumptions Simon made about appropriate theory and methods, though they never invoke his name.

And so another anomaly of scientific administration becomes apparent. Its emphasis falls not upon the phenomenological reality of administrators—neither upon the realities of those who wield power nor upon the perceptions of those who suffer its consequences. Such science chooses to study a greater reality, one that lies beyond the awareness of individuals: the reality of the organization itself. Even if we can assume the reality of the organization, and even if we assume that knowledge of that reality is in some way useful, we must still ask why administrative science has failed to explore the second of Simon's concerns: "the logic and psychology of human choice." The answer, as Hodgkinson (1978a, p. 272) suggests, is "perhaps for the basic and stupefyingly simple reason that the central questions of administration are not scientific at all. They are philosophical." Here Hodgkinson is using "science" to mean an objective, imperial Science that is presumed to live only within the limits that positivism has placed upon it: a limit that reduces values to epiphenomena and that precludes Science from speaking about values at all.[5] If such limits are accepted, then Science cannot presume to tell any of us that we should go to work today, let alone what we should do when we get there. But there is another and larger sense of science that sees it simply as truth, as reliable knowledge, and not as a particular method for arriving at knowledge (Schumacher, 1977). But what knowledge is reliable? Perhaps in the end we must be content simply with knowledge that lets us get through the day, preferably happily (Greenfield, 1983).

The De-evaluation of Administrative Studies

The scientific movement is closely connected to the notion that a value-free science of administration is not merely possible, but at hand. With the elimination of values, consideration of the conduct of organizations is reduced to technicalities. The substance of decisions is not important—only the manner of the making of them. As Bates (1983a, p. 8) points out, this approach brings with it a separation of problems in administration from problems in education. It also brings, as Tipton (1985) argues, the isolation of theory in educational administration from other academic studies that bear powerfully on its professed concerns and interests. Many texts in the field bear the unimaginative title, *Educational Administration*,[6] and from this emphasis one would expect that they should address uniquely educational issues. Not so. Readers look in vain for any substantive educational discussion. They may be told how to lead, motivate, communicate, develop morals,

---

[5] I use "Science" to denote the narrower, but imperial inquiry that claims objectivity and value-neutrality and that stands in contrast to the broader search for reliable knowledge that characterizes all inquiry (Schumacher, 1977).

[6] For example, Hoy and Miskel (1982).

and maintain the organization in dynamic equilibrium, but they will find no discussion of an issue that they must bring judgement. Radical and conservative critiques of school structure and curriculum, disputes over religion and language of instruction, the virtues of private versus public schools, class and cultural bias, unions, women, dicipline, dress codes—of all these and the many other issues that beset education, there is no murmur of comment. Not even the major controversies about the meaning and reliability of administrative science are discussed in these texts.[7]

Hidden Values of Administrative Science

Despite its claim to objectivity, the science of administration is usually to be found on the side of the status quo. It starts from a standpoint of things as they are, and then asks why they are so. It does not question whether that which is ought to be. The argument here is not that conventional society or the status quo are necessarily wrong, but that positivist science cannot and *should not* attempt to validate social reality without revealing the weakness of its credentials for doing so. But despite its claims to neutrality, Science cannot seem to resist taking on the role of social validator, and, in fact, is often well paid for its neutered conscience. This criticism has been launched against positivist social science generally, but in administration it has particular potency, for the state is the ultimate organization; it has almost unrestricted power over the individual—even the power that can ask and get an individual's life. But if Science conceives the state (and all organizations of lesser puissance) as an objectified reality that is beyond question by the science of organization, then its students have no recourse but to serve their organizations with all the skill and devotion of which they are capable. In Hobbesian terms, the administrative scientist becomes a servant of the General Will—of the Sovereign. The General Will is, of course, to be interpreted by the Sovereign, not by the scientist whose role is limited to that of a technician skilled in applying a kind of physics of sociation—the impersonal and objective science of social organization and administration.[8]

A science of administration limited by the assumptions of positivism can produce experts in technique, not experts in value. If, however, the positivists are right, and values are merely an illusion or an affect that registers only in the psyche of individuals, then no real problem exists, for there is no objective way of expressing or arbitrating between competing claims of perceived value. The physics of sociation would then suffice as a basis for

---

[7] In a text devoted wholly to theory in educational administration, Silver (1983) devotes not even a footnote to the controversies that have shaken educational administration for over a decade.

[8] These ideas are elaborated in Greenfield (1984, pp. 147–51).

understanding and evaluating social reality. But if values are real, and if they
are beyond the scope of positivist science, then a science of social order that
claims to be value-free must remain silent in the face of the central issues of
organizational and administrative life. But remain silent it does not. The
mantle of objectivity permits scientists to intervene on the behalf of values
without seeming to do so, and to move readily from commenting on the way
things are to advocating the way they should be. In the contemporary field,
such scientists are everywhere: for example, administrators who, following
Hoy and Miskel (1982, p. vii), want to make their practice "less of an art and
more of a science," the agent of educational change and implementation, the
consultant on organization development who promises to improve the
"health" of the organization, and now the purveyors of excellence in organization and designs for effective schools. Indeed, all *experts* in organization
theory who claim their prescriptions stand on objective Science are open to
challenge, for their values, not their Science, constitute the real foundation of
their knowledge.   The difficulty that arises from a belief in the possibility of
a de-valued notion of rationality and decision-making is well illustrated with
a metaphor from Hodgkinson: the sandwich of rationality. Closely following
his explication of three levels of reality and three types of values, Hodgkinson
(1983; 1985; 1986) draws attention to *levels* of reality and value in rationality
itself. In this view, any human choice is made up of three elements. One is
cognitive and limitedly rational in Simon's sense of the calculation of factual
relationship between ends and means. This calculation constitutes the
"meat" of the sandwich, but it is held in place by two slices of bread made up
of subrational affect on the one hand and another slice made up of superra-
tional ideology and transrational value. The sandwich metaphor thus recognizes that human beings are driven by their desires and fears, by their hopes
and ideals, as much as by their rational calculations. And who is to say that
such drives are not also a kind of rationality?

Angels and other rationalists say it. For as William Blake said:

> I have always found that Angels have the vanity to speak of themselves as the only
> wise. This they do with a confident insolence sprouting from systematic reasoning.

This point urges not that we dispense with systematic reasoning, but only
that we recognize it as a compact with an individual's ideology, ideals,
commitment, and preference. What the angels of systematic reasoning and
administrative science must comprehend is that issues great and small—
whether to die for love of one's country, whether to close a school in the face
of falling enrollments, whether to stop smoking today—are decided by people
who bring all their belief, passion, habit, frailty, or nobility to the choice that
faces them. Whatever the choice before them, they are unlikely to make it on
the basis of a calculated, fact-driven rationality alone. Or as I have argued,
facts *are*, but they do not tell us what to do (Greenfield, 1980, p. 43). Indeed,

the facts alone decide nothing; it is we who decide about the facts. This realization comes as no surprise to historians and artists who deal with what men and women do, not with what the "angels of reason" (see Huxley, 1954) would have them do. But scientists of administration continue to be surprised, and spend much effort pointing out how the world would be better if people only behaved "rationally." This then is the failure of administrative science. Instead of providing, as it claims, an objective description of the world and of human choice, administrative science offers merely another value-driven prescription. Apparently despairing over the irrationality of the world, many otherwise encouraging critiques of administrative science offer expressions of hope that stronger research methodologies will yet plumb the depths of its mystery and find Simon's fact-only rationality at the bottom (see Haller and Knapp, 1985; Hoy, 1982).

Science-Validated Training Programs

New Movement science fosters and legitimates programs for training and certifying administrators. During the 1950s, a foundation-supported drive began in the United States to transform the old-style training programs into new ones based upon the assumptions of modern organization theory and administrative science (Tope et al., 1965). These programs were designed to bring New Movement administrative science to bear upon the practical problems of education. Such programs have since spread through the proselytizing efforts of university-based advocates to other countries, notably the English-speaking Commonwealth countries, but increasingly to Third World countries as well.[9] To criticize the spread of such programs is not to suggest that the training of administrators is futile and unnecessary; rather, it is to argue that many university-based training [programs], captured by a narrowly defined concept of administration, restrict the possibility of productive inquiry into administration.

Sovereign powers, in the form of state departments of education and other public and private authorities, have long had a role in the choice and validation of administrators for educational institutions. As Gronn (1985b) has shown, the selection of administrators is driven by a rationality that sweeps far beyond the logic of fact-driven choice. How could it be otherwise? Administrators are essentially value-carriers in organizations; they are both arbiters of values and representatives of them. Those who select and evaluate administrators are not so naive as to ignore their surface characteristics. Indeed, they likely see all that meets the senses—dress, speech, custom—as

---

[9] For further critique of this advocacy, see Riffel (1986) and Greenfield (1975; 1979/80).

expressions of the administrator's deeper values and commitments. But administrative science, holding up the ideal of the administrator as technician, is likely to argue otherwise. It offers the Sovereign the possibility of choosing the "certified" decision-maker, the one who uses science to bring excellence, effectiveness, or efficiency—as though these conditions had no value content—to whatever organization employs him.

And so administrative science again plays into the hand of the social system. While the scientifically-based training program claims to produce technicians skilled in decision-making and organization building, the Sovereign looks beyond such froth to the prospective administrator's values and character. But the froth is not irrelevant either; if for no other reason, it is politically advantageous to be seen standing with Science. Therefore we see authorities increasingly turning to science-driven training programs. The result is a happy one for both sides of the bargain. The Sovereign can claim a scientific validation of its decisions, and Science gets privileged access to the benefits the Sovereign can bestow.

Callahan (1964) has identified four stages in the historical development of administrative programs for American school superintendents, and he shows how each stage was shaped by a characteristic ideal. In this development, we may also see the values that now generally pervade programs for the training of educational administrators in the United States. And—thanks to the international network that promulgates science-based training in educational administration—we may see these same values in similar programs in Canada and in many other countries as well. Callahan describes the stages through which belief in the value of science-based programs for the training of educational administrators developed in the United States:

The superintendent as scholarly educational leader, 1865–1910.
The superintendent as business manager or school executive, 1910–1930.
The superintendent as statesman in a democratic school system, 1930–1954.
The superintendent as applied social scientist, 1954–present.

Khleif (1975) has reported an illuminating study of the socializing process and values of an exemplary program for the training of an elite cadre of educational administrators in administrative science. He found that more of the effort of the program was devoted to the inculcation of values than it was to the training of students in science. Indeed, he found that under the guise of training in social science, the neophyte administrators were offered a new persona and introduced to a set of values congenial to prospective employers. Students were carefully chosen for the program and schooled at length in their roles. After an appropriate time, the neophytes were certified as experts in the social scientific knowledge needed to administer schools and were introduced to mentors who then recommended them for jobs in the power system of education. Thus, particular social values were advanced under the guise of a training program dedicated to science.

As Khleif (1975, p. 307) explains:

The program is a high-speed course in social mobility. . . . The program is a school for statesmen or—if one is uncharitable—politicians. Candidates acquire an upper-middle-class demeanor, dress, and presentability. Candidates become more socially polished, masters of small talk, alert politicians with—if necessary—a talent for intrigue and little arts of popularity. They become adept at self-manipulations and manipulations of others.

With respect to the values in the four historical stages identified by Callahan, Khleif says the science-based program:

puts an emphasis on the three latter types of superintendency and definitely discourages or ignores the first type. Attention to school finances, a smooth facade of democratic leadership and pieties about it, and a realistic training in the ways of community power exemplify the historical heritage and current culture of this profession.

It is not likely that training programs of the intensity and selectivity described by Khleif exist today. Such programs have been the victims both of a new stringency in university budgets and of a diminishing faith in the ideology that inspired them. But many programs of lesser purity and intensity undoubtedly remain, carrying on in the spirit noted by Khleif. Indeed, training programs for educational administrators have surely increased in number and enrollment over the past twenty years. They have consolidated their presence and have gained even stronger acceptance by sovereign powers. Such programs nurture Simon's conception of rational administration and decision-making. The pity of this situation is that such conceptions of administrative training block the development of programs that might deal more openly and helpfully with the value problems that confront all those who manage organizations. For administration is not a science in Simon's terms. It is better conceived as Hodgkinson (1978b, p. 100) does:

While it has at its disposal a managerial quasi-technology, it is essentially a philosophical endeavour, a kind of humanism. Its overriding mission is the civilization of power.

The Alternative

The criticisms I have made of the conventional practice of administrative science can be summed up in a few brief points. First, administrative science does not work as science; it has not brought us increased understanding and control of organizations. Yet this outcome is what both early and contemporary proponents of the science of administration claim to be its whole justification. Administrative science was to provide useful and powerful knowledge. This was the very criterion by which the fledgling science of administration rejected all previous knowledge in the field. Second, administrative science has ignored power relationships and has been content to deal with administrative problems that ignore substantive problems in education. Third, administrative science has focused its efforts not upon the phenomenological realities of administration—upon the experience of wielding power and making decisions—but upon the organization. It has been content to regard organizations rather than people as the real actors in society. And finally, administrative science has de-valued the study of human choice and rationality. It has insisted that decision-making be dealt with *as though it were* fully explainable in rational and logical terms. This has allowed administrative science to deal with values surreptitiously, behind a mask of objectivity and impartiality, while denying it is doing so.

For these reasons, I believe it is a fair judgement to say that administrative science is in decline. Whether it has also fallen is a moot point. Some might argue that it does not matter whether the body of the science is dead or dying; it matters only that scholars and practitioners bahave as though it were alive. Faith in administrative science certainly inspired the creation of the earliest models of science-based training programs (Khleif, 1975), and a similar if somewhat diminished faith surely continues to maintain them.

New directions are apparent in theory that again places value questions as central in administration (Hodgkinson, 1978b; Scott and Hart, 1979). What then is the alternative to a science- and fact-driven definition of the field? Though I have elaborated an answer elsewhere (Greenfield, 1983; 1985a), let me suggest again its dimensions.

1. Organizations are not things. They have no ontological reality, and there is no use studying them as though they did. They are an invented social reality of human creation. It is people who are responsible for organizations and people who change them. Organizations have reality only through human action, and it is that action (and the human will driving it) that we must come to understand. The alternative I am proposing rejects theory that explains human behavior as though a depersonalized organization and its de-valued, nonhuman environment *caused* it. The alternative theory grants a measure of free will to individuals, and so places a measure of responsibility upon them for their action. People do not exist in organizations. Organizations exist in and through individuals. The concept of organization should be understood as a moral order deeply imbedded in each of us—an order that is arbitrary, nonnatural, and often backed by enormous power, even by violence. But that power may be redeemed by love, that is, by a dedication to better values.

2. Organizations are a nexus of freedom and compulsion. As invented social realities, they can be not only created but also manipulated. The creation and maintenance of this illusion is the root of what the world understands as leadership; although in less dramatic forms, it could as well be called administration. The metaphors of production and technical control, appropriate to systems, organisms, and other physical or biological unities, are not appropriate to understanding and administering organizations. We need new metaphors to describe organizations and administration. Perhaps most important would be to rid ourselves of the concept of an equilibrating system responding to benevolent environmental control. I suggest the metaphor of the Bonsai tree. This image is particularly apt for education. The gardener does not let the young tree simply "develop its full potential." Instead, he acts upon his own view of what constitutes a proper expression of the tree's potential, and he keeps clipping and pruning until the tree manifests that form. Since in education the "full potential" of a child (or of a teacher or administrator) could be anything from Charles Manson to Albert Schweitzer,[10] the gardener keeps pruning until the desired form is produced. The difference between the gardener's task and the task of the leader or administrator is that trees never learn. People do, and that is where organizations and human culture itself come from.

3. The world of will, intention, experience, and value is the world of organizations and administration. The building of a new science of administration will depend on our ability to understand these realities. It will require that we recognize their complexity (Hodgkinson, 1983, pp. 57–91) and their personal and subjective dimensions (Greenfield, 1985a). Such a science will require methods and instruments that are adequate to these realities. As Schumacher (1977, pp. 39–60) points out, the question of what constitutes adequate methods and instruments for understanding the world is essentially a philosophical one. And as Gronn (1982, 1984) has shown, our assumptions about adequate methods and instruments for studying administrators not only will reflect what we think administration is, but also will shape powerfully how we see administrators and understand what they do.

4. Conflict is endemic in organizations. It arises when different individuals or groups hold opposing values or when they must choose between accepted but incompatible values. Administrators represent values,

---

[10] Near one end of this continuum, there surely stands Jim Keegstra, the small-town Alberta teacher who until recently taught and examined his students on a history whose central "facts" proved that Hitler's "final solution" was purely a hoax perpetrated by Jewish conspiracy.

but they also impose them. Administrative science must come to understand these complexities if it is to speak meaningfully to the world of practice. Only then may it begin to help administrators understand and cope with the personal and existential stress of conflict. The texts of administrative science are suffused with metaphors that portray organizations in terms of equilibrium, stability, adjustment, and harmony. We need other metaphors to bespeak the reality of stress and conflict.

5. The ideas and insights of Barnard (1938), the scholar-practitioner, were largely swept aside in the rush to make the study of administration embrace the rationality of Simon's science. What Barnard focused upon was not rationality and the enhancement of it, but an essential value phenomenon in organizations: commitment. For him, the building of commitment was the fundamental task of administration. This view raises the question, "How can administrators be moral?" rather than Simon's question, "How can they be rational?" Simon would make the administrator a technician; Barnard would have him be a moral leader. Barnard speaks of the moral complexity of the leader. If we return to Barnard's view, we need again his insights as well as new metaphors to ground the science of administration. To help us begin to think of leaders in moral terms, we should recognize that they are representatives of values: indeed, they are both creators of values and entrepreneurs for them.

6. The ethical dimensions of administration come constantly to the fore once we free ourselves from the metaphors of harmony, optimism, and rationality that administrative science imposes upon organizational reality. What amazes in all of this is to read the science-based texts and to mark how positive and optimistic they are about human nature and the human condition. Administrative science lives in a world of pristine goodness, and so its knowledge can be of little use to those who face the perplexities of the world—perplexities that come readily to those who do no more than reflect upon their own experience or who simply read the newspapers or literary portrayals of life in organizations. Those, like Hodgkinson, who observe life in organizations in a clear-eyed fashion find that things often go wrong in them; they are beset by conflict, self-interested action, and the debasement of value through compromise. He lets us see the power of commitment, the polestar quality of transcendent values, and the madness they may bring with them. He repeats Saul Bellow's simple but fundamental question: "With everyone sold on the good, how does all the evil get done?" Of an earlier generation, Barnard speaks of the "moral complexity" of the leader by which he seems to mean the leader's wisdom in knowing when to raise moral issues and when to defuse them. Reflecting on such

questions and building answers to them must become an essential and pervasive purpose of administrative studies. If Science cannot answer questions of what constitutes right action in social contexts—if it cannot speak of praxis—then it is time to begin again with a conception that sees administration as a set of existential and ethical issues. If inquiries launched from this premise lead to an understanding of administration in moral terms, and if this knowledge helps administrators see themselves and their tasks more clearly and responsibly, we may then have reliable knowledge and a sound guide for action in the world. Although this is exactly the kind of knowledge that Simon found wanting and hoped to provide in a rational and control-oriented Science of Administration, could we not still call such knowledge "science" in humbler form?

An Agenda for the Future

Scholarship in administration has been bound for more than a generation by the power of Simon's thought. While a weakening of this remarkable uniformity is now apparent in all branches of the field, orthodoxy still struggles tenaciously to maintain its grip. In educational administration, defenders such as Willower (1985) meet the challenge by repeating positions only slightly modified from Simon's philosophical assumptions about the nature of administration and the proper means for inquiry into it. Most scholars will surely continue in the path that Simon pioneered, but others are now beginning to question that direction. They seek an alternative way and, therefore, an alternative conception of science to guide them. They, too, may call theirs the way of science, though they will likely abandon the assumptions and methods that Simon espoused as proper for scientific inquiry into administrative and organizational realities.

What is needed now in the study of educational administration is, first, the honesty to face the intellectual disarray of the field and, then, the courage to begin inquiry in a new mode. To guide such inquiry, we need only turn to an existing tradition of interpretive science that recognizes both subjectivity in the construction of social reality and the inevitability of interpretation in science. Though this mode of inquiry is still largely unknown and unused in administrative studies, it is at hand; it offers the best alternative to the narrow and increasingly sterile path of rationalism and positivistic science.

Administration is about power and powerful people. The study of administration must stand therefore upon a resolute examination of people as they strive to realize their ends. Administrative Science has too often yielded to the temptation of power and desired to wield it, not just to study it. Those who stand close to sovereign powers readily find reason to assist them. An adequate science of administration, however, must study power while resisting its pull. The new science of administration must be free to talk about the values that power serves, but free it cannot be if it is closely dependent upon the Sovereign (Ramos, 1981). To escape that dependency, the new science should abjure those activities that are most likely to endear it to the Sovereign—recognizing that the Sovereign, like the Devil, can take many forms. The certification of future administrators is one such endearing activity.

For more than a quarter of a century, a fact-driven model of decision-making and rationality has dominated training programs for educational administrators. To the extent that these programs embrace technically oriented notions of administration, they offer less than they espouse. They miss the meaning of human action and most of what saves the study of administration from inducing a state of ennui in its students. They oversimplify administrative problems and overstate the claim that science can solve them. Yet such programs recognize virtually no limit on what can be done through academic study to prepare candidates for administrative responsibility. Only by suffering through their perhaps intentionally boring training do students of science-based training come to glimpse the meaning of administrative power and its scope for good and evil (Greenfield, 1980, pp. 47–48).

A more fruitful training may be achieved through approaches that work with practising administrators and aim to give them deeper insights into the nature of their craft—into its dilemmas and possibilities— through study of its realities and through reflection upon them. We must seek new models for administrative training—ones that acknowledge responsibility, right judgement, and reflection as legitimately and inevitably part of administrative action. Such programs would lead the field of study toward what Scott (1985, p. 156) has called "revolutionary moral discourse" and away, therefore, from instruction in a putative science of organization and administration.

When I first took up the study of educational administration, nothing I learned cast a scintilla of doubt upon the certainty and power of administrative science; its objectivity and probity were simply assumed as were the benefits that were supposed to flow from its application. Certainly I did not doubt these apparent truths. What then is to be said now? Would the world be the worse without an administrative science? Probably not. But the issue is not simply science versus something else—versus the humanities, philosophy, or doing nothing at all. The issue is rather, "What kind of science?" Toulmin (1983) has observed the progress of modern science and noted the transformation of the scientist from an observer of reality to a participant in its construction. Where scientists once worried only to do the measurement right, they now find an even greater problem: to do the right measurement—that is, to make the right observation. Thus the inevitability of subjective choice and interpretation enters science, and the possibility of a value-free science disappears. We must seek a new definition of science in administration—one that can accommodate the view that values pervade the entire realm of administration and, indeed, constitute the proper focus of study. Toulmin explains how a demand for neutrality in scientific method and observation came to limit the very kinds of problems that scientists could think of as proper for study:

This demand for value neutrality played two separate roles in the sciences. On the one hand, it required the modern scientist to approach all the intellectual problems that properly fell within the scope of his methods with a clear head and a cool heart. On the other hand, it served to demarcate those issues that were properly the subjects for "scientific" investigation and discussion from those that were, rather, matters of human taste, choice, or decision. To begin with, these two aspects were not always distinguished in people's minds. [1981, p. 81]

If nothing else, we must understand that the new science of administration will be a science with values and of values.

What is required now is a transformation of the administrative scientist's attitudes toward the reality he studies. Scientists inspired by positivism approach administrators with the conviction that their theories and methods enable them to know administration in a way mere practitioners never could. The reverse assumption now seems a better point of departure: administrators know administration; scientists don't. The point of such inquiry would be to enable scientists to come to know what administrators know and to bring a fresh and questioning perspective to it. To accomplish this purpose, we might well return to one of Simon's original starting points and seek to understand the logic and psychology of human choice. But that will require the study of decisions, will, and intention in all their depth, perplexity, and subjective uncertainty. The new science will surely also require giving up the notion that decisions and organizations themselves can be controlled by science. Greater insight such science may offer, but greater control, no.

A possible research agenda of the new science is apparent:

1. How is the social reality of the organization built and maintained? What do administrators and others contribute to this process?
2. What is the role of language in the building of administrative reality? We might begin to answer this question by taking seriously Hodgkinson's propositions (1978b, pp. 199–222): Two of these state, "Language is the basic administrative tool" and "Language *has* power and cloaks power."
3. The character of administrators is clearly of great importance. We may study it through biography and history.
4. Law is built upon the arbitration of value conflict. Let us emulate its methods and learn from the substance of its knowledge.

5. We must consider more fully such philosophical issues as the nature of value and the question of right values. What constitutes good or right in administrative affairs and how can administrators gain knowledge of it?
6. Questions of what constitutes good and right action in administration must be answered not simply for themselves, but in context and with specific educational issues and policies.
7. We must understand more deeply the administrative career. Who administers our schools? What motivates them to climb the ladder of administration? What happens to them as they do? What routes lead upward? In the recent past, there was truth in the dictum: women teach and men administer. What made that dictum true? Is there a better truth and how may it be realized? What are the consequences of these truths for women and for men, and how do they shape the organizations we understand as schools?
8. We need to understand the existential realities of leading and following in organizations. We need to understand the wielding of power and the making of decisions when much is on the line. And we need to appreciate what it is to suffer the decisions of such power.

This is a minimal agenda for research, but it stands in contrast with much of what has gone before. If we could achieve it only partially, we would have some basis to say a valid and valuable science of administration is emerging.

References

Barnard, Chester. (1938). *The functions of the executive.* Cambridge: Harvard University Press.
Bates, Richard J. (1983a). *Educational administration and the management of knowledge.* Victoria, Australia: Deakin University Press.
Bates, Richard J. (1983b). Morale and motivation: myth and morality in educational administration. *Educational Administration Review* 3 (1).
Bates, Richard J. (1985). Towards a critical practice of educational administration. In T.J. Sergiovanni and J.E. Corbally (Eds.), *Leadership and organizational culture,* pp. 260–74. Urbana: University of Illinois.
Bauman, Z. (1978). *Hermeneutics and social science.* London: Hutchinson.
Boethius. (1969). *The consolation of philosophy.* Translated by V.E. Watts. Penguin Books.
Boyd, W.L., and Crewson, R.L. (1981). The changing conception and practice of public school administration. In D.C. Berliner (Ed.), *Review of Research in Education,* 9:311–73. Washington: AERA.
Callahan, R.E. (1964). Changing conception of the superintendency in public education: 1865–1964. Fifth Alfred. Simpson Lecture in Education. Cambridge, Mass.: New England School Development Council, Harvard Graduate School of Education.

Campbell, Roald F., and Lipham, James M. (Eds.) (1960). *Administrative theory as a guide to action*. Chicago: Midwest Center, University of Chicago.

Culbertson, Jack. (1983). Theory in educational administration: Echoes from critical thinkers. *Educational Researcher* 12(10):15–22.

Eisener, E.W. (1983). Anastasia might be alive, but the monarchy is dead. *Educational Researcher* 12(5):13–24.

Fields, M.W. (1985). Exploratory data analysis in educational administration: Tempering methodological advances with a conservative note. *Educational Administration Quarterly* 21(3):247–62.

Foster, William P. (1985). Towards a critical theory of educational administration. In T.J. Sergiovanni and J.E. Corbally (Eds.), *Leadership and Organizational Culture*, pp. 240–59. Urbana: University of Illinois.

Giddens, Anthony. (1976). *New rules of sociological method: A positive critique of interpretive sociologies*. London: Hutchinson.

Greenfield, Thomas B. (1975). Theory about organization: A new perspective and its implications for schools. In M. Hughes (Ed.), *Administering education: International challenge*, pp. 71–99. London: Athlone.

Greenfield, Thomas B. (1978). Reflections on organization theory and the truths of irreconcilable realities. *Educational Administration Quarterly* 14(2):1–23.

Greenfield, Thomas B. (1979/80). Research in educational administration in the United States and Canada: An overview and critique. *Educational Administration* 8(1):207–45.

Greenfield, Thomas B. (1980). The man who comes back through the door in the wall: Discovering truth, discovering self, discovering organizations. *Educational Administration Quarterly* 16(3):26–59.

Greenfield, Thomas B. (1983). Against group mind: An anarchistic theory of organization. In R.L. Rattray-Wood (Ed.), *Reflective readings in educational administration*, pp. 293–301. Victoria, Australia: Deakin University Press.

Greenfield, Thomas B. (1984). Leaders and schools: Wilfulness and nonnatural order in organizations. In T.J. Sergiovanni and J.E. Corbally (Eds.), *Leadership and organizational culture*, pp. 142–69. Urbana: University of Illinois.

Greenfield, Thomas B. (1985a). Putting meaning back into theory: The search for lost values and the disappeared individual. Paper presented to the Annual Conference of the Canadian Society for the Study of Education, Montreal.

Greenfield, Thomas B. (1985b). Theories of educational organization: A critical perspective. In T. Husén and T.N. Postlethwaite (Eds.), *International encyclopedia of education: Research and studies* 9:5240–51. Oxford: Pergamon.

Griffiths, Daniel E. (1979). Intellectual turmoil in educational administration. *Educational Administration Quarterly* 15(3):43–65.

Gronn, Peter C. (1982). Neo-Taylorism in educational administration? *Educational Administration Quarterly* 18(4):17–35.

Gronn, Peter C. (1983). *Rethinking educational administration: T.B. Greenfield and his critics*. Victoria, Australia: Deakin University Press.

Gronn, Peter C. (1984). On studying administrators at work. *Educational Administration Quarterly* 20(1):115–29.

Gronn, Peter C. (1985a). After T.B. Greenfield, whither educational administration? *Educational Management and Administration* 13:55–61.

Gronn, Peter C. (1985b). Notes on leader watching. In R.J.S. Macpherson and H. Sungaila (Eds.), *Ways and means of research*, Armidale, N.S.W.: University of New England.

Gronn, Peter C. (1986a). Choosing a deputy head: The rhetoric and the reality of administrative selection. *Australian Journal of Education* 30(1).

Gronn, Peter C. (1986b). *The psycho-social dynamics of leading and following*. Victoria, Australia: Deakin University.

Haire, Mason, ed. (1959). *Modern Organization Theory*. New York: Wiley.

Haller, E.J., and Knapp, T.R. (1985). Problems and methodology in educational administration. *Educational Administration Quarterly* 21(3), 157–68.

Halpin, Andrew W., ed. (1958). *Administrative theory in education*. Chicago: Midwest Administration Center, University of Chicago.

Halpin, Andrew W. (1966). *Theory and research in administration*. New York: Macmillan.

Halpin, Andrew W. (1970). Administrative theory: The fumbled torch. In A.M. Kroll (Ed.), *Issues in American education*, pp. 156–83. New York: Oxford.

Hodgkinson, Christopher. (1978a). The failure of organizational and administrative theory. *McGill Journal of Education* 13(3):271–78.

Hodgkinson, Christopher. (1978b). *Towards a philosophy of administration*. Oxford: Basil Blackwell.

Hodgkinson, Christopher. (1983). *The philosophy of leadership*. Oxford: Basil Blackwell.

Hodgkinson, Christopher. (1985). Confucius, Wittgenstein, and the perplexing world of administration. Lecture, Ontario Institute for Studies in Education, Toronto.

Hodgkinson, Christopher. (1986). The value bases of administrative action. Paper read to the Annual Conference of the American Educational Research Association, San Francisco.

Hoy, Wayne K. (1982). Recent developments in theory and research in educational administration. *Educational Administration Quarterly* 18(3), 1–11.

Hoy, Wayne K., and Cecil G. Miskel. (1982). *Educational administration. Theory, research, and practice*, 2nd ed. New York: Random House.

Huxley, Aldous. [1954] (1977). *The doors of perception*. Reprint. Frogmore, England. Triad/Panther.

Khleif, B.B. (1975). Professionalization of school superintendents: A sociocultural study of an elite program. *Human Organization* 34(3):301–08.

Lakomski, G. (1984). On agency and structure: Pierre Bourdieu and Jean-Claude Passeron's theory of symbolic violence. *Curriculum Inquiry* 14(2):151–63.

Lakomski, G. (1985a). Critical theory and educational administration. Problems and solutions. Paper read to the American Educational Research Association, Annual Conference, Chicago.

Lakomski, G. (1985b). The cultural perspective in educational administration. In R. J.S. Macpherson and H.M. Sungaila (Eds.), *Ways and meanings of research in educational administration*. Armidale, Australia: University of New England.

Lakomski, G. (1985c). Theory, value, and relevance in educational administration. In Fazal Rizui (Ed.), *Working papers in ethics and educational administration*, pp. 35–64. Victoria, Australia: Deakin University.

March, James G. (Ed.) (1965). *Handbook of Organizations*. Chicago: Rand McNally.

Phillips, D.C. (1983). After the wake: Postpositivistic educational thought. *Educational Researcher* 12(5):4–12.

Rabinow, P., and Sullivan, W.M. (Eds.) (1979). *Interpretive social science: A reader.* Berkeley: University of California Press.

Ramos, A.G. (1981). *The new science of organizations: A reconstruction of the wealth of nations.* Toronto: University of Toronto Press.

Riffel, J.A. (1986). The study of educational administration: A developmental point of view. *Journal of Educational Administration* 24(2):152–72.

Schumacher, E.F. (1977). *A guide for the perplexed.* New York: Harper and Row.

Scott, William G. (1985). Organizational revolution: An end to managerial orthodoxy. *Administration and Society* 17(2):149–70.

Scott, William G., and Hart, David. (1979). *Organizational America.* Boston: Houghton Mifflin.

Silver, P. (1983). *Educational administration: Theoretical perspectives on practice and research.* New York: Harper and Row.

Simon, Herbert. [1945] (1957). *Administrative behavior: A study of decision-making process in administrative organization.* 2nd ed. New York: The Free Press.

Szasz, T. (1976). *Heresies.* Garden City, N.Y.: Anchor/Doubleday.

Tipton, B.F.A. (1985). Educational organizations as workplaces. *British Journal of Educational Sociology* 6(1):35–53.

Tope, D.E., et al. (1965). *The social sciences view educational administration.* Englewood Cliffs, NJ: Prentice-Hall.

Toulmin, Stephen. (1981). The emergence of post-modern science. In R.M. Hutchins and M.J. Adler (Eds.), *The great ideas today*, pp. 69-114. Chicago: Encyclopedia Britannica.

Toulmin, Stephen. (1983). From observer to participant: The transformation of twentieth century science. Lecture, University of Toronto.

Willower, Donald J. (1979). Ideology and science in organization theory. *Educational Administration Quarterly* 15(3):20–42.

Willower, Donald J. (1980). Contemporary issues in theory in educational administration. *Educational Administration Quarterly* 16(3):1–25.

Willower, Donald J. (1985). Philosophy and the study of educational administration. *Journal of Educational Administration* 23(1):7–22.

Wolcott, Harry. (1985). On ethnographic intent. *Educational Administration Quarterly* 21(3):187–203.

14

Talking up and Justifying Organisation: The Creation and Control of Knowledge About Being Organised

R.J.S. "Mac" Macpherson

Recent research concerned with how people come to believe they are organised for educational purposes has identified the crucial role that talk plays. The first section of this paper describes how administrators gain control over aspects of social reality and the moral and organisation knowledge deemed to be policy.

Administrators' Talk and Control

Verbal Rehearsals to Build Policy

What are the processes used by influential administrators to generate ideas, understandings, and agreements about collective action? There is

Reprinted with permission from *Studies in Educational Administration*, Commonwealth Council of Educational Administration, No. 41, May, 1986. Armidale, Australia: University of New England Printery.

relatively little material available from direct research into administrators' practice to assist this examination, simply because it has been so difficult to obtain (see Macpherson, 1985a). The evidence that exists tends to confirm that educational administrators use talk as the major tool of that aspect of their work which they label "organisation" and "development." Three studies have been selected to illuminate the potency of talk.

Gronn's (1983) case study investigated how senior administrators in an institution decided on the deployment of staff. They talked about "deployment," about controlling "deployment," and about the language games they later played to retain control of the rationale of "deployment." Talk, in this sense, was an instrument (Hodgkinson, 1978, p. 204; 1983, pp. 26–29) serving clarification, decision-making, and implementation. It was therefore catalytic and the vehicle for the creation of taken-for-granted knowledge about being deployed and organised. But how was this finding reached?

Two crucial questions guided Gronn's research in an Australian school: what was the nature of the control accomplished by the words of the administrator and those administered; and, how did the words accomplish that control? In the school, "Corridor Work" initiated the action on neutral ground. Issues were raised here for informal treatment. Architectural and interactional factors contributed to an ambiguous chumminess between staff. Status had been temporarily suspended. Later, when administrators analysed political and professional options, their thinking was riddled with shifts in concern between their own and others' interests. Gradually, the articulation of ideas among this elite group led to the creation of a taken-for-granted stock of administrative knowledge about deployment. These premises were later evident as the basis of the principal's operating assumptions. These assumptions could, however, be fully understood by only those who took part in their creation, as with any cultural artefact.

Eventually, of course, the emerging construction, labelled "policy," became public knowledge. It was embedded in the principal's opening statement at a staff meeting and was really an invitation for all staff to define "the deployment situation" as they saw it. Rather than refuse the invitation, or ask for its value base, some sought amendments to achieve their own particular needs. The micropolitics of opportunism shrouded ends.

The origins of the principal's definition of policy related to earlier institutionalised stocks-of-knowledge such as last year's practices, vestiges of system policy, and legal and economic contexts. It was also interesting to note that although either of the two senior administrators could claim to be speaking authoritatively on deployment given their experience in such matters, the principal's definition had the weight of positional authority and thus was allowed to prevail as the accepted view. This is not to argue that the principal was above influence. His subjective definitions of the situation and deployment futures had to be articulated and discussed (and thus negotiated) as a result of corridor talk. The rules-for-success for this principal emerged and implied that:

Teachers who become administrators have to adjust to having teachers attempt to control them. This means listening to staff speaking as authorities before replying authoritatively. They have to listen . . . and be verbally parsimonious in exercising their control by making their own words count and knowing when to make them count. [Gronn, 1983, p. 18]

The particular value of this study was the way it portrayed how the principal's informal "corridor talk" and other verbal rehearsals gradually created knowledge that provided a basis to policy agreed at the staff meeting and later used to justify action. Such is the work of talk. How does it unfold in more formal settings? Another piece of research offers many clues.

Conclusions-All-Must-Accept

Four people in a large public-sector institution were expected by their appointment duties to consider " . . . the job potential of a person employed by the Organisation" (Silverman and Jones, 1976, p. 155). From a detailed analysis of the language the four senior public administrators used, a three-stage process was identified. The three stages discovered bear a remarkable similarity to the process described by Gronn (1983).

The first stage was concerned with the articulation of a "corpus of data" that had to be taken seriously—the Premises-All-Can-Accept. Conversational banter like "corridor work" did not have to be presented as objective; indeed the status of informal utterances were accepted by the panellists as opinions or expressions of prejudice. But, most notably, when "the speaker attends to the proper location of the [same] judgments in the assembling of a conversation, he can offer his 'views' without 'substantiation' or location in a 'wider picture' and need not anticipate present or subsequent challenges to the reliability of his account' (Silverman and Jones, 1976, p. 155). Opinions, if presented with subtlety, stood as facts!

The basic technique used by all four panellists involved was to assemble a few unchallengeable "facts" on which subsequent judgment could be grounded, if necessary. Facts were arranged only so that they (not the panel) could "speak for themselves." Whenever alternative interpretations were possible, the "proper reading" was discussed at length and eventually negotiated so that the most "objective" account of the pattern of data (consistent with community rules) could be added to the corpus of facts already agreed on. In this way "facts" and "interpretations" were compounded incrementally into "obvious" "truths." "Data" plus "proper reading" could "speak for themselves." Throughout this and all stages, members of the panel rigorously demonstrated to each other how communal, how rule-governed, how objective, and how serious their work was.

Once the Premises-All-Can-Accept had been negotiated, the next stage was to reaffirm the community rules about Steps-All-Can-Follow to justify the report. Here the concern of the panel of administrators was to do not with the individual case, but with the procedural niceties of setting an audit trail, and *being seen* to have provided for accountability. Communal standards in this regard were invoked to review the assemblage and presentation of "facts" in an impersonal, irrefutable logic. It was concluded by Silverman and Jones (1976, p. 169) that "facts are resources for the communities of bureaucracy and science." Even when common sense dictated a short cut, or levity threatened the sanctity of the process, procedural rules were invoked (out of order, let's get down to business) to create an objective, logical rationale for the presentation of findings. This rationale mirrored the official ideology of the organisation. It was a bureaucratic rationality.

The third and final stage was the application of this framework, to produce Conclusions-All-Must-Accept. Here the panel members worked assiduously to display "the rule-governed character of their proceedings and of their conclusions" (Silverman and Jones, 1976, p. 161). The use of standardised report forms served well to foster the impression of a neutral process, and along with panel consensus created the situation where any charge of bias would reinforce rather than threaten the community and its rules.

The consequences of the panel's approach and the nature of their report was then fully evident. They had, in effect, co-opted the language and rules of the Organisation to the extent where the Conclusions-All- Must-Accept on display not only borrowed from but reinforced the authority of *any* member of the collective. Put simply, the de-authored speech of the panel's report had adopted the authoritative language of the Organisation. Any challenge to the report would challenge the official discourse and rationality of the Organisation itself. So what happens when this process breaks down?

Contested Realities

To understand what occurs when the realities of administrators encounter alternative "facts" and organisational fictions, we can turn to Leila Berg's *Risinghill: Death of a Comprehensive School* (1968). Her investigations into corporal punishment in an English county revealed substantial inconsistencies between administrative policy and practices. She published preliminary findings, and then sought access for a follow-up article:

On the date fixed, I arrived at County Hall. . . . In the Chief Inspector's ante-room I was introduced by his secretary to several heads. We were then all shown into the Chief Inspector's room. He opened the meeting. His words were "I think it is very kind of us to give up this beautiful summer morning to come and talk to Miss Leila Berg" . . .

"I'm so sorry, Dr Payling, I'm afraid that's me."
A brief silence. Then—
"I didn't know you were here already. You look like a headmistress."
"I would just like to remark on what you've just said—"
"NO! NO! Wait till I've finished! I will not have you speaking whenever you feel like it! You'll listen to me!" [Berg, 1968, pp. 202-03]

The Chief Inspector then reiterated the public policy that was inconsistent with privately sponsored practices, and he ended by flourishing the brown booklet, *Punishment in Schools*, and shouting:

"I don't suppose Miss Berg has seen this!" When he had finished, I said I was sorry he had prevented me from speaking. I had merely wanted first to say that I resented his deliberate whipping up of hostility against me, and secondly, to give the heads the correct information that it was not I who had forced them to "give up this beautiful summer morning," but the L.C.C. as the Chief Inspector knew perfectly well. . . . And I recounted the steps that had led up to this meeting. Then I said "I have, of course, seen the fairly pleasant brown booklet, that is fairly easily obtainable. I have also seen this, which is not so pleasant, not so easily obtainable, but was reissued seven years after that brown booklet was published," and I held up a white double-leaflet headed *Corporal Punishment*. [Berg, 1968, p. 203]

This exchange exhibited the elements of knowledge creation in the Gronn and Silverman and Jones cases examined above. Talk here was also being used in an attempt to re-establish control over policy-making and to legitimate that control largely by assertion. Berg's unintended penetration and dismantling of assumptions about territory and authority demonstrate how central the acceptance of hierarchical relationships is to the control of negotiations over realities and administrative knowledge. Unchallengeable "facts," so necessary for subsequent judgments, were demonstrably challengeable. The Chief Inspector held to premises Berg would not accept. She refused to follow his logic and, worse, confronted him with an "inhouse" contradiction to his public policy, his public Conclusions-All-Must-Accept. Predictably, his only defence was to fall back on the formality of office, the sanctity of confidentiality, and to claim privileged rights to knowledge on behalf of the London City Council:

"That is highly confidential!"
"I know. It says so on the outside. Why is it?"
"This is intolerable! This is grossly improper! I don't know who gave you the document! Nobody has the right—"
"Why would you call it improper for anyone to know that their children in school can be hit with a cane of the approved pattern? Why do you think I, a parent and a citizen, have no rights to know—." [Berg, 1968, p. 205]

It should not be drawn that the evidence reviewed above is representative of all organisers in education, but it does offer valuable insights into the creation of administrative assumptions and operational realities. The evidence provides examples of talk being work.

Talk-as-Action

There is a substantial body of literature following Mead (1964), Schutz (1964), and the work of Berger and Luckman (1966) that has explored the role of symbolic meanings in creating, sustaining, or changing assumptions about organisation.

From this literature it seems reasonable to infer that as each individual in an organisation strives to control the symbolism of roles, structure, and context there is a struggle to expand a personal zone of discretion in the social phenomena known as "the organisation" (Silverman, 1970). By talking with others, and by taking other actions, each person is party to a pattern of interaction that builds up over time into ordered sets of practices. Formalised and institutionalised, ordered patterns of relating to others are usually referred to metaphorically as "structure." These patterns of practices reflect the initiatives and the routines of individuals, the consequences of actions taken, and the stock of knowledge people bring to each situation. The point here is that we should consider "role" as re-created practices and define "action" as the symbolic meanings of behaviour. There is an often overlooked but substantial difference between behaviour, like raising one finger, and the significant cultural meanings of such an action. It is the symbolism of the words that convey meanings and, hence, accomplish the work of talk in administering meanings. The symbolism, of course, varies with each organisational culture (Connell, 1983).

Let me review the argument to this point. The first study, Gronn's, demonstrated how central talk is in the achievement of control and how talk is the medium through which realities are sustained and renegotiated. It also introduced the essence of "organisation" and "development." They are cultural artefacts, however seemingly real and far reaching their consequences in peoples' lives. Verbal rehearsals were shown to be a major tool used to create and negotiate operational fictions, fictions that would later be posed as "policy," underpinned with "facts," and used to justify and sustain changes to what were collectively known as "organisation" and justified as "development." Policy is thereby defined as a subset of organisational culture that has been operationalised.

The Silverman and Jones research examined the work of a panel of administrators in a large public-sector organisation. Their three-stage explanation of processes included Premises-All-Can-Accept, Steps-All-Can-Follow, and Conclusions-All-Must-Accept. Most notably, an enormous amount of time was given over to defining what was significant, and thus served to foreclose alternative ways of valuing "job potential." The attention given to mutual reassurance on procedures spoke of doubts about the value base used as the primary source of legitimation. They were driven, as it were, by the dominant metaphors of their organisation. They were impelled to demonstrate their absolute objectivity and neutrality, and to reaffirm the "organisation" values. This was accomplished by giving disproportionate weight to objective and scientific "facts" in explanations. In a phrase, a bureaucratic rationality ruled.

The Berg study, of challenged realities, also demonstrated how some types of administrators' talk, along with other practices, lead them into mind-sets which puzzle or annoy others with alternative assumptions. Although it is clear by now that the symbolic meanings of action, such as talk, serve to sustain and change organisational realities, the control of what is seen as educationally significant and right now deserves closer attention. The next section will therefore examine how power and structure are used to control significance and legitimacy in educational organisations.

The Powerful in Action

Aspects of social organisation are constantly obvious in recent portrayals of highly successful educators. For example, before his appointment, Frank Tate (appointed Victoria's first Director of Education in 1902 when only thirty-eight years old) had "shown himself to be eager for office, tough and resourceful, a shrewd operator of the Department machine, persuasive" (Selleck, 1982, p. 134). Crucial were the actions Tate used to create influence. One example must suffice. In 1908 he campaigned for the extension of State secondary schools. He:

seized every opportunity to push home his advantage. He stalked the lobbies and took his convictions, his persuasiveness and his copious lantern slides around the state [to argue] . . . that "school- power" was an "imperial necessity." For all his admiration of British institutions Tate did not behave as civil servants were supposed to do. He was not an anonymous administrator endeavouring to implement a government's policies. [Selleck, 1982, p. 189]

Power often appears to be a phenomenon associated with a series of personality traits made significant by action. It is also associated with an ability to organise, sustain, or dramatically alter the operational assumptions in the minds of others. A biographical example comes from ancient times:

It was evident to me that my first task was to destroy the enemy army in Africa. And here I found myself handicapped by mutiny in these legions upon whose loyalty I had counted most. . . . They and I were indispensable to each other and this was a fact they knew well. Yet they were now presuming to trade on this fact of our interdependence. . . . Could they not see that if I were to obey and they were to command, the whole nature of the enduring bond between us would be broken and transgressed? I asked to hear their complaints and then listened to speech after speech dealing with the same themes—their wounds, their hardships, their great deeds, the rewards they expected, their claim to be demobilised. . . . When I did speak, I surprised them. I announced, in as indifferent a tone as possible, that they would all be demobilised at once. . . .

As I spoke I could feel how bitterly the soldiers were wounded by my words. They resented the thought that they would not take part in the final [African campaign] triumph; but what chiefly distressed them was the thought that I could do without them. . . . They were used, of course, to being addressed as "Comrades" or "Fellow-Soldiers." Now, with great deliberation, as though to emphasise that I had already discharged them, I used the word "Citizens. . . . At this there was an immediate outcry. The mutiny was over. Soon the men were begging me to punish the ringleaders. . . . I told them I would forgive all except the Tenth Legion. Later I received deputations from the men of the Tenth begging that the whole legion should be punished by decimation and then again allowed to serve with me. I would not, of course, agree to so cruel and so unjust a punishment; but I did, in the end, forgive the men. Then, with the utmost speed . . . I began to make preparations for the invasion of Africa. [Attributed to Julius Caesar, in Warner, 1967, pp. 324–45]

To understand power it is evident that we must look closely at the actions of the powerful, mindful of their setting. Consider Tate for a while. It was noted above that Tate had personality characteristics that set him apart from his peers. He was persuasive, persistent, and utterly purposeful. But his power to sustain change was also due to his ability to organise and fix others' thinking. Like Caesar, he had a sophisticated grasp of management technique. For example, Tate ensured the loyalty and service of his staff. His ". . . determination to control his Department showed in his careful attention to office procedure" (Selleck, 1982, p. 249). He knew well that to design and to insist on particular routines served to give life to (or operationalise if you will) particular assumptions. Hence certain values (Tate's) were institutionalised and defended, at cost to others'. It was noticeable how, over time, reformism was replaced by a defensive bureaucratic ideology:

Tate grew to be jealous of the expertise which he and his professional colleagues had. The Department knew best. This belief, the wariness brought about by the constant struggle against governments who cared little for education, and his personal identification with policies he had helped develop made him edgy with critics and as the years went by inclined to speak of loyalty. He encouraged the able, the adventurous and the independent, but he liked to be the one who criticised educational policies; in fact, he grew particularly anxious if criticism came from internal sources. Moreover, while he tried to increase the Department's influence . . . he resisted efforts to bring the Department under independent scrutiny. He would not submit the Department to the checks he was anxious to impose on others. . . . He built a powerful Department by being swift to increase its influence and equally swift to resist the efforts of others to gain influence over it. [Selleck, 1982, p. 263]

This pattern of attending to the installation of selected values is reminiscent of the consequences of the administrative style of another famous Australian, General Monash. Cuttack (cited in Serle, 1982, p. 383) wrote that Monash's staff "found themselves committed to the most continuous hard work they had ever done in their lives. . . . He left nothing to chance which industry and foresight could make certain. He made no plans until he had exhausted the ideas of all staff and subordinate commanding officers; then he would suggest a scheme which embraced the good points of all." While his subordinates found his ability to synthesise ideas formidable, and thus one source of his power to persuade, it is important to realise that Monash himself knew the crucial consequence of his style. Indeed, as he declared on becoming a Corps Commander, "his first task was 'to acquire a moral ascendancy' over his senior commanders and staff," and thus:

> to secure complete domination over their thoughts, action and policy. The first consideration was the creation of complete unity and thought, and complete unity both of administrative and tactical policy. This could not be ensured without . . . inculcating high ideals, high aims, and a high standard of conduct. In particular, it was necessary to create and foster among all officers, and particularly among junior officers, a sense of responsibility to themselves, their commanders, their comrades, their men, their country and their cause.
>
> These results were achieved by close personal contact with hundreds of officers, by the holding of conferences, by lectures and addresses, and by a constant process of critical supervision. [Monash, in Serle, 1982, p. 383]

Without labouring the point with further examples, such actions can be interpreted as the deliberate control of moral and organisational culture. Are these processes of policymaking and policy implementation so distant from the leadership work of educational administrators? While educators might despair at some of the values being served by these techniques, the patterns of efficient leadership are now evident enough to underpin reflection on the nature of power itself and, in particular, on three different approaches used to understand power (after Luke, 1974).

As these portrayals of "Great Men" emphasise, power *can* easily be thought of as a tangible resource that allows some to be more influential than others. When educators talk of *others* as being "powerful," they usually mean "fuller of power" than themselves. In this way of speaking power is being conceived of as a highly efficient catalyst, and as such can, like any real substance, be collected, stored, and then applied, almost like a magical lubricant. Further, this one-dimensional view of power is straightforward because it means focussing on the behaviours of influential people, watching for cause and effect in decision-making, and then identifying how key issues, observable conflict, subjective interests, and participation reveal policy preferences.

The basic problem with this approach to understanding power is that because it is so clear-cut an approach, much is missed. For example, by taking a behaviouralist stance to understand the decision-making power of individuals, the researcher too easily adopts the biases of the political system under observation and tends, therefore, to be blind to the ways in which the political agendas themselves are being controlled behind the displays of powerful behaviour.

A two-dimensional view of power is doubly subtle by comparison—it focusses on decision-making *and* non-decision-making, issues *and* covert conflict, as well as subjective interests, but again, all seen as policy preferences or grievances. A two-dimensional view points the way to examining bias and control in political processes, although conceiving of them too narrowly. It lacks a sociological perspective with which the administrator can examine not only decision-making and non-decision-making power, but also the effects of multiple social contexts and how bias is systematically mobilised in the broader settings of systems and institutions.

The third approach, which Luke (1974, p. 25) advocates, encourages a focus on decision-making assumptions and patterns to establish *how political agendas are controlled*. This means carefully noting the origins, nature, and consequences of issue making and conflict (both observable and latent) and noting how subjective and real (perhaps unrealised) interests arise and fade. To do this means interpreting the effect of political processes in terms of their multiple-host social structures. Some of the implications of this third approach can be illustrated by a selective discussion of my own research (Macpherson, 1984a, 1984b) with particular reference to the control of patterns of relationships and practices.

Structure

I set out to portray what it was to be a Regional Director of Education (R.D.E.) in Victoria in 1983 by interpreting events, using the meanings accorded by informants to their administrative action. Data was also illuminated by how each person's relationships with position and context were in turn related to wider host "structures" and how these relationships changed over time. From this exercise came a new description of structure.

How each administrator defined his "position" and the "structure" about him were therefore considered crucial data. But where role theory suggested that action is the product of role expectations and personal dispositions, it was found in my study that the traditional explanation failed to account for the crucial reciprocal relationship between the symbolism of actions and their context. The reciprocal relationship was evident, for example, in the evolving nature of the local "structure" within which the actions of the

R.D.E.s were given and, in turn, gave meaning. Giddens (1979), however, had argued that understanding structure should not rest at this level but should also consider the "structuration" of social systems. What did he mean by this? He defined "structure" as rules and resources organised as properties of social systems. Three major properties of social systems were memory traces of knowledge of "how things are to be done," social patterns organised through repeated use of that knowledge, and the abilities people need to produce those properties. These properties were very evident in the "talk" cases reviewed above. "System" was therefore given a particular meaning; reproduced relations between actors or collectives organised as regular social practices. "Structuration" was defined as the conditions governing the continuity or transformation of structures and, therefore, the reproduction of systems.

There are particular assumptions in this line of argument. For example, social systems are constructed not of parcels of functions termed roles, but of reproduced practices. A "role" is not a neutral element of organisation. It is a normative concept that transmits personal perceptions of expected or intended action. Another assumption is that the social system into which incumbency is embedded is in turn embedded in wider host "structures." These assumptions are quite inconsistent with the traditional and structural-functional view of organisation that systematically avoids questions of power, rightness, and how the actions of individuals relate to structure and context. Indeed, Salaman (1978) argued forcefully "that organisational power and control must be seen in terms of the nature and priorities of the 'host' society rather than as consequences of particular forms of work process or technology."

In my study this meant considering the ostensibly neutral forms and processes of organisation and the nature and purposes of prevalent ideologies in order to capture the relationship between them and the society in which they were located. Personal histories and cultural affiliation were therefore considered highly relevant, and, indeed, personal and biographical sources were found to underpin much of the inner development and purposes each informant had.

And what drove the twelve R.D.E.s? Although operational facets of their administration, such as attention-giving, did derive from formal and external sources, each R.D.E. was alert for shifts in others' allegiance, in "policy," and in the language used to portray "the situation." While little movement from each R.D.E.'s fundamental purposes was seen, the great shifts in tactics seen and discussed came from "hot" information and, in particular, from interaction. When an R.D.E. was not alone working on communicated knowledge, he was compulsively moving from one key forum to another, massaging knowledge about "structure" to the extent he could. The net impression gained was that being a Regional Director meant an all-consuming involvement, a form of participation that invoked the deepest aspects of self, values, and personal development. It will also be clear by now that the term "structure" itself was found to be an overworked metaphor in the setting. This phenomenon requires a detailed explanation.

The political context of regionalisation was fraught with contradictions. A series of studies (for example, Rizvi, 1984; Angus, Prunty, and Bates, 1984; Macpherson, 1986c) have indicated that restructuring events largely constituted symbolic politics at the regional level. While political intervention in 1983 continued to be justified (Fordham, 1983) in terms of requiring educational administrators to serve a socially-critical ideology, the data suggested that events enhanced the power of metropolitan elites. My interpretation (Macpherson, 1986c) led to three propositions:

a. Faced with ideological challenges to their assumptions about order, control, and the hierarchical distribution of wisdom, power, and knowledge, some educational administrators at central and regional levels were responding with resistance strategies. These included devices such as new coping alliances, elaborated organisation, and consultative processes to re-create a sense of adequate legitimacy.

b. In the absence of systematically developed and formal reference groups that articulated regional mandates, the purposes being served by educational administration at regional levels were principally mediated by the values of each Regional Director.

c. Those individuals who represented parents, principals, teachers, and "the Centre" on the State Board of Education also recognized that if Regional Boards became the mouthpiece of localist perspectives, then they would have their power bases expropriated.

How then was "power" and "structure" evident in this contest over what would count as the new orthodoxy of administrative practice? Mythmaking was a constant feature of R.D.E.s' actions directly related to "structure." Indeed, the twelve incumbents were often in a position of having to counter the effects of others' myths. For example, a political verbal symbol of great potency for a period was "twelve mini-bureaucracies." It was typically employed by centralists to counter calls for regional discretion and ironically incorporated two contradictions: that bureaucracy must, of itself, always serve wrong ends, and that each interest group already represented at "the Centre" was not itself organised as a mini-bureaucracy.

Nevertheless this myth served centralism well by retarding the establishment of Regional Boards and the consequent claims about democratic legitimacy in system politics. Such claims by regionalists were contesting both rampant and covert neo-centralism. The major verbal political symbols used by R.D.E.s appeared in their constant claims of being at the latter end of four value dimensions: centralism—localism; metropolitan elitism—

rural/local fellowship; academic education—practical community education; and management by crises—administrative statesmanship. The rituals in the R.D.E.s' practices (information processing, advocacy, generating techno-rational images of the regional office in the minds of subordinates) all spoke of attempts to control knowledge and conceptions, specifically to publicly present the regional office as a local educational service centre directly supporting school operations and governance. A favourite one-liner was "a one-stop shop." How then did "structure" relate to the R.D.E.s' actions?

Seven meanings of "structure" were apparent (Macpherson, 1985b). Although structure is from a Latin word "to build," and refers to the construction, the composition, or the inherent patterns in concrete, observable, mechanical, or organic systems, all meanings used by R.D.E.s were figurative. They were social constructs inferred from events over time. Converting the abstract to concrete, reification was widely evident, despite the metaphorical nature of the term. In some settings reification went even further, into deification.

The first and locally important meaning of structure was to convey the nature of *actions*, practices, and processes of creating networks and assumptions. The second, again specific to administrative action, referred to *the manner* of organising relationships and organisational knowledge. The third meaning sought to interpret regionalism and centralism. It was concerned with how the *symbiosis* of constituent parts were *arranged* to coexist as a whole. The fifth and sixth meanings were manifest in definitions of the system's characteristics: structure integral to "the system," that is, simply *an edifice* or, more broadly, *a framework of organised and real units*. The seventh meaning of "structure" was biological in nature. It emphasised the *interdependence* of organisational parts of "the system," often, for example, by referring to an organic Department's survival and life. Here, "structure" was the skeleton to which "the system" gave life. Together, organisational "life" was possible. When its values were to be worshipped, deification had been achieved.

Strikingly consistent with these seven usages of the metaphor "structure" would be organisational analysis in terms of institutional structures and functions, norms, roles, and groups, whilst presuming these concepts were virtually static and determining realities of organisational life. In other words, this metaphor was being used to sustain a natural systems view of organisational reality, to perpetuate a bureaucratic rationality, and to legitimate a structural-functional way of valuing practices.

Such a departure from a metaphorical definition, however, ignores the evidence above that "structure" is a figure of speech transferring *significance to a perceived pattern* in social events (of relative stability) in a setting of vigorous micro-politics. Interaction, in what was conceived of as organisational life, occasionally settled to an extent, but only for a period, into social and cultural arrangements that allowed the development of temporary rule-for-success. How power relates to structure in the setting explored can now be summarised.

"Structure" was being used metaphorically to portray and control the concerted imaginations of organised men. It was a theoretical construct sustained and repeatedly constituted by complex transactions in an environment of micro-politics and contested values. Hence the myriad of definitions necessarily existed as the contest went on. The significant aspects of these definitions were differentiated on many dimensions, sometimes simultaneously. Only the longer-standing, shared assumptions persisted as norms, mandates, and standard operating procedures. It was concluded that in order to defend preferred assumptions about organisation, in an environment of alternative values, the reification of "structure" clearly served as a major administrative strategy.

There were, of course, good reasons why these processes were unusually evident. Given the ambiguous mandate for regionalism in Victoria, and the eroding political and bureaucratic support for regionalisation in late 1983, order, rules, and "structure" were being continuously negotiated. Definitions were debated, redefined, bent, ignored, or suppressed as the potential inherent in each situation was perceived and weighed. Hence the intimate interrelationship discerned between the production and maintenance of three forms of "structure": images of organisation; patterns of practice; and, most subtle of all, preferred and discrete systems of knowledge with their own methods of justification. The upshot of understanding organisation in this manner is that the traditional concepts of "structure" and "function" are no longer adequate. Further, just as the arguments above indicated the utility of "action" as compared to behaviour, we now also require the most eclectic concept of culture to accommodate the subtleties of imagery, practices, and systems of knowledge found in perceptions of organization.

Cultural Tools, Theory, and Outcomes

Culture

A cultural explanation of administrative practice needs to take account of two crucial definitions. To elaborate the definition in the abstract above, culture is held to be:

> an interdependent and patterned system of valued, traditional, and current public knowledge and conceptions, embodied in behaviours and artefacts, and transmitted to present and new members, both symbolically and non-symbolically, which a society has evolved historically, and progressively modified and augments, to give meaning to and cope with its definitions of present and future existential problems. [Bullivant, 1984, p. 4]

If culture is thereby defined as a form of civilisation, and ideology as a system of beliefs belonging to a culture, then another term is required to denote how a culture is internalised in an individual. This term, which is "habitus," is defined as each individual's "system of durable transposable dispositions which functions as the generative basis for structured, objectively unified practices" (Bourdieu, 1979). Habitus is a particularly useful concept, for it allows a distinction to be drawn between the actions and ideologies of group culture and the way in which each individual makes sense of (and justifies) his or her experience. The dispositions of the habitus are mediated by the structures of relationships and assumptions in the setting and, in turn, mediate how the situation is seen and what meaning and purposes are given to practice. Perception is also affected by past situations in a reciprocal manner. Based on Bourdieu's notions of habitus, a cyclical model of elaboration has been envisaged (see Figure 14–1 below).

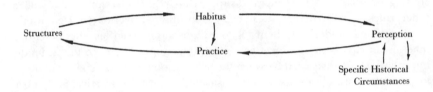

Figure 14–1
Reproduction and Change
(Harker, 1984)

An example will help clarify this model. The R.D.E.s I researched were found to have three major operational selves (labelled System Man, Structure Man, and Political Man) and a fourth deeper self — Reflective Man (Macpherson, 1986a). These four selves together constituted the general nature of each R.D.E.'s habitus and substantially influenced how each situation was understood and acted on. The perception that each R.D.E. had of his position and context was, to a degree, idiosyncratic and particularly evident in two ways.

First, when confronted by an unexpected situation, each R.D.E. rapidly switched between, and then selected and rigorously applied, one operational self and its set of rules-for-success. Second, the idiosyncracies of disposition were very evident in nuances of administrative style. It was notable, for example, that the major facets of political style were found to be derived from each R.D.E.'s first major success in organisational politics. The most important consequence of this foundational experience was that it predisposed each R.D.E. to analyse political situations in particular ways. This accounted for the different consequences of the nature and outcomes of their personal rituals and, to an extent, interaction with others.

The crucial point here is that the habitus played a significant role in the reproduction and the changes in the meanings accorded to the metaphors of organisation between settings. As the imparting of cultural knowledge is actually achieved by individuals, it is now appropriate to take up the questions of purpose and rightness.

Although evidence is still relatively limited, my closing argument is that the emergent implications are powerful enough to suggest that all administrators should develop a socially-critical awareness of their practices, especially with respect to the administration of cultural capital, and yet be mindful of the relativity of this form of awareness.

Cultural Capital

Capital, in commerce, is the total value of a business, property or stocks. To "make capital of" is to turn something to one's advantage. Both meanings derive from an ideology about the economic, industrial, and social organisation of society, namely capitalism. Capitalistic organisation means the ownership, control, and direction of production of privately-owned business organisations. While socialism emphasises the value of communally-owned organisation, most societies today have mixed economies of private, state, and communal ownership.

The phrase "cultural capital" has been coined to convey how aspects of culture can advantage and disadvantage an individual in society. Watkins (1984) and his co-researchers used ethnographic research methods to understand how a negotiated reality (called Christian Boys College) facilitated students' access to the workplace. It was made evident that the action of administrators served to impart and defend a selected set of cultural traits, assumptions, and social conventions. The actions, principally cultural in consequence, were also found to be closely related to the capitalistic demands of the school's setting and to the philosophies prevailing in the social and religious networks of the clients. It was particularly noticeable how cultural assets displaced (in the social group studied) property and wealth as the most important factor reproducing their culture and how school-based actions substantially controlled those processes.

What are the implications with respect to understanding administrative practice? First, the school's educational administrators were deeply involved in organising and controlling a cultural function much in the ways found in the studies reviewed above. Second, their cultural work had a specific outcome in their clients, namely an interesting mixture of Irish Catholicism and capitalism, which in turn implied that alternative outcomes were possible. Third, the cultural work of these administrators was made possible by the existence of structures of assumptions in the social context of the school, and their cultural work served to sustain the existence of those structures. Fourth, it was clear that there was potential in the cultural agency of these administrators to facilitate changes to the assumptions that mediated practices, to alter acquired knowledge about society, and to change the access clients had to social resources (Watkins, 1984).

There exists, therefore, the need for educational administrators to be aware of the role they play in the distribution of cultural capital. However unwitting their past involvement, they need to become critically aware of the range of social purposes served by their actions. They need to examine their administrative habitus and the ideologies served by their practices. But the particular value of Watkins' report, apart from the research effort it represents, was how it established the case that educational administrators are deeply engaged in the administration of cultural capital. The final issues addressed in this paper are therefore the ideas that will assist the process of becoming critically aware of the social consequences of practices, and how valuable the socially-critical form of awareness is in a relative sense.

Socially-Critical Administration

Educational administration, as a field of enquiry, has been reluctant to use socially-critical ideas because of the strength of earlier taken-for-granted values and world views of practice. As argued above, especially in the discussion on power and structure, the foundational tenets of the behavioural science tradition in the field of educational administration have tended to perpetuate and justify a bureaucratic rationality. Briefly, the enduring management-oriented traditions have it that organisation is a natural system, that practice reflects the values embodied in the organisation itself, and that knowledge about practice and organisation in education can be limited to and defended by the ideology of structural-functionalism. But there are a number of reasons why alternative perspectives have supplemented the philosophical and theoretical sophistication of the field.

First, Greenfield (1975, 1985) has effectively demonstrated that the keystone of the behavioural science account, natural systems ideology, has reflected the perspectives of but one doctrine (instrumentalism) and that it relied on myths (such as "organisational effectiveness") and symbols (such as administrator-as-leader) to create a rationality, an approach to legitimation, and an accepted set of practices consistent with the ideology. Second, my own research (Macpherson, 1984b) has indicated that the limited epistemological relativity of the behavioural science approach should be acknowledged and reflected in explanations of practice.

By this I mean that while the behavioural approach was adequate to the task of interpreting the world of "System Man," it could not comprehend the reconstructive realm of "Structure Man," nor cope with the interactional subtleties of the "Political Man" mode. Indeed, when in the Reflective mode, R.D.E.s were able to point to the advantages and disadvantages of imposing a behavioural science account of administrative phenomena. To "play the neutral bureaucrat," as one put it, in a particular setting, was a very effective micro-political strategy. Finally, it was demonstrated that the epistemological relativity of these different modes of being could be established for the three Regional Directors of Education in terms of conceptual realms, fundamental concerns, ideal-typical roles, origins of ideologies, and basic orientations to means-ends and to values.

Whether or not other educational administrators also live in diverse realms is yet to be conclusively established, although considerable evidence does exist, and my own experience has often suggested that it is generally the case. Lee (1966) did offer strong evidence to suggest that administrators are dependent on (and sometimes captive of) their major reference groups for identity and self-esteem, implying the need for Goffmanesque masks. Also consistent with the multi-realm nature of the Regional Directors' work-world are findings on gestalt-switching dynamics that produce the different administrative postures and strategies (Crozier, 1964) used to maintain and develop power arenas and to produce negotiated illusions of order (Strauss et al., 1963). It therefore follows that working with and within multiple realms is likely to be a common experience amongst senior administrators. If, as I demonstrated with regard to three R.D.E.s, each realm has its own approach to the justification for knowledge, then the use of an ideologically exclusive form of interpretation is inappropriate.

The third reason for being aware of alternative ways of valuing practice is that a socially-critical perspective presumes that the educational administrator is central to the negotiation of order and structure and should be held accountable for social ends thus served by his agency. Key assumptions here are that order is constructed in schools and systems through the dynamics of culture (myths, metaphors, rituals, language, ceremony, and structuration) and through the systematic structuring of knowledge (selection, organisation, transmission, distribution, control, and justification). As these mechanics have been related by Bates (1981a, 1981b, 1982a) to the administrative practices of dividing knowledge, pupils, teachers, time, and locations, and to the assembling of different forms of social and epistemological order, what are the implications?

Socially-Critical Thought

The greatest impact of the socially-critical approach to interpreting educational administration lies in the realm of demystification, prosecuted, for example, by Bates, at two levels. At the first level he was able to show that "professionalism" is a metaphor for control and authority serving centralist interests (Bates, 1980a) and that the rationalities behind "education systems" are interrelated structures of social, cultural, epistemological, and educational activities (Bates, 1980b, 1980c). The second level of demystification became evident when Bates (1982a) turned to two concerns of classical organisation theorists: motivation and morale. Just "as the culture of the school is . . . the product of conflict and negotiations" (Bates, 1982b, p. 12), so could the epistemological pedigrees and behavioural-science orientations of theoretical accounts of administrative action be explained and contested.

Bates (1982b, p. 2) attacked the "mainline theorists" who used positivistic approaches to reproduce "pathological" theories. His charge was that a behavioural-science approach was but one ideology and encouraged a non-reflective social technology of control. The effect of this, he argued, was to divert attention from educational issues, such as inequities in education and society. It thus became too easy for administrators to merely manage and to reproduce knowledge about practice without realising the potential they have to democratise communication, relationships, and culture, and thereby transform practices and outcomes. At the very least, the "demystificationalists' " agenda is consistent with presenting "an alternative definition of organisations and with explain(ing) how well-meaning people . . . participate in the fiction of intended rationality in the service of official goals" (Perrow, 1978).

It must be stressed that despite the cautions that follow, the point should not be overlooked that although socially-critical theorising in educational administration is comparatively recent, it is acquiring international respect in the understanding of organisation and development. Moreover, this accomplishment has been the contribution of relatively few, when compared to the massive intellectual and institutional resources that often appear devoted in Australia, the U.S.A., and the U.K. to the furthering of more traditional perspectives. Nevertheless, some limitations to the approach derive in part from the very recency of the ideas. For example, the first problem is the way claims are made for the approach.

Two major concepts in the socially-critical approach to understanding are "demystification" and "emancipation." Both concepts are used in challenges mounted against the hegemonic nature of behavioural science accounts of practice. It is therefore something of a paradox that the socially-critical account is itself ideologically exclusive, often couched in mystifying language and, further, proposing an alternative hegomony. Why is this the case?

"Emancipation" is a concept from a different paradigm of enquiry from "demystification." The former derives from radical humanism or radical structuralism whereas the latter is more consistent with interpretivism (Morgan, 1980). The difficulty here is that while on one hand the socially-critical approach to interpreting practice might serve to reveal the existence of multiple selves and systems of justification by demystifying practice, there is, on the other, also the strong likelihood of a new "functionalism of the Left." By this is meant that it is very tempting to argue for the installation of but one approach to practice, that of the "Socially-Critical Man." "Emancipation" implies the imperatives of a neo-Marxist, socio-political movement (Bates, 1985) that brooks no contradiction. In contrast, "demystification" emphasises illuminative purposes without necessarily challenging the nature of the existing order.

The problem is that idealism and realism appeared to coexist. For example, when unravelling the work experience of R.D.E.s, I found (Macpherson, 1986a) that a continuum of emancipation–enslavement provided an inadequate conceptual basis for explaining changes in administrative selves, practices, outcomes, or assumptions. Instead of relying on the presumed rightness of a specific moral posture, my study suggested that the central dynamic of "beingness" has to do with an elaboration of selves and their knowledge systems in pragmatic, socio-political, and biographical as well as ethical contexts. In other words, the Regional Director's real world of pragmatic eclecticism could not be squared with the *a priori* unilateralism of a Socially-Critical Man, despite his challenging ideals. And yet, the "reflective man" was often intensely socially critical in his thinking.

Concluding Note

The real problem now seems to be to explain and account for the eclecticism of practice and reflection, rather than to dismiss it or deride it using one valuable perspective. Another task awaiting the attention of philosophers is to advise how administrators might compromise in a morally-defensible manner when facing socially-critical, economically-critical, managerially-critical, and educationally-critical imperatives. The field of educational administration has been singularly lacking in this type of philosophical machinery (Macpherson, 1986b) although there are strong indications in the Commonwealth (for example, Rizvi, 1985; Miklos et al., 1985) that this challenge has been taken up.

To conclude, "organisation" has been conceived of as a cultural process whereby an administrative habitus influences the reproduction and elaboration of asumptions in other peoples' minds about "being organised." It follows from the discussion of "power" and "structure" above and elsewhere (Macpherson, 1986c, 1985c) that "development" and "reform" are metaphors for a dialectical process embedded in social contexts (Watkins, 1985) whereby a facet of social reality is being reconstructed.

In these processes, the centrality of "talk" as an administrative tool is constantly reaffirmed. Indeed, as demonstrated above, the particular value of cultural explanations of administrative practice is that organisational change can be portrayed as social reality being transformed. It is being renegotiated because of influential peoples' actions impacting on the patterns of others' assumptions about practices, context, and rightness.

References

Angus, L.; Prunty, J.; and Bates, R. J. (1984). *Restructuring Victorian education: Regional issues*. Geelong: Deakin University Press.

Bates, R. J. (1980a). Bureaucracy professionalism and knowledge: Structures of authority and structures of control. *Education Research and Perspectives* 7: 66–76.

Bates, R. J.(1980b). New directions—The new sociology of education. *British Journal of Sociology of Education* 1: 67-79.

Bates, R. J. (1980c, August). The functions of educational administration in the process of cultural transmission. Paper presented to the Conference on the Origins and Operation of Educational Systems, International Sociological Association, Paris.

Bates, R. J. (1981a). General Introduction. In EED 443/733, *Management of resources in schools*. Geelong Open Campus Program, Deakin University Press.

Bates, R. J. (1981b). What can the new sociology of education do for teachers? *Discourse* 1: 41–53.

Bates, R. J. (1982a). Motivation and morale: Myth and reality in educational administration. Keynote Address, Annual Conference of the Australian Council of Educational Administration, Sydney.

Bates, R. J. (1982b, September). Towards a critical practice of educational administration. *Commonwealth Council for Educational Administration*, Studies in Educational Administration, No.27.

Bates, R. J. (1985, March). A Marxist theory of educational administration. A paper given to the symposium on "Critical Theory, Marxism and Educational Administration" at the A.E.R.A. Conference, Chicago.

Berg, L. (1968). *Risinghill: Death of a comprehensive school*. Ringwood: Australia.

Berger, P. C., and Luckman, T. (1966). *The social construction of reality*. Ringwood: Penguin.

Bourdieu, P. (1979). *The inheritors: French students and their relations to culture*. Chicago: Chicago University Press.

Bullivant, B. M. (1984). *Pluralism: Culture maintenance and Evolution*. Avon: Multilingual Matters.

Connell, R. W. (1983). The Concept of role and what to do with it. In Connell, R. W. *Which Way is Up?* Chap. 10. Sydney: Allen and Unwin.

Crozier, M. (1964). *The bureaucratic phenomena*. Chicago: Chicago University Press.

Fordham, R. (1983). *Ministerial papers 1–4*. Melbourne: Ministry of Education.

Giddens, A. (1979). *Central problems in social theory*. London: Macmillan.

Greenfield, T.B. (1975). Theory about organizations: A new perspective and its implications for schools. In M. G. Hughes (Ed.), *Administering education*, pp. 71–99. London: Althone Press.

Greenfield, T. B. (1985). Theories of educational organisation: A critical perspective. In *International encyclopedia of education: Research and studies.* Oxford: Pergamon.

Gronn, P. C. (1983). Talk as the work: The accomplishment of school administration. *Administrative Science Quarterly* 28: 1–21.

Harker, R. K. (1984). On reproduction, habitus, and education. *British Journal of Sociology* 5: 117–127.

Hodgkinson, C. (1978). *Towards a philosophy of administration.* Oxford: Basil Blackwell.

Hodgkinson, C. (1983). *The philosophy of leadership.* Oxford: Basil Blackwell.

Lee, A. M. (1966). *Multivalent man.* New York: Braziller.

Luke, S. (1974). *Power: A radical view.* Studies in Sociology: British Sociological Association. Hong Kong: Macmillan.

Macpherson, R. J. S. (1984a). On being and becoming an educational administrator: Some methodological issues. *Educational Administration Quarterly* 20: 58–75.

Macpherson, R. J. S. (1984b). *Being a regional director of education.* Unpublished doctoral thesis, Monash University.

Macpherson, R. J. S. (1985a). Some problems encountered boswelling elite educational administrators. *Canadian Administrator* 24: 2.

Macpherson, R. J. S. (1985b). Structure and the action of regional directors. *The Administrators Notebook* 31: 8.

Macpherson, R. J. S. (1985c). The administration of timetabling as cultural agency. *The Forum of Education* 44: 26-34.

Macpherson, R. J. S. (1986a). System and structure man, politician and philosopher: Being a regional director of education. In R. J. S. Macpherson (Ed.), *Ways and Meanings of Research in Educational Administration.*

Macpherson, R. J. S. (1986b). Values in the journal of educational administration: Towards making an ethic of moral compromise. In F. Rizvi (Ed.), *Working papers: Ethics and educational administration.* Geelong: Deakin School of Education.

Macpherson, R. J. S. (1986c). Reform and regional administration in Victoria's education: 1979–1983. *The Australian Journal of Public Administration* 45: 216–29.

Mead, M. G. (1964). *On social psychology.* A. Strauss (Ed.) Chicago: University of Chicago Press.

Miklos, E. (1985, May). Comments on the re-emergence of values and the transformation of administrative theory; Holmes, M., the Revival of traditional thought and its effects on educational administration: The case of decision making; Hodgkinson, C., New directions for research and leadership: The triplex bases of organisation theory and administration; and Greenfield, T. B., putting meaning back into theory: The search for lost values and the disappeared individual. Papers presented at the Canadian Society for the Study of Education Conference, Montreal.

Morgan, C. (1980). Paradigms, metaphors, and puzzle-solving in organisation theory. *Administrative Science Quarterly* 25: 605–22.

Perrow, C. (1978). Demystifying organisations. In R. D. Sarri and Y. Hasenfeld (Eds.),*The management of human science organisations*, pp. 105-200. New York: Columbia.

Rizvi, F. (1984). Problems of devolution in Victorian education. *Regional Journal of Social Issues* 15: 24–31.

Rizvi, F. (Ed.). (1985). *Working papers: Ethics and educational administration.* Geelong: Deakin University School of Education.

Salaman, G. (1978). Towards a sociology of organisational structure. *Sociological Review* 26: 519–54.

Schutz, A. (1964). *Collected papers II: Studies in social theory.* A. Rederson (Ed.) The Hague: Martinnus Nijhoff.

Selleck, R. W. J. (1982). *Frank Tate: A biography.* Carlton: Melbourne University Press.

Serle, W. (1982). *John Monash: A biography.* Melbourne: Melbourne University Press.

Silverman, D. (1970). *The theory of organization.* London; Heinemann.

Silverman, D., and Jones, J. (1976). *Organizational work: The language of grading/the grading of language.* London: Collier MacMillan.

Strauss, A., et al. (1963). The hospital and its negotiated order. In E. Griedson (Ed.), *The hospital in modern society.* Chicago: The Free Press.

Warner, R. (1967). *Julius Caesar.* London: Collins.

Watkins, P. (1984). Culture, cultural resources, and the labour market: A study of a Christian boys college. *The Australian Journal of Education* 28: 66–77.

Watkins, P. (1985). *Agency and structure: Dialectics in the administration of education.* Geelong: Deakin University Press.

SECTION IV

The Practice of Educational Administration

The papers in this section raise three important policy questions about the future of the practice of school administration: Will sufficient numbers of talented persons be available to assume leadership in the near future? What will be an appropriate relationship between and among the skills and character necessary for future leaders in administration? What part will information technology play in the work of educational leaders? James Bliss's paper is an examination of the supply of and demand for future administrators. He ends with a cautious estimate of oversupply and with a more general conclusion that state records in this area are inaccurate. He suggests that a major contribution to oversupply is the relatively low cost of obtaining an administrative license. Richard Gousha and his colleagues' paper, which examines state requirements, lends powerful support to Bliss's speculation that state requirements for licensure are dismally low, a point made by the Commission also. The two papers suggest that state licensing requirements rest on an open-door policy. The papers by Roland Barth and William Greenfield address the issue of the moral character of school administration. Greenfield argues that "moral imagination" is a necessary characteristic of successful school leadership. Barth contends that schools in the United States are driven by a "list logic" and share many of the traits of flocks of sheep: they are joyless, uninterested, and uninteresting. Barth would prefer a community of learners with some of the characteristics of goats, who are smart, playful, independent, and demanding of attention. Finally, the paper by Muriel Mackett and her colleagues raises questions about future policy regarding the use of computer technology in education. Examining the scope of the potential effects of the use of computers in schools, they conclude with a series of recommendations for the preparation of administrators, who should be able to make use of the powers of computer technology. The papers in this section are consistent with the ideas of the Commission members. Not everyone has sufficient talent or moral fiber to become an educational leader. Those who do must be identified and nurtured, and the process of identification and nurturance must be anchored in a vision of schools as communities of learners.

15

On Sheep and Goats and School Reform

Roland S. Barth

When I was growing up on a farm, my favorite companion was a goat. She was smart, friendly, playful, unpredictable, with a mind of her own that would not discern between a snack of grass and the carefully tended flowers surrounding our house. She was a most agreeable companion, until confined by a wagon harness, when she became most ornery. In short, our goat asked for a lot but contributed a lot in return.

A generation later, when my two daughters sought a farm companion, we took on five sheep. They lived happily within a fence, caused little trouble — and brought disappointingly little joy. "Mary Had a Little Lamb" notwithstanding, the sheep turned out to be docile, dumb, unaffectionate, uninterested — and uninteresting. They asked for little and contributed less.

Last fall I had the chance to spend a month with the Department of Educational Studies at Oxford University. I went to learn about things in another country, particularly about the professional development of headmasters. I visited schools and talked with many educators, and I returned

Reprinted with permission from *Phi Delta Kappan*, No. 4 (December 1986): 293–96. © 1986 by *Phi Delta Kappan*.

from England with new thoughts about education in my own country — and about sheep and goats.

It became clearer to me, while 2,500 miles away, that our public schools have come to be dominated and driven by a conception of educational improvement that might be called "list logic." For instance, the intention of one state legislature is to "identify competencies of effective principals through research and develop training, certification, selection, and compensation procedures that recognize and support these competencies." These kinds of conceptions seem to rest on several assumptions:

— Schools do not have the capacity to improve themselves; improvement must therefore come from sources outside of schools, such as universities, state departments of education, and national commissions.

— What needs to be improved about schools is the level of pupil performance and achievement, best measured by standardized tests.

— Schools can be found in which pupils are achieving beyond what might be predicted. By observing teachers and principals in these schools, we can identify their characteristics as "desirable."

— Teachers and principals in other schools can be trained to display the desirable traits of their counterparts in high-achieving schools. Then their pupils will excel, too.

— School improvement, then, is an attempt to identify what schoolpeople should know and be able to do and to devise ways to get them to know and do it.

This conception of school improvement has led to an extraordinary proliferation of lists. Lists of characteristics of the "effective principal," the "effective teacher," the "effective school"; lists of minimum pupil competencies and of behavioral objectives for teachers; lists of new certification requirements, mandates, and regulations. The list logic has begotten a list sweepstakes to see whose is the best list. Advocates argue that *their* vision of a desirable school, their vision of the desirable characteristics of schoolpeople, and their vision of the methods for attaining these ends rest on the firmest ground.

These myriad lists are making some valuable contributions. Lists provide a coherent nucleus around which to build a conception of an ideal school. Lists are ready vehicles that enable those outside schools to approach the important matters inside schools. Embedded in each list is usually some fresh thinking about schools that widens the universe of alternatives available for improving schools. Each list usually enlists a band of believers who will take the next step and use the list to address the problems of some real schools. And each list that succeeds in improving a single school holds the promise of improving all schools.

In short, the list logic of educational change seems simple, straightforward, and compelling. Its only flaw is that it doesn't seem to work very well.

I suspect that there may be several reasons why this is so. For one thing, the widespread belief that schools do not have the capacity to improve themselves is not unknown to those who work in schools. Most teachers and principals respond to even enlightened lists not with renewed energy, vigor, and motivation, but rather with feelings of oppression, guilt, and anger. The vivid lack of congruence between the way schools are and the way others would have them be causes most schoolpeople to feel overwhelmed, insulted, and inadequate — hardly building blocks for improving schools or the teaching profession.

The assumption that "strong leadership" and "effective teaching" are whatever brings about high student test scores suggests a very limited — and demeaning — view of both students and their educators. Good education is more than the generation of good scores on tests. Furthermore, what causes teachers and principals to spring out of bed at 6 A.M. is not the preparation for, administration and scoring of, and remediation after tests. Tests lead to a preoccupation with production, workbooks, worksheets, and drills, whereas teachers report that the major reward they derive from teaching is promoting the growth and development of their students.

Lists tend to be prescriptions for other people and for other people's children. Most external lists constitute a suffocating description of a teacher's job, a principal's job, or a pupil's job. They create roles that few of the list makers are apt to want for themselves or for their own children. We might do better to take the good advice of E.B. White: "If a person is in health, he doesn't need to take anybody else's temperature to know where he's going."

Moreover, I doubt that we would find that many teachers, principals, and students in high-achieving schools comply closely with a list of any kind. As Ronald Edmonds often said, we know far more about the features that characterize an effective school than we know about how a school becomes effective in the first place. Why, then, do we try to force schools we don't like to resemble those we do like by employing means that have little to do with the evolution of the kind of schools we like?

And finally, I think the list logic breaks down because it depends for its success on the existence of bright sheep. We read proposals every day suggesting ways to attract, train, retain, and retrain the best and the brightest to work with our children in school. Yet on the very next page we read more and more demands that such individuals comply with the requirements of externally controlled, predetermined, routinized, carefully monitored jobs.

Only bright sheep can pull that off. But sheep don't come that way, and neither do people. As I learned on the farm, you can have dumb, plodding, pedestrian, undistinguished, compliant sheep — or you can have bright, discriminating, questioning, willful goats. You may have both in one school, but you cannot have both within a single individual.

Thus it's not surprising that many successful teachers and principals — goats at heart — report keeping "two sets of books." They keep a close eye on what others expect of them: prescribed curricula, minimum student competencies, criteria against which they will be evaluated. They may appear to meet the specifications of these external lists. They also keep a careful eye on what they want to accomplish in their work, according to their own vision of a good school or classroom. Unfortunately, the dissonance created by merely living with, much less reconciling, these two sets of books too often obliterates any good that might be inherent in either set. This leaves many adults in school agreeing with one veteran Chicago-area principal who lamented, "You know what I want to be in my next incarnation? An *educator*."

Higher salaries may lure some young people with high test scores and class rank to submit to the indignities of public school life, but money alone will do little to make working in the schools a profession. Teachers with responsibilities for dozens of human lives 190 days each year and principals who run complex schools with budgets in the millions of dollars do not want to be run themselves, especially badly. Lists of desirable characteristics are a good idea, but they have been taken too far. Logic has become a pathologic.

There are two good reasons for the perseverance of list logic as the driving force in education reform. First, it *is* a logic and thus is defensible in solemn presentations before school boards and state legislatures. Second, it enjoys face validity. As one state education department's list of "the 91 characteristics of the effective principal" suggests, lists show that we know where we are going and that we're taking steps to get there. They allow us to determine which individuals and which schools have arrived, and they offer political cover for educators who are higher up in the administrative chain of command. In short, lists promise change, legitimacy, and accountability to an enterprise in need of all three.

Still another reason why list logic seems so compelling is that the alternatives are not compelling. Anarchy? Independent schools? Free schools? No schools? Accepting schools as they are? Precious few alternatives to the logic of lists spring to mind. And as long as no other conceptions of school improvement emerge, lists will continue to dominate education reform. The debate will swirl around which elements belong on each list (Was "parent involvement" a part of Edmonds' list or not?); which list is best (Rutter's, Boyer's, the list proposed in *A Nation At Risk*?); which are the best ways of choosing one list to rely on rather than another (pedigree of the panelists? rigor of the research cited?); and who should make these decisions (superintendents? chief state school officers? legislators? academics?).

Many educators — both within and outside the schools — are growing weary of the logic of lists and would prefer that their own common sense be honored. Indeed, I see in a number of educational projects about the U.S. the outlines of a conception of school reform markedly different from list logic. The Bay Area Writing Project, what is becoming a "thinking skills movement," Circles of Learning from Minnesota, the Triad at the University of Connecticut, the Coalition of Essential Schools, and the development of principals' centers across the country are all examples of separate educational groundswells beneath which a common vision seems to lie — a vision of a school quite unlike a center of production for principals, teachers, and pupils.

Those who take part in these and similar efforts seem to value and honor learning, participation, and cooperation above prescription, production, and competition. I see in these kinds of endeavors the concept of the school as a *community of learners*, a place where all participants — teachers, principals, parents, and students — engage in learning and teaching. School is not a place for big people who are learn*ed* and little people who are learn*ers*, for important people who do not need to learn and unimportant people who do. Instead, school is a place where students discover, and adults rediscover, the joys, the difficulties, and the satisfactions of learning.

We talk constantly about the importance of student achievement, of teachers' staff development, and of the professional growth of principals as if they occur on different planets during different epochs. In a community of learners, adults and children learn — at the same time and in the same place — to think critically and analytically and to solve problems that are important to them.

An anthropologist friend tells me that the most dramatic, profound learning takes place in societies in which people of all ages, generations, and positions — grandmother, father, child, adolescent, grandchild — work and learn together, simultaneously. This kind of yeasty environment for learning is evident in one primary school in the Boston area that decided to explore the Charles River. Everyone — students, teachers, parents, and administrators — set about to discover all they could about the river. They worked together to learn about history, geology, pollution, geography — and about the power of collective inquiry. They became a community of learners.

I see elements of a community of learners in a Massachusetts high school in which the principal and teachers meet periodically to share their writing and their ideas and to make connections between their writing experiences and their work with students.

Many conditions appear to foster learning, such as posing one's own problems, risk taking, humor, high standards coupled with low anxiety, collaboration with another learner, and the importance of modeling. It is astonishing to me how these and other conditions associated with learning attract so little attention from list makers and how infrequently they appear in schools, the places in which learning is supposed to take place.

Communities of learners seem to be, above all, committed to discovering the conditions that support human learning and to providing these conditions. Whereas many attempts to improve schools dwell on adult working conditions, on the control of students, and on the production of student achievement, the central question for a community of learners is not, What should students, teachers, and principals know and do and how do we get them to know and do it? Instead, the question is, Under what conditions will principal and student and teacher become serious, committed, sustained, lifelong, cooperative, learners?

A community of learners seems to work from a set of assumptions fundamentally different from those of the list makers:

— Schools have the capacity to improve themselves, if the conditions are right. A major responsibility of those outside the schools is to help provide these conditions for those inside.

— When the conditions are right, adults and students alike learn.

— What needs to be improved about schools is their culture, the quality of interpersonal relationships, and the nature and quality of learning experiences.

— School improvement is an effort to determine and provide, from without and within, conditions under which the adults and youngsters who inhabit schools will promote and sustain learning among themselves.

Taking these assumptions seriously leads to some fresh thinking about the culture of schools and about what people do in them. For instance, the principal need no longer be the "head teacher" pretending to know all, one who consumes lists from above and propagates lists to those below. The more crucial role of the principal is as head *learner*, engaging in the most important enterprise of the school — experiencing, displaying, modeling, and celebrating what it is hoped and expected that teachers and pupils will do. As a participant in one principals' center put it, "Since I've joined the center, I've noticed that teachers in my building have become much more committed to their own staff development." *That* a principal is learning something is far more important to the school than any list of *what* a principal should know.

Teachers in a learning community, such as the Prospect School in Bennington, Vermont, are not "inserviced." Instead, they engage in continuous inquiry about teaching. They are researchers, students of teaching, who observe others teach, have others observe them, talk about teaching, and help other teachers. In short, they are professionals. Colleagues helping one another provide a powerful source of recognition and respect both for the helpers and for those who are helped. And teachers find that, when they engage in serious learning themselves, their students take learning more seriously. As one teacher put it, "Learning is not something like chicken pox, a childhood disease that makes you itch for a while and then leaves you immune for the rest of your life."

Implicit in many of the lists of school reforms is a vision of school as a place where students learn and adults teach, where the role of educators is to serve, not be served. Because schools and those who work in them are accountable for pupils' achievement and because no amount of pupil achievement is sufficient to place every student in the top half of the class, pupil learning usually pre-empts adult learning. Yet only a school that is hospitable to adult learning can be a good place for students to learn. The notion of a community of learners implies that school is a context for lifelong growth, not only for growth among students. Adult learning is not only a means toward the end of student learning, but also an important objective in its own right.

Many lists pose the questions, problems, and tasks that those in school are expected to address. Lists have also specified who has responsibility for monitoring these tasks — the state department for school systems, the superintendent for principals, the principal for teachers, and the teacher for pupils.

In a community of learners, on the other hand, a different set of relationships prevails. Adults and youngsters often pose their own questions and enlist others as resources to help answer them. The assumption is that the knowledge base for improving schools is fed not by one but by two tributaries: social science research *and* the craft knowledge of schoolpeople. Research and national reports are valuable not as lesson plans for schoolpeople but for the help they offer in clarifying practitioners' own visions of the way schools and classrooms should be and of how to make then that way. Or, as one principal put it, "I came to the Institute looking for a formula — to put things together so that we could be anointed an 'effective school.' What I have come to realize is something I really knew all along. We are a pretty effective school already, and any answers or solutions that are reached will come from within."

Our preoccupation with lists seems to be bucking increasingly heavy tides these days, as teachers and principals become adept at circumventing prescriptions. The notion of the school as a community of learners may be moving with a different tide, but it, too, is accompanied by a host of tough questions: How can we overcome the taboo that prevents teachers from making themselves, their ideas, and their teaching visible to other teachers? How can principals become active learners when learning implies deficiency? How can students learn to work more cooperatively and less competitively? Can we have more (and higher) standards for adults and students without more standardization? In what ways can those outside the schools, by working with those in the schools, contribute to the development of a community of learners? From whence comes legitimacy and accountability? How can we unlock the extraordinary idealism, vision, and energy that are sealed within teachers and principals? And how can a conception such as the community of learners avoid becoming yet another set of prescriptions, another list to be imposed on teachers, principals, and students?

But unlike the problems of transforming goats into sheep and sheep into goats, trying to find answers to questions such as these is invigorating both for young people and for the adults charged with educating them. And it leads to the improvement of their schools.

Many advocates of the effective schools movement have observed that, when a school becomes effective, it remains to become good. I wonder whether it's possible to *start* with a good school. Once a school is good, I suspect that it will also be effective.

16

Public School Administrators in the United States: An Analysis of Supply and Demand

James R. Bliss

Introduction

In February 1986 the National Commission on Excellence in Administration commissioned a study of the supply of school administrators relative to the demand for school administrators. At the outset of the study, three possible relationships between supply and demand were identified: demand exceeds supply, demand equals supply, and supply exceeds demand. It was assumed that if supply exceeded demand by a large, growing margin, pressures would soon rise either to change the qualifications for administrative positions or to create new positions. Until such changes occurred, it would become increasingly difficult to bring top administrative talent into the profession.

The lack of reliable data on the supply of educational administrators at a given time is a major obstacle to reforming the profession. Thus, reliable data on the supply of educational administrators are needed; without such data, university chairmen and deans will be unwilling to promote appropriate voluntary adjustments in their admission standards, curricula, and teaching strategies. At the outset of the study, consolidated information on the supply of school administrators was unavailable. We expected, however, that state certification offices would have extensive electronic files and would easily be able to calculate at least the total number of current administrative certificate holders in their states. Even though supply issues cannot be completely resolved by counting the total number of administrative certificate holders, this total is a useful starting point.

The lack of reliable data on the demand for school administrators is likewise a major obstacle to reforming the profession. If more were known about replacement rates and about the ways in which the number of administrative positions may grow in the near future, better planning could take place. As a first approximation to the demand for school administrators, we chose to estimate only the number of current administrative positions in the schools. We assumed that this figure would be an upper limit on the current demand. Furthermore, we thought that asking uncomplicated questions about the demand, as well as the supply, would offer the best chance for quickly gaining an impression of how well the states are able to keep track of these issues.

Questions

The main research question was this: "What is the relationship between the current supply of public school administrators and the current demand for public school administrators in the United States?" This question was divided into four subquestions:

1. What is the current supply of public school administrators?
2. What is the current demand for public school administrators?
3. How large is the difference between the current supply of public school administrators and the current demand for public school administrators?
4. How large is the difference between the current supply of public school administrators and the current demand for public school administrators, relative to the demand for public school administrators?

Methods

Data were collected from two sources: state certification directors and the Center for Educational Statistics (U.S. Department of Education). In May 1986 a questionnaire was mailed to every state certification director in the United States. A covering letter explained the purpose of the study and requested that respondents estimate the number of persons currently certified for service as administrators in the public schools. Second requests were mailed to the certification directors four weeks later, and some directors were contacted by telephone. Through telephone conversations with directors, we learned that many directors can only guess the number of administrative certificate holders in their states. We also learned that the amount of paperwork in teacher certification offices is staggering. New Jersey, for example, has collected approximately 268,000 certification records since 1960. Some directors were even unable to offer a guess regarding the current number of school administration certificate holders.

Data concerning the current demand for school administrators were obtained from the Center for Educational Statistics. We requested from the center up-to-date totals of central-office administrators and school building administrators in each state. The center provided a table entitled "Staff employed in public school systems, by type of assignment and by state: Fall 1984." This table provided a breakdown of public school system employees including district staff, school staff, and support service staff. The numbers of school *district* administrators and school *building* administrators were added to obtain an estimate of the maximum current demand for public school administrators.

The analysis consisted of tabulating the estimates for supply and demand (Table 16–1) and calculating the means of four variables: (1) the number of certificate holders, (2) the number of position holders, (3) the number of certificate holders less the number of position holders, and (4) the number of certificate holders minus the number of position holders, all as a fraction of the number of position holders.

Results

What Is the Current Supply of Public School Administrators?

Only thirty-two (63 percent) of fifty-one certification directors were able to estimate the number of persons certified for service as public school administrators in their own states. According to Table 16-1 (column 1), estimates of the number of certificate holders ranged from 507 in Hawaii to 55,434 in New York State. Michigan does not currently certify public school administrators, but may do so as of July, 1990.

The mean estimated number of certificate holders per state is 9,753 (excluding New York State, an outlier in the data set with its estimated 55,434 certificate holders, the mean estimated number of certificate holders per state is 4,487.) The estimated total number of certificate holders in the United States is at least 312,108. This figure is based on estimates from only thirty-two of fifty states plus the District of Columbia. No extrapolations or imputations were made. The data were insufficient for estimating an upper limit of the total number of certificate holders in the United States. (A future study could request information on the total number of school personnel certification records on file.)

Table 16–1
Number of School Administrators by State: 1985

State	Certificate Holders (1)	Position Holders (2)	Certificate Holders less Position Holders (3)	Column 3/ Column 2 (4)
Alabama	*	2704	*	*
Alaska	*	537	*	*
Arizona	4798	2270	2528	1.11
Arkansas	*	2447	*	*
California	35642	23969	11673	0.49
Colorado	4300	2716	1584	0.58
Connecticut	9000	2290	6710	2.93
Delaware	836	493	343	0.70
Dist. of Colum.	*	720	*	*
Florida	31279	7416	23863	3.22
Georgia	*	3982	*	*
Hawaii	507	559	−52	−.09
Idaho	*	802	*	*
Illinois	25000	5924	19076	3.22
Indiana	5200	3476	1724	0.50
Iowa	*	2031	*	*
Kansas	1300	1898	−598	−0.32
Kentucky	*	2999	*	*
Louisiana	16243	4090	12153	2.97
Maine	2775	1324	1451	1.10
Maryland	3000	2529	471	0.19
Massachusetts	*	4171	*	*
Michigan	*	14107	*	*
Minnesota	5396	3109	2287	0.74
Mississippi	6730	1928	4802	2.49
Missouri	16112	4747	11365	2.39
Montana	2591	694	1897	2.73
Nebraska	*	1567	*	*
Nevada	*	465	*	*
New Hampshire	*	642	*	*
New Jersey	14640	7325	7315	1.00
New Mexico	2795	1562	1233	0.79

Table 16–1, continued

New York	55434	10303	45131	4.38
North Carolina	4100	5133	−1033	−0.20
North Dakota	1000	735	265	0.36
Ohio	*	9862	*	*
Oklahoma	*	2923	*	*
Oregon	3700	2251	1449	0.64
Pennsylvania	*	6353	*	*
Rhode Island	*	658	*	*
South Carolina	12154	2676	9478	3.54
South Dakota	1053	579	474	0.89
Tennessee	*	5014	*	*
Texas	14696	13188	1508	0.11
Utah	1110	1219	−109	−0.09
Vermont	1170	867	303	0.35
Virginia	2996	4618	−1622	−0.35
Washington	15000	3238	11762	3.63
West Virginia	4551	1763	2788	1.58
Wisconsin	7000	2978	4022	1.35
Wyoming	*	810	*	*

Source of data on certificate holders: state certification directors.
Source of data on position holders: U.S. Department of Education, Center for Educational Statistics, survey of "Common Core of Data."

What Is the Current Demand for Public School Administrators?

Table 16–1 (column 2) shows that the number of administration positions ranged from 465 in Nevada to 23,969 in California. The mean estimated number of administration positions held per state is 3,738.

The number of positions in Table 16–1 (column 2) represents not only the demand for certified administrators, but the total demand for administrators, that is, 190,652 positions. Thus, the table overestimates the actual demand for certified people. The differences between the supply of certified administrators and the demand for certified administrators are even greater than the differences reflected in Table 16–1 (column 3)

How Large Is the Difference Between the Current Supply of Public School Administrators and the Current Demand for Public School Administrators?

The oversupply was calculated for only states that submitted the number of certificate holders (Table 16–1, Column 3). It ranged from -1,622 in Virginia to 45,131 in New York. A negative figure would suggest a "shortage" of certified school administrators. However, the numbers that suggest a shortage of certificate holders should be treated with caution. The mean oversupply of school administrators per state, based on Table 16–1 (column 3), is 5,758.

How Large Is the Difference Between the Current Supply of Public School Administrators and the Current Demand for Public School Administrators, Relative to the Demand for Public School Administrators?

What matters most about the oversupply is not the extent of oversupply in absolute terms, but the extent of oversupply relative to the number of "available" positions. Table 16–1 (column 4) indicates that the extent of oversupply relative to positions varies from -0.35 in Virginia to 4.38 in New York. The estimated mean oversupply relative to positions per state is 1.34. The oversupply is more than large enough to replace all incumbent school administrators.

Discussion

The inability of many state certification directors to provide accurate data on the number of certificate holders is symptomatic of a widespread crisis of information management within state certification offices. Although computers are beginning to make an impact on the way in which certificate records are managed, many directors indicated that the information requested could be obtained only by conducting a manual search of conventional files at a substantial cost. Others indicated that computer listings of certificate holders were available, but that descriptions by particular employment categories were unavailable. In addition, records are often not well maintained. Individual certificate holders relocate to other states, but information systems usually fail to register these changes.

On the other hand, it would be inappropriate to completely discount the estimates that were provided by state certification directors; these estimates are presented in Table 16–1. Along with information on the number of positions held, these estimates are reasonably consistent in suggesting a vast oversupply of school administrators in the United States.

The results of this study indicate that the supply of public school administrators in the United States is at least two and one-third times the number of available administrative positions.

What accounts for this seemingly vast oversupply? A number of possible explanations have been offered, including a whole range of monetary and nonmonetary incentives (Gerritz, Koppich, and Guthrie, 1984). One explanation for the apparent oversupply of school administrators is that market forces may be weak with respect to public school administrators. For example, New York is a high-spending state in its average expenditures per pupil for public education. New York spends 159 percent of the national per-pupil average (Plisko and Stern, 1985). To the extent that high spending translates into high administrative salaries and other benefits, high-spending states create incentives for teachers to obtain administrative certificates. Yet these incentives, while encouraging the production of more and more certificate holders, do not react to an ever-growing oversupply, at least in part, because the extent of the oversupply is concealed. According to this argument, we would expect at least a modest correlation between the extent of the oversupply of public school administrators and the levels of spending across the United States.

Another explanation for the apparent oversupply is that the oversupply may be illusory in the following sense. Graduate-level courses for credit can often be arranged in such a way that state certification requirements can be easily met, even though the student has no intentions of becoming a school administrator. The direct costs of gaining administrative certification over and above another specialization within the field of education may be quite low. Thus, the pursuit of a certificate as a supervisor, as a general administrator, or even as a principal may often take place as a large ancillary activity of those who merely wish to keep their options open. Although a substantial proportion of classroom teachers seek graduate training and the number of potential certificate holders now seems almost unlimited, not all certificate holders would either seek or accept an administration position if one were offered.

References

Gerritz, William; Koppich, Julia; and Guthrie, James W. (1984). *Preparing California school leaders: An analysis of supply, demand, and training.* Berkeley: University of California.

Plisko, Valena White, and Stern, Joyce D. (Eds.)(1985) *The condition of education: 1985 edition.* Washington, D.C.: U.S. Department of Education.

17

Report on the First Annual Survey Certification and Employment Standards for Educational Administrators

Richard P. Gousha, Peter L. LoPresti, and Alan H. Jones

Purpose of the Study

The First Annual Survey of Certification and Employment Standards for Educational Administrators was initiated in the fall of 1984 to gather information on the status of requirements for preparation, certification, and employment of individuals in educational administration positions in the public schools across the United States. As the directors of the study, our intention was that this information would be disseminated as widely as possible following its analysis during the 1984–85 school year, and that similar data collection, analysis, and dissemination would be done each subsequent academic year.

Structure of the Study

The survey instrument was prepared in three versions, specifically to address state certification officials, large public school district officials, and program directors at institutions of higher education that offer doctoral degrees in educational administration. Each of the versions included questions concerning such issues as state certification for service as a public school administrator; required competencies for preparation, certification, and employment as a school administrator; the use of testing and examinations in the preparation, certification, and employment of school administrators; the use of performance assessment and requirements for field experience in the preparation, certification, and employment of school administrators; whether classroom teaching experience is required for preparation, certification, or employment as a school administrator; whether there are continuing education requirements for certified or employed school administrators; and the history of enactment and revision of standards for preparation, certification, and employment of school administrators, and the nature and direction of such changes in requirements.

Response to the Study

Survey forms were sent to the officials who direct certification activities in each state government plus the District of Columbia and Puerto Rico, who coordinate personnel in the thirty-two large public school districts that compose the Council of Greater City Schools, and who direct departments of ecucational administration at one hundred institutions of higher education that offer doctoral degree programs in educational administration. Of the one hundred institutions of higher education, eighty were public universities and twenty were private, and there was at least one institution in each state.

Completed responses were received from certification officials in thirty-nine states (a 75 percent response), from personnel officials at sixteen large public school districts (a 50 percent response), and from directors of graduate study programs at fifty-two institutions of higher education (a 52 percent response). Of the responses from higher education, forty-three were from public universities and nine from private institutions, located in thirty-three different states. Of the total of 107 responses (a 58 percent response), there was at least one from each of forty-six states. The information collected does, therefore, widely reflect preparation, certification, and employment activities in educational administration across the United States.

In the following sections the findings of the survey are described for each of the major topics examined: certification, competencies, examinations, performance assessment and field experience, teaching experience, continuing education, and revision of standards.

Certification

Each official in the constituencies surveyed was asked whether his or her state has governmental standards for certifying school administrators. Of the thirty-nine state certification officials responding, all but one replied that they did have such standards for certifying school administrators. Of the officials at the sixteen large school districts who responded, all but one said that their states had standards and procedures for certifying school administrators. Of the directors of graduate programs of fifty-two institutions of higher education who answered the survey, fifty stated that their states certified school administrators. In each case the negative responses were from the state of Michigan—the Michigan Department of Education, the Detroit Public School District, Michigan State University, and Wayne State University. The combined responses from the three groups of officials covered forty-six states, and the *Manual on Certification and Preparation of Educational Personnel in the United States*, published in late 1984 by the National Association of State Directors of Teacher Education and Certification, further confirms that Michigan is the only state that does not have certification requirements and procedures for school administrators.

Of the thirty-eight other state officials responding to the survey, thirty-five reported that their certification procedures differentiate between the certification for superintendents and other central office administrators and the certification for school building principals and other site administrators. Specific responses indicated that twenty-seven of the states have separate certification for superintendents or chief district administrators, nineteen states differentiate between elementary and secondary principals in their certification, and a handful of states also certify separately such administrators as business officers and administrators of certain types of academic programs.

Of the officials from fifty institutions of higher education not located in Michigan who responded to the survey, forty-nine indicated that they offer programs of study leading to state certification as school administrators. The University of Hawaii officials responded that while they do not have a specific program leading to state certification, they do offer courses in support of state requirements for persons preparing to satisfy those state standards. Of the institutions with programs of study in educational administration, thirty-seven have standards and requirements for their programs that exceed the state certification standards in their state. Of the sixteen large public school districts participating in the survey, thirteen have employment standards for administrators in their districts that exceed state certification requirements for administrators.

Competencies

Each official in the three constituencies was asked if specific competencies were required for certification, employment, or preparation as school administrators. Of the officials from the thirty-eight states that certify school administrators, sixteen replied that they specify competencies to be met for certification, twenty indicated they do not have required competencies, and two stated that specific competencies were currently under consideration. Twelve of the sixteen large public school district officials replied that they have required competencies to be met before employment as a school administrator; the other four stated that they do not require specific competencies. Of the directors of graduate study programs for school administrators in institutions of higher education, thirty-two stated that they do have a list of required competencies, seventeen indicated that they do not, and three did not offer a response to this question.

Examinations

Each official in the three constituencies was asked if any form of examination or testing is used in evaluating candidates for certification, employment, or training in school administration. Eleven of the responding state officials answered that they do use an examination as part of the certification process, while twenty-eight said they do not. Of the eleven, three stated that they use the administration and supervision section of the National Teachers Examination battery; the other eight use some form of examination developed by or for that specific state.

Of the sixteen school district officials, eight stated that they use an examination in evaluating candidates for employment as school administrators; the other eight said they do not. Two of the districts use the NTE examination, while the other six have locally developed and administered tests or interviews. Of the directors at institutions of higher education engaged in preparation of school administrators, thirty-six indicated that they use some form of examination in addition to course work and field-experience requirements, while fifteen stated that they do not use examinations in this way, and one campus did not respond to this question.

Of those campuses using examinations of any sort, the most commonly used is the Graduate Record Examination, employed by thirteen institutions. Eight campuses use the Miller Analogies Test, and in many other cases locally developed tests or interviews are used, or state examinations are required. Directors at only two campuses stated that they use the NTE administrative examination. Sixteen indicated that they use some form of comprehensive or qualifying written examination as part of their advanced degree program for school administration; four reported requiring an oral examination upon completion of the program.

Performance Assessment and Field Experience

Each official in the three constituencies was asked to describe the role of performance assessment and field experiences in the certification, employment, and preparation of school administrators. Of the thirty-nine responding state certification officials, six reported that their state requires a performance assessment of candidates prior to certification; twenty-one states require some form of field experience or internship. The other eighteen responding states have no specific field experience requirements.

Of the sixteen responding large public school districts, ten require evidence of field experience or internship work prior to employment as school administrators, and the other six do not have such specific requirements. Of the fifty-two institutions of higher education, forty-three have some field experience requirement as part of their training program for school administrators. The types of field experience vary from campus to campus, with seventeen requiring internships and the others using some form of supervised field work.

Teaching Experience

Each official in the three responding constituencies was asked to indicate whether classroom teaching experience was required prior to certification, employment, or training in school administration. Of the state certification officials, thirty-two reported that their state requires teaching experience for certification as school administrators; seven indicated that they do not. Fourteen of the large public school district officials reported that they require classroom teaching experience of applicants for school administration employment, one district official said teaching experience is required in some cases, and the other responding district official stated that the district does not have such a requirement.

Of the directors in institutions of higher education, twenty-eight stated that classroom teaching experience is required for graduate study in school administration, twenty-four indicated it is not. However, many of those twenty-four suggested that they encourage students of school administration to have classroom teaching experience, since it is often required for state certification and employment. Three years of teaching was most commonly required by all three constituencies—by twenty states, six districts, and fifteen campuses in the sample. Two years was next most common length of teaching service required by states and institutions of higher education, and six of the large school districts require five years of teaching experience.

Continuing Education

Each official in the three responding constituencies was also asked if they have continuing education requirements relevant to certification, employment, or preparation as school administrators. Of the thirty-nine responding states, certification officials in twenty-one reported that they have continuing education requirements for persons holding certification as school administrators. Officials in the other eighteen states indicated that they do not have such continuing education requirements. The nature of the requirements in the twenty-one states ranges from graduate study, continuing education units, and clock hours of staff development to be completed within a period of time from one to ten years, depending on the state.

Twelve of the sixteen large school distlricts in the sample also require some form of continuing education for all school administrators in their employement, while the other four do not. In most cases the requirements involve participation in staff development or continuing education programs coordinated by the district.

The directors of the institutions of higher education were asked whether they offer continuing education or staff development programs in educational administration in which their employed graduates can participate. The officials from thirty-four of the fifty-two institutions stated that they do offer such programs.

Revision of Standards

All of the respondents were asked to indicate the date when their current standards and procedures for certification, employment, or preparation of school administrators were enacted, when they were most recently revised, and whether any further revisions were currently being considered, and, if so, what the nature or direction of the revision would be. Of the thirty-nine state certification officials responding, eighteen reported that their state standards had been revised at least once during the 1980s, and twenty-four stated that some type of further revision was currently under consideration. These current discussions were described as involving a total review of certification procedures in some cases and fine tuning of specific competencies, examinations, or assessment procedures in other instances.

Of the sixteen large public school districts in the sample, fourteen reported that their criteria and procedures for employment of school administrators had been revised at least once during the 1980s, and six of the districts stated that further revisions were currently under consideration. The nature of such current considerations involved development of new standards for employment and creation of new performance assessment procedures.

Of the directors at the fifty-two institutions of higher education responding to the survey, forty-two stated that their graduate study programs in school administration had undergone revision during the 1980s, and thirty-five reported that further program revisions were currently under consideration. Many campuses indicated that they have a continual process of revision for such programs, involving review and evaluation of the program and its graduates; others stated that they were currently responding to new state requirements, reviewing standards, considering new examinations to be used, raising required scores or competencies, adding field experience requirements, and considering such areas as multicultural education and law-related education.

Although there appears to be no specific common thread to the considerations of the states, districts, and campuses, it is obvious that there is much activity with respect to updating and revising programs and procedures for certification, employment, and preparation of school administrators. Of the total sample of 107 respondents, seventy-four (or 69 percent) have undergone some form of revision of standards for school administrators during the current decade, and sixty-five (or 61 percent) are currently considering additional revisions. Thus it would be an understatement to suggest that the procedures and standards for the preparation, certification, and employment of public school administrators is a dynamic and volatile field of study.

18

Moral Imagination, Interpersonal Competence, and the Work of School Administrators

William D. Greenfield

Introduction

The three-fold purpose of this paper is to (1) examine aspects of the relationship between certain features of the school work situation and the personal qualities of school administrators, (2) briefly discuss formal and informal processes and outcomes of role socialization and their relationship to preparing individuals to work effectively as school administrators, and (3) examine the implications of these ideas for the preparation of educational administrators, particularly school principals. The paper concludes with a summary of the major ideas and a set of tentative propositions regarding the preparation of effective school principals.

Three central assumptions underlie the ideas to be discussed. First, one's effectiveness in a work role, such as that of school principal, is primarily a

Portions of this paper appear in W. Greenfield (ed.), (1987), *Instructional Leadership: Concepts, Issues, and Controversies*, pp.56–73, and in A. Blumberg and W. Greenfield (1986) *The Effective Principal: Perspectives on School Leadership* (2nd ed.), pp. 223–40, and are published with permission of Allyn and Bacon, Inc.

function of the degree of match or "fit" between one's personal qualities and the demands of the work situation itself. If this fit is close, then one is likely to be effective in a given work role. Second, the school work setting is a normatively complex and highly ambiguous social situation characterized by multiple and frequently conflicting standards of goodness; these standards are maintained or changed primarily through interpersonal interactions among participants in the situation. Third, the school work situation reflects a social order negotiated within a complex set of professional, organizational, cultural, and environmental constraints and opportunities, and is always subject to renegotiation; thus it is a "temporary" order in that it is highly susceptible to internal and external threats to stability.

There are other assumptions, of course, but these three are fundamental and serve to guide the discussion in this paper. The ideas expressed here are offered in a speculative vein in an effort to reconceptualize the way we think about the work of school principals and about efforts to enhance their effectiveness on the job, particularly as it relates to the improvement of instruction in schools.

Where Are We?

The current "image" of principals' effectiveness is one entwined with the idea of instructional leadership, the assumption being that schools will be more effective to the extent that the school principal emphasizes the importance of academic achievement and provides teachers with instructional supports (Edmonds, 1982; Achilles, 1987). This concept of instructional leadership is a *very narrow* view of the work of school principals, particularly to the extent that it suggests that working *directly* with teachers is what effective principals actually do (Bossert et al., 1982).

The question *not* being asked is "Why do school principals spend their time as they do?" Prescriptions calling for principals to be instructional leaders confound the issue by implying that the way they do spend their time is inappropriate. The thesis advanced in this paper is that principals are doing their work as they know it *must* be done, given the demands of the work situation. The framework developed in this paper is intended to be responsive to what principals actually do, rather than to prescribe what they should be doing.

The literature is pretty clear about what principals actually do at work and indicates that most school principals spend very little time *directly* supervising or observing teachers in classrooms (Gorton and McIntyre, 1978; Byrne, Hines, and McCleary, 1978; Wolcott, 1973; Peterson, 1978; Blumberg and Greenfield, 1980, 1986; Morris et al., 1981; Lortie, Crow, and Prolman, 1983; Dwyer et al., 1983; Dwyer, 1984; Goldhammer et al., 1971; Greenfield, 1982; Martin and Willower, 1981; Willower and Kmetz, 1982;

Dwyer et al., 1985; Little, 1982; and others). Basic conclusions that can be derived from these and other studies is that a principal's work is largely social in character, occurs outside classrooms, and involves a lot of verbal, face-to-face interaction with multiple actors on the school scene. For example, one recent set of studies indicates that most of the work activity of the elementary principal involves *communicating* with teachers, students, supervisors, and other actors in the school, and with parents and various persons and groups external to the school; the second most time-consuming work activity includes *monitoring*—reviewing, watching, being present, and assessing (without any intended formal evaluation) what is occurring vis-à-vis work structures, student and staff relations, plant and equipment, and safety and order concerns (Dwyer et al., 1985). Dwyer and his colleagues' recently completed in-depth studies of seven principals at work indicate that more than 60 percent of an elementary principal's behavior is focused on the routine activities of communicating and monitoring, and that these at best are only *indirectly* (but importantly) related to instruction.

In short, reforms that call for principals to work more closely and directly with teachers on instructional matters are somewhat misleading and based on a normative rather than an empirical conception of the work of principals. Principals who interpret that call to mean that they should spend more time working directly with teachers are likely to frustrate themselves and, indeed, may do their staffs and the children they serve a real disservice (Deal, 1987). There is much that a school principal must do in order to administer a school well, and relatively little of that is related to working directly (one on one) with teachers in classrooms. What the school principal does spend most of his or her time doing is what might be called responding to "situational imperatives"—events and activities that demand immediate attention—which if not attended to have a high potential to threaten the stability of the school situation (including the capacity of teachers to teach and the opportunities for youngsters to learn).

Not only is the concept of instructional leadership misleading, it is ambiguous and reveals little about the work of principals or what is required of principals in order that they be effective in the school situation. As suggested earlier, being effective as a principal requires responding appropriately to the demands of the school situation. Understanding the nature of the school situation holds the key to understanding *why* principals behave as they do, and *why* some schools and some principals are more effective than others (Greenfield, 1987). A more complete empirical understanding of a principal's work situation will help to (a) explain *why* principals behave as they do, and (b) *prescribe* changes in behavior (or requisite knowledge, skills, and personal dispositions) directed at a more appropriate fit between the requirements of the situation and the actions and orientations of the principal.

The call for more and better instructional leadership is a "prescription" that reflects virtually no understanding or recognition of the realities of the school principal's work situation. A brief sketch of important aspects of the school administrator's actual work situation is offered next, followed by a more detailed examination of "moral imagination" and "interpersonal competence"—two lower-order concepts that illuminate important dimensions of the work of principals and are grounded in an understanding of the nature of the school work situation.

The Work Situation in Schools

As stated earlier, the notion of effectiveness guiding this discussion is one that focuses attention on the match or the "degree of fit" between the demands of the situation and the knowledge, skills, and dispositions of the actor in that situation, in this case the school principal. Any effort to describe or explain what school administrators do at work must conceive of that behavior as a function of the individual's perception of and interaction within the school situation (Lewin, 1951; Blumberg and Greenfield, 1986). Ten features of the school principal's work situation are briefly outlined below:

1. The relationship between a school and its system, the district, is loose. Each school is a more or less self-contained entity, and its primary concerns are its immediate participants and setting. The relationships between principals are transitory and tend to be based on interpersonal friendships. The focus of the principal is inward, giving primary attention to what is occurring in his or her school. In Weick's (1976) terms, schools are loosely coupled to one another and, by and large, to the central office.

2. The dominant values in the larger system are "peace-keeping" and loyalty. Keeping the school and the district running smoothly and communicating loyalty to superiors are uppermost in the minds of school administrators, and serve to foster the stability of an organization that is extremely susceptible to parental and community pressure and other *external* influences.

3. The demands placed on the school principal are frequent and varied, and call for quick responses. This fosters a reactive stance on the part of the principal, and much that occurs does so unpredictably. The work setting is full of uncertainties. The school principal never knows what the next demand will be, how problematic it will be, or whether it will be associated with a teacher, student, parent, or some other actor in the system; in addition to "people" demands there are those that might be termed mechanical or physical (malfunctioning equipment and school support facilities). As Wolcott (1973) observed, virtually every problem that arises is viewed as important by a school principal.

4. Teachers have total responsibility for production (instruction) in their classrooms; the effect of one teacher's work on another is hard to discern. What occurs between one teacher and another or between a teacher and the principal has no necessary bearing on what happens elsewhere in the school, and how well a teacher does his or her job bears little immediate relation to the effectiveness of other teachers. The teacher views the school not as a place of organizational membership but rather as "a place where I teach." There is little concern by most teachers for what occurs beyond their classroom door.

5. The work effort of the principal tends to focus on individuals rather than on groups, and this is reinforced by the norms of teachers as a group. Efforts to introduce change tend to emphasize changes in individual behaviors, not group norms. As noted both in early conceptions of the administrator's role and in more recent studies, its essentially dyadic character is central to understanding the nature of their work (Coladarci and Getzels, 1955; Griffiths, 1959; Dwyer et al., 1985; Blumberg and Greenfield, 1986).

6. Schools are under attack, reflect a culture built on a history of vulnerability to the public, and are not very secure environments. School goals often are ambiguous, it is difficult to demostrate effectiveness to the public, and schools often are unsure of their very reason for being. Schools are ontologically insecure organizations (Blumberg and Greenfield, 1986).

7. In part due to multiple and ambiguous goals and a relatively low level of codified technical knowledge about effective teaching practices, teachers and principals confront a normatively complex situation characterized by competing and sometimes conflicting standards of good practice. This is exacerbated by a heterogeneous clientele, a teacher culture that values individual autonomy in teaching practices, and a tradition that emphasizes "learning-by-doing," "doing it on your own," and "getting through the day." It is not a reflective culture, and places a low value on technical knowledge and evaluation of practice, essentially abdicating group standards. There is little discussion of or consensus about standards of good practice.

8. The work that occurs in schools is mediated through dyadic and larger-group interactions. The school is a highly normative social situation, and this places a heavy reliance on interpersonal exchanges as the primary vehicle through which teachers and principals influence one another, children, and others. Communication is primarily oral and face-to-face.

9. The social order in schools is transitory, highly vulnerable to internal and external threats to stability, and always subject to renegotiation. A complex of professional, organizational, cultural, and environmen-

tal forces come together in a school, and there is ongoing competition for and conflict over the distribution of ideological and other resources. The school is a political arena, and principals and teachers are critical political actors in the game of schooling, with some having more influence than others (Wiles, Wiles, and Bondi, 1981; Burlingame, 1987).

10. Unlike counterparts in other sectors, school principals tend to have few assistants or specialized (nonteaching) staff under their immediate control, particularly in elementary schools. While middle and secondary schools usually have larger administrative staffs, the size generally is small given the overall size of the enterprise. It is not uncommon, for example, for an elementary principal to supervise thirty or more teachers with no assistant principal. The average span of control of supervisors in industry and other work sectors is considerably more narrow.

These are only some of the features of the work situation encountered by a school principal. There are other features, and many school researchers have written much more extensively and insightfully about these matters (Waller, 1932; Bidwell, 1965; Jackson, 1968; Goslin, 1965; Dreeben, 1970; Becker, 1980; Lortie, 1975; Lortie, Crow, and Prolmon, 1983; Wolcott, 1973; Burlingame, 1979; Morris et al., 1981; Little, 1982; Little and Bird, 1987; Dwyer and Smith, 1987; Sarason, 1971; Sarason and Klaber, 1985; Cusick, 1983; Sergiovanni and Corbally, 1984). The point I wish to emphasize is that a great deal is known about the character of the school as a work setting. Yet, in discussions or studies of administrator and school effectiveness, little attention is given to what might be called the "situational imperatives" in schools.

One may agree or disagree that the described situation is or is not desirable, but that misses the point. While there clearly is a need to reform and improve working conditions in most schools (for school administrators as well as for teachers), the reality is that for the present moment in any given school, the school principal is given a set of circumstances to which he or she *must* respond. Calling for new responses without a recognition of what the situation *actually* demands of school principals is futile vis-à-vis efforts to improve schools or to make principals more effective. School principals *can* be equipped with the knowledge and skills needed to lead and manage schools well and to improve teaching conditions for teachers and learning opportunities for children. And, if the way the school is administered is not changed, there will be no discernible changes in the school situation itself; schools in the year 2036 will look much like schools do today, and as they did in 1936. However, proposed changes in the professional preparation of principals and in the way schools are to be administered will be effective only to the extent that they are responsive to *the actual demands* of the present work situation.

In order to change the way schools are administered, it in part will be necessary to equip principals with knowledge, skills, and dispositions responsive to the actual demands of the work situation. In short, it will be necessary to attach much greater importance to the match between the personal qualities of principals and the demands of the work situation than has been the practice. Many personal qualities may be important, but only two are discussed here. These include the acquisition and development of moral and interpersonal knowledge and skills that will enable principals to more effectively respond to *certain* features of the school situation: (1) that there are competing standards of goodness regarding effective and acceptable practice in schools; and (2) that the school is fundamentally a normatively complex and ambiguous social situation, and in order to influence the school situation or classroom teaching practices the principal must work with and through teachers. These ideas are explored as an extension of the concept of "vision" (Blumberg and Greenfield, 1980), a much touted quality of effective principals. First, however, I shall discuss personal qualities more generally.

Personal Qualities of the Principal

The thesis advanced is that an understanding of the antecedents to effective school administration can be gained by focusing more attention on understanding the personal qualities of administrators, which are the knowledge, skills, beliefs, and personal dispositions characterizing the individual, and the relationships between those qualities and the demands and characteristics of the work situation itself. That is, the presence or absence of certain personal qualities may influence an individual's ability to be effective in specific work environments. For example, numerous studies describe the work situation of the principalship as highly ambiguous, suggesting that administratiors with a high tolerance for ambiguity will be more likely than others to cope effectively with such circumstances (Foskett, 1967; Goldhammer et al., 1971; Wolcott, 1973; Byrne, Hines, and McCleary, 1978; Gorton and McIntyre, 1978; Dwyer et al., 1983; Morris et al., 1981).

Studies of effective schools and the work of school principals increasingly point to the significance of aspects of the work itself and contextual properties of the school, its environment, and its history as important determinants of the activities of principals and teachers and instructional outcomes for children (Cuban, 1984; Manasse, 1985; Dwyer and Smith, 1987). However, while these are important new directions and are to be encouraged, personal qualities of the individual teacher or the principal continue to receive extremely limited attention both from researchers and from those concerned with staff-development programs and associated efforts aimed at improving the day-to-day performance of professional educators. The issue is not to emphasize the importance of traits, attitudes, and other individual characteristics per se (Bridges, 1982), but rather to understand the relationships

between the knowledge, skills, and dispositions of individuals *and* the characteristics of the situation in which they work. This strategy assumes that
individual effectiveness in a given situation is in large part a function of the
degree of match between the demands of the situation and the knowledge,
skills, and dispositions of the individual (Becker, 1964; Schein, 1978).

While relationships between the personal qualities of school administrators and the elements of the school work culture and organizational context
are not well understood, evidence does suggest that the principal's character
is central to leading a school well (Blumberg and Greenfield, 1986). Our
initial study (1980) identified vision, initiative, and resourcefulness as three
key elements associated with a principal's effectiveness, and led to the
development of a "grounded" or middle-range theory of leading and managing a school. Given certain features of the role of principal, which derive both
from the larger system and from the school itself, we speculated that several
personal qualities characterize the principal who would lead a school well:

Being highly goal oriented and having a keen sense of clarity regarding instructional
   and organizational goals
Having a high degree of personal security and a well-developed sense of themselves as
   persons
Having a high tolerance for ambiguity and a marked tendency to test the limits of the
   interpersonal and organizational systems they encounter
Being inclined to approach problems from a highly analytical perspective and being
   highly sensitive to the dynamics of power in both the larger systems and in their own
   school
Being inclined to be proactive rather than reactive — to be in charge of the job and not
   let the job be in charge of them
Having a high need to control a situation and low needs to be controlled by others —
   they like being in charge of things and initiating action
Having high needs to express warmth and affection toward others, and to receive it —
   being inclined toward friendliness and good-natured fellowship
Having high needs to include others in projects on problem solving, and moderate to
   high needs to want others to include them [Blumberg and Greenfield, 1986, pp.
   181-185]

Our discussion of the results of a follow-up study of the principals who
participated in the original investigation emphasizes the "embeddedness" of
the principalship in the school culture, and lends additional support to the
idea that the personal qualities of school principals are instrumental determinants of their success in coming to terms with a school's culture, the value
orientations of teachers as a social group, and the larger organizational and
community context in which the school is situated (Blumberg and Greenfield, 1986).

Although there has been only limited study of the specific "qualities of
person" presumed to characterize those who would enact an instructional

leadership conception of the principalship (DeBevoise, 1984), current images of that role usually contain three key ideas: (1) that the effective principal holds an image or a vision of what he or she wants to accomplish; (2) that this vision serves as a general guide for the principal as he or she sets about the activities of managing and leading a school; and (3) that the focus of the principal's work activity should be on matters related to instruction and to the classroom performances of teachers (Manasse, 1985; Strother, 1983). Like many others, I agree that a school principal can and should be instrumental in determining the direction and effectiveness of school programs, and that "vision" is a critical antecedent to effective school administration.

Why is this so? What is the relationship between this personal quality of the principal and the nature of the school work situation? The purpose of the next section is to examine the concept of vision and to explore its fuller meaning vis-à-vis the nature of the school as a work setting. The discussion will then turn to a consideration of what may be instrumental in the development of school administrators capable of vision and committed to leading and managing schools well and improving instruction.

School Administration: Values in Action

School administration is referred to here as actions undertaken with the intention of developing a productive and satisfying working environment for teachers and desirable learning conditions and outcomes for children. Administrators are effective to the extent that these broad purposes are achieved in a particular school or school district. The following discussion centers on school principals, although the elements and conditions to be described are also relevant to understanding efforts by teachers, department heads, and others committed to school effectiveness.

Interpersonal Competence and Moral Imagination

Two aspects of the work situation of principals appear critical. First, decisions must be made and actions must be taken, usually in the face of competing and conflicting norms. That is, the standards by which others will judge whether the decision or action chosen by the principal is appropriate or effective may be unknown, unclear, or different from those employed by the principal. Second, the principal's work world is a highly interpersonal one. Frequent verbal exchanges and face-to-face interaction with teachers, students, parents, supervisors, and other adults on the school scene (aides, custodians, cafeteria workers, and security personnel, for example) characterize much of the work of a principal. The capacity of a principal to influence instructional and organizational arrangements thus depends to a large degree on his or her ability to work effectively with and through people. Action has both a factual and a value component. Decision or action alternatives always require the assignment of values to facts and the exercise of judgment in arriving at an alternative—to embark on one line of action as opposed to another, or to choose one decision alternative over another (Simon, 1957). These often are choices of habit and may not necessarily involve deliberate and conscious choice between competing facts and values, but action always requires that a judgment be made. Whether by habit or by deliberation, judgments are made as values are assigned to facts and as decision or action alternatives are evaluated (Dewey, 1957).

School administration as it is conceived here thus involves the assignments of values to facts and the necessity to select one decision or course of action over another. Decisions and action alternatives often confront the principal with competing standards of goodness—the criterion one uses as the basis for judging that one alternative is to be preferred over others. Will it be a standard of efficiency, friendship, good educational practice, convenience, political expediency, or some other standard? In this sense there is a moral component to action, and principals or others may frequently be confronted with moral dilemmas (Schrag, 1979; Blumberg and Greenfield, 1986; Greenfield, 1986). The concept of "moral imagination" is discussed next to suggest aspects of the processes by which one evolves a vision regarding the educational or organizational arrangements in one's school.

Moral Imagination

Moral imagination refers to the inclination of a person to see that the world, in this case the school and the associated activities of teaching and learning, need not remain as it is—that it is possible for it to be otherwise, and to be better (Green, 1984). It is the ability to see the discrepancy between how things are and how they might be—not in terms of the ideal, but in terms of what is possible given a particular school situation. This is the element of "imagined" possibility.

It is "moral" imagination because the discrepancy, the possibility envisioned, is rooted in an awareness of and a commitment to the standards of good practice, of effective schools and good teaching, that characterize membership in the normative community of educators. Thus, it is "moral" in that it is the application of some standard of goodness that illuminates the discrepancy between the present and what is possible, and better.

Evolving a vision thus entails the exercise of moral imagination. The latter is a process that involves observing the current state of affairs in a school and making a judgment about whether the current state is satisfactory. Implicit in the activity of making a judgment is the application of some standard of goodness. This involves a consideration of what is observed, in light of the standard applied, that results in a decision either to leave things as they are or to try and change them for the better. Engaging in this process is thus requisite to the development of a vision of what might be both possible and better in a particular school situation.

Given the desire to pursue some more desirable alternative, relative to what is observed in the present, the principal must then act to realize those objectives. He or she must articulate the vision to others, and must then move others to action aimed at achieving or at least working toward the desired state. Because the school setting is essentially a social situation, the principal's primary means of influencing what happens in a school is to work with and through teachers and others. "Interpersonal competence" thus is central to articulating one's vision to others and influencing others to act on that vision (Argyris, 1962).

Interpersonal Competence

The daily work of the principal is characterized by a seemingly endless series of brief interpersonal encounters and exchanges with students, teachers, parents, superiors, and others (Peterson, 1978). To paraphrase a recent study of principals, "talk is the work" (Gronn, 1983). The medium of the work is verbal, and the work involves frequent face-to-face interaction (Wolcott, 1973). The social order negotiated by the principal is highly complex and often is characterized by competing norms and expectations, and it is not unusual that misunderstandings, conflict, and miscommunication occur (Dwyer, 1984; Dwyer et al., 1985; Lortie, Crow, and Prolman, 1983; Morris et al., 1981).

Interpersonal competence refers to the knowledge and skills that enable an individual to shape the responses he or she gets from others (Foote and Cottrell, 1955; Argyris, 1962). In an extension of that idea, Weinstein (1969) conceptualizes interpersonal competence as the interrelation of ten basic elements:

Interpersonal task—The response one actor is intending to elicit from another
Interpersonal competence—Being able to achieve interpersonal tasks
Lines of action—What one actor actually does to elicit a desired task response from another
Encounter—Any contact between people that involves an interpersonal task by at least one party to the exchange
Situation—All the potentially meaningful stimuli present in an encounter
Defining the situation—The process by which participants in an encounter select and organize situational stimuli into a coherent understanding of what is actually occurring during an encounter
Projected definition of the situation—These are lines of action by one actor intended to influence another actor's definition of the situation
Working consensus—This is the definition of the situation to which participants in the encounter jointly subscribe

Situational identity—All relevant situational characteristics determining who the
actors are and what they represent to one another

Identity bargaining—The process by which actors influence their own or each
other's situational identity [Pp. 754–58]

The last concept, that of identity bargaining, is pivotal (Weinstein, 1969, p.
757). Identity bargaining is the process through which one shapes the
situational identity projected and maintained for one's self and for others,
and it is this situational identity that determines one's ability to influence
another; that is, to get the desired response. The challenge for the principal is
to develop a working consensus among teachers as to what the situation is
and what needs to be done given that definition of the situation.

Critical to successful identity bargaining is the ability of the principal to
take the role of the other and to predict the effect of certain actions on the
other. Being able to establish and maintain an identity that will enable one to
successfully influence another requires the ability to view and understand the
situation from the other's perspective (Goffman, 1959). This is what enables
a principal to determine which lines of action will be most effective in
eliciting the desired response. Being able to successfully influence a teacher
thus depends to a large degree upon being familiar with an extensive set of
possible actions.

School contexts differ, and what is possible in one setting may not be
possible in another. A school in a relatively homogeneous rural farming
community, with stable student enrollment and low faculty turnover, represents conditions different in many respects from those one might find in an
inner-city school populated by poor children and characterized by high
turnover among both students and faculty. They each represent somewhat
different potentials for what might be achieved instructionally and for
organizational arrangements. Similarly, all teachers are not the same, and
each will differ to some extent in how he or she defines a given school or
classroom situation and in his or her resources, such as certain knowledge,
skills, or attitudes. What works with one teacher in a given situation may not
be effective in another situation, or with a different teacher.

Being interpersonally competent therefore requires that one possess a
fairly extensive set of possible actions. Thus the idea of being interpersonally
competent as a principal not only implies a good deal of familiarity with the
work of teachers, but also requires that the principal be knowledgeable about
teachers' views of themselves, their students and colleagues, and their work.

To summarize the discussion to this point, two major ideas have been
suggested as the cornerstones of effective school administration. The ability
to exercise moral imagination underlies one's capacity to develop a compelling vision of what is possible and desirable to achieve in a given school
situation, vis-à-vis more effective instructional practices and organizational

arrangements. "Interpersonal competence," the ability to elicit desired task responses from another, refers to the knowledge and skills needed to influence teachers and others in desired directions.

In each instance a judgment must be made. One must apply some standard of goodness as the basis for choosing a course of action. The chosen course of action may be aimed at eliciting a desired task behavior from someone in the immediate situation, such as influencing a teacher to experiment with an alternative method of instruction or another way to manage student behavior. On a larger scale, it may be aimed at cultivating or maintaining a more encompassing vision of what is possible and desirable in a given school, vis-à-vis organizational and subgroup norms and practices associated with effective instruction, improved school-community relations, or other activities or outcomes. In both cases, standards of goodness are applied and a judgment is made.

Neither the exercise of moral imagination nor being interpersonally competent occurs in a contextual vacuum. In both cases one is constrained by and must be sensitive to the realities and the limits characterizing a particular school, a group of students, or a particular teacher or group of teachers. The exercise of moral imagination thus is the ability to see the discrepancy between how things are and how they might be—*not* in terms of the ideal, but in terms of *what is possible* given a particular individual, group, or school situation.

In order to administer a school well, it is proposed that one must have a vision of what is desirable and possible in that school's context, and that one must also be able to mobilize others to work to achieve those possibilities. Administering a school well thus requires that one be knowledgeable about and committed to the standards of good educational practice and that one be interpersonally competent and able to articulate those possibilities to others, and thereby able to move others to action to work toward those goals.

Developing Interpersonal Competence and a Capacity for Exercising Moral Imagination

How do school administrators become interpersonally competent, and how do they develop their capacity to exercise moral imagination? If, indeed, these two personal qualities are antecedent to one's ability to manage and lead a school well, can the development of these qualities be guided or cultivated by a school district or by a professional preparation program in educational administration? I believe that the second question can be answered affirmatively, and that knowing how to cultivate these two personal qualities depends upon answering the first question—how are these qualities developed, and by what processes? Socialization theory offers a number of useful ideas and serves as a general framework guiding the discussion to follow.

Socialization refers to the processes and conditions that mediate the acquisition of knowledge, skills, beliefs, and personal dispositions required to perform a given role satisfactorily (Brim and Wheeler, 1966). This occurs through formal and informal processes. *Formal processes* refer to role-learning situations in which both the role of the learner and the material to be learned are specified in advance. One example is a professional preparation program designed to train and develop prospective school administrators. Another example is found in staff development programs and in-service education activities sponsored by school districts and professional associations.

Informal socialization processes refer to those in which neither the role of the learner nor the material to be learned are specified. One example is the process encountered by a newcomer to the school setting. Although neither the "learner" role nor the "lessons to be learned" are formally specified in advance, the rookie teacher quickly learns the "do's" and "don'ts" of what it means to be a teacher in that school. The informal group norms are passed on fairly quickly by the "old hands," and the "rookie" who deviates from those norms is likely to experience difficulty in gaining acceptance by the group. Another example is the informal learning that occurs as one makes the transition from teaching to administration. Upwardly mobile teachers take on more and more of the values and orientations of the administration group, and they begin to develop administrative skills and values as they engage in administrative activities and interact more frequently with administrators (Greenfield, 1985a). In both cases the learner role and the material to be learned are not clearly specified—yet much role-relevant learning occurs nevertheless.

In addition to these formal and informal role-learning processes, socialization theory points to important variations in the "content" to be learned. Socialization outcomes can be characterized as moral or technical (Bidwell, 1965). *Moral outcomes* are the sentiments, beliefs, standards of practice, and value orientations characterizing the reference group in which one holds or seeks membership. *Technical outcomes* are the instrumental knowledge and skills required to satisfactorily perform tasks associated with a given role or status.

Moral and technical learning outcomes can be influenced by formal as well as informal socialization processes. In educational administration, as in many other fields of practice, efforts to develop the capabilities of prospective practitioners tend to emphasize technical knowledge and skills, and depend primarily upon formal rather than informal processes. However, moral socialization outcomes generally receive little explicit attention through formal processes, and thus the development of beliefs, values, and role-relevant sentiments and personal dispositions tends to occur informally in school

Socialization Outcomes

	Technical	**Moral**
	Cell I:	Cell II:
Formal	Technical knowledge and skills in preparation programs	Codes of ethics
	Workshops sponsored by professional associations	National reports on excellence and reform
	Staff development activities in school districts	Standards of practice promoted by professional associations
	Administrative internships	Case studies, simulations, role-playing and modeling focused on values and standards

Socialization Processes

	Cell III:	Cell IV:
	Learning the ropes (the tasks)	Learning the ropes (the group's norms)
Informal	Sponsor-protege relationships	Aspiring to become an administrator
	Engaging in administrative duties	Associating with administrators
	Committee assignments at the school and district level	Resolving value conflicts

Figure 18–1

**Influences Shaping Socialization Processes and Outcomes in
Educational Administration**

(Based on Brim and Wheeler, 1966).

settings. As a result, what one learns is highly variable and depends upon the character of the individuals with whom one associates, what kind of work one does, and the culture that characterizes a particular work group or school setting (Greenfield, 1985b).

Four basic relationships describe the conditions that influence the socialization of school administrators, and these are depicted in Table 18–1 as the interaction between the nature of the material to be learned (moral and technical) and the processes by which such learning occurs (formal and informal). Cell I represents the current focus of formal efforts to help school administrators acquire the technical knowledge and skills needed to perform administrative tasks and duties. The examples reflected in this cell are illustrative of the kinds of formal activities employed to influence the technical role-learning of administrators. Cell II suggests potential sources of formal moral development, but tends not to be fully exploited in current practice; the formal learning that occurs is likely to be rather limited in scope and rarely is an explicit socialization target in either graduate programs or in-service programs.

Cells III and IV represent informal "on-the-job" learning opportunities, with technical knowledge and skill being the focus in Cell III, and group norms, individual values, and standards of practice being the focus in Cell IV. These two cells represent the most complex learning conditions for two reasons. First, the material itself is not formally specified. What is learned comes through informal association with others and as a result of doing particular tasks. Second, in actual practice there is often a moral dimension to the technical skill or knowledge to be acquired. In other words, some techniques or ways of doing things are preferred over others. They may or may not be more effective in an empirical sense, but they frequently are assumed to be effective, and they almost always are viewed as "appropriate" or "better" than another alternative. This may occur for several reasons. The emphasis on some skills, but not others, and the value attributed to some facts, and not others, may be influenced by various elements: a school's history and its immediate context; the culture of the work group; the values and disposition of influentials in the setting; traditions within the community; and perhaps the reality that a given practice works—or at least appears to given the criteria applied by the actors involved.

The preceding discussion identified formal and informal processes by which the development of moral imagination and interpersonal competence are believed to occur. The framework depicted in Figure 18–1 suggests that the knowledge and skills requisite to developing and articulating a vision of desirable instructional and organizational arrangements in a school have both a technical and a moral component, and to the extent that one develops the knowledge, skills, and attitudes requisite to the exercise of moral imagination and interpersonal competence, those personal qualities currently tend to be learned informally rather than deliberately.

Implications for Administrator Preparation

The school is a normatively complex and ambiguous organizational setting wherein one encounters numerous moral dilemmas. A principal is regularly confronted by the necessity to take action or make a decision in the face of competing and often conflicting standards of goodness; hence the importance of the ability to exercise moral imagination. Further, the school situation is essentially social, and if the principal is to influence instructional and organizational arrangements, he or she is constrained by the necessity to work closely with and through people; hence the importance of being interpersonally competent. The discussion to follow suggests that the two personal qualities of moral imagination and interpersonal competence can be deliberately developed and cultivated, and that graduate preparation and staff development and in-service programs *can* be more effective than they currently are in helping school administrators develop these qualities.

Developing Moral Imagination

Moral imagination requires technical skills in observation and analysis as well as formal knowledge about alternative standards of good practice—the criteria by which one judges the desirabililty of a given situation, relative to what is possible. The technical skills of observation, data collection, and analysis could be the focus of formal learning activities in Cell I, and proficiency would be fairly easy to determine. Standards of good practice, the criteria applied in the process of determining the value of alternatives and judging which alternative is to be preferred, would be the province of formal learning in Cell II. An individual's knowledge of standards (normative as well as empirical) and skills in developing and defending competing arguments related to those standards could be assessed rather easily through oral or written examination, or perhaps through evaluation of a number of short "position papers" or "cases" written or analyzed by the candidate.

I do not suggest that prospective or practicing administrators be indoctrinated, but rather they be deliberately introduced to competing empirical and normative standards of effective practice and provided with formally designed opportunities to apply those standards in simulated conditions: to practice resolving value conflicts; to engage in discussions of standards; and to prepare defenses of the relative merits of one standard of practice or line of action over another. In short, formal moral socialization efforts (Cell II) would attempt to assure that prospective school administrators become informed of competing standards of good practice and that they have opportunities to practice making and defending the decisions or actions they believe would be most desirable in given situations.

Administering and leading a school requires acting and deciding, and doing so involves reliance on both moral and technical knowledge and skill. I propose that providing administrators with deliberately conceived opportunities to acquire and use knowledge about competing standards of good and effective practice will increase their capacity to exercise moral imagination, and will increase the likelihood that they will be able to manage and lead a school well.

Developing Interpersonal Competence

How do school administrators develop interpersonal competence? As depicted in Cells III and IV, the dominant mode occurs informally, although it is true that limited opportunities exist in some preparation programs and through some in-service programs (workshops in conflict management, communications, group dynamics, and interpersonal skill development, for example). However, those formal opportunities that do exist are for the most part found in only a few preparation and in-service programs, and the focus is likely to be limited to only the interpersonal *skill* dimension.

As described in the preceding section, interpersonal competence not only calls for certain skills, but also requires a great deal of formal and informal *knowledge* about the work activities and perspectives of the person whom one desires to influence. Thus, to be interpersonally competent as a school administrator, one needs certain skills as well as a great deal of *knowledge* about teachers, the teaching task, and teachers' views of themselves, their students, and their work. A substantial formal knowledge base exists for all these areas (Wittrock, 1986), and much could be done through Cell-I types of activities to introduce individuals to this knowledge and to provide them with opportunities to practice using that knowledge *and* the related interpersonal skills.

While the centrality of interpersonal competence (skills *and* knowledge) to influencing others in a school setting may seem obvious, it is an aspect of the administrator's role that is largely unattended to by those concerned with understanding administrator effectiveness. This aspect of the work of school administrators requires critical skills and knowledge that are basically ignored by those most concerned with the selection, training, and continuing development of school administrators.

The discussion thus far has suggested several points of intervention through formal processes. It is also possible to intervene in informal processes, and to do so without reducing the special "potency" that accompanies such learning conditions. The key strategy available to school districts, which is where the bulk of the informal learning occurs, is to attend more carefully to the general conditions associated with the processes employed to recruit, select, and develop prospective and practicing administrators. Interventions might occur in several ways: by being sure that prospective administrators have many practice opportunities to make judgments about instructional and organizational arrangements and to work closely with teachers; by being sure that district and school expectations for administrator and teacher practices are clearly communicated and reinforced and that they reflect what is known empirically about effective practice; and by being sure that prospective leaders are exposed to good role models—those who have demonstrated their capacity to exercise moral imagination and interpersonal competence with teachers and others. The basic issue is not to "formalize" the informal, but rather to capitalize on what is known to occur informally by shaping and structuring the circumstances through which those learning processes unfold (Greenfield, 1984 and 1985b).

Implications for Research and School Improvement

The basic thesis explored thus far is that the school work setting presents an administrator with "situational givens" to which he or she must respond in order to act responsibly and effectively. It was suggested that one's capacity to respond appropriately to two pervasive aspects of the work setting—its largely social character and the competing standards of goodness to be evaluated in choosing among decision and action alternatives—is largely determined by one's capacity to exercise moral imagination and to be interpersonally competent. Finally, it was argued that these two personal qualities of the administrator are shaped, in varying degrees, by formal and informal socialization processes.

The discussion to follow proceeds on the assumption that there should be a direct relationship between the administrative knowledge, skills, and value orientations cultivated in preparation programs and the empirical and theoretical understanding of schools, the work of teachers and administrators, the process of school improvement, and the like that evolve from systematic study of those and related phenomena in education and the social sciences generally. The alternative explored next is proposed as an addendum to the traditional methods used by researchers in educational administration to generate understandings about schools and their administration. It is believed that more substantive understandings of the administrator's work world are needed, and that doing school-based research that teachers and administrators view as useful in addressing relevant problems of organizational, instructional, and administrative practice can contribute much to advancing administrator preparation, theory development, and the improvement of schools (Lawler et al., 1985).

Social behavior is the fundamental element in school organization and in the administration of schools. Researchers in education have emphasized study of the antecedents and consequences of social behavior in the work place (studies of organizational climate, organizational size and structure, and leader behavior, for example), but the methods and the targets of inquiry associated with most of the research in educational administration have not focused on the day-to-day social behavior of school participants in situ. Examples of several exceptions include the work of Waller, 1932; Becker, 1980; Cusick, 1973, 1983; Wolcott, 1973; Lortie, 1975; Blumberg and Greenfield, 1986; Morris et al., 1981; and Dwyer et al., 1985.

The research tradition in educational administration is somewhat analogous to the approach taken by the person who wants to understand the differences in technique between a gourmet chef and a good cook and proceeds by sampling and distinguishing among the various finished products those persons create. The issue here is that while one can distinguish the difference between the appearance or the taste of the dishes served, being able to differentiate such qualities tells one very little, perhaps nothing at all, about differences in the preparation or baking processes and techniques themselves. While the ingredients may be very similar, differences in the processes by which they are put together can result in very different outcomes. In educational administration we know something about manifest appearances and outcomes, but very little about the *social processes* underlying those results.

Social behavior in work settings can be studied in a variety of ways, ranging from close-up observation over extended periods of time to large-scale surveys that are cross-sectional or longitudinal in design. Direct observation is probably the most profitable source of basic descriptive explanations of social behavior, although it has the disadvantages of high personnel costs, few available researchers skilled in collecting and analyzing such data, and a high risk associated with producing something useful from a policy or scientific perspective. Despite these disadvantages, it is nevertheless important to employ such strategies if one expects to develop substantive descriptions and explanations of what actually occurs at the individual or group level in schools.

Understanding and description that meet the dual criteria of (1) being grounded in the everyday social reality of school life and (2) being informed by and contributing to the development of theories of practice are fundamental to advancing the knowledge base in educational administration. Theory grounded in the daily work of teachers, administrators, and other actors in the school setting is the necessary prerequisite to developing and testing useful hypotheses about administrative work, social processes in administration, the relation of setting to process variables, and the like. The discussion turns next to a brief exploration of the potential of action-research partnerships for the development of grounded theories of practice and effective strategies for school improvement.

Developing effective partnerships with school administrators and teachers has been difficult for those in universities, particularly when the primary goal of the university professor in seeking the partnership is access to school settings for scientific research purposes—research that often produces little of immediate benefit to the teachers and administrators in the partnership. Many schoolteachers and administrators view the research being done as too often having little or no practical use in solving the daily problems they face.

One research strategy that has not received much recent attention in educational administration, and which lends itself quite well both to the social phenomena to be studied and to the conditions under which they must be studied, is action research (Corey, 1953; Sanford, 1970; Clark, 1972; Clark, 1976; Susman and Evered, 1978). The roots of action research are deep, and while the ends of action research frequently are not reviewed as scientifically useful, this need not necessarily be the case. Applied research, and educational administration *is* an applied field of study and practice, has as its primary goal the systematic collection of information designed to solve applied problems. Within this tradition, action research is often viewed as more partisan in its orientation, with the aims of this particular strategy being actions, training, and decision making intended to bring about social change. Action research *can* be an effective strategy for accomplishing instructional and organizational improvement, although most school administrators are not equipped with the knowledge and skills needed to effectively employ such an approach. Organizational development, for example, is a change strategy that is specifically grounded in action research and has been successfully used as a school improvement strategy (Schmuck et al., 1985).

A potential strategy for departments of educational administration that could result in a more effective partnership between schools and research agencies, and in research that has both scientific and practical value, is to develop the capability and interest of administrators and teachers in action research at the local school site that is targeted to immediate problems of an applied nature. While many scholars do not view action research as "real" research in a scientific sense, there is no reason not to encourage such inquiry by public school educators—persons who *are* concerned with action, training, decision making, and social change. In fact, encouraging such research is likely to lead to better-informed and more effective actions and decisions than no research at all, and it is unlikely that even the most staunch traditionalist would argue against such consequences. The benefit to scientific researchers of encouraging and developing the capabilities of school practitioners to do problem-centered action research of immediate practical value is that it can provide applied and basic scientists with access to settings of interest and can build credibility and legitimacy for the related but different kind of research that is of interest to traditional scholars in educational administration. Also, the results of such research can provide organizational and administrative theorists with new insights about such processes and structures.

Developing a partnership whereby skilled action researchers work in liaison with school practitioners to develop their capability to engage in problem-centered research, to guide them regarding the collection and interpretation of data, and to advise them of the results of scientific research studies or social theories related to the particular problem being addressed has potential for all parties involved and could do much to help bridge the current chasm between the work of researchers and school practitioners.

From the perspective of the university-based researcher serving in such an advisory capacity, the benefits of such a contribution include long-term access to settings for scientific social research. Presently, a fundamental limitation of research aimed at describing and explaining social behavior in schools or the role of the school principal, for example, is that circumstances often permit only a cross-sectional glimpse of phenomena. The reality in schools is that the activities, behaviors, values, and attitudes of school participants, such as the school principal, unfold over time; events and actions have antecedents and consequences that cannot be understood in a week or two of observation or through a series of cross-sectional interviews or observations.

To summarize, the perspective offered above encourages researchers in educational administration to broaden their definition of what constitutes "useful inquiry," to focus more of their research on the work contexts and day-to-day social behavior of school participants, and to employ research strategies appropriate for investigating essentially *dynamic* phenomena. The related problems of obtaining long-term access to school settings and bridging the chasm between action and research on administrative and school problems were briefly discussed, and the potential of developing an action-research partnership was explored as a strategy that holds promise for generating scientifically useful knowledge and for promoting effective school improvement strategies based on problem-centered inquiry by teachers and administrators.

Conclusion

The purpose of this paper has been to call attention to the salience of the school work situation and its bearing on administrator effectiveness, to note the importance of the "fit" of school administrators' personal qualities with the demands of the work setting, and to suggest that it is possible to identify those qualities and to intervene in their development. Vision was noted as an important element in leading and managing a school, and moral imagination and interpersonal competence were discussed as lower-order qualities associated with the school administrator's ability to respond appropriately to the demands of the school work situation.

Several points of intervention were noted whereby school districts and professional preparation programs might influence the development of these and other personal qualities. The school was described as a socio-cultural situation in which school administrators must work with and through people, in a context of competing standards of goodness, to influence school programs and learning outcomes for students. It was noted that these realities of the administrator's work world have not been addressed to any great extent by researchers, and that a continued failure to study the work situation itself and to incorporate that knowledge in preparation programs and intervention strategies will mitigate efforts to understand or improve administrator effectiveness.

More attention by researchers to understanding the connections between the personal qualities of administrators and the demands of the school work situation promises to yield much useful knowledge about the work of school administrators and the nature of leadership in schools. Efforts by school districts and by professional preparation programs to intervene more deliberately in the processes by which administrators learn their roles promises the possibility of increasing their capability to be effective in leading and managing instruction.

This paper concludes with a call for action-research partnerships between school districts, universities, and national or regional research and development laboratories. Such partnerships promise the possibility of *problem-centered school-based research* that can (1) help school teachers and administrators solve pressing problems of practice, (2) enable school researchers to gain continuing access to school work settings, thereby permitting sustained observation and analysis of the social dynamics of day-to-day life in schools, and (3) foster the development of grounded theories of administrative and school practices that serve to inform both the preparation of school administrators and the development of the knowledge base in educational administration.

References

Achilles, C.M. (1987). A vision of better schools. In W. Greenfield (Ed.), *Instructional leadership: Concepts, issues, and controversies*, pp. 17–37. Boston: Allyn and Bacon.

Argyris, Chris (1962). *Interpersonal competence and organizational effectiveness*. Homewood, Ill: Dorsey Press.

Becker, H.S. (1964). Personal change in adult life. *Sociometry* 27 (1): 40–53.

Becker, H.S. (1980). *Role and career problems of the Chicago public school teacher*. New York: Arno Press.

Bidwell, C.E. (1965). The school as a formal organization. In J.G. March (Ed.), *Handbook of organizations*, pp. 972–1022. Chicago: Rand-McNally.

Blumberg, A., and Greenfield, W. (1980). *The effective principal*. Boston: Allyn and Bacon.

Blumberg, A., and Greenfield, W. (1986). *The effective principal*, 2d ed. Boston: Allyn and Bacon.

Bossert, S.; Dwyer, D.; Rowan, B.; and Lee, G. (1982). The instructional management role of the principal. *Educational Administration Quarterly* 18 (3): 34–64.

Bridges, E. (1982). Research on the school administrator: The state of the art, 1967–1980. *Educational Administration Quarterly* 18 (3): 12–33.

Brim, O.G. Jr., and Wheeler, S. (1966). *Socialization after childhood: Two essays*. New York: John Wiley and Sons.

Burlingame, M. (1979). Some neglected dimensions of the study of educational administration. *Educational Administration Quarterly* 15 (Winter): 1–18.

Burlingame, M. (1987). Images of leadership in effective schools literature. In W. Greenfield (Ed.), *Instructional leadership: Concepts, issues, and controversies*, pp. 3–16. Boston: Allyn and Bacon.

Byrne, D.; Hines, S.; and McCleary, L. (1978). *The senior high school principalship: Vol. 1*. Reston, Va.: National Association of Secondary School Principals.

Clark, A.W. (1976). *Experimenting with organizational life*. New York: Plenum Press.

Clark, P.A. (1972). *Action research and organizational change*. New York: Harper and Row.

Coladarci, A.P., and Getzels, J.W. (1955). *The use of theory in educational administration*. Stanford, Calif.: Stanford University Press.

Corey, S.M. (1953). *Action research to improve school practices*. New York: Teachers College, Columbia University.

Cuban, L. (1984). Transforming the frog into a prince: Effective schools research, policy, and practice at the district level. *Harvard Educational Review* 54(2): 129–51.

Cusick, P. (1973). *Inside high school*. New York: Holt, Rinehart and Winston.

Cusick, P. (1983). *The egalitarian ideal and the American high school*. New York: Longman.

Deal, T. (1987). Effective school principals: Counselors, engineers, pawnbrokers, poets . . . or instructional leaders? In W. Greenfield (Ed.), *Instructional leadership: Concepts, issues, and controversies*, pp. 230–45. Boston: Allyn and Bacon.

DeBevoise, W. (1984). Synthesis of research on the principal as instructional leader. *Educational Leadership* 41(5): 14–20.

Dewey, J. (1957). *Human nature and conduct*. New York: Random House.

Dreeben, R. (1970). *The nature of teaching*. Glenview, Ill.: Scott, Foresman, and Co.

Dwyer, D. (1984). The search for instructional leadership: Routine and subtleties in the principal's role. *Educational Leadership* 41 (5): 32–37.

Dwyer, D.C.; Lee, G.V.; Barnett, B.G.; Filby, N.N.; Rowan, B.; and Kojimoto, C. (1985). *Understanding the principal's contribution to instruction: Seven principals, seven stories*. Volumes 1–8. San Francisco: Far West Laboratory for Research and Development.

Dwyer, D.; Lee, G.; Rowan, B.; and Bossert, S. (1983). *Five principals in action: Perspectives on instructional management*. San Francisco, Calif.: Far West Laboratory for Educational Research and Development.

Dwyer, D., and Smith, L. (1987). The principal as explanation of school change: An incomplete story. In W. Greenfield (Ed.), *Instructional leadership: Concepts, issues, and controversies*, pp. 155–78. Boston: Allyn and Bacon.

Edmonds, R. (1982). *Programs of school improvement: A 1982 overview*. Unpublished manuscript, Michigan State University, School of Education, Lansing.

Foote, M., and Cottrell, L. (1955). *Identity and interpersonal competence*. Chicago: University of Chicago Press.

Foskett, J. (1967). *The normative world of the elementary school principal*. Eugene, Oregon: The Center for the Advanced Study of Educational Administration.

Goffman, E. (1959). *The presentation of self in everyday life*. Garden City: Doubleday and Company.

Goldhammer, K.; Becker, G.; Withycombe, R.; Doyel, F.; Miller, E.; Morgan, C.; DeLoretto, L.; and Aldridge, B. (1971). *Elementary school principals and their schools: Beacons of brilliance and potholes of pestilence*. Eugene, Oregon: Center for the Advanced Study of Educational Administration.

Gorton, R., and McIntyre, K. (1978). *The senior high school principalship: Vol. 2.* Reston, Va: National Association of Secondary School Principals.

Goslin, D. (1965). *The school in contemporary society.* Glenview, Ill.: Scott, Foresman, and Co.

Green, T. (1984). *The formation of conscience in an age of technology.* Syracuse, New York: The John Dewey Society.

Greenfield, W.D. (1982). *Empirical research on principals: The state of the art.* Paper presented at the American Educational Research Association annual meeting, New York City.

Greenfield, W.D. (1984). *Sociological perspectives for research on educational administration: The role of the assistant principal.* Paper presented at the American Educational Research Association annual meeting, New Orleans.

Greenfield, W.D. (1985a). *Being and becoming a principal: Responses to work contexts and socialization processes.* Paper presented at the American Educational Research Association annual meeting, Chicago.

Greenfield, W.D. (1985b). The moral socialization of school administrators: Informal role learning outcomes. *Educational Administration Quarterly* 21 (4): 99–120.

Greenfield, W. (1986). Moral, social and technical dimensions of the principalship. *Peabody Journal of Education* 63 (1): 130–49.

Greenfield, W. (Ed.). (1987). *Instructional leadership: Concepts, issues, and controversies.* Boston: Allyn and Bacon.

Griffiths, D.E. (1959). *Administrative theory.* New York: Appleton-Century Crofts.

Gronn, P.C. (1983). Talk as the work: The accomplishment of school administration. *Administrative Science Quarterly* 28 (1): 1–21.

Jackson, P.W. (1968). *Life in classrooms.* New York: Holt, Rinehart and Winston.

Lawler, E.E.; Mohrman, A.M.; Mohrman, S.A.; Ledford, G.E.; Cummings, T.G.; and associates (1985). *Doing research that is useful for theory and practice.* San Francisco: Jossey-Bass.

Lewin, K. (1951). Frontiers in group dynamics. In D. Cartwright (Ed.), *Field theory in social science: Selected theoretical papers.* New York: Harper and Row.

Little, J.W. (1982). Norms of collegiality and experimentation: Workplace conditions of school success. *American Educational Research Journal* 19 (3): 325–40.

Little, J.W., and Bird, T. (1987). Instructional leadership close to the classroom in secondary schools. In W. Greenfield (Ed.), *Instructional leadership: concepts, issues, and controversies,* pp. 118–38. Boston: Allyn and Bacon.

Lortie, D.C. (1975). *Schoolteacher: A sociological study.* Chicago: University of Chicago Press.

Lortie, D.C.; Crow, G.; and Prolman, S. (1983). *The elementary school principal in suburbia: An occupational and organizational study.* (Contract No. 400-77-0094). Washington, D.C.: National Institute of Education.

Manasse, A.L. (1985). Improving conditions for principal effectivenes: Policy implications of research. *The Elementary School Journal* 85 (3): 439–63.

Martin, W.J., and Willower, D.J. (1981). The managerial behavior of high school principals. *Educational Administration Quarterly* 17 (1): 69–70.

Morris, V.; Crowson, R.; Hurwitz, E.; and Porter-Gehrie, C. (1981). *The urban principal: Discretionary decision-making in a large educational organization.* Chicago: University of Illinois at Chicago Circle.

Peterson, K. (1978). The principal's tasks. *Administrator's Notebook* 26 (8): 1–4.

Sanford, N. (1970). What ever happened to action research? *Journal of Social Issues* 26: 3–23.

Sarason, S.B. (1971). *The culture of the school and the problem of change.* Boston: Allyn and Bacon.

Sarason, S.B., and Klaber, M. (1985). The school as a social situation. *Annual Review of Psychology* 36: 115–40.

Schein, E.H. (1978). *Career dynamics: Matching individual and organizational needs.* Menlo Park, Calif.: Addison-Wesley.

Schmuck. R.A.; Runkel, P.J.; Arends, J.H.; and Arends, R.I. (1985). *The third handbook of organizational development in schools,* 3rd ed. Palo Alto, Calif.: Mayfield Publishing Company.

Schrag, F. (1979). The principal as a moral actor. In D.A. Erickson and T.L. Reller (Eds.) *The principal in metropolitan schools,* pp. 208–32. Berkeley, Calif.: McCutchan Publishing.

Sergiovanni, T.J., and Corbally, J.E. (Eds.). (1984). *Leadership and organizational culture.* Urbana: University of Illinois Press.

Simon, H.A. (1957). *Administrative behavior* (2d ed.). New York: The Free Press.

Strother, D.B. (Ed.). (1983). *The role of the principal.* Bloomington, Indiana: Phi Delta Kappan.

Susman, G.I., and Evered, R.D. (1978). An assessment of the scientific merit of action research. *Administrative Science Quarterly* 23 (4): 582–603.

Waller, W.W. (1932). *Sociology of teaching.* New York: John Wiley.

Weick, K. (1976). Educational organizations as loosely-coupled systems. *Administrative Science Quarterly* 21 (1): 1–19.

Weinstein, E., (1969). The development of interpersonal competence. In D. Goslin (Ed.), *The handbook of socialization theory and research,* pp. 753–75. Chicago: Rand-McNally.

Wiles, D.K.; Wiles, J.; and Bondi, J. (1981). *Practical politics for school administrators.* Boston: Allyn and Bacon.

Willower, D.J., and Kmetz, J.T. (1982). *The managerial behavior of elementary school principals.* Paper presented at the American Educational Research Association annual meeting, New York City.

Wittrock, M.C. (Ed.). (1986). *Handbook of research on teaching.* 3rd. ed. Riverside, N.J.: Macmillan.

Wolcott, H.F. (1973). *The man in the principal's office: An ethnography,* New York: Holt, Rinehart and Winston.

19

Computers and Educational Excellence: Policy Implications for Educational Administration

Muriel Mackett, Frederick Frank, Peter Abrams, and Jeri Nowakowski

Computers have become part of everyday life in much of modern society, revolutionizing our abilities to access, use, exchange, and manage information. Computer applications such as word processing, communications links, data management, record keeping, and graphics can be found in virtually every setting — education, business and industry, the social services, government, the military, and home and community. Robotics, computer optics, interactive video, and other high-technology computer applications also are developing rapidly. The ability of individuals to be fully employed and to otherwise participate productively in modern society is becoming more and more tied to computer literacy and skills. The power and pervasiveness of computers make them a driving educational, political, economic, and social force (Beam, 1986; Logan, 1986; National Task Force on Educational Technology [NTFET], 1986).

This raises a number of fundamental policy questions related to educational excellence that our society should address. What should our schools teach about computers? How can computers be used to improve delivery of instruction and other student services? How can computers be used to manage schools more effectively? How should schooling be redefined as computers extend the instructional process far beyond school walls? (Culbertson and Cunningham, 1986; NTFET, 1986) The educational community must redouble its efforts to address these questions thoughtfully and systematically if the schools are to keep pace with society's needs.

It is particularly fitting for educational administrators to assume a leadership role in addressing such policy questions, because computer use bears directly on the effectiveness of the entire educational enterprise. Computers are not only extending and enriching the learning experience and creating new options for instruction and service delivery (Bork, 1987; Kinzer, Sherwood, and Bransford, 1986). They are also putting in the hands of educational administrators more-sophisticated and powerful tools for managing the educational process (Bruno, 1986; Caffarella, 1985; Frank, Mackett, Abrams, and Nowakowski, 1986; Lotus Books [TM], 1984).[1]

The recommendations offered here to guide the educational leadership effort called for by the computer revolution deal with (1) optimizing computer use; (2) understanding possible computer applications; (3) addressing key policy issues related to accountability; and (4) instituting appropriate training programs for administrators. Each recommendation is followed by a brief supporting discussion and a statement of implied imperatives for the field of educational administration.

The Field of Educational Administration Should Initiate a Systematic, Nationwide Effort to Develop a Long-Range Plan for Optimizing the Use of Computers in Education

The field of educational administration should begin to view development and application of computer technology in education as a compelling responsibility for both the present and the future. Although there is much evidence of computer use throughout education, the scale of computer applications in the field is far too small and the range far too limited relative to the potential (Crawford, 1985a, 1985b; NTFET, 1986; Silverman, 1986). The intensity of computer-related activity in the field, however, suggests that progress is being made in the productive use of computers in education.

For example, The United States Department of Education has recently called for a "radical restructuring" of its educational information system (Mirga, 1986, p.1). In addition, the nation's chief state school officers have

---

[1] Lotus Books (TM) is a registered trademark of Lotus Development Corporation, 55 Cambridge Parkway, Cambridge, Massachusetts 02142.

undertaken efforts to " . . . conduct rigorous assessments of their policies and their students' educational progress" (Sirkin, 1985, p.1). Although not limited to computer-based data systems, such efforts will need to rely heavily on computer technology for maximum productivity and cost effectiveness.

More directly related to the educational process, a national task force commissioned by the United States Department of Education has recently released a report on ". . . the integration of appropriately integrated technology to improve learning in our nation's schools" (NTFET, 1986, p.1). The National Governors' Association also has released a report stating that now is the "time for results" in American education (Alexander, 1986; Nathan, 1986; National Governors' Association Center for Policy Research and Analysis [NGACPRA], 1986). Both of these reports contain major recommendations for the better use of computers in educational improvement.

Further, a number of educators and public-policy makers are currently working to develop more sophisticated information systems for educational management and to make possible the expansion of computer networking technologies to link students, staff, schools, curriculum resources, and information bases across the country and internationally. The goal of such efforts is to foster educational excellence and consequent social benefits (Frank, Mackett, Abrams, and Nowakowski, 1986; Montague, 1986; Snider, 1986a). Finally, it should be clear to even the most casual observer that the field of education is virtually exploding with all manner of curriculum materials, scholarly and technical publications, courseware and other software, and informal communications, all dealing in some fashion with computer use in the schools.

But in spite of the high level of attention and energy being devoted to educational computing, a clearly articulated leadership effort to shape computer policy and practice has not yet emerged. In short, there has not yet been a systematic, nationwide effort to consider policy, implementation, and professional training needs related to optimizing the use of computers in the curriculum, instruction, and management; for increasing educational opportunity; or for the broad purposes of educational reform. This is an essential and timely undertaking.

The past two decades have produced dramatic developments in computer technology. Among the most important changes is that the architecture of the microcomputer and associated software support a far more "user-friendly" environment, which permits users who are comparative beginners to computing to accomplish far more and different things with a microcomputer than they could with a mainframe. Worthy of note was the appearance in 1986 of the Intel (TM)[2] 32-bit 80386 microprocessor, which, at a mini-

---

[2] Intel (TM) is a registered trademark of Intel Corporation, 5200 NE Elam Young, Building TOD, Hillsboro, Oregon 97124.

mum, doubles the capacity of desktop microcomputer's and rivals the capacity of many mainframes of just a decade ago (Petzold, 1986). Coming decades, moving well into the twenty-first century, should produce even more elaborate and sophisticated computer technologies and applications that will have the potential for making a much broader impact on how schooling content and processes can be conceived, delivered, and managed.

Because the potential of computers to promote change is so great, they can increase substantially the administrator's ability to play an important role in improving educational programs. Expanded use of these technologies, especially more systematic and intensive applications of these technologies to curriculum, instruction, and educational management, will also enable educators to individualize educational interventions, monitor individual student achievement, and, as a result, be more accountable for the effectiveness and equity of educational experiences (NGACPRA, 1986; NTFET, 1986).

Two sets of cautions, however, apply to this and the following recommendations. First, computer technologies are not a panacea. They can, however, help educators to solve or to do a better job of coping with both old and new educational problems. We should expect neither too much nor too little of these technologies, and we should acknowledge the continuing importance of craft wisdom, intellect, values, socialization, and professional experience to educational excellence. In the immediate future many elements of the school culture may be touched only peripherally by computer technologies. Ultimately, however, the most important contributions of computer technology will likely be to help students learn and to help teachers, administrators, and other educational leaders access and use good information to sustain student achievement and support the school culture within the modern school organization (Bolman and Deal, 1984; NTFET, 1986).

Second, if computer technologies are to achieve their potential to contribute to educational excellence, a fundamental shift in thinking about the training of educational leaders and the practice of administration will need to occur. Briefly, administrator preparation has been built on two basic approaches: study and application of the "craft wisdom" (Blumberg, 1984) of the field and, more recently, study and application of content from the "theory movement" (Sander and Wiggins, 1985). The shift that must now occur is to include the study and application of computer technology as an ongoing part of educational management. Computer technology represents a third generative branch on which to base future administrator preparation and practice.

The implied imperative for the field of educational administration is to understand the central role of computers in society and their power to improve education; to sort out what computers can and cannot be expected to help accomplish, now and in the future, in the curriculum, in instruction, and in management; and to understand as well the broad implications of computer technology for administrative preparation and practice.

The Field of Educational Administration Should Undertake Data-Based Planning to Determine the Kinds of Computer Applications in the Curriculum, in Instruction, and in Educational Management That Can Improve the Educational Process and Be Supported by Current and Emerging Computer Technologies

The primary applications of virtually all currently available computer technologies involve access, use, exchange, and management of information for educational purposes. While the extent of the use of computer technology varies widely from classroom to classroom and from school to school, computer applications in the curriculum, in instruction, and in management are evident across the nation.

The computer technologies currently available to support educational applications parallel those in general use, including mainframe and mini-computer hardware and software, the microcomputer (personal computer), user-friendly microcomputer software, local and remote computer networking, and other emerging technologies such as interactive video. It is evident, however, that the full potential of this technology for educational applications has far from been achieved in the curriculum, in instruction, or in management. This is due chiefly to lack of adequate training of professional and support staff, lack of standards in the field for equipment compatibility and software to support educational needs, and lack of resources to support computer purchase and use (NTFET, 1986).

New hardware and software computer technologies also will present unique challenges for supporting educational computer applications. Although it is difficult to speculate what new technology might be available twenty, ten, or even five years hence, current trends point to developments that will vastly expand current capabilities to access, use, exchange, and manage information for educational purposes and to promote the proliferation of producers, applications, and users of computer technology in education and throughout society (Logan, 1986). Major emerging development evident throughout the marketplace and in the trade literature include:

— Greater *accessibility of equipment* through reduced cost, reduced size, greater portability, and greater compatability of hardware and software.
— More *powerful equipment* through expanded memory and data storage and retrieval, increased speed of operation, expanded local and site-to-site

remote networking, and increasingly sophisticated software packages, including graphics.
— More *flexible equipment* through simplified computer programming languages and more *flexible use of equipment* through the creation and adaptation of software at the local level.

The unrealized potential in education of currently available technology, together with these emerging revolutionary developments in computer hardware and software, suggest that a much broader range of curricular, instructional and educational management applications of computer technology can and should be supported.

Curriculum and Instruction

The chief application of computers in the curriculum and in instruction and other educational services has been computer-assisted instruction (CAI) (Becker, 1982; Tobias, 1985), which often uses microcomputers as stand-alone systems in conjunction with prepackaged or specially developed software designed to meet specific curricular or other educational objectives. Information libraries and data banks such as CompuServe (R)[3] and The Source (SM)[4], accessible through phone lines or microwave transmissions, and adaptive computing for handicapped populations (Snider, 1986b) also are playing increasingly important roles in curricular and instructional computer applications. New curricular applications in reading, language arts, mathematics, and science also are proliferating in the nation's schools (Bork, 1987; Neill, 1986; Pogrow, 1985b; Sununu, 1986). Currently, however, there are few instances where curricular and instructional computer applications are systematically articulated across the K–12 curriculum. All of those kinds of applications tend to focus on the student as the primary user, rely more on materials that are prepackaged rather than specifically tailored to support local instructional objectives, and involve different degrees of classroom-, building-, or district-level coordination, depending upon local needs or preferences.

Current and emerging computer technologies allow greatly expanded curricular and instructional applications, including opportunities for students to learn about computers and computer applications in the curriculum and to learn other curricular content by using computers in the instructional

---

[3] CompuServe (R) is a registered trademark of CompuServe, Incorporated, 5000 Arlington Center Boulevard, Columbus, Ohio 43220.
[4] The Source (SM) is a registered trademark of Source Telecomputing Corporation, 1616 Anderson Road, McLean, Virginia 22102.

process (Hawkins and Sheingold, 1986; Walker, 1986). Because of computer networking and applications such as interactive video, more communication is now possible between students, teachers, and administrators within schools and at different school sites. In these applications, the computer extends the educational process and exposes students and professional colleagues to a much wider range of thinking, learning activities, teaching strategies, curricula and curricular materials, instructional management strategies, and research findings.

Students and teachers can also expand their access to current information and updated print materials through a growing number of computer libraries and electronic bulletin boards and increasing capabilities to up- and download information from more powerful computers to less powerful ones. This allows teachers and administrators to play a much more active role in developing computer-based instructional materials suited to specific, locally defined learning objectives or learner capabilities. This also promotes wide sharing and testing of materials and development of "best practice" models. Through microcomputers and corresponding software, much greater individualization of instruction is possible, including the capability to better match students' learning needs with support materials. This expands learning opportunities in virtually all curricular areas for all categories of students, including gifted and talented, regular education, handicapped, and disadvantaged students (Sununu, 1986; Tobias, 1985).

As computer technologies proliferate, mature, and decrease in cost, these kinds of applications will become more widely feasible, allowing computer-related communication across states and nations, contact with politically and culturally diverse populations, and access for learners who for whatever reason do not or cannot attend school. Because of advances in computer technology, we are now closer than ever before to being able to consider new, nontraditional definitions of schooling in the public and private sectors. Schooling may soon be able to extend far beyond school walls with much greater quality and cost efficiency than has yet seemed possible. New frontiers are accessible. Educators, particularly educational leaders, will determine the degree and nature of our exploration.

Educational Management

For educational management, computer applications have focused largely on student and financial control tasks such as scheduling, record keeping, accounting, and budgeting (Pogrow, 1985a). Use of local, centrally controlled mainframe systems has tended to dominate management applications, although use of microcomputers as stand-alone systems is increasing very quickly, as is use of the local and remote networking capabilities of both mainframe and microcomputer systems. Microcomputer software designed for word processing, data-base management, file systems, spreadsheet functions, and statistical analysis of school data also are being applied more frequently to educational management. Typically, all of these kinds of management applications focus on the administrator as the primary user of the technology. They tend also to be directed toward providing information for fairly discrete management tasks and decisions rather than for integrated strategic planning for curriculum development and delivery of instruction and other services in the district (or other unit) as a whole.

As with curriculum and instruction, existing and emerging computer technologies allow greatly expanded educational management applications (Frank, Mackett, Abrams, and Nowakowski, 1986). As the most salient example, administrators can create and access much richer data banks about student and teacher performance and better integrate students, personnel, instructional, fiscal, and organizational information for decision making. The capability to tie these management areas together into integrated information systems is truly revolutionary and makes possible resource allocations and budgets that are more programmatically defensible. It is now possible for administrators to use these data banks and information systems to undertake more comprehensive strategic planning based on multiple, and more reliable and valid, measures of student and staff performance. With the microcomputer, virtually all of the computer aspects of this work can be done from the administrator's own office, and with much greater control than ever before over the kinds of information to be considered in planning. Administrators should therefore be able to better evaluate the learning environment and provide leadership for shaping that environment in ways that promote student achievement, quality of the educational experience, and educational equity (NTFET, 1986).

Again, as computer technologies and software proliferate, mature, and decrease in cost, these kinds of computer applications will become more feasible. It should soon be possible for educational administrators to create and access district, state, and national data banks to inform their thinking and provide a broader basis for testing, comparing, and improving educational processes and outcomes across the nation, and ultimately internationally. It is now possible for educational administrators to work toward these goals with an expanded repertoire of computer-based management tools and with more substantial assistance from increasing networks of peers and other experts. These new opportunities will require redefinition of traditional administrative roles and may well lead to new "information management" roles not previously defined (Mackett, Frank, Nowakowski, and Abrams, 1986). As with curriculum and instruction, management of schooling may soon be extended far beyond district boundaries, with much greater benefit and cost efficiency than has yet seemed possible.

The implied imperative for the field of educational administration is to understand the vast potential for computer applications in the curriculum, in instruction, and in educational management and to develop in the field's cadre of preservice and in-service administrators and in the professoriate those computer and other professional skills necessary to provide leadership for these types of applications to flourish in the school and extended-school setting.

The Field of Educational Administration Should Address Key Policy Issues Related to Accountability for Effective Computer use in Education and to Appropriate Administrator Preparation to Support That Use

The great potential for computers to contribute to increased educational excellence suggests three major sets of policy issues that bear on the field of educational administration (Culbertson and Cunningham, 1986; Frank, Mackett, Nowakowski, and Abrams, 1986; Lieberman and McLaughlin, 1982). These issues are equal opportunity in accessing and benefiting from educational computer applications, the extent and character of government responsibility for computer applications, and privacy and autonomy related to the use of computer information.

The first of these issues, equal opportunity in accessing and benefiting from educational computer applications, applies to students in the educational system as well as to the society that supports that system. Unless educational systems put in place effective mechanisms to assure access to high-quality computer applications in the schools, then educational, economic, and social disparities will emerge between those who can afford them and those who cannot. Since educationally handicapped and disadvantaged students will tend to require a greater expenditure of resources to achieve access equal to that of other students, efforts to assure equity in computer use will also likely encourage intense competition for resources. Further, if curricular, instructional, or management use of computers in the schools unknowingly incorporates any systematic bias in the treatment of students or the images of people in society, then computers can become powerful tools for perpetuating bias and inequities within the educational system and in society (NGACPRA, 1986; NTFET, 1986; Sununu, 1986).

These possibilities point to a number of important policy questions. How can equal access to high-quality computer applications be assured? What level of public resources should be assigned to education technology development and access to that technology? How can education motivate product developers in the private sector to invest in quality computer applications for the vast education market? How can education influence the shape and content of computer applications to assure that a full range of high-quality products is available to meet the needs of *all* students, including special-needs students? Should education attempt to establish guidelines for equipment compatibility and software quality? What kinds of computer expertise should professional educators have, and what expertise should be drawn from the private sector? How can the effects of computer applications on different populations and in different domains of the educational process be evaluated?

Without educator involvement in the development of computer hardware and software, it will be virtually impossible—at any cost—for education to make optimal use of computer technology (Komoski, 1984). And without equity in computer access and benefits, computer applications in education—or the absence of them—will perpetuate inequity for those who have traditionally been disadvantaged.

The second policy issue, the extent and character of government responsibility for educational computer applications, applies to both individuals and individual educational units such as schools or districts and the choices each should have with respect to computer access and use in the school setting. The essential policy question is whether society has the right and responsibility to require that educational systems "turn out" people who are literate and skilled in computer use (Logan, 1986; NGACPRA, 1986; NTFET, 1986; Olson, 1986).

There are several dimensions to this issue. Should education about computers and computer use be required in all schools, public and private? Should minimum standards for computer literacy and use be set for all students and staff? Should standards be set at the state or local level? Should individual students, teachers, and administrators have the option *not* to be involved in computer use where it is available? Should schools and districts have this option? Should individual parents have the right to secure publicly supported computer access for their children when such access is not routinely available through the school or district? Should school or district leaders be empowered to obtain computer access when such access is not provided by the state? Further, since allowing or requiring access to computers in the schools must be tied to a substantially increased financial commitment to support computer applications in education, how should funding be provided?

Even though there are no clear or certain answers to the issues that fuel such questions, policy guidelines must be developed, particularly since these issues are fundamental to the rights of children to access educational programs and to the responsibilities of government to provide universal education in a democratic society. For instance, without some resolution of the issue of the government's responsibility in computer access and use, it is all but certain that schools will continue to seriously limit computer applications in the educational experience and to turn out students who may not be prepared to function in a technological and computer-oriented society (Olson, 1986). It should also be expected that any failure to resolve these issues will contribute to unequal educational opportunity and increase still further educational, economic, and social disparities for students who are at risk.

The third policy issue, privacy and autonomy related to computer information, has to do with the use and potential abuse of information that accompanies educational computer applications. Computer-based electronic information networks allow for vastly increased scope, exchange, and manipulation of information about individuals and the educational process, and this possibility also prompts a number of important policy questions (NGACPRA, 1986; NYFET, 1986; Rodman, 1986).

What information should educational policymakers and professional educators be able to access about students, teachers, administrators, the educational process, and educational outcomes? What information should students, parents, and the community be able to access about student and school performance? To what extent should teachers, administrators, and other professional staff be evaluated on the basis of student-performance data? Who should have the power to make these decisions? How should privacy of computer information be defined? What security measures need to be instituted to assure privacy? How can we assure that information will be used for the purposes for which it was collected? How can we assure that the information used to make educational decisions incorporates both computer-based and other information? Given the need for accountability, how can professional judgments be supported when they may seem to be contrary to a powerful but incomplete information base? How can we expand our ability to account for variance in educational outcomes?

As with the government responsibility issue described previously, there are at present no definitive answers to such policy questions. Without policy guidelines to assure that extensive computer (and other) information bases can be used productively and fairly—and to minimize the strong potential for intentional or unintentional abuse of this information—computer applications in education will not be developed to their fullest potential, and the benefits of applying the technology will be unnecessarily delayed.

The implied imperative for the field of educational administration is to understand the educational and social consequences of computer technology and to develop educational policies and practices that will optimize the effectiveness of computer applications for educational excellence and equal educational opportunity and minimize the risks of abuse or increasing inequity.

The Field of Educational Administration Should Institute Administrator Preparation Programs That Prepare Leaders to Optimize Use of Computers in Education as an Essential Part of Achieving Greater Educational Excellence

As computer applications in education mature, computers will make it far easier to include information as part of educational planning and decision making. Also, goals of schooling will expand to include accountability for computer literacy and skills. Curricula will broaden, and alternative organizational structures and delivery systems will emerge. Traditional teaching and administrative roles will be redefined. Computer communication capabilities will make it possible for students, teachers, and administrators to reach beyond the classroom to other local, regional, and ultimately national and international resources to carry out the schooling process.

In this broad context, then, what specific actions should the field of educational administration take to institute programs that will prepare administrators to provide leadership for computer use in education? In addition to the actions stated or implied in the three previous recommendations, two specific actions are indicated.

The Field of Educational Administration Should Undertake Data-Based Planning to Develop Computer Applications Content in Administrator Preparation Programs

There is much for administrators and professors to learn about computer applications in education (Clinton, 1986; Mackett et al., 1986). Content could be defined at the awareness level, the user or "hands on" level, and the problem-solving level so that administrators have the opportunity to learn about issues related to computer use and how computer technologies function, how to use the technology individually and with other people, and how to apply the technology to the educational process. At a minimum, administrators need to learn computer fundamentals (such as word processing), desktop publishing, software evaluation and adaptation, computer-supported curriculum content and instructional strategies, information-library access, spreadsheet and other data-management functions, statistical and other procedures for data analysis, and computer networking and communications. Ultimately, use of such applications as computer decision models and artificial intelligence also will need to be incorporated into administrator preparation programs (Johnson, 1986; Tanner and Holmes, 1985). The focus of this training should be on preparing administrators to integrate information for student and personnel, instructional, fiscal, and organizational decisions, drawing on local, state, and national data banks. As part of this effort, model programs should be developed and implications for certification and accreditation for educational administration (and other professional preparation) should be addressed.

The Field of Educational Administration Should Advocate Resource Mechanisms Designed to Assure That Appropriate Administrator Preparation in Computer Applications Can Occur

At present, requisite computer knowledge and skills are not incorporated into most preservice administrator preparation programs, in-service practitioner training, or in-service training for professors of educational administration. Thus, large-scale training efforts are called for immediately (Clinton, 1986; Mackett et al., 1986). The content and intensity of computer training for these three groups will need to be quite similar at first. As the current cadre of administrators and professors becomes trained, intensive efforts can be directed toward preservice administrators, while practicing administrators and professors will require periodic updates to keep pace with rapid product development and new applications. Some professors and advanced graduate students likely will move quickly into computer-related research and evaluation domains.

Clearly, the kind of training effort required to meet these needs far exceeds the available resources in public or private K–12 education or higher education. While some reallocation of existing funds may be possible, major efforts will need to be made to secure new funds to support equipment and training costs, as well as costs for students and teachers to use computers in the curriculum and in instruction. Whether these sources should be primarily public or private, target amounts and specific means to make these funds available should be considered as an integral part of implementing these recommendations (Levin, 1986; NTFET, 1986).

The implied imperative for the field of educational administration is to understand the complexity and immediacy of the need to provide high-quality preparation in computer applications in the curriculum, instruction, and management for the field's cadre of preservice and in-service administrators and the professoriate, to develop model programs, to support computer networking across district and state boundaries, and to advocate resource mechanisms necessary to make these efforts successful.

Where will implementation of all these recommendations take education and the field of educational administration? Although computer applications are proliferating in the curriculum, in instruction, and in the management of schools across the nation, education has not yet come to terms with the need to fully integrate computer applications into the educational process. The culture of the school can and should be built around the premise that computer technology can make a major contribution to educational excellence and equal educational opportunity. The recommendations presented here suggest a means for the field of educational administration to lead this effort. Optimizing computer use, understanding possible computer applications, addressing policy issues related to accountability, and instituting appropriate administrator preparation programs are steps that must be taken for the schools to become modern organizations and to best serve all of their clients in a computer-oriented information society (Logan, 1986; Olson, 1986). Not to take these steps is to ignore a clear and present need and to lose a major opportunity to contribute to educational excellence.

References

Alexander, L. (1986). Time for results: An overview. *Phi Delta Kappan* 68: 191–96.

Beam, A. (1986). The USSR: Atari Bolsheviks. *The Atlantic* 257 (3): 28–32.

Becker, H (1982). *Microcomputers in the classroom: Dreams and realities.* (Report No. 319). Baltimore: Center for the Social Organization of Schools, John Hopkins University.

Blumberg, A. (1984). The craft of school administration and some other rambling thoughts. *Educational Administration Quarterly* XX (4): 24–40.

Bolman, L.G., and Deal, T.E. (1984). *Modern approaches to understanding and managing organizations.* San Francisco: Jossey-Bass.

Bork, A. (1987). *Learning with personal computers.* New York: Harper and Row.

Bruno, J.E. (1986). *Designing education information systems using dBase II and the Apple II.* Palo Alto, Calif.: Blackwell Scientific Publications.

Caffarella, E.P. (1985). *Spreadsheets go to school: An administrator's guide to spreadsheets.* Reston, Va.: Reston Publishing Company.

Clinton, B. (1986). Who will manage the schools? *Phi Delta Kappan* 68: 208–10.

Crawford, C.W. (1985a). Administrative uses of microcomputers, part I: Needs evaluation. *NASSP Bulletin* 69 (479): 70–72.

Crawford, C.W. (1985b). Administrative uses of microcomputers, part II: Specific tasks. *NASSP Bulletin,* 69 (480): 53–61.

Culbertson, J.A., and Cunningham, L.L. (Eds.). (1986). *Microcomputers and education.* Eighty-fifth Yearbook of the National Society for the Study of Education. Chicago: NSSE.

Frank, F.; Mackett, M.; Abrams, P.; and Nowakowski, J. (1986). The education utility and educational administration and management. In D.D. Gooler, *The education utility: The power to revitalize education and society,* pp. 94–107. Englewood Cliffs, N.J.: Educational Technology Publications.

Frank, F.; Mackett, M.; Nowakowski, J.; and Abrams, P. (1986). Policy implications of applying integrated information systems to educational management. *Thresholds in Education* 12 (2): 34–36.

Hawkins, J., and Sheingold, K. (1986). The beginning of a story: Computers and the organization of learning in the classrooms. In J.A. Culbertson and L.L. Cunningham (Eds.), *Microcomputers and education,* pp. 40–58. Eighty-fifth Yearbook of the National Society for the Study of Education. Chicago: NSSE.

Johnson, G. (1986). *Machinery of the mind: Inside the new science of artificial intelligence.* New York: Times Books.

Kinzer, C.K.; Sherwood, R.D.; and Bransford, J.D. (1986). *Computer strategies for education: Foundations and content-area applications.* Columbus, Ohio: Merrill.

Komoski, P.K. (1984). Educational computing: The burden of insuring quality. *Phi Delta Kappan* 66: 244–48.

Levin, H.M. (1986). Cost and cost effectiveness of computer-assisted instruction. In J.A. Culbertson and L.L. Cunningham (Eds.), *Microcomputers and education*, pp. 156–74. Eighty-fifth Yearbook of the National Society for the Study of Education. Chicago: NSSE.

Lieberman, A., and Mc Laughlin, M.W. (1982). *Policy making in education.* Eighty-fifth Yearbook of the National Society for the Study of Education. Chicago: NSSE.

Logan, R.K. (1986). *The alphabet effect.* New York: William Morrow.

Lotus Books (TM). (1984). *The Lotus guide to learning Symphony (TM).* Reading, Mass.: Addison-Wesley.

Mackett, M.; Frank, F.; Nowakowski, J.; and Abrams, P. (1986). Preparing educational administrators. In D.D. Gooler, *The education utility: The power to revitalize education and society*, pp. 118–35. Englewood Cliffs, N.J.: Educational Technology Publications.

Mirga, T. (1986). 'Radical' overhaul offered for E.D. data collection. *Education Week* V (20): 1, 10, 11.

Montague, B. (1986). Rural educators say 'networking' key. *Education Week* VI (6): 5, 17.

Nathan, J. (1986). Indications for educators of *time for results*. *Phi Delta Kappan* 68: 197–201.

National Governors' Association Center for Policy Research and Analysis (NGACPRA). (1986). *Time for results: The governors' 1991 report on education.* Washington D.C.: NGACPRA.

The National Task Force on Educational Technology. (1986). *Transforming American education: Reducing the risk to the nation.* A Report to the Secretary of Education. Washington D.C.: United States Department of Education.

Neill, G.W. (Ed.). (1986). *School Tech News* (Issue), 3 (6): 1–8.

Olson, Lynn. (1986). New study raises concerns about adult literacy: Many said unable to cope in technological society. *Education Week* VI (4): 1, 16.

Petzold, C. (1986). Intel's 32-bit wonder: The 80386 microprocessor. *PC Magazine* V (20): 147, 148, 150, 152–55.

Pogrow, S. (1985a). Administrative uses of computers: What is the ideal system? What are the trends? *NASSP Bulletin* 69 (485): 45–53.

Pogrow, S. (1985b). Instructional uses of computers: Stress problem-solving skills to capitalize on potential. *NASSP Bulletin* 69 (484): 47–5.

Rodman, B. (1986). Ranking teachers on students' test scores sparks furor, legal action in St. Louis. *Education Week* VI (2): 1, 18.

Sander, B., and Wiggins, T. (1985). Cultural context of administrative theory: In consideration of a multidimensional paradigm. *Educational Administration Quarterly* XXI (1): 95–117.

Silverman, F. (1986). An educational imperative: Advances in technology translate into new opportunities. *NASSP Bulletin* 70 (488): 50–56.

Sirkin, J.R. (1985). Nation's school chiefs complete plans to gauge states, students. *Education Week* 5 (13): 1, 14.

Snider, W. (1986a). Improved access to technology is coalition's goal: An 'electronic pipeline' for low-cost services. *Education Week* VI (6): 1, 17.

Snider, W. (1986b). Pioneers are harnessing computers to unlock learning for handicapped. *Education Week* V (371): 1, 10.

Sununu, J.H. (1986). Will technologies make learning and teaching easier? *Phi Delta Kappan* 68: 220–22.

Tanner, C.K., and Holmes, C.T. (1985). *Microcomputer applications in educational planning and decision making.* New York: Teachers College Press.

Tobias, S. (1985). Computer-assisted instruction. In M.C. Wang and H.J. Walberg (Eds.), *Adapting instruction to individual differences*, pp. 105–34. Berkeley, Calif: McCutchan Publishing.

Walker, D.F. (1986). Computers and the curriculum. In J.A. Culbertson and L.L. Cunningham (Eds.), *Microcomputers and education*, pp. 22–39. Eighty-fifth Yearbook of the National Society for the Study of Education. Chicago: NSSE.

Section V

Preparation Programs

The papers in this section analyze some important issues of the preparation of school administrators. The authors examine the state of university preparation programs, suggest needed reforms, and call attention to serious social policy issues.

Bruce Cooper and William Boyd assert that current preparation programs are so similar that they constitute a national model. This program model is state controlled, closed to nonteachers, mandatory for aspirants, university based, credit driven, and certification bound. Daniel Griffiths reconstructs the changes in the past twenty years in the nature of university departments of educational administration. As a result of hard economic times for the departments, the number of faculty has been reduced and academic specialities have been replaced with more general offerings. At the same time the mix of professors has changed, as has the focus of academic attention. The sum of these multiple changes has left the field in intellectual turmoil, bordering on chaos.

In their papers M. Scott Norton and Frederick Levan argue two important conditions now affecting departments. The first is that departments of educational administration have experienced major structural changes in the past twenty years. They are now most likely to be components of larger, more-complex structures within colleges of education. They have been merged, reorganized, and, in general, submerged as a result of efforts to economize. Faculty members see both the advantages and the disadvantages of the new structures. The second condition is that doctoral study in educational administration lacks a coherent core across universities. It appears that the field of study has yet to be sufficiently defined to permit a systematic examination of what graduates should be expected to know.

Martha McCarthy's paper reports a major study of the professoriate. According to the data, faculty are aging Anglo males with relatively high salaries who are satisfied with their lives and with the condition of the field. Younger and female faculty are substantially less satisfied with their departments and with the field in general. Charol Shakeshaft provides glimpses of possible sources of female administrators' discontent. Research on the behavior of educational administrators has largely focused on male administrators. Shakeshaft argues, however, that significant behavioral differences between male and female administrators exist. However, the attention to these differences is not part of the core of the typical preparation curriculum, even though at least half of the graduate students are female. Barbara Jackson's paper is also in response to the domination of the field by Anglo males. Arguing that education from a Black perspective has implications for administrator preparation, she recommends significant changes in preparation programs in order to prepare administrators for more successful practice in urban areas.

The authors of the remaining papers in this section also make recommendations for change. John Peper defines appropriate clinical experiences for administrators, noting that linking theory to practice is hard but important work. Leonard Valverde and his colleagues address preparation for superintendents, describing in their paper the cooperative superintendency program of the University of Texas at Austin.

Daniel Griffiths, Robert Stout, and Patrick Forsyth developed their paper from background papers they had written for members of the Commission. Their paper includes a set of propositions about the state of preparation in educational administration. Originally, the propositions were offered to Commission members to provoke discussion; this intent was realized during subsequent meetings of the group. Nancy Pitner's paper on the training of school administrators is similarly provocative. She bases her criticisms of current practice on research about what administrators do. She then examines selected efforts to revise preparation and closes with a set of suggestions for future efforts.

Two major threads run through the papers in this section. The first is that preparation for educational administration is in ferment. Multiple forces have converged to require thoughtful reexamination of developments during the past twenty years. Some of what had been developed is sound. Much of it is vulnerable to criticism. The second thread is that new ideas are available and, in some measure, in place. The newer ideas, whether of the definitions of what is to be studied or of methods of teaching it, represent an opportunity for restructuring preparation. As Cooper and Boyd conclude, ". . . the training of administrators must look to modify the system, to make training more rigorous, more interesting, more enticing, and more integrated into the real school problems."

20

The Evolution of Training for School Administators

Bruce S. Cooper and William L. Boyd

Introduction

A nearly universal model for the training of school administrators and supervisors has evolved in America in the last half-century. In this "One Best Model," training is state controlled, closed to nonteachers, mandatory for all those entering the profession, university based, credit driven, and certification bound.[1] The model involves "training, most often accomplished at a university in a graduate program in educational administration that affords a broader view of education systems, familiarity with a body of knowledge . . . and an introduction to an array of conceptual, technical, and human relations skills" (Silver, 1979, pp. 49–50; see also Silver and Spuck, 1978). For all the decentralization among the four hundred educational administration training programs, which serve fifty different states and around 15,500 public school systems nationwide, requirements for licensure are amazingly similar, both in process and content, throughout the United States. (See Miklos, 1983; Reavis, 1946.)

Entry to the field is restricted, and the training process is rather rigidly

---

Revised by the authors and reprinted with permission from Chapter 1 in Joseph Murphy and Phillip Hallinger (Eds.), *Approaches to Administrative Training.* © 1987 by the State University of New York Press.
[1] On the history of the development of school administration, see Pierce (1939); Callahan (1962); Callahan and Button (1964); and Campbell and Newell (1985).

prescribed (Nunnery, 1982; Peterson and Finn, 1985; Russell, 1969). Only licensed teachers with at least three years in the classroom may be certified. They must attend a graduate school of education to take a sequence of prescribed courses, approved by the state education department as appropriately "administrative" or "supervisory" in content. In fact, not only is each course scrutinized, but so are the graduate programs themselves, to ensure that offerings are in line, emphases are correct. and sufficient faculty have degrees from similar programs in educational administration (Culbertson and Hencley, 1962, 1963; Hills, 1965).

The One Best Model is driven by state requirements, including a set number of courses, certain degrees, and, most important, state licensure. As Peterson and Finn (1985, p. 44) recently commented, "these requirements are nearly always stated in terms of paper credentials supplied by colleges of education—transcripts and credit hours that must parallel those on a list maintained by the certification bureau of the state education department." Usually, too, the road to licensure leads to a master's or professional diploma; some 96 percent of all school administrators have master's degrees (Silver and Spuck, 1978). This path to the school administrator's office is so long and narrow that latecomers and outsiders are almost never welcome. Indeed, the One Best Model rests on the belief that only licensed teachers (after paying their dues at the chalkboard), trained in state-sanctioned, university-based programs, are qualified to become administrators. It is virtually impossible, with this model in place, to be an administrator without coming through the proper door, with the common certificate, after having climbed the same professional ladder.

Further, the content of these courses of study is basically similar. The programs typically focus on the study of administration, leadership, and supervision, and include an introduction to school law, planning, politics and negotiation, finance and budgeting, and some gesture at research methods and evaluation. These courses generally rely on a small number of rather similar textbooks, cite articles from the management and educational administration journals, and are taught by professors from this same tradition. (See Campbell and Newell, 1973.) As we shall discuss shortly, the programmatic content of the One Best Model now rests on an intellectual paradigm borrowed from social psychology, management, and the behavioral sciences. The philosophical base of the One Best Model, one that evolved alongside the programmatic component, is an abiding belief in empiricism, predictability, and "scientific" certainty, taught by professors steeped in this approach.[2]

In sketching in broad strokes the main features typical of training pro-

---

[2] On the history of the rise of empiricism in the study and teaching of educational administration, see Griffiths (1964); Miklos (1983); and Willower (1981).

grams in school administration today, we acknowledge that our portrait of the field neglects the variation in programs and emphases that does exist in some places. Also, consistent with the temper of the times, our discussion focuses on the problems with the One Best Model, even though it has some undeniable strengths as well. For instance, while the rigidities of the present training and certification requirements narrowly restrict entry to the field, thereby greatly reducing the pool of talent available, they also prevent untrained charlatans from preying on the unsuspecting. Thus, while the One Best Model encourages inbreeding, and probably promotes mediocrity more often than brilliance, it also reduces the likelihood of outrageous abuses, such as those that occur from time to time in the child care and nursing home industries. When it comes to the education of our children—and the same should apply to child care and nursing homes—we are risk aversive; we want to "play it safe." In this respect and some others, the One Best Model has seved us well. At present, however, it appears that the national needs for educational reform and improvement demand not simply an overhaul of the teaching profession but also an improved and rejuvenated cadre of educational managers.

The book for which this paper was originally prepared (Murphy and Hallinger, 1987) offers alternative models for the training of school administrators. Like all alternatives, they are not without some risks. But these departures are best understood—and must be judged—in comparison to the prevailing training approach in the field: the state-controlled, university-based, licensure-driven model, which is centrally directed at the state level, lockstep, and widely accepted. By contrast, Murphy and Hallinger's volume offers options that are sometimes local, experimental, and directed by the users in close cooperation with the providers. Thus, whereas the One Best Model is stipulated by state departments of education, options discussed in Murphy and Hallinger's work often are directly controlled by school administrators themselves, in cooperation with neighboring universities. Whereas the One Best Model usually focuses attention on administrators-in-training as they amass sufficient credits for certification, the alternatives presented in Murphy and Hallinger's volume include the possibility of career development without great concern for licensing or whether a candidate for a leadership job has been a teacher. Whereas the dominant model assumes a technical, behavioral sciences approach, Murphy and Hallinger's volume offers alternatives that include the idea that other approaches—for example, studying philosophy, economics, literature, and drama—might enhance our understanding of school leadership in modern society (compare Farquhar and Piele, 1972; Walton, 1962).

This paper describes the evolution of the predominant training model for public school administrators and its origins, development, and shortcomings, leading to suggestions for possible improvements and alternatives. Paralleling the programmatic history and development, this paper also explores the content of school administration training, from "trait theories" of leadership (during the administrator-as-statesman–philosopher phase, 1865–1900[3]) through "efficiency" theories in which administrators were seen as "executives" (1900–1920) plagued with concerns for scientific and then human relations management.[4] Finally, we take a brief look at the social science approaches and their shortcomings, leading to some thoughts on the latest "policy sciences" view of administration.[5]

In fact, we shall make an argument for a relationship between the evolution of the One Best Model and the theories of administration taught in these programs. As the schools became more complex, larger, more highly specialized and structured, researchers needed more complex paradigms to describe and analyze what school leaders do, their environment, interrelationships, decision making, staffing, and, most recently, their productivity. The current content of courses, taught within the One Best Model, has a kind of orthodoxy not unlike the approaches to training themselves. Thus, to change and improve the models (who controls them, where they occur, to what ends, taught by whom), one must also consider new theoretical viewpoints. Just as the "cult of efficiency" was an important force in the birth of scientific management, perhaps now notions of political economy and hermeneutical or interpretive approaches to human behavior will parallel the introduction of new ways of understanding the organization and training leaders for it.

Evolution of School Administrator Programs and Theories

The formal training of school administrators is a recent development; superintendents and principals had been introduced in city school systems for fifty years or more before a semblance of training programs appeared (Campbell and Newell, 1985; Halpin, 1966). Although William H. Payne probably wrote the first book on administration in 1875 and taught the "first college-level course in school administration" in 1879 (Callahan and Button, 1964), professors of educational administration were unknown until the early 1900s, and the first two doctorates were awarded in 1905 at Teachers College, Columbia University to Ellwood Cubberley and George Strayer (Callahan, 1962; Silver, 1979).

---

[3] See Callahan and Button (1964); Suzzalo (1906).
[4] See Callahan (1962); March (1974, 1978).
[5] For critiques of mainstream social science approaches to educational administration, see Bates (1983) and Foster (1983).

Table 20–1 shows the stages in the development of school administration from 1865 to 1985, including the roles, programs, philosophical bases, training, and degrees awarded. While it is neither possible nor necessary to review the histories of these developments in great detail (a growing literature on the subject already exists), it is important to see the evolution of the One Best Model and the nature of competing approaches to the preparation of administrators. Certainly, it was not preordained that the university classroom be the site, the state the overseer, and the credit the unit. However, once the demand for administrators increased, the credentializing process began, and the complexity of American schools grew, it seemed inevitable that the standard, state-sanctioned program would take hold. Or, as Silver (1979, p. 49) explains, the forces affecting preparation programs included "the massive migration of populations to urban centers, the growth and increasing complexity of schools and school systems, advances in technical knowledge in business and industry, increasingly stringent certification requirements, and changing cultural values."

Table 20–1 demonstrates that training programs increased in formality, structure, and complexity in much the same way as the school system developed: from amateur to professional, from simple to complicated, and from intuitive to "scientific," under whatever the rubric, that is "efficiency," "business management," "scientific management," and later the "behavioral sciences."

Phase 1: Philosopher-Statesperson (Or the Happy Amateur)

Little is known about the lives of early superintendents and principals, and still less about their preparation for their positions (See Chancellor, 1904, 1908.) What do survive are biographies of educator-statemen (few, if any, were women) like William Torrey Harris (the St. Louis superintendent and U.S. Commissioner of Education) and William H. Payne (writer, professor, and Michigan superintendent). It is no wonder, then, that the first teachings to prospective administrators were "theories" about exemplary school leaders, which were then rarefied into "Great Man" and "trait" theories (Bobbitt, 1913; Dutton and Snedden, 1908). What set Harris and Payne apart from the pack, however, were their philosophical leanings (Harris was the leading Hegelian of his time) and their genuine search for meaning.

Their formal training for administration included some basic pedagogy and a life-long search for the "ideal" education, but not much self-consciousness or thought about their own roles as leaders, statesmen, administrators. (See, for example, Spaulding, 1910.) Hence, they attended no courses, received no credits, and applied for no licenses in educational administration. The One Best Model was the furthest thing from their minds. These early school leaders were practical men (concerned about

Table 20–1
The Evolution of Training in School Administration

Approx. Dates	Role or Title	Program Content–Background	Philosophy	Training	Degrees and Licensure
1865–1900	Philosopher–educator	Teacher training, no formal training in administration	Pedagogy, classics, liberal arts, philosophy	Informal, as teachers	No special degrees or licenses
1900–1912	Educator–capitalist	Teacher training and experience	Business ethos, "cult of efficiency," no administrator training	No formal training	No degrees or licenses in administration
1913–1915	Business manager	Business, techniques of accounting, graphing, and some philosophy	Mix of pedagogy, philosophy, and efficiency	Beginnings of programs in educational administration	First degrees offered – no license required

1915–1929	School executive	Administration based on rudiments of scientific management, business	Cult of efficiency business methods	Formal, university based	Master's, some state licensing
1930–1950	Social agent	Social foundations, administrator as mediator	Social philosophy, economics, change, "democratic" administration	Formal, required, university based	Master's and license
–ONE BEST MODEL–					
1950–1985	Behavioral scientist	Management, organization theory, leadership theory	Behavioral, empirical	Formal, state controlled. Set credits for various licenses	Master's and credits, building and district level licenses, state run

Adapted, in part, from Raymond E. Callahan and H. Warren Button, "Historical Change of the Role of the Man in the Organization: 1865–1950." In Daniel E. Griffiths (ed.), *Behavioral Science and Educational Administration*, pp. 73–92. Sixty-third Yearbook of the National Society for the Study of Education. Chigaco: University of Chicago Press, 1964.

finding enough teachers, books, classrooms, and pupils) as well as lofty, idealistic, noble philosophers seeking the inner meaning of education and pedagogy.

Phase 2: Educational Capitalists

As the "business ideology was spread continously into the bloodstream of American life," the leaders of education were expected to use modern business methods and efficiency in the schools (Callahan, 1962, p. 43). Immigrants glutted the schools, putting extraordinary pressure on schools in a time (1900–1913) of rising inflation, all against a background of demands for doing more for less. Like a bombshell, in the fall of 1910 the "scientific management system" of Frederick Taylor became social gospel, further squeezing schools to cut waste, improve managerial efficiency, and *be like business*. By 1913, administrators who were untrained in the managerial philosophy of Taylor were falling like flies. The *American School Board Journal* reported that, *"No recent year has seen such wholesale changes in superintendencies and other high school positions* [as 1913] ... *there has been a perfect storm of unrest culminating in wholesale resignations, dismissals and new appointments"* (as quoted from Callahan and Button, 1964, p. 80, their emphasis). Administrators had no formal training, no preparation to be the new educational managers. The state and university were standing by, watching the bloodbath. The years of playing philosopher-king were over; the hard realities of little money, few qualified staff, crowded schools, and little sympathy from communities took their toll. Teacher training was hardly enough to qualify one as an administrator.

Phase 3: Business Manager

For those who survived, the one hope was to learn from business. They would manage their schools, as Newton, Massachusetts, superintendent, Frank Spaulding (1910, p. 3) wrote, on "simple and sound business principles." Once the business model was adopted, universities began to establish courses and programs in administration, stressing economy and efficiency. Significantly, the first major address to the Department of Superintendence of the National Education Association, given by Spaulding (1913), was entitled "Improving School Systems through Scientific Management." However, Spaulding really seemed more concerned about larger classes and lower pay than effective education, but gave a facade of "science" to his work.

It is worth noting that the link between practice, "science," and school management was made in the early 1900s, laying the groundwork for further attempts to quantify the administration of schools, whether through dollar amounts, IQ scores, achievement scores, or the most recent efforts to measure "effectiveness." The foundation, then, of the One Best Model had been laid; now universities had something firm to teach and state depart-ments something for which to hold administrators accountable. And to make efficiency possible, as Franklin Bobbitt and Ellwood Cubberley explained, the system must control the behavior of teachers and thus required, in Bobbitt's (1913, p. 7) words, the "centralization of authority and definite direction by supervisors of *all* processes performed." The pieces were all in place: the glow of "science," the language of "management," the goal of "efficiency," and finally the need for central control and authority.

Phase 4: The School Executive

Between 1915 and 1929, as Callahan and Button (1964, pp. 85–86) relate, the notion of formal graduate training for school administrators was increased and institutionalized, under, for example, Cubberley at Stanford University, and George Strayer at Teachers College, Columbia University (Cubberley, 1916; Strayer, 1925). These were the heady days of the powerful, almost "superhuman" school superintendent, the new professional, armed with new knowledge, who gives direction to boards, teachers, the public. He was, in Cubberley's words, a "Captain of Education." As such, the training was practical, applied, and direct. Still missing —to come in later phases— was a comfortable intellectual base around which to conceptualize, study, and instruct the budding school administrator. At Teachers College, for example, Strayer stressed basic techniques of graphing, calculating, and accounting, not elaborate theories of behavior. Business, not the social sciences, was still the model (Cremin et al., 1954).

Phase 5: Administrator as Social Agent

During the Great Depression and World War II, the optimism and undiluted worship of business declined; administrators were then forced to think about social and economic issues. The era of the social conscience led to a consideration of the role of schooling (and administration) in a broader context. Administrators were expected to mediate "between classroom learning-teaching and the purpose or function of schools" (Callahan and Button, 1964, p. 91; Moehlman, 1940). So while a majority of school administrators did some graduate work, and while thirty-eight states by 1950 required a graduate degree in administration for superintendents and princi-pals, the One Best Model was not quite complete. Training was still highly practical, with a blend of "plant management," "scheduling," and "budget-ing" interspersed with courses on "schools and the social order." Missing still were academic respectability and a sense of full professionalism; these were to come in the next phase with the rise of social science in education.

Phase 6: Administrator as Behavioral Scientist

By the late 1950s and 1960s administrators were being trained to be applied social scientists. For, as Daniel Griffiths and others explained in the 1964 classic, *Behavioral Science and Educational Administration*, "administration is susceptible to empirical research", using the "concepts and theories of human behavior, research designs, statistical insights, computers, and the logic of these modes of inquiry" (p. 3). At last, the subject for the study of administration was the administrator (in contrast to earlier concerns with the social order, the teacher, the program). At last, school administration had evolved into the possibility of academic respectability within the academy, on a rough par with business management and public administration studies. Or, as Boyan (1963, pp. 11–12) observed, "The more the professor of school administration looked at the social sciences for help . . . , the more the process of administering schools appeared to be like the processes of administering other organizations. The skills applicable to understanding, predicting, and controlling human behavior appeared to hold with generality in administering organizations of all kinds."

While scholars of school administration had come at last to a common belief in the "applied social sciences," there was less consensus on research problems, methods, and implications of findings. The common framework did allow researchers, trainers, and administrators-in-training to benefit from the evolution of behavioral research, from Taylor to Likert, Gulick to Drucker. A few professors of education administration, notably scholars like Andrew Halpin, were widely cited in the general organizational leadership research. (See, for example, Hersey and Blanchard, 1982, pp. 91–93.) But placing educational administration in the mainstream of social research did not seem to solve the dilemmas of what to teach practitioners; hence the concern through the 1970s and 1980s about preparation programs.

In sum, the training of school administrators had evolved, changed, and grown. From a period when leaders were born, not bred, through times when the businessman was king and the superintendent a captain, school administration was given professional legitimacy by an alliance with the scholars of leadership and organizational behavior. This central role was strengthened by the monopoly over training that schools of education enjoyed between 1950 and now, one in which the state departments of education required attendance at a graduate school, while they attempted to accredit the program and training in those graduate schools.

The One Best Model, then, had official sanction, a measure of academic respectability, and nearly absolute control over the field. Now the system of training was capable of supplying a near-endless supply of trained, licensed administrators for a wide variety of school and central office positions. While the course offerings at various graduate schools were widely diverse (Culbertson, 1962), the basic assumptions about human behavior and the social sciences held much in common. The Model—its content and program—was firmly established and accounted for more master's degrees than any other field in the nation (Peterson and Finn, 1985).

The Model Under Attack

Most orthodoxies are easy targets; they can be readily blamed for being the status quo when problems occur. And the One Best Model for the training of school administrators is increasingly under attack. Some, like Michael Nunnery (1982, p. 46), have asserted "that no meaningful reform will occur until education administration preparation is freed from many of these traditional academic practices," including reliance on credits, classroom instruction, current program content, and program control.

Peterson and Finn (1985) argue in *The Public Interest* that these professional training programs are both too mindlessly rigid and rule bound on the one hand and too soft and ineffective on the other. They feel so strongly about the improvement of preparation programs and administrative practices that they provide a maxim: "Practically never does one encounter a good school with a bad principal or a high-achieving school system with a low-performance superintendent" (p. 42). But, they ask, "Is there a valid relationship between what individuals do in universities in order to become licensed as educational administrators and the actual knowledge, skills, and competencies that they need to be effective unit managers and system leaders in the public schools?" (p. 48). Similarly, John Hoyle (1985), in calling attention to the severe shortcomings of current training practices, suggests that most administrators receive fragmented, overlapping, and often useless courses that add up to very little.

Trying to categorize the barrage of complaints presents certain difficulties, since these criticisms come from many quarters in many forms. In one way or another, they seem to be attacking some aspect of the One Best Model. The following are some of the complaints.

1. *Poor Candidates.* A number of the critics of the major way administrators are prepared point to the inadequacies of candidates for training. Having to be a trained, licensed, and experienced teacher rules out some talented people with fresh perspectives. Peterson and Finn (1985, p. 49) wonder how to separate the effects of training "from the consequences of this severe limitation on the pool of potential candidates." As education became a less and less popular career among the better graduates from college, the pool of possible trainees became still thinner. The worst-case scenario might show few able, talented, and creative people initially entering the field of education; the first few years of teaching then weed out most of the small group of creative, bright people because they find the work too tedious and the school

bureaucracy too uncaring. Then, from those surviving, some pursue training in school administration and encounter graduate courses they frequently deem irrelevant and uninspiring. Those who don't drop out become the next generation of leaders. Fortunately for the schools, this worst-case scenario does not always occur. We continue, somehow, to get some very good people into school administration, but does this happen because of or *despite* the One Best Model?

2. *Low Admission Standards.* Schools of education depend on a steady flow of trainees to maintain their programs. With the drop, until very recently, in teacher training and school populations, graduate schools have become concerned about the need for more trainees. What few standards of admission that might have existed were weakened, and "eased entry," to use Dan Lortie's term, became even easier. "If entrance requirements exist at all," Peterson and Finn (1985, p. 51) note, "they are not very competitive and most applicants are accepted, this in marked contast to the situation facing prospective matriculants to most law and medical schools." One in thirty applicants in California is rejected from administration programs, according to James Guthrie (as reported in Peterson and Finn, 1985, p. 51).

This ease of admissions has several negative effects. First, it lowers the level of training and experience possible, since courses are often geared to the background and intelligence of the students. Second, "eased entry downgrades the status of the students in the eyes of the populace" (Peterson and Finn, 1985, p. 51). Third, the candidates themselves realize that anyone can get in and almost everyone will get the license if he or she keeps paying for credits. In part, this lack of rigor at entry reflects a lack of clear criteria for training or a clear vision of what candidates and graduates will look like, and the realization that the graduate school experience itself is not very demanding. Efforts to create special, elite, high-powered programs with tough admissions standards are rare and typically end up training the next group of professors of educational administration, since they often produce few graduates truly interested in practice.

3. *Incoherent Programs.* Once candidates are admitted (even before in some cases, because some graduate programs allow teachers to take up to twelve credits without even applying for admission, they often confront a confusing mélange of courses that has no clear meaning, focus, or purpose. More criticism has been directed at the graduate training programs in educational administration—their curriculum, experiences, pedagogy, and activities—than to any other aspect of administrative education.

The problems in this area have been clearly delineated by Michael Nunnery (1982), who raises a number of important questions about the curriculum in university-based preparation programs. From a national survey (by Silver and Spuck), and other probes of the program, Nunnery (1982, p. 48) concludes that no clear means of educating administrators is apparent:

The variance in informed opinion about what educational administrators need to know, the different preparation program practices, and the apparent incongruities between preparation and what practitioners are spending much of their time doing call attention to a major inadequacy in the knowledge base for educational administration. If the knowledge base is conceived of as a continuum from conventional wisdom to the results of carefully designed and conducted research, far too much of the knowledge base is near the conventional wisdom end of the continuum.

Criticism seems to come from four sources: those who believe (1) that what programs teach is not what candidates need to do their jobs; (2) that the research base on which training is based in inadequate to guide practice; (3) that administrators cannot strike a useful balance between general learning (applicable to all administrative posts) and specialized training (for jobs as curriculum specialist, budget finance director, personnel/labor management relations specialist, and the like); and (4) that the courses themselves are taught in boring, unapplied, and unchallenging ways.

In fact, many critics wonder whether the means of teaching so evident in the One Best Model (classroom based, part time, geared to credit hours) are necessary for good administration at all. Certainly, the mood emerging from the *A Nation At Risk* report and others makes one wonder to what ends all the hours, credits, and licenses lead. The basic elements of the prevailing approach have not been enough. Administrative "science" has been thwarted by the increasingly political nature of school leadership, since much of social psychology and other behavioral sciences assumes that administrators have the autonomy and choice to make the best decisions.

Those who try other approaches, such as "human relations" and "human development," find themselves accused of ignoring the "bottom line," that is, the achievement and testing results of students. Or, if they are successful in getting the staff to be productive, they are accused of being "manipulative" and controlling. Even the more scientific administrators find themselves worrying about research that may not fit the conditions in their school. A bad case of "analysis paralysis" can occur when administrators take too seriously the tenets of "good" administration and decision making: (1) set goals, (2) gather possible options, (3) assess and rank options, (4) calculate outcomes for each option, and (5) select and implement the "best" line of action. Such paradigms are fine for operations researchers in a laboratory with a bank of computers; but for the line administrators making hundreds of decisions daily, the "science of administration," according to Bridges (1977) and, earlier, Lindblom (1959), becomes the cause of inaction and failure.

Solutions

The papers in Murphy and Hallinger (1987) suggest ways of reconceptualizing the training of school administrators. This paper has argued that the field has a prevailing model of training, one that is orthodox, accepted, supported by states, universities, and school districts alike. The One Best Model rests on the assumptions that a standardized, university-based, classroom-focused, credit-driven, and licensure-directed approach to preparation is best, given the demands of the field. Perhaps, at one time, this was true: when shortages and growth demanded large numbers of leaders for far-flung districts and in a hurry.

But, times have changed. Observers are beginning to question the results of the One Best Model, wondering if other means for training administrators would work better. Remedies seem of two types. A number of writers are suggesting modifications, improvement in the training systems, the *Better One Best System*. Others, seeing the essential problems and rigidities of making the system work as is, are suggesting new arrangements, some of which are detailed for the first time in Murphy and Hallinger (1987). The former approach assumes that centrally controlled, university-based modes can be improved with better technology, clearer purposes, and stronger doses of the same medicine. Supporters of alternative models believe that until the basic structure of the prevailing model is changed, the results will not be appreciably improved. Still others think that a blend of the elements of the One Best Model and new, innovative means may be the most desirable route.

The "Better" One Best Model?

Much of the reform in the current system of training is consistent with the development of the One Best Model. That is, universities and state departments of education are working together to expand (more credits in new subjects) or modify the process of training (to focus, for example, on the development of measurable "competencies"). Most important, perhaps, among current reformers is John Hoyle, a professor who works closely with the American Association of School Administrators, the national superintendents' organization. In an article preceding his new textbook, *Skills for Successful School Leaders*, Hoyle puts his faith in an improvement in competencies and related skills. He "believes that the use of competencies and related skills can bring structure and continuity to administrator preparation programs" (Hoyle, 1985, p. 72). Then, as though he realizes that a list of competencies will hardly overcome the problems of the training of administrators, he adds, "Although some may feel that this approach can be shallow and lead to fragmentation, there are others who think that school leaders who possess the competencies and skills set forth in the American Association of School Administrator (AASA) guidelines will have the cognitive structure necessary for gaining deeper understanding of the practice of administration" (p. 72). But gaining a deeper understanding hardly qualifies one as an effective leader; being able to apply the skills, in complex organizational settings, is the other half of the equation. Moreover, even if the competencies of good leadership could be identified and taught, the problem of recruiting talented new blood (including those without teaching experience), despite the barriers to entry and the low standards and prestige of many educational administration programs, still remains.

Hoyle includes competencies and accompanying skills such as the following: "Designing, implementing, and evaluating a school climate improvement program that utilizes mutual staff and student efforts to formulate and attain school goals" (p. 71). Then, under this rubric (which reads more like an assignment for a term paper in school administration than like a competency) he lists a whole set of skills that sound amazingly like Luther Gulick's 1937 patterns of POSDCoRB (planning, organizing, staffing, directing, coordinating, reporting, and budgeting). Hoyle lists skills in human relations, organizational development, and leadership; collaborative goal setting and action planning; participative management; and improving the quality of relationships to enhance learning. This "wish list" includes every good technique in management, from assessment through motivation and communications. Most of the ideas are old, and the list is unrealistic. Under his "program delivery components," he urges preparation programs to include the following:

1. Diagnosis capability
2. Design capability
3. Instructional capability
4. Resource capability
5. Program evaluation capability

Again, nothing new: old wine in old bottles. It sounds very much like thinking, planning, doing, and figuring out whether it worked.

Hoyle's approach stands clearly in the rational, "scientific," controlling world, though he does include a "political theory" and "political skills" competency. But little thought is given to the political economy that drives behavior within the present context of public schools. Instead, the approach reads like good advice to superintendents about public relations ("communicating and projecting an articulate position for education . . . and comprehending the role and function of mass media . . ." [p. 78]), and there is nothing about the reciprocal relationship of the schools and the social order.

In Hoyle's approach, the One Best Model goes unchallenged; the existing course content is simply listed and justified: an organization of the status quo with little thought to who controls courses, licensure, and programs, who might join together to improve schools, and how administration might redirect itself to outcomes. While the ideas are comprehensive, well-organized, and thorough, they have limited promise for really improving the pool of trainees, program standards, or administrators' real skills and performance.

Another way of rejuvenating the One Best Model is found in programs reorganized around a "policy sciences" approach to training. The analytical focus in this approach is concerned with "the nature, causes, and effects of alternative public policies" (Nagel, 1980, p. 391). The approach emphasizes assessing and choosing the best policy from a number of alternatives, with explicit recognition of the realities involved in implementing the policy. The policy studies approach is especially relevant and useful for training in school administration because much of the earliest and best research in the field deals with educational policy questions. (See Williams, 1980, p. 10.)

At its best, the policy sciences approach has the potential (1) to bridge the perennial gap between theory and practice and (2) to link organizational and administrative processes to organizational outcomes, countering the troublesome tendency toward goal displacement in educational organizations (see Boyd and Immegart, 1979; Nagel, 1983). Moreover, the theory of organizational behavior most prevalent in contemporary policy studies—the public choice model of political economists (Wildavsky, 1985, p. 29)—can reveal much of the fundamental dynamics of organizations by showing the skeleton of incentives beneath the blubber of platitudes and professional rhetoric (Boyd and Immegart, 1979).

The potential of the policy studies approach for connecting theory and practice is most obvious in the rich contribution of studies focusing on the "bottom-heavy, loosely-coupled" realm of the implementation process (Elmore, 1983). The literature in this domain is full of insights about administration and the realities of designing effective policies (Elmore, 1983; Mann, 1978; Williams, 1980). More broadly, the activist, field-oriented approach taken in public policy schools could provide a model for reinvigorating training programs in educational administration. It is the ethos of the schools, according to Wildavsky (1985, p. 32), that is more important than their curriculum: "From the first week, students are placed in an active position. They analyze, grub for data, reformulate problems, write and write again to communicate with their clients. Fieldwork is their forte. An analyst with clean hands . . . is a contradiction in terms."

Despite its potential, the reality of applying policy studies approaches to the training of school administrators may be another matter. Since the mid 1970s the policy studies approach has been something of a bandwagon movement. Unfortunately, the approach means many things to many people. And so far very few faculty members in educational administration have been trained in public policy schools. Consequently, all too often it appears that the approach is being implemented only in rather superficial and symbolic ways. Still, its rich potential remains available.

New Directions

Departures from the One Best Model

Nunnery (1982) is doubtful that the state will relinquish control over the licensing process. Rather he argues that "what may possibly change is the basis upon which the state education agency issues a certificate or an endorsement in educational administration" (p. 48). That might be a starting place: breaking the mold of requiring university courses only; recognizing activities and programs sponsored jointly by school districts, universities, and professional associations, for example. The AASA National Academy for School Executives provides such an avenue and has in a few cases given its own "credits" though using the faculty and research of schools of education.

Another alternative might be an internship "in a Commission-approved program of in-service training in administrative services," as Woellner (1981, p. 30) proposes. Or, as in New Hampshire, competencies can take the place of credits and courses: "candidates for certification who have gained the competencies, skills, and knowledge through other means . . . may request teaching, administrative, or educational specialist certification on the basis of demonstrated competencies and equivalent experiences" (Woellner, 1981, p. 30).

Thus, a number of new roads to administrator training open up, once the One Best Model is understood and challenged. Murphy and Hallinger (1987) present a rich collection of examples, some speculative, others now functioning. Some of their qualities are described next.

1. *New Recruitment Practices.* Already, search committees from private schools are reaching out to "former professors, quondam deans, clergymen, and even the occasional business executive" (Peterson and Finn, 1985, p. 44). Public schools, too, might consider recruiting mid-career professionals from outside the ranks, giving them a year or two of training and perhaps some classroom work and pushing them into key positions, particularly as leaders in new areas like technology, planning, budgeting, and development. What would a Lee Iacocca do with a city district or high school? What approaches, resources, and ideas could such a person bring to the job?

2. *Higher Standards.* Entry into administration should indicate more than perseverance and time served. It should indicate that some of our best, most well-prepared, and most creative people have entered the field, not the bottom of the barrel. Why not take a more elite approach to selecting and training school administrators? Peterson and Finn (1985, p. 55) agree: "A good program would have stringent entry requirements, high standards during coursework and other training experiences, and opportunities for candid, precise feedback to students about their performance." Such quality would create a sense of esprit, importance, and excitement during training,

raising the expectations of professors, trainees, and school district personnel as well.

3. *Integrated, High-powered, and Exciting Training.* Currently, administrators-in-training accrue credits, licenses, and stamps for approval from the university and state. It is not uncommon for middle-level administrators to have two master's degrees, one in their pedagogical field and one in administration, plus dozens of additional credits toward a possible doctorate and the fulfillment of state requirements for "relicensing," which periodically are increased. So, credits qua credits are not the answer to the improvement of administrator training. In fact, somehow we must invent ways to wean administrators away from "credit-itis" and more toward the concept of "life-long" education and improvement. Heads of Fortune 500 corporations spend weeks in the Colorado mountains, at some great expense, studying literature, drama, and philosophy at the Aspen Institute, putting themselves into a totally different framework and stretching their minds and imaginations in ways new to men and women trained on diets of finance, banking, corporate law, advertising, and production. Clearly, school administrators, like other managers, could benefit from such an escape into the world of ideas. But, while many school administrators would jump at the opportunity, how many school systems would finance their study at the Aspen Institute?

Peterson and Finn (1985) make some interesting suggestions for training, many of which might break prospective administrators out of the credit/licensure chase and into a concern for values, ideas, concepts, on the one hand, and the world of apprenticeship, real theory, and real human problems, on the other. They explain:

> It may well be that piecemeal reform is simply inadequate to the task of overhauling the training, licensure, and professional standards of school administrators. It may also be that the profession lacks the fortitude or the perspective for a thoroughgoing, self-induced overhaul. Perhaps governors, business leaders, and blue ribbon commissions will need to bring school administration under the same kind of intense scrutiny that they have applied to school teaching. Maybe one state needs to burst from the pack with a radically different model of training, licensure, selection, evaluation, and recruitment into this field. Perhaps the universities need a modern day Flexner to map their route through a systematic—and system-wide—reformulation of the precepts and practices of administrator training. [P. 62]

Such alternatives are worth considering; many are suggested in Murphy and Hallinger (1987). These changes, radical or otherwise, include some of the following: a formal program that is coherent, focused around real-world problems, and both practical and theoretical—the action sciences at work.

"Coursework should naturally span the best current research and theory in the field," Peterson and Finn (1985, p. 56) declare, "and faculty members should expect students to acquire—and to demonstrate that they now possess—both the requisite knowledge and the skills by which that knowledge can be analyzed, synthesized, and applied." There is nothing new in this admonition, except the degree of their emphasis on the *application* of knowledge. Peterson and Finn stress that since administration is a way of thinking and acting—not usually of doing research, the heavy emphasis on research in training programs should be modified to include much more attention to the art of doing, convincing, exploring, and thinking about problems in schools.

And the intellectual paradigms also need some attention. Besides reaction against overreliance on the scientific, behavioral model for research and action, interest is increasing in "naturalistic" studies, those that actually bring the researcher and objects (or "subjects") of study eye to eye. Thus ethnographic approaches, case studies, and program evaluations have lifted the student of school administration out of the armchair and into the school environment. But the teaching of administration rarely takes full advantage of these close-up views. How often are candidates shown videotapes—not of teachers in classrooms—but of school leaders working, influencing, supporting? How often do classes, workshops, seminars actually take on a school as a laboratory organization, looking, learning, and helping? Schools are all around us, but we sit in classrooms and talk about schools and leadership. Finally, the false certitude that pervades much of research on school administration needs a good dose of reality. Leaders do not work in neutral, safe settings; political pressures and realities come crashing in. But while these realities loom large in courses on educational politics, the central paradigms of school administration still lean toward the rational, scientific mode.

In conclusion, school administration and its intellectual, political, and institutional bases have grown and developed since the first principals were appointed, the first doctorates granted, and the first programs created. Powerful interests now control the preparation of school leaders: state agencies, universities, and local school systems. They have opted for a system of convenience, the One Best Model, which allows trainees to accumulate credits over time at various universities, all applied toward a statewide license. This system was a long time in coming. It has served well the needs of the burgeoning local districts that needed administrators trained quickly, and with minimal disruption (most were able to continue working while going to graduate school).

Now, however, the need is not for numbers but for quality and effectiveness. Thus the training of administrators must look to modifying the system, to making training more rigorous, more interesting, more enticing, and more integrated into the real school problems. The collection of papers in Murphy and Hallinger (1987) suggests what can be done when associations, districts, schools of education, state departments of education, and administrators themselves collaborate in facing the problems of school leadership and improvement.

References

Bates, R. (1983). *Educational administration and the management of knowledge.* Geelong, Victoria, Australia: Deakin University Press.

Bobbitt, J.F. (1913). *The supervision of city schools: Some general principles of management applied to the problems of city-school systems.* Bloomington, Ill.: National Society for the Study of Education.

Boyan, N.J. (1963). Common and specialized learnings for administrators and supervisors: Some problems and issues. In D.J. Leu and H.C. Rudman (Eds.), *Preparation programs for school administrators.* East Lansing: Michigan State University.

Boyd, W.L., and Immegart, G.L. (1979). Education's turbulent environment and problem-finding: Lines of convergence. In G.L. Immegart and W.L. Boyd (Eds.), *Problem-finding in educational administration.* Lexington, Mass.: D.C. Heath.

Bridges, E.M. (1977). The nature of leadership. In L.L. Cunningham, W.G. Hack, and R.O. Nystrand (Eds.), *Educational administration: The developing decades.* Berkeley, Calif.: McCutchan Publishing.

Callahan, R.E. (1962). *Education and the cult of efficiency.* Chicago: University of Chicago Press.

Callahan, R.E., and Button, H.W. (1964). Historical change in the role of the man in the organization, 1865–1950. In D. Griffiths (Ed.), *Behavioral science and educational administration.* Chicago: University of Chicago Press.

Campbell, R.F., and Newell, L.J. (1973). *A study of professors of educational administration.* Columbus, Ohio: University Council for Educational Administration.

Campbell, R.F., and Newell, L.J. (1985). Administration, history of. In *International encyclopedia of education,* Vol. 1, pp. 52–59. Oxford, England: Pergamon Press.

Chancellor, W.E. (1904). *Our schools: Their direction and management.* Boston: D.C. Heath.

Chancellor, W.E. (1908). *Our schools: Their administration and supervision.* Boston: D.C. Heath.

Cremin, L., et al. (1954). *A history of Teachers College, Columbia University.* New York: Columbia University Press.

Cubberley, E.P. (1916). *Public school administration.* Boston: Houghton Mifflin Co.

Culbertson, J.A. (1962). New perspectives: Implications for program change. In J.A. Culbertson and S.P. Hencley (1962). *Preparing administrators: New perspectives.* Columbus, Ohio: University Council for Educational Administration.

Culbertson, J.A. and Hencley, S.P. (1963). *Educational research: New perspectives.* Danville, Ill.: Interstate.

Dutton, S.T., and Snedden, D. (1908). *The administration of public education in the United States.* New York: Macmillan.

Elmore, R.F. (1983). Complexity and control: What legislators and administrators can do about implementation. In L.S. Shulman and G. Sykes (Eds.), *Handbook of teaching and policy.* New York: Longman.

Farquhar, R.H., and Piele P.K. (1972). *Preparing educational leaders: A review of the literature.* Columbus, Ohio: University Council for Educational Administration.

Foster, W. (1983). *Loose coupling revisited: A critical view of Weick's contribution to educational administration.* Geelong, Victoria, Australia: Deakin University Press.

Griffiths, D.E. (Ed.) (1964). *Behavioral science and educational administration.* Chicago: University of Chicago Press.

Halpin, A.W. (1966). *Theory and research in administration.* New York: Macmillan.

Hersey, P., and Blanchard, K. (1982). *Management of organizational behavior.* 4th ed. Englewood Cliffs, N.J.: Prentice-Hall.

Hills, J. (1965). Educational administration: A field in transition. *Educational Administration Quarterly* 1: 58–66.

Hoyle, J.R. (1985). Programs in educational administration and the AASA Guidelines. *Educational Administration Quarterly* 21 (1) (Winter): 71–93.

Lindblom, C.E. (1959) The science of 'muddling through.' *Public Administration Review* 19: 79–88.

Mann, D. (Ed.) (1978). *Making change happen?* New York: Teachers College Press.

March, J.G. (1974). Analytical skills and the university training of educational administrators. *Journal of Educational Administration* 12 (May): 17–44.

March, J.G. (1978). American public school administration: A short analysis. *School Review* 86 (February): 217–45.

Miklos, E. (1983). Evolution in administrator preparation programs. *Educational Administration Quarterly* 19 (3) (Summer): 153–77.

Moehlman, A.B. (1940). *School administration.* Boston: Houghton Mifflin Co.

Murphy, J., and Hallinger, P. (Eds.) (1987). *Approaches to administrative training.* Albany: SUNY Press.

Nagel, S.S. (1980). The policy studies perspective. *Public Administration Review* 40 (July/August).

Nagel, S.S. (Ed.) (1983). *Encyclopedia of policy studies.* New York: Marcel Dekker.

Nunnery, M.Y. (1982). Reform of K–12 educational administrator preparation: Some basic questions. *Journal of Research and Development in Education* 15 (2): 44–51.

Peterson, K.D., and Finn, C.E., Jr. (1985). Principals, superintendents, and the administrator's art. *The Public Interest*, No. 79 (Spring): 42–62.

Pierce, P.R. (1939). *The origin and development of the urban school principalship.* Chicago: University of Chicago Press.

Reavis, W.C. (1946). Educational administration as a profession. In W.C. Reavis (Ed.), *Educational administration: A survey of progress, problems and needs.* Chicago: University of Chicago Press.

Russell, G.T. (1969). Preparation of administrators. In R.L. Ebel (Ed.), *Encyclopedia of educational research*, 4th ed, pp. 93–104. New York: Macmillan.

Silver, P.F. (1979). Administrator preparation. In H. Mitzel et al. (Eds.), *Encyclopedia of educational research*, 5th ed, Vol. 1, pp. 49–50. New York: The Free Press.

Silver, P.F., and Spuck, D.W. (Eds.) (1978). *Preparatory programs for educational administrators in the United States.* Columbus, Ohio: University Council for Educational Administration.

Spaulding, F.E. (1910). *The aims, scope, and method of a university course in public school administration.* Iowa City: National Society for College Teachers of Education.

Spaulding, F.E. (1913) *Improving school systems through scientific management.* Proceedings of the Department of Superintendence, National Education Association, pp. 249–79. Washington, D.C.: National Education Association.

Strayer, G.D., et al. (1925). *Problems in educational administration.* New York: Teachers College, Columbia University.

Suzzalo, H. (1906). *The rise of local school supervision in Massachusetts.* Teachers College Contribution No. 1. New York: Teachers College, Columbia University.

Walton, J. (1962). The education of educational administrators. In J.A. Culbertson and S.P. Hencley (Eds.), *Preparing administrators: New perspectives.* Columbus, Ohio: University Council for Educational Administration.

Wildavsky, A. (1985). The once and future school of public policy. *The Public Interest,* No. 79 (Spring).

Williams, W. (1980). *The implementation perspective.* Berkeley: University of California Press.

Willower, D.J. (1981). Educational administration: Some philosophical and other considerations. *Journal of Educational Administration* 19 (2) (Summer): 115–35.

Woellner, E.H. (1981). *Requirements for certification.* Chicago: University of Chicago Press.

21

The Professorship Revisited

Daniel E. Griffiths

Twenty-one years ago I wrote a paper that was given at the University Council for Educational Administration (UCEA) seminar at Penn State on the professorship. In that article I presented some thoughts on the professor of educational administration and on the environment of the department and of the school in which it was located. Some of the ideas have worn well, some need revision, but others appear ridiculous when viewed now. For example, I accepted without question the following recommendation of the American Association of School Administrators (AASA) as it appeared in *Professional Educators for America's Schools*: (Griffiths, 1964, pp. 29–46).

> To staff adequately an institution preparing administrators, it is anticipated that the following faculty and supplementary personnel will be needed in the area of educational administration if the average annual number of full-time students is sixty:
>   Three senior faculty members . . .
>   Five associate faculty members . . .
>   Two assistant faculty members . . .
>   Ten assistants . . .
>   Seven secretaries . . .
> [The terminology is somewhat awkward: the first three refer to professorial ranks; the assistants are graduate students.]
> I am talking about a relatively large department in a school of education within a university: a department of ten professors and sixty full-time students. The professors would be housed as a unit with individual offices of a minimum size of

ninety-six square feet, a large seminar room, a library of basic reference materials
and periodicals, a large room with a desk for each of the assistants, and secretarial
and reception areas planned for optimum use. [AASA, 1960, p. 215]

Seven secretaries! Ten assistants! Ten professors for sixty students! Remember, the recommendation appeared in 1960 in the middle of the golden age of
educational administration. Since I was one of the authors of the yearbook, I
probably devised the scheme, and I'm stuck with it. Keep it in mind as we
proceed.

Typology of Professors

I next devised a categorization of professors of educational administration
shaped after the work of Alvin Gouldner and Burton Clark (Table 21–1).
First, it seemed that the cosmopolitan-local dimension was appropriate. The
second dimension was one that I concocted. There are many professors who
conduct meetings, conferences, or classes, but who do not contribute anything of substance. They carve out careers as arrangers, moderators, or
chairmen. When they do talk to a topic, they discuss how to do it rather than
what to do. When they attend national conferences, they generally keep
quiet, since someone else has arranged the meeting; others, usually of higher
prestige, do the moderating. This dimension appears to me to be independent of the local-cosmopolitan orientation. The dimension seems to run from
those who "conduct" at one extreme to those interested in substance at the
other. This is called the conductor-scholar dimension. Combining the two
dimensions produces six types of orientations. They are abstract, and some
are extreme. Some professors can be classified as more than one type; under
certain circumstances they may move from one type to another.

In 1964 I described the types of professors as follows:

The Teacher is often characterized as the professor who stays home and tends to
the store. He generally has the maximum teaching load and often has classes with
the most students, since they are the core of foundation courses. He carries a heavy

Table 21–1
**Types of Professors of Educational Administration as Derived from Two
Dimensions of Professorial Activity**

	Scholar to Conductor Orientation		
Local to Cosmopolitan Orientation	Teacher	Demonstrator	Conductor
	Researcher	Consultant	Entrepreneur

load of doctoral students for both program and thesis advisement. He is oriented to the subject matter of his courses although he often uses buzz sessions, small groups, and other techniques of letting students share their experiences. He writes little and does no research. The Teacher is loyal to the university and does not seek positions elsewhere. He is a member of the inner reference group.

The Demonstrator may be the retired school administrator who joins the department staff. He supervises the interns, conducts field trips, and tells the students how he did it out there on the firing line. He does no writing or research. He is essentially a local, although he may have strong ties to the profession through his work with AASA. Because of his short tenure, he does not exercise very much influence on the inner reference group in his department, nor does he get to be well-known in the university. His loyalties are essentially to the school of education rather than the profession.

The Conductor is generally a local, although some do conduct at the regional and national level. He may be in charge of the department's program of work-shops and conferences, or he may do his conducting through planning and operating field trips. When a Conductor teaches a class, he may use the vaudeville technique of bringing in a succession of visiting lecturers or moderate the exchange of student views of the world. His idea of good instruction is to have every student say something. Other Conductors manage trips abroad, acting as amateur travel agents. When Conductors write they generally produce a travelogue or an idealized description of how they conducted a workshop or class. They do no research. They are locals largely because there is little or no market for Conductors; generally they are rather influential with the inner reference group.

The Researcher is a cosmopolitan absorbed in the study of administration and caring little where he does his work. He generally specializes in the study of one aspect of administration. He writes a great deal, usually articles, pamphlets, or chapters of specialized books. Occasionally he writes a textbook. He has a small teaching load, and although he spends most of his time doing research, he does not have many thesis advisees. There are many reasons for the small number of thesis advisees, among them being the fact that the Teacher takes as many as he can get. Since he also does the doctoral program advising and sees the student first, he gets first choice. The Teacher uses his large number of doctoral advisees as a way of wielding influence with the administration. The Researcher does not need to do this and so does not compete for thesis advisees. Further, most students do not want to get mixed up with a Researcher when they do their doctoral study. The Researcher owes his allegiance to the study of administration and gains his stimulation from social scientists and others outside the department. He is active in national organizations and centers his loyalty on them rather than his department. He will take another job for more money or better working conditions and is very mobile.

The Consultant is the big-time professional man, the man of the professional school who has a national reputation and mobility. Like the Demonstrator, he is primarily concerned with practice, the application of knowledge, rather than disinterested study. . . . He is also busy with his outside commitments, more than the research cosmopolitans, since he consults with outside organizations and is caught up in the committee system of his profession. As a professional educator, for example, he consults with school systems locally and throughout the nation, attends a meeting of a committee of the National Education Association in Denver this week, gives an address to a state association of high school principals in Milwaukee the next. He has expertise, and will travel (Clark, 1962).

In addition, he generally writes the textbooks, and, in fact, often gains his reputation through the books he writes. His books do not reflect deep analysis of the subject matter, but "cover" all aspects of the topics, generally using secondary sources for references.

The Entrepreneur is the extreme of the cosmopolitan and "conductor" orientations. He performs services to schools and other agencies for a fee. The Entrepreneur is generally found in the large university and, upon attaining tenure, is as little involved with it as possible. He sometimes operates alone, but more often conducts a business enterprise involving a number of others, generally those categorized as Consultants. He does surveys, conducts studies, and writes educational materials, all generally based upon his background of experience. His major contribution to education is the introduction of modern ideas into school systems. He might also write for popular magazines such as *Women's World* or the *Ladies' Home Journal*. The Entrepreneur has an outside reference group, often the AASA. He wields little influence on the affairs of the department, since he is not a member of committees and interacts little with other department personnel. He often holds views which differ widely from those of others in the department, but these views do not influence the program or activities of the department to any visible extent. [Griffiths, 1964, pp. 39–41]

At the time, my guess was that the environment of a department would be shaped by the kinds of professors in it. Of course, this is a bit circular because the types of professor hired by a university would also be a contributing factor. So, if a department hired only teachers, one could assume that the environment would differ from a department of entrepreneurs. I would also assume that if a university wanted to shape the environment of a department, one might give some thought to the kind of department wanted and then hire professors who would fit the concept.

Two Departments of Educational Administration

The Composition of the Departments in 1961

I went on to describe two departments I knew rather well at the time (1961), which were the largest in the country. I shall present those descriptions and then give you a description of both departments as they were in January 1984.

Department A was composed almost exclusively of Entrepreneurs, Consultants, Demonstrators, and Conductors. It was a large department, with some twenty professors and several hundred students, 10 percent of whom were full-time. Its staff members spoke at every major and many minor functions all over the country. The Entrepreneurs did surveys in all of the states and some of the territories. Large numbers of practicing administrators came to workshops and conferences arranged by the several Conductors in the department. The programs consisted of a succession of speakers drawn from both within and without the university. The department members were highly influential at the national level, but had little or no influence in their school. The control at home was in the hands of departments more liberally populated with locals. The department in question had only one professor who could be categorized as a Teacher. He had an inordinately large teaching load, a high number of program and thesis advisees, and made the least money. The department was originally recruited so as to be populated with Consultants and Entrepreneurs, and since then basically employed its own graduates. The students complained bitterly because they never knew who would be conducting their classes, and they were unable to see their professors for advice on their theses (one student drove his professor to the airport as his sole means of getting advice). Further, they felt that there was no real program of studies, since duplication was rampant and many lectures consisted of narrations of the professor's last trip. The department produced a large number of textbooks, but little research.

Department B was also large, but it was composed of Teachers, Demonstrators, Conductors, and a single Consultant. It was in a large school of education which saw its role as a service agent to the local community. Most of the students were part-time and came from close by. All of the professors had heavy teaching-loads, but program advisement and thesis consultation were divided evenly among staff members. The students commented favorably on the accessibility of professors and on the practical advice they were given in class. Many objected to the so-called "group-dynamics" approach to teaching, used by many of the professors: they would have preferred to draw on valuable faculty experience. Although the department had placed large numbers of superintendents and principals, it had few professors of educational administration in the country's universities. With the exception of the Consultant, the department exercised no influence on national groups, but was influential in its school, with members being elected to the Faculty Council and University Senate. The professors had an inner reference group orientation and knew and were known by large numbers of university faculty members. Department B produced a few textbooks, little other writing, and practically no research. It performed the service role expected by the university through its teaching and student advisement. There were few conferences or workshops; when held they met for credit within the regular course structure. The Consultant "brought in" the superintendents and principals and he also conducted the workshops and conferences. (Teachers, Demonstrators, and Consultants alike are rewarded for their efforts, since they meet university expectations.) The department recruited its members largely from the ranks of both superintendents who retired early and practicing administrators. There was never a Researcher as a staff member. [Griffiths, 1964, pp. 42, 43]

Present-Day Composition of the Departments

Department A is composed of seven full-time professors classified as follows:

Two teachers
Four researchers
One demonstrator

Each of the professors has a specialization, such as the elementary principalship, politics of education, school business administration, and psycho-social aspects of administration. One of the researchers started as an anthropologist, but undertook training as a psychologist and now has a private practice in addition to his professorship. Another has an MBA, and a third specializes in the management of information systems and high technology. One of the researchers should be more properly categorized as a researcher-consultant. He explains that consulting is necessary in order to get an adequate income. He points out, however, that consulting provides funds and access to funds for research. Another researcher should be called a researcher-developer because virtually all of his work is in development, not research.

There are some 30 full-time students, largely supported through grants held by individual professors, and approximately 250 part-time students. A major revision of the curriculum for this department is now underway.

Department B has seven full-time professors, six part time, and two part timers who supervise interns. There are 2 full-time students, about 200 part time on campus, and 90 registered in off-campus residence centers. The categories of professors are as follows:

Four teachers
Two researcher-consultants
One demonstrator

The specializations of full-time professors include organizational theory, organizational development and organizational climate, secondary school administration, research, special education administration, futures, policy-making and politics of education, and administrative applications of microcomputers. Several members of the program are active in the AASA, the American Educational Research Association (AERA), the Collegiate Association for the Development of Educational Administration (CADEA), and other state, national, and international groups. The researcher-consultants have published extensively, and the department has hosted the *Educational Administration Quarterly*.

This educational administration program is located in the Department of Organizational Studies together with educational sociology, human relations, and higher education; some courses are taught by professors from the other programs. There has been some redesigning of aspects of the program in the past year.

The drastic changes in two departments over a twenty-five-year period led me to wonder about other programs in the state. I contacted professors, usually the department chair, at four other doctoral-granting institutions and compiled descriptions of each department. Remember that my data for the present composition are from the departments, while the 1961 report was based on my own observation. The data are contained in Table 21–2, and the following observations seem appropriate:

— The two largest departments in 1961 were also the two largest in the country. Their size now is what appears to be the mode for doctoral-granting institutions in the state. The two largest programs in the country (in numbers of professors) now appear to be SUNY-Albany and Northern Illinois.

— The number of students has declined drastically.

— As a result of the modal size (seven), some specializations are uncovered and professors teach out of license.

— The most significant changes might be those in faculty composition:

There is a substantial increase in the number of researchers.

The researcher-consultant has emerged as a new type.

There are fewer demonstrators and conductors.

The lack of conductors might be the result of changes in what is taught.

There are three women professors among the schools surveyed and at least two more in the state. I believe there was one in the country in 1961: Professor Evelyn B. Martin of Florida A & M.

There is an increase in the number of professors with no training in education or administration, but with Ph.D.'s in sociology, psychology, economics, and other behavioral sciences.

There appear to be few ex-superintendents and ex-principals on the faculties of educational administration departments. Some have none; the one with the most has three.

— The number of full-time students in the departments varies markedly. As many as 50 percent of the students are women, in marked contrast with 1961. There are more foreign students in more universities. (One up-state university noted they previously thought a foreign student was one from Long Island.)

— Respondents reported program revision underway in most universities. Cost-cutting is the rationale of some; for example, several finance courses might be combined into one, and some courses might be weeded-out.

Table 21-2
Composition of Six New York State Departments of Educational Administration in 1984 Contrasted with Two Departments in 1961

	Teacher	Demonstrator	Conductor	Researcher	Consultant	Entrepreneur	Total Faculty Full-time	Total Faculty Part-time	Students Full-time	Students Part-time
A	1	X	X		X	X	20	NA	40 (App.)	1000
B	X	X	X		1		20	NA	NA	1000
A'	2	1		4*****			7*	None	30	250
B'	4	1		2****			7	8	2	290
C	3			4***			7	None	35	200
D	3			3			6	3	16	90
E	2	3		2			7	2	3	310
F	4			10	1	1	16**	4	20	200

(1961: rows A, B) (1984: rows A', B', C, D, E, F)

* One woman
** Two women
*** One researcher-consultant
**** Two researcher-consultants
***** One researcher-consultant

— One university reported the faculty in educational administration has doubled since 1974, while student enrollment has declined.

— While the number of researchers has increased rather dramatically, I have not noticed any increase in either the quality or quantity of published research.

Problems Confronting Professors of Educational Administration

Professors of educational administration have been battered by all of the problems that have hit education and the schools, plus some of their own making. There has been the decline in enrollment, which has resulted in fewer schools and, of course, fewer administrators. The decline in achievement has brought about a decline in public confidence, resulting in the lack of growth in resources. Schools of education have fallen on hard times, and educational administration departments have had it as hard as any. Personally, I do not see the light at the end of the tunnel in spite of the rash of interest generated by the twenty-four national studies of education, the survival of the Department of Education, the impending shortage of teachers, and President Reagan's newly found interest in education.

The unique problem for professors of educational administration is the attack on the discipline—on the substance of what is taught and the methodology of the research that is done.

We are, in our research methodology in educational administration, in a period in which we acknowledge the weakness of positivism, but we have not yet entered the period of post-positivism. We appear to be rejecting the approach that gave the world its greatest scientific productivity and are now seeing a raft of approaches such as phenomenology, ethnomethodology, symbolic interaction, neo-symbolic interaction, and the sociology of the absurd. Probably the only assumption these approaches share is that human beings create their own social reality in interaction with others. We are also becoming very aware of the obvious shortcomings of traditional organizational theory, a topic I shall touch on later. Then, too, there is a variety of Marxist approaches that appeals to many social scientists.

The present period in the philosophy of science has been termed "chaotic" by Suppe (1977). Many of the ideas and concepts that once seemed so certain to theoreticians are no longer held. Take the word "theory," for instance. Shapere (1969, p. 209) sums up the present by saying, "There is today, no completely—one is almost tempted to say remotely—satisfactory analysis of the notion of a scientific theory."

The chaotic situation in organizational studies has come about because of the inadequacies of present theories to account for what is observed in organizations. In my paper "Intellectual Turmoil in Educational Administration" I attempted to catalogue and analyze the criticisms of organizational theory (Griffiths, 1979, pp. 43–65). The criticisms range widely, from addressing the fact that organizational theories ignore the presence of unions and fail to account for the scarcity of women and minorities in top administrative positions to noting the failure of those theories to account for the degree of external control that is exercised over practically all organizations. Organizational theories also strive to be universal, but end up with only limited applicability. Then there is the criticism of Perrow (1978), now accepted by many, which questions the long-held assumption that organizations ". . . are, or can be, rational instruments of announced goals" (p. 247). The rejection of this assumption is central to what Perrow terms "demystifying organizations." The rise of ideologically based theories such as Marxism, the introduction of new research methodologies such as ethnographic studies, and the popularity of phenomenology all add up to a confusing picture. C.P. Snow (1971, p. 56) has said, "The scientific process has two motives: one is to understand the natural world, the other is to control it." This statement is as true for the organizational theorist as it is for the physical scientist. At present, we can neither describe our organizations nor control them, and this is at the heart of the present situation.

Probably the most significant, and positive, analysis of the present state of affairs in the study of organizations is that of Burrell and Morgan (1980). It is their contention that studies of organizations fall into four paradigms, each with its own assumptions and methodologies, and each raising different questions. It would seem that no one paradigm holds the only key to understanding organizations, but each offers particular insights important to students of organizations. They are suggesting that the study of organizations be conducted through the use of all paradigms, not one; rather than having competition among the paradigms there should be cooperation. They advocate an era of paradigm diversity or, to put it more positively, the use of multiple paradigms. Such an approach might well result in a different academic content for educational administration, one which would not be as subject to numerous criticisms as is the present content. While the current scene in educational administration is chaotic, there does seem to be a way of rendering it more orderly. We should welcome the era of multiple paradigms.

In summary, we have different professors today than we had in 1961. We have a different content than we had in 1961. This content is under attack and will doubtless be changed. The crucial question, however, is this: "Are we producing better school administrators?" The jury is still out on that one.

References

American Association of School Administrators. (1960). *Professional educators for America's schools*. Washington, D.C.: The Association.

Burrell, G., and Morgan, G. (1980). *Sociological paradigms and organizational analysis*. London: Heinemann.

Clark, B.R. (1962). Faculty culture. In T.R. Lunsford (Ed.), *The study of campus cultures*, pp. 39–54. Berkeley: University of California Press.

Griffiths, D.E. (1964). The professorship in educational administration: Environment. In D.J. Willower and J. Culbertson (Eds.), *The Professorship in Educational Administration*, pp. 29–46. Columbus, Ohio: University Council for Educational Administration.

Griffiths, D.E. (1979). Intellectual turmoil in educational administration. *Educational Administration Quarterly* 15 (3) (Fall): 43–65.

Perrow, C. (1978). Demystifying organizations. In Y. Hasenfeld and R. Saari (Eds.), *The management of human services*. New York: Columbia University Press.

Shapere, D. (1969). Notes toward a post-positivistic interpretation of science. In P. Achinstein and S.F. Barker (Eds.), *The legacy of logical positivism*. Baltimore: The Johns Hopkins Press.

Snow, C.P. (1971). The two cultures, a second look. *Public affairs*. New York: Charles Scribner.

Suppe, F. (1977). *The structure of scientific theories*. Urbana: University of Illinois Press.

22

The Preparation of Educational Administrators

Daniel E. Griffiths, Robert T. Stout, and Patrick B. Forsyth

Across the nation educational administrators face difficult, complex, and continually changing problems. Needed are highly qualified, well-prepared administrators who can place these daily administrative problems in the context of a long-term vision of what excellent education can be and find solutions to nagging problems. But more than that, education needs administrators who can create the environments and secure the resources to release the creative talents of teachers. Also needed are graduate-level programs of varied form and content that offer bright students a sound theoretical base, a knowledge of administration in an educational setting, an understanding of basic educational issues, a substantial exposure to the realities of educational administration, and training in the skills of administration. For such programs to be devised, departments of educational administration must be restructured and upgraded. Even the nature of the doctorate in educational administration needs to be reconsidered. All these changes are necessary to assure that the schools receive the leadership they will need in the twenty-first century.

284

Criticisms of Educational Administration

"Superintendent bashing" in American public education is not a recent phenomenon (Callahan, 1962; Campbell et al., 1985; Griffiths, 1966; Tyack and Hansot, 1982). However, in the last decade, criticisms have intensified as a result of such reports as *A Nation At Risk* (National Commission on Excellence in Education, 1983) and *Time for Results* (National Governors' Association, 1986). The criticisms have had two foci. First has been the criticism that educational administrators are simply not as competent as administrators in other fields. The second is that school administrator behaviors have not kept up with changing public expectations of the purpose of schools and for administrator behavior.

Modern criticisms of public school administrators stem from the current mood of dissatisfaction with public schooling in general. If public schools are not of sufficiently high quality (however defined), then perforce the blame must rest with the schools' administrators. Consequently, superintendents and principals are criticized for lack of leadership, lack of vision, lack of modern management skills, and lack of courage to do the things that must be done in order to make schools more effective.

Because the criticisms range widely, we will not fully explore them all here. However, some of the most noteworthy will be reviewed. Among the most telling of the criticisms is that preparation programs for school administrators are of low quality and irrelevant for practice. Peterson and Finn (1985) disparage preparation programs for their "Mickey Mouse" courses, for following an arts and sciences model rather than a professional school model, for low admissions standards, and for poor clinical training. Haller and Knapp (1985) argue that the research capability of education administration professors and their students is limited at best. Erickson (1979) and Bridges (1982) both argue that the focus of research is misdirected. Griffiths (1979) has argued that the theoretical underpinning of school administration practice is under attack on a number of grounds. Summary reports by Hawley (1988), Pitner (1982), and McCarthy (1987) describe a collection of serious difficulties in the preparation of school administrators in the United States.

Superintendents are criticized for being timid and wedded to status quo policies and procedures. As Achilles (1984) states:

> When most of today's superintendents were still classroom teachers . . . they were quiescent, conservative, and respectful of authority. Those who didn't accept these norms dropped out.
>
> Surviving male teachers, then, tended to become more politically conservative and to develop an unusually high need for respect, an exaggerated concern for authority, and a personal rigidity and fear of risk-taking behavior.

Superintendents are also criticized for high-handed and manipulative behavior toward policymakers (Zeigler, 1973; Boyd, 1976) and for failing to help school board members take appropriate policymaking roles (Carol et al., 1986). Other criticisms contribute to the picture of general lack of leadership in a low-performing system (Cuban, 1976; Pitner, 1981).

School principals as well face increasing scrutiny. Recent studies have pointed out that all too often principals are not able to lead teachers and students to high performance levels. Principals who cannot are described as lacking in vision, unable to express a vision to others, reluctant to try to make needed changes, unwilling to monitor teachers' work and unwilling to intervene in the business of the school (Russell et al., 1985; Rutherford, 1985). In effect, too many principals are unwilling or unable to assume positions of active, future-oriented school leadership (Martin and Willower, 1981).

While it may be argued that such criticisms are unjust, inaccurate, or applicable to only a few administrators, the general call for reform in administrator behavior has been substantial. State and local policymakers have acted and are acting as though the criticisms are valid.

A Concept of Educational Administration

There has been little interest since the 1950s in developing a comprehensive concept of educational administration. In the 1950s, with the extensive funding of the Kellogg Foundation and the interest of social scientists and professors of educational administration, considerable time and effort were devoted to working out sophisticated concepts of educational administration (Moore, 1957, p. 25). Since the 1950s, however, attention to the concept of educational administration has been sporadic, driven by fads, and marked by attention to splinters, not wholes.

The competency-based movement lasted for about ten years in the 1960s and 1970s. The idea was that the job of the administrator could be broken up into a large number of ill-defined items called competencies. These could be taught to students who would then, somehow, put them together and understand administration. While interest has waned in the competency movement, there are still those who consider it worthwhile. In actuality, the competency movement was a lost decade in the search for a concept of educational administration.

More recently interest has turned to administrators as leaders, and a great deal is being said about the need for principals to be "instructional leaders" (Edmonds, 1979). This view is based on the assumption that schools cannot improve themselves, that state legislatures or departments of education must tell them what they must do. The role of the administrator is, apparently, to see to it that the schools do what they are told to do. The concept could well be called "the effective school manager," based as it is on the research studies on effective schools. These studies recommend strong administrators who set goals, monitor student and teacher performance, build a stable climate, develop job descriptions, set rules and policies that ensure reliable behavior, attempt to control all aspects of the school, and emphasize centralization and efficiency. Effective school principals, it is said, should spend most of their time being instructional leaders. The critics contend that education would improve tremendously if we had "effective school managers" as principals. In fact, "instructional leader" and "effective school manager" seem to be used as synonyms for "strong leader."

On the other hand, as Greenfield (1988, this volume) points out, "The concept of instructional leadership is a *very narrow* view of the work of school principals, particularly to the extent that it suggests that working directly with teachers is what effective principals actually do." He refers to fourteen studies that indicate that most school principals spend very little time directly supervising or observing teachers in classrooms. Greenfield concludes, "The call for more and better instructional leadership is a 'prescription' that reflects virtually no understanding or recognition of the realities of the school work situation encountered by the principal."

Should we look, however, to the studies of what principals do on the job, then we are faced with another dilemma. Pitner (1982, and this volume) has concluded: " . . . while we know to the minutest detail the length of every phone call made and meetings attended by the administrator, the people with whom he or she interacted, and the locations of these encounters, we know very little about what impact these activities have on the school organization and, specifically, on student achievement."

Gronn (1982) is even more emphatic in his evaluation of what he calls the reincarnation of Taylorism. In an analysis of the work of eight researchers purporting to study what principals actually do, he writes:

> Never at any state was it established what principals, superintendents, or program managers do. Invariably, the researchers suggested that such persons sit at their desks, go on tours, walk up and down corridors, write, attend meetings, talk, and so on. . . . The question still remains: What do the administrators *do* at their desks, *do* with their talk, *do* in the corridor, *do* on tours, and *do* with their writing? [P. 24]

Many of those who study modern successful organizations say that administrators should be quite the opposite of the "effective school manager" prototype. Drawing heavily on Peters and Waterman's work (1982), *In Search of Excellence*, and on Kanter's (1983), *The Change Masters*, Astuto and Clark (1988) draw a remarkably different picture of what school administrators should do. They say successful administrators strive for activity (numerous trials and innovations), culture building, divergent behavior, reinforcement of creativity, commitment of teachers and other participants, loose coupling, and productivity and innovation. These administrators believe that if the creativity of the faculty can be released and guided and if resources can be provided, then schools will improve. This concept of an administrator is very similar to one developed by those in the human relations movement. The modern name for such an administrator is "culture builder."

Because the literature does not offer unequivocal guidance to an accepted concept of the principalship or the superintendency, the door is open to all comers. We accept the invitation. As we combine long observation with discreet selections from the literature, a picture of desirable administration emerges.

In order not to make the common mistake of settling on a single narrow approach to conceptualizing educational administration, we start by noting Brooks Adams' definition, written in 1913. In spite of the archaic and sexist language the thrust is modern. In fact, it is more modern in stressing the scope and significance of administration than most of what is written today. He said:

> Administration is the capacity of coordinating many, and often conflicting, social energies in a single organism so adroitly that they shall operate as a unity. This presupposed the power of reorganizing a series of relations between numerous special social interests, with all of which no single man can be intimately acquainted. Probably no very highly specialized class can be strong in this intellectual quality because of the intellectual isolation incident to specialization, and yet administration or generalization is not only the faculty upon which social stability rests, but it is possibly the highest faculty of the human mind. [P. 216]

Putting these thoughts into the education context, we believe the administrator must deal with a wide variety of problems and situations and with many kinds of people and must have a wide array of abilities. While the administrator must be a leader, that is, must develop a sense of purpose within the school and community to bring about the necessary changes, the administrator must also have the technical skills needed to make the organization function effectively and efficiently and, in addition, the human relations talents to maximize the production and creativity of all those in the organization.

What an administrator does at a given time is heavily dependent on the situation in which the administrator works. If, for instance, we accept the premises of the Holmes Group (1986) or Carnegie Forum (1986), then the school organization and staff will be very different from those in present-day conventional schools. Some teachers (those who are highly educated and highly competent) would have considerable input regarding curriculum decisions, supervision, and school policy. Administration in such a school would differ greatly from that in a school with poorly educated and incompetent teaching staff.

In the first school the principal would be well advised to provide resources, develop with the teachers a sense of purpose, encourage staff, deal with superiors and the external environment, but otherwise stay out of the way. In the second school the instructional leader type of administrator would most likely be successful. The rule appears to be: The less qualified the teachers, the more strong leadership is needed; the more qualified the teachers, the less strong leadership is needed.

There is, of course, more to administration than saying, "It all depends. . . ." The setting is important and, many times, crucial. In fact, there are settings in which no administrator can be successful, and there are settings in which almost any administrator can succeed. The setting determines the parameters in which one works and establishes the limits of what can be accomplished. Superintendents, in particular, and principals, to an extent, spend a great deal of time working with the setting, that is, the environment in which the schools function.

One of the most insightful discussions of what the setting has done to educational administration is that of Fritz Hess (1983), Superintendent of Schools in East Syracuse, New York. He summarizes as follows:

> In the last analysis, the evolution of the practice of educational administration during the period 1959–1981 has been an evolution of roles. Sweeping alterations in American society, in student enrollments, in personnel, in regulation, in finance, and in technology have changed school executives from the leaders of an unquestioned institution to conflict managers and advocates in an intensely competitive environment. The transformation has been a dramatic one. It has been accompanied by considerable stress and dislocation. It continues to unfold in many areas; yet it has already encompassed trends that have totally reshaped the assumptions on which administrative practice in 1959 was based. [P. 245]

Since special interest groups, clients, workers, and governmental officials all believe they have legitimate roles in the management of schools, superintendents are not so much managers as they are politicians attempting to resolve conflicting demands on the organization. They use negotiation and persuasion as their major tools.

The Preparation Program

In this section we discuss the broad outlines of a desirable program for the preparation of school administrators, which we do *not* suggest is the *only* program possible. Within the guidelines advocated in this paper many different variations are possible. Only the creativity of professors and school administrators limit the number of variations. Because recruitment and selection of potential administrators is so important, we begin with a discussion and recommendations that should lead to better students in administrator preparation programs and, thus, to better administrators.

Recruitment and Selection

Bright people with proven leadership potential must be attracted to the ranks of educational administrators. Presently this is not happening. In fact, most programs have "open admissions," with a baccalaureate degree the only prerequisite. Those who enter educational administration programs are either self-selected (the vast majority) or tapped by superiors (a small, but significant number). The Graduate Record Examination (GRE) is the single best indicator of the mental ability of graduate students. Table 22–1 compares the average scores on the verbal, quantitative, and analytical tests of those in several professional fields with the mean scores of all those taking the GRE. Computer science is, next to psychology, the most popular graduate major, while medicine, law, business and commerce, and public administration are other majors with large numbers of students. Students in only three major fields—physical education, social work, and home economics—have lower scores than do students in educational administration. In fact, of the ninety-four intended majors listed in *Guide to the Use of the Graduate Record Examination Program, 1985–86* (1985, pp. 22–26), educational administration ranks fourth from the bottom. Certainly, the principalship and superintendency demand more in intellectual ability than the current crop of students has demonstrated.

Careful recruitment and selection from the pool of teachers would result in enrolling educational administration graduate students with much higher intellectual ability. A clue to the size of this pool can be found in the scores of education graduate students on the Graduate Record Examination (GRE). About 35 percent of these students taking the GRE score above the means on each general test: verbal, quantitative, and analytical. Efforts should be made by boards of education, superintendents and principals, state education departments, and other professional organizations to induce these people to consider becoming administrators. Lest some think too much emphasis is placed on the intellectual criterion for educational administrators, they should be reminded that there are no recorded examples of good dumb principals or successful stupid superintendents.

In addition to the intellectual dimension, those wishing to become educational administrators should have demonstrated some capacity for leadership during their high school and college years. Those who were or are Scout leaders, team captains, or presidents of clubs or classes should receive special attention. After all, the best predictor of whether people will become effective leaders is the fact that they have led.

Although there is no definitive research evidence that other characteristics

Table 22–1
Comparison of Graduate Record Examination Score Means of Students in Selected Intended Major Graduate Fields with Total Means (1981–1984)

Intended Major	Means/Majors		Total Means	Difference
Physics	V	555	472	+ 83
	Q	696	539	+ 157
	A	615	505	+ 110
				+ 250
Computer Science	V	489	472	− 17
	Q	646	539	+ 107
	A	582	505	+ 77
				+ 167
Medicine	V	499	472	+ 27
	Q	578	539	+ 39
	A	554	505	+ 49
				+ 115
Business and Commerce	V	458	472	− 14
	Q	536	539	− 3
	A	517	505	+ 12
				− 5
Law	V	466	472	− 6
	Q	479	539	− 60
	A	502	505	− 3
				− 69
Public Administration	V	466	472	− 6
	Q	476	539	− 63
	A	494	505	− 11
				− 80
Educational Administration	V	435	472	− 37
	Q	468	539	− 71
	A	486	505	− 19
				− 127
Physical Education	V	417	472	− 55
	Q	474	539	− 65
	A	484	505	− 21
				− 141

Note: V = Verbal test score
        Q = Qualitative test score
        A = Analytical test score

are necessary to become a successful administrator, informed observers agree that certain characteristics are valuable. These include social skills, the ability to speak and write clearly and persuasively, emotional maturity, adequate health, decent character, vision, understanding of America's varied cultures, sensitivity to change, and motivation (Miskel, 1983).

Although many graduate programs require applicants to submit GRE scores and occasionally Miller Analogies Scores, they do not use the scores to select students. Others do use the scores and have established varying cut-off scores; a few require a combined score on the verbal and quantitative tests of at least 1,000 and others required a combined score of as low as 800. Some universities may require evidence of other leadership and administrative traits, but we do not know of any.

Since school administrators deal with a wide array of topics, subjects, and problems, they need to have had a good general education. If they do not have such a background, they should be required to take arts and science courses that will give them a good general education background.

Enrollment of women in educational administration programs nationwide is approaching 50 percent, a trend that should be encouraged. Enrollment of minorities in such programs has, however, declined and is now at 2 or 3 percent. Strenuous efforts should be made to recruit into educational administrative programs those minority students who meet the above standards.

In summary, every program in educational administration should have extensive recruitment and intensive selection. Students should be drawn from those with GRE scores in the upper 50 percent and who have displayed leadership in their high school and college years and in their professional careers. Selection is far more important than most universities acknowledge. Training programs are not so powerful that they can make strong administrators out of people who lack intellectual and personal abilities. The old saw is right, "You cannot make a silk purse out of a sow's ear."

The Program

An extremely high percentage (as high as 95 percent) of all graduate students in educational administration attend part time, which is one of the major reasons for many of the problems that afflict programs. Courses are not sequential; and students do not develop esprit de corps, do not use libraries, computer facilities, and the like, do not develop close relationships with professors, and do not have the opportunity to participate in field research projects. In short, students do not really experience the benefits available to full-time students.

Even though some difficulties are involved, the study of educational administration should be a full-time endeavor, as it is in most of the other professions, and students should move through the program as cohorts. If the difficulties are too great, alternatives to full-time study should be developed that will guarantee the benefits available to full-time students. Boston College, New York University, and the University of Alberta have made progress in this direction.

The responsibility for preparing educational administrators should be shared with the profession and the public schools. Each should do what each can do best. The university should provide the intellectual dimension of preparation. As March (1974) notes:

> Universities do as good a job as anyone at most aspects of management training. They do better at providing the basic knowledge, at identifying general problems, at isolating and providing broad experience in the necessary and intellectual skills, at discussing value issues, at encouraging risk-taking and initiative, at building social and personal sensitivity, at exposure to conflicting ideas and sentiments, and at building a sense of self-esteem. [P. 24]

The profession and the public schools are best at the clinical aspects of the program and should bear major responsibility for supervising field activities, which include the internship, and for solving practical problems in university classes.

Planning for the program should involve both professors and practitioners. The program should be conceived in the framework of the professional school model, not the arts and science model, meaning that the program should prepare students not merely to think about administration but to act, and should, therefore, stress clinical training but not neglect the intellectual aspects of preparation.

The program for preparing educational administrators should include courses from many different departments in the university, not just those offered exclusively in the department of educational administration. Universities are honeycombed with offerings in administration and with courses that could help students become better administrators. Some of these courses are psychology, philosophy, sociology, and anthropology in the arts and science department; budgeting, accounting, and systems analysis in the school of business; social agencies in the school of public administration; and education law in the school of law. No department of educational administration in the world can match the resources of a university. By using appropriate university offerings, programs can become much richer. Furthermore, the latest technological developments in teaching should be used. Advanced computer simulations, computers, films, and recordings should all be employed.

The program should be composed of five strands or themes. Just how these strands are handled could well vary from university to university, since each strand can be realized in many different ways; thus we give the details of each strand for illustrative purposes only. The strands are:

1. The theoretical study of educational administration
2. The study of the technical core of educational administration
3. The solution of problems through the use of applied research and the development of administrative skills
4. Involvement in supervised practice
5. The demonstration of competence

These strands, with the exception of the demonstration of competence, can be taken concurrently because they need not be sequential. Some courses in each strand might be taken in other schools in the university, or professors from other parts of the university might be induced to teach in the department of educational administration.

Strand 1. The Theoretical Study of Educational Administration. While administration is the performance of an action or, more accurately, many actions, these actions have an intellectual and value basis found in administrative science, the behavioral sciences, philosophy, and experience. Since these fields of study are vast, it is necessary to choose and construct courses that focus on administration. Simply sending a student to a graduate course in sociology or philosophy is not likely to contribute much to their preparation as administrators.

The course work in administrative theory should include the now-traditional study of social systems, decision making, contingency theory, bureaucracy, and the Barnard-Simon equilibrium theory. These are the functionalist theories, and by studying them, students can gain an understanding of modern organizations. Equal attention should be given to the new theories and approaches to understanding organizations. These include ethnography, phenomenology, naturalistic inquiry, as well as neo-Marxist theories. The former theories look at organizations from the point of view of management, while the latter view organizations from the position of an organizational member. In order to understand organizations, both views are necessary. In addition, the exploration of a variety of new metaphors for thinking about organizations and of such ideas as paradigm diversity would be useful (Burrell and Morgan, 1979). The following is a good guide for structuring the courses in administrative science:

> We propose that organizational analysis has been evolving . . . toward more complex, paradoxical, and even contradictory modes of understanding. Instead of monochromatic thinking, we suggest an interpretive framework more like a rainbow—a "code of many colors" that tolerates alternative assumptions. . . . For organizational analysis, we need to be able to perceive and understand the complex nature of organizational phenomena, both micro and macro, organizational and individual, conservative and dynamic. We need to understand organizations in multiple ways, as having "machine-like" aspects, "organism-like" aspects, and others yet to be identified. We need to encourage and use the tension

engendered by multiple images of our complex subject. [Jelinek, Smircich, and Hirsch, 1983, p. 331]

Few courses offered at the present time accomplish these objectives. Strand 1 should also give attention to the broad underlying issues that confront educational administrators, such as the nature of the curriculum, moral and ethical issues, how to deal with children with AIDS, minority questions, poverty in society, and the changing American society. These issues might be dealt with in a cohort seminar taught by a multidiscipline faculty using the case method.

This strand also includes work in the behavioral sciences, with each student taking courses in sociology, psychology, economics, or anthropology as his or her background demands.

Strand 2. The Technical Core of Educational Administration. Every profession has a core of technical knowledge that its practitioners must possess. Educational administration is no different. It too has a core of technical knowledge with which the educational administrator must be familiar. (Note we did not say master or be expert in.) Most superintendents and principals will have staff people who are experts in the various aspects of the technical core. The superintendent and principal need to know enough of the technical core to be able to direct and monitor the work of others who are, presumably, experts. March (1974), in his Cocking Lecture of 1973, discusses in considerable detail the management of expertise. Having an understanding of the technical core is one aspect of that ability.

Most programs have one of more courses in each aspect of the core such as school finance or law. It would make more sense if a single course of a year's duration were constructed to include the whole core and focus on how to manage experts in each core area. The components of the course would include supervision of instruction, curriculum building and evaluation, finance, law, personnel, school-community relations, pupil personnel, physical facilities, and school business management.

The technical core might well be augmented by course work in other departments of the school of education and in other schools of the university. These courses would be particularly valuable to those aspiring to the superintendency and those wishing to fill staff positions in school business administration. They include:

Arts and Science
  –Sociology of Complex Organizations
  –Demography
  –Philosophy—Values
  –Urban Sociology
  –Urban Anthropology

School of Public Administration
  –Information Systems for Public Organizations
  –Financial Decision Making for Public, Nonprofit, and Health Organiza-
    tions.
  –Urban Poverty
School of Social Work
  –Institutional Racism: Perspectives for Social Values
  –Treatment of Adolescents
  –Social Issues in Clinical Social Work
  –Social Work Practice in Child Welfare
School of Business
  –Managing Organizational Behavior
  –Operations Management
  –Financial Management
  –Systems Analysis and Design
  –Information Systems: Concepts and Issues
School of Education
  –Philosophy of Education
  –Sociology of Education
  –Computers
  –Psychology of Children
  –Curriculum Theory
  –Curriculum Evaluation

We remind the reader that this list is merely suggestive of the resources available in the university that can be used to prepare educational administrators. Offerings differ from university to university, so a careful study should be made of what is available and then the offerings incorporated in appropriate ways.

Because both the principal and the superintendent must be consummate educational politicians and negotiators, they should take at least one course in the politics of education and one in negotiations. The latter should not merely be a "book" course, but should include supervised practice in negotiating.

Strand 3. The Solution of Problems Through the Use of Applied Research and the Development of Administrative Skills. This strand would be taught both at the university and in the schools. The problems might well be posed through use of computer simulations, cases, and filmed incidents, and actual problems in the schools might be examined. Successful school administrators should be employed as adjunct professors to aid in the instruction. The students would be taught how to solve problems through the use of both quantitative and qualitative research methods as well as decision-making techniques. The substance of the problems should include ethics, values, human relations, curriculum, school-community relations, finance, and in-school problems such as student discipline.

Probably more school administrators fail because of poor skills than any other single reason, yet programs in educational administration fail to do anything about it. It's as though a baseball team in spring training gave the players books to read and lectures on the theory of baseball and did not have the players practice hitting and fielding. Administrators have to perform, and in order to perform well, they must have basic administrative skills:.

–Effective speaking
–Writing (memos, announcements, public relations, releases, and the like.)
–Conducting meetings of various sizes
–Conducting interviews
–Computer literacy
–Class scheduling
–Negotiating
–Supervising teachers
–Working with the board of education

It is recommended that each department establish an administrative skills center and that each student be tested on each of the skills and then tutored if found lacking to reach the desired level of performance. No academic credit should be granted for skills development.

The center could take several forms, depending on the resources available. In some instances the center would be administrative only, contracting with appropriate parts of the university for appropriate instruction, and in other cases it could be a physical site staffed with specialists. The former is a more likely choice.

Strand 4. Involvement in Supervised Practice. This strand could well be the most critical phase of an administrator's preparation. The student would start this clinical experience almost from the first day of graduate study. Starting with observations of school board meetings and administrators in action, the student would move through a series of short, special-purpose internships with a master administrator. Through these experiences, the student would develop a feel for administration and would start to acquire the background that will enable him or her to solve future problems.

The clinical experiences might well be organized by a university professor, but the students should be supervised by top administrators.

Strand 5. The Demonstration of Competence. The culminating experience would not be a research thesis, which is usually required. Rather, it would be a demonstration that the student has really learned something about performing as an administrator, which could be demonstrated by the student formulating a large computer simulation, partaking in a field test, or handling a large case. The student should also be required to do a field study either individually or in a group.

The student should be expected to demonstrate a philosophy of education and administration, a sensitivity to people, an awareness of ethical values, and technical competence.

The Professional Doctorate

We now ask, what is the nature of the degrees that should be given for the program we have discussed? Given that virtually all administrators will have been teachers and will have a master's degree in their teaching field, the degree should be a doctorate. The master's degree in educational administration should be dropped. After all, the program should take three years to complete and is post-master's. The doctorate is commonly the one earned by administrators: somewhere between one-third and one-half (depending on who does the counting) of the superintendents now have a doctorate. Since the program is heavily clinical and resembles professional doctoral programs in dentistry, medicine, and psychology, the degree should be a professional doctorate.

The original idea of the Ed.D. was that it would be education's professional doctorate. But professional educators have so bastardized the Ed.D. that one university's Ed.D. is another's Ph.D., and vice versa. A very respectable professional doctorate, whether it be called an Ed.D., D.Ed. Adm., or some other name, could be built on the recommendations we have made here. We believe that such a doctorate would, after a time, be accepted in the universities. Universities expect professional schools to have their own doctorate and express alarm at the present state of affairs. The attempt by professional educators to develop a pseudo arts and science doctorate has been met with scorn in most universities. It's high time we build what is expected: a professional doctorate.

The Role of the Department of Educational Administration

In 1973 the authors of a major study of professors of educational administration were perplexed by the complacence of professors in the face of recognized problems with administrator preparation, particularly the poor intellectual climate of the department (Campbell and Newell, 1973). Today, those professors continue to be complacent (McCarthy et al., in press). Fewer and older, these professors are faced with insufficient resources and small enrollments; they are less able and probably less disposed to improve administrator preparation now than they were in 1973.

Another concern expressed in the 1973 study, the dismal quantity and quality of research in educational administration, has been addressed by the "publish or perish" norm affecting the work of those entering the professorate in the last decade, especially in major universities. Unfortunately, channeling the young energy of departments into the pursuit of tenure by publication has, by and large, left the rethinking and renewal of preparation programs to those characterized as complacent. When efforts to change have emerged, they have often been superficial, reactive, and cosmetic.

Perhaps the single most destructive trend affecting professional preparation in school administration during the last thirty years has been domination by an arts and sciences model rather than a professional school model of education. The consequent failure to develop a sophisticated knowledge base for practice and divorce of preparation from the school setting are at least partly the result of this domination. The school of education has been cast in the role of the ugly stepsister of arts and sciences instead of taking its place with the other professional schools housed in the university.

At the major universities domination by arts and sciences has tended to establish a single, narrowly construed research path to tenure. The junior professors' concern for review and renewal of the preparation program, for the development and supervision of the clinical aspects of administrator preparation, for overseeing recruitment and selection, for instructional development and innovation, and for providing liaison with professional practice groups have been wholly displaced by the single-minded pursuit of publication. Yet, all these are vital concerns in the regeneration of administrator preparation.

Clearly, a focus on research has been necessary during the last thirty years. The resulting corpus of empirical and theoretical knowledge has value for further research as well as for practice. The extension of the knowledge base must continue to be a critical concern, but to strengthen departments and professors attention must be given to the cumulative effects the neglect of curriculum revision, clinical experiences, and advisement can have on administrator preparation. A research-oriented faculty can result in a collection of individuals rather than a cohesive department. In such a situation faculty members work independently and have little need or desire to interact with colleagues or students; the critical entity of faculty and students engaged in the study of school administration has given way to process without substance. The care of the preparation program may be left to the department secretary, and faculty members may concern themselves with the program primarily as reaction to university directive, legislative mandate, or market fluctuations in enrollment.

How might the vitality and intellectual climate of departments be enhanced? First, the notion of department leadership as a temporary and reluctant service must be discarded as an anachronism. Departments are not romantically conceived clusters of eccentrics governed by benevolent anarchy. The creation of a dynamic, effective setting for the study of schools and the preparation of school administrators is not a chance happening. Scholars who reluctantly serve as chairs are unlikely creators of the appropriate setting; election by peers does not often result in strong leadership. Departments preparing administrators need chairs who devote significant time to the programs of the departments and constantly propose change, adaptation, and renewal. The preparation of professionals requires constant adjustment to changing technology and to evolving notions of best practice, particularly in educational administration where the clinical knowledge base is in its infancy. For these same reasons, we would question the recent trend to combine educational administration with other areas of education in an artificial administrative unit.

Second, schools of education must stand with the other professional schools, which argue that the university has a mission broader than scholarship; it should include the preparation of practitioner educators as well as lawyers, architects, and doctors. The reward structure for professors in professional schools must reflect important responsibilities connected with professional life. Ultimately, roles in departments of educational administration need to be differentiated by both scholarly focus and responsibility for the many aspects of a professional preparation program.

Specialties that depart radically from the arts and sciences are appropriate for professional schools (Schein, 1972, pp. 139–49). *Information specialists*, for example, might be nonteaching professors concerned with student admission (recruitment, screening, assessment) as well as with testing and the student data system. The information specialist's research could involve periodic program evaluation, student data analysis, and test consulting with colleagues. In other words, the research area would be directly related to program role. *Field specialists* might be concerned primarily with the clinical aspects of administrator preparation. They would supervise interns, run the weekly intern seminars, and coordinate opportunities for colleagues and students to solve problems in the field. Their research would center on applied studies, the effects of administrator intervention, and case analysis. These professors might also teach field-study methods, case analysis, and other clinical studies. Despite the nontraditional nature of these roles, all professors would be expected to produce new knowledge directly related to school administration.

Third, the intellectual climate of the departments needs tending. The knowledge base of educational administration was borrowed from the theory and research of the social sciences. Unfortunately, it never evolved into a unique knowledge base informing the practice of school administration. Unlike medical research, which is often focused on specific problems of professional intervention (treatment), the research done by scholars in educational administration has followed the methods and organization of sociology. Like the sociologist, the researcher in educational administration has chosen to study schools and administration as they exist without examining the methods, possibilities, and consequences of professional intervention or standards of practice.

A knowledge base, organized around problems of practice, that includes administrative intervention and its consequences for teaching and learning must be developed. This implies the embrace of new research methods, information retrieval and display systems, and taxonomies of practice. Also implied are new partnerships between schools and universities for the collection, storage, retrieval, and analysis of information related to the professional practice of school administration. The traditional division between preclinical and clinical study might be abandoned (Hughes et al., 1973, p. 34). Contingent on these changes is the development of instructional materials, texts, and clinical learning opportunities consistent with the preparation of adult learners for the informed practice of school administration.

Technological developments require that professors rethink their primary responsibilities, such as the dissemination of professional knowledge. Computers, and the networking potential they afford, have important implications for what professors do, how they do it, and with whom they do it. Data about schools, new ideas about schools, and other kinds of information can be sent and received instantaneously and manipulated, displayed, and used in decision-making simulations by a multitude of simultaneous users. The processes of and new knowledge about school administration, and knowledge about practice and intervention can be disseminated in unprecedented ways. Practitioners, researchers, graduate students, and teachers can be effectively linked together to pose and address the complex problems of schooling. The constraints of time and restricted information have been dissolved by technological advances.

Without abandoning the belief that professional preparation is, at best, an intense, prolonged, and rigorous experience, we must push at the constraints and find new ways to deliver high-quality preparation to worthy candidates. Proceeding through programs as a cohort, students should experience the university community as dynamic; that is, professors should be there and be available, and journal clubs, guest scholars, research projects, and debate should be evident.

Colleges of education must work to restore a cadre of research and graduate assistants to the department. School districts must share responsibility for administrator preparation. Sabbaticals, paid fellowships, release time, and intern sponsorship are ways districts can assure themselves and the profession of a superior pool of administrator candidates. The revival and expansion of university study councils can provide relevant part-time employment for students within the university environment. Cooperative programs between the state department of education and the university can provide an enriched preparation program that combines salaried responsibilities in the state department with continuous residency within the university. In short, aggressive efforts can win the resources to make administrator preparation full-time academic and clinical work.

Departments and schools must also give new attention to the development needs of individual professors. Budget restrictions of the last decade have had a depressing effect on development opportunities as the professorate has grown older and less mobile. Travel to professional meetings and support for research, two of the primary means through which professors can develop have all but disappeared at many universities. A combination of old and new approaches, such as services to improve instruction, sabbaticals, exchange programs, retooling opportunities, career development services, and fellowship programs, may meet current needs.

In other professional schools professors keep current by continuing to practice. However, unlike a professor of dentistry, a professor of educational administration cannot practice school administration intermittently. The business professor maintains currency by maintaining a consulting practice. With careful planning and university coordination, this approach might keep administration professors current and provide the additional benefits of creating university-district linkages and locations where students and professors can jointly study schools. We underscore the need for departmental sponsorship, assignment, and quality control of consulting activities.

New mechanisms are needed to stimulate and disseminate changes in research methods and focus. For example, an academy for the advanced study of school administration might bring together professors and practitioners for summer programs. The nation's top educational administration scholars could refocus research through the dissemination of new procedures for studying organizations and administrator intervention.

In summary, departments of educational administration are in need of structural and disciplinary adjustments. Most adjustments concern building and incorporating a knowledge base of administrative practice and formalizing rigorous clinical experiences as part of administrator preparation. In addition, the intellectual climate of departments requires rejuvenation for both professors and students.

References

Achilles, C. (1984). Forecast: Stormy weather ahead in educational administration. *Issues in Education* 2: 127–35.

Adams, B. (1913). *The theory of social revolution.* New York: The MacMillan Company.

Astuto, T., and Clark, D. (1988). *Achieving effective schools.* This volume.

Boyd, W. (1976) The public, the professionals and educational policy making: Who governs? *Teachers College Record* 77 (May).

Burrell, G., and Morgan, G. (1979) *Sociological paradigms and organizational analysis.* London: Heinemann.

Callahan, R. (1962). *Education and the cult of efficiency.* Chicago: University of Chicago Press.

Campbell, R.; Cunningham, L.; Nystrand, R.; and Usdan, M. (1985). *The organization and control of American schools.* 5th ed. Columbus, Ohio: Charles E. Merrill.

Campbell, R. F., and Newell, L. J. (1973). *A study of professors of educational administration.* Columbus, Ohio: The University Council for Educational Administration.

Carnegie Forum. (1986). *A nation prepared: Teachers for the 21st century.* New York: Carnegie Forum on Education and the Economy.

Carol, L.; Cunningham, L.; Danzberger, J.; Kirst, M.; McCloud, B.; and Usdan, M. (1986). *School boards.* Washington, D.C.: The Institute for Educational Leadership.

Cuban, L. (1976). *Urban school chiefs under fire.* Chicago: University of Chicago Press.

Edmonds, R.(1979). Effective schools for the urban poor. *Educational Leadership* 37(1): 15–24.

Greenfield, W. (1988). Moral imagination, interpersonal competence, and the work of school administrators. This volume

Griffiths, D. E. (1966). *The school superintendent.* New York: Center for Applied Research in Education.

Griffiths, D. E. (1979). Intellectual turmoil in educational administration. *Educational Administration Quarterly* 15(3): 43–65.

Gronn, P. C. (1982). Neo-Taylorism in educational administration. *Educational Administration Quarterly* 18(4): 17–35.

Guide to the Use of the Graduate Record Examination Program. (1985). Pp. 22–26. Princeton, N.J.: Educational Testing Service.

Hawley, W. D. (1988) Universities and the improvement of school management: Roles for the states. This volume.

Hess, F. (1983). Evolution in practice. *Educational Administration Quarterly* 19(3): 245.

Hughes, E. C.; Thorne, B.; DeBaggis, A. M.; Gurin, A.; and Williams, D. (1973). *Education for the professions of medicine, law, theology, and social welfare.* New York: McGraw-Hill.

Jelinek, M.; Smircich, L.; and Hirsch, P. (Eds.). (1983). Organizational culture. *Administrative Science Quarterly* 28(3).

Kanter, R. M. (1983). *The change masters.* New York: Simon and Schuster.

March, J. G. (1974). Analytical skills and the university training of administrators. *The Journal of Educational Administration* 1(8): 30–54.

Martin, W. J., and Willower, D. J. (1981). The managerial behavior of high school principals. *Educational Administration Quarterly* 17(1): 69–90.

McCarthy, M. M.(1987). UCEA Presidential address. October 1987.

McCarthy, M. M.; Kuh, G. D.; Newell, L. J.; and Iocona, C. M. (in press). *Professors of educational administration: 1973–1988.* Tempe, Ariz.: The University Council for Educational Administration.

Miskel, C. (1983). The practicing administrator: Dilemmas, knowledge, and strategies for improving leadership. In W. N. Hird (Ed.), *The practicing administrator:*

Dilemmas and strategies, pp. 1–21. Brisbane, Australia: Bardon Professional Development Centre.

Moore, H. A., Jr. (1957). *Studies in school administration*. Washington, D.C.: American Association of School Administrators.

National Commission on Excellence in Education. (1983). *A nation at risk*. Washington, D.C.: United States Department of Education.

National Governors' Association. (1986). *Time for results*. Washington, D.C.: National Governors' Association.

Peters, T. J., and Waterman, R. H., Jr. (1982). *In search of excellence*. New York: Harper and Row.

Peterson, K. D., and Finn, C. E., Jr. (1985). Principals, superintendents, and the administrator's art., *The Public Interest* 79: 42–62.

Pitner, N. J. (1981). Organizational leadership: The case of the school superintendent. *Educational Administration Quarterly* 17(2): 45–65.

Pitner, N. J. (1982). *Training of the School Administrator: State of the Art*. Eugene, Oreg.: Center for Educational Policy and Management.

Russell, J. S.; Mazzarella, J. A.; White, T.; and Maurer, S. (1985, June). Linking the behaviors and activities of secondary school principals to school effectiveness: A focus on effective and ineffective behaviors. Eugene, Oreg.: Center for Educational Policy and Management.

Rutherford, W. L. (1985). School principals as effective leaders. *Phi Delta Kappan* 67(1): 31–34.

Schein, E. H. (1972). *Professional education: Some new directions*. New York: McGraw-Hill.

The Holmes Group. (1986). *Tomorrow's teachers: A report of the Holmes Group*. East Lansing: The Holmes Group, Inc.

Tyack, D., and Hansot, E. (1982). *Managers of virtue*. New York: Basic Books.

Ziegler, L. (1973). Creating responsive schools. *Urban Review* 6.

23

Education from a Black Perspective with Implications for Administrator Preparation Programs

Barbara L. Jackson

Education from a Black Perspective

Before public policy can be developed, an issue or problem must be defined. Those in power generally define the issue according to their own values, and from their own perspective. The assumptions underlying these values will not be questioned unless other groups participate in redefining the issues on the basis of their own perspectives.

Developing public policy is particularly difficult when it concerns issues that have implications for the distribution of economic benefits and power or that are at the core of the decision makers' value system. Race has been such an issue in America. It has permeated American society since the first

---

The first section of this paper is adapted from an earlier work by the same author, which was the chapter entitled "Urban School Desegregation from a Black Perspective" in *Race and Schooling in the City* (1981). In that chapter the information on the black perspective was used as background for a description of the Atlanta, Georgia, school desegregation case. The basic ideas, however, are equally pertinent to higher education and administrator preparation programs.

Africans were brought to this country. For black Americans, race is all-pervasive—and this is difficult, if not impossible, for those who are part of the majority to comprehend. Because of the legacy of the peculiar institution of slavery followed by legal segregation, the situation of African Americans and the response of policymakers have been different in kind, not just in degree, from those involving all other immigrant groups. Fundamental value questions as well as economic and political power are at stake. For the educational administrator, values are important because they are the basis on which decisions are made.

Desegregation at all levels of the educational system continues to be defined and assessed from changing perspectives. During the battle to eliminate the laws that required segregation, blacks reached a consensus that could be called a black perspective. In the period since the 1954 *Brown* decision, that perspective has changed, primarily in response to white society's reaction to desegregation. While there are still issues to resolve at. the public school level, attention has shifted to higher education, as evidenced in the *Bakke* case, and to state plans based on the *Adams* case.[1]

One fact seems clear: the issue of race, with us since the founding of this country, will not easily be resolved. I am convinced, after looking at past efforts to create an integrated society under the rules written by others, that a new approach is needed—one that no longer attempts to erase differences between blacks, whites, and other ethnic-cultural groups, but accepts them, respects them, and encourages each to perpetuate what it values.

The heritage of slavery and the legal segregation that forced the establishment of parallel and separate institutions, not only in education but in virtually every phase of life for the freedmen and their progeny, were primarily responsible for the creation of a black perspective. Perspective is a particular vantage point from which phenomena are viewed that grows out of the value system and the position of a group in society. A black perspective is a view of a group that has been victimized. It arises not solely from a study of books but also from "the bones and spirits of those who have stood at the bottommost point of the pit of humiliation and dehumanization." (Smith, 1976). A black perspective grows out of the historical-cultural heritage of African Americans and their struggle to become citizens. To ignore one's history or to be robbed of it is to lose self-understanding and the roots of one's past so necessary for pride in self and group. A brief review of the significant differences between African Americans and all other immigrant groups will give further meaning to a black perspective.

---

[1] Cases cited are *Brown v. Board of Education of Topeka* 347 U.S. 483 (1954); *Regents of the University of California v. Allan Bakke* No. 76–811, June 28, (1978); *Adams v. Califano* 430 F. Supp. 118 D.C. Cir. (1977).

First, the ancestors of African Americans were forcibly brought to this so-called land of opportunity and subsequently enslaved. As stated by Justice Thurgood Marshall in the *Bakke* decision:

> Three hundred and fifty years ago, the Negro was dragged to this country in chains to be sold into slavery. Uprooted from his homeland and thrust into bondage for forced labor, the slave was deprived of all legal rights. It was unlawful to teach him to read; he could be sold away from his family and friends at the whim of his master; and killing or maiming him was not a crime. The system of slavery brutalized and dehumanized both master and slave.

What made slavery and the segregation that followed so enforceable was the badge of color. Black skins made identification easy and at the same time prevented those of African descent from disappearing into the dominant society as other immigrants had done. As time went on, however, the activities of masters and mistresses became evident in the range of skin colors among the slaves and their children, making identification more difficult and creating a value-laden color consciousness that still exists.

A second factor that contributed to the development of a black perspective was the justification used to perpetuate slavery. Some of the reasons were religious, quasi-scientific, and environmental. But the definition of slaves as property was the most ingenious and has had the most far-reaching effects. And now only blacks are accused of separateness and withdrawal from society when they choose to perpetuate their own customs. Other groups are applauded for still celebrating, for example, their St. Patrick's Day. In fact, as all other immigrant groups became Americanized, they were permitted and at times encouraged to keep some of the old-country ways. For them, it was recognized as legitimate that group identity was important in developing individual identity. Some of these differences in treatment may have been based on the presumption that the Negro had no culture and, therefore, had nothing to preserve—assimilation into the majority culture was his only option. We know now that the African heritage was rich; we know now that many traditions were continued despite the efforts of the masters to destroy the past. One positive outcome of the turbulent 1960s was the reconnection of many African Americans, especially some who had "arrived" into the middle class, with their African heritage.

Third and perhaps most significant in creating a black perspective was the drocess through which the slave, and later the segregated African American, was enculturated into American society. Because of the slave's position in society, he had to adapt to two cultures simultaneously. In the world of the white master, his role as slave was determined by others; he was forced to develop certain behaviors in order to survive physically and psychologically. But the slave also lived in the world of his own community, and later in black communities segregated explicitly by law in the South and subtly by law and custom in the North. It was with his own group that some sense of humanness could be nurtured: "The most important aspect of this group identification was that slaves were not solely dependent on the white man's cultural frames of reference for their ideas and values . . . the slave's culture bolstered his self-esteem, courage, and confidence and served as his defense against personal degredation" (Blassingame, 1972, p. 96).

One result of this heritage, shared by all whose ancestors came from Africa, is an individual identity based primarily on group membership in direct conflict with the philosophical basis on which this country and its democratic form of government were founded. DuBois (1961, pp. 16, 17) defined this phenomenon as a "double consciousness . . . a sense of always looking at one's self through the eyes of others, of measuring one's soul by the tape of a world that looks on in amused contempt and pity." It is more than ironic that the present administration and some scholars are now asking that blacks be judged as individuals, each solely on his or her own merits—in effect, thus, they are no longer members of the group that for centuries was labeled inferior and assigned low status in the society.

Another outcome of this double life was the way slaves responded to the white society. Being part of the master's world—working in the big house—meant access to better food, an easier life in many ways than working in the fields, and at times being treated almost as a human being. It meant exposure to another culture. But it also meant compromising who they were, especially as they were subject to the prerogatives of the masters and the mistresses that produced a new species of "coloreds" and the value-laden color consciousness that gave status to light skin. Entering the dominant society today brings some of these same opportunities, potential benefits, and disadvantages. For now, as then, it is often believed that the only way African Americans can succeed is not through integration, which as defined here includes retaining some differences, but rather through assimilation—giving up all traces of their African heritage and even contact with their own group in order to be truly acceptable. Since so much of the socialization and enculturation of young children occurs in schools, this aspect of the black perspective deserves attention and high priority as decisions are made about staff, curriculum, and organization in education.

One more outcome of this master-slave relationship is the distrust, at times hostility, that prevents honest discourse and impedes progress. A major problem today is finding ways to develop trust among black folk, their leaders, and the larger society. This is not easy because distrust in black communities is so deep seated, and, unfortunately, conditions have not yet changed enough to make suspicion unnecessary. Other immigrant groups were not faced with the same dilemma. Their leaders could retain credibility within the group while trying to gain power and influence in the dominant society. The white power structure too often designated black leaders. Thus distrust arose between the designated black leaders and their constituencies and, in turn, for white society itself. Whatever else might have been accomplished during the turbulent 1960s, the gap of distrust between and among black and white society failed to close, which is evident in blacks' questioning the very legitimacy and authority of many societal institutions, including the schools. The presence of black Americans in positions of authority, such as the school superintendency, has helped overcome some of the distrust—but not completely.

Finally, the road to citizenship for African Americans was unique—no other immigrant group had to establish its humanity as a condition for citizenship. Blacks were handicapped from the beginning by their status, for not only were they not citizens, they were not even human beings. As the Supreme Court declared in the 1857 *Dred Scott* case:

> The question is simply this: can a negro, whose ancestors were imported into this country, and sold as slaves, become a member of the political community formed and brought into existence by the Constitution of the United States, and as such become entitled to all the rights, and privileges and immunities, guaranteed by that instrument to the citizen? . . .
>
> We think they are not, and that they are not included and were not intended to be included, under the word "citizen" in the Constitution . . .
>
> They had for more than a century before been regarded as beings of an inferior order, and altogether unfit to associate with the white race, either in social or political relations; and so far inferior, that they had no rights which the white man was bound to respect; and that the negro might justly and lawfully be reduced to slavery for his benefit. He was bought and sold, and treated as an ordinary article of merchandise and traffic, whenever a profit could be made by it. . . .[2]

A civil war, three Constitutional amendments (the thirteenth, the fourteenth, and the fifteenth), and a period of reconstruction were required to establish that first condition—yes, the former slaves were human beings. Thus, a beginning was made toward securing the right to exercise the privileges associated with citizenship. After the Reconstruction, however, advances in the opportunity for African Americans to exercise these rights were blocked by the legislative and executive branches of the government. With the 1896 Supreme Court decision in *Plessy v. Ferguson*,[3] it appeared that there was no legitimate route to gain the rights of citizenship, even through the judiciary. The Supreme Court confirmed the legality of Jim Crow laws that segregated every aspect of life for the Negro in the South. For those who lived in the North, there was also a segregated existence, with barriers to participation erected in ways that were more subtle but just as effective in

---

[2] *Dred Scott v. Alex Sandford, Saml Russell, and Irene Emerson* 60 U.S. 393 (1857).

[3] *Plessy v. Ferguson* 163 U.S. 537 (1896).

achieving the subjugation of the total group and in denying equality of opportunity.

But the African American was now a citizen and no longer defined in law as property; and this was a government of law in which citizens had certain guaranteed rights. Slow but steady pressure, primarily through the courts, eliminated the legal barriers created by the other branches of government. With the *Brown* decision in 1954 came an end to one chapter of race relations—"separate but equal" was no longer the law of the land. A new era in race relations was about to begin with great promise and hope, promising to resolve the American dilemma and fulfill the American dream for all its citizens.

In the more than twenty-five years since that historic decision, progress and change have occurred, but not without continued court action and new modes of protest that took place in the 1960s. In education, more young people are attending college than ever before—more blacks attend the traditionally white colleges than the historically black ones, which were once the only way to attain a higher education.

A significant change pertinent to educational administration is in the number of African Americans holding superintendencies. The study by Charles Moody in 1970 found only seventeen black superintendents, and none of them in major urban areas. Today there are more than one hundred—still few in absolute numbers because there are close to 16,000 school districts, but important in a relative sense and in view of where some are located. Black superintendents head some of the largest urban school systems and those with a majority of black students: Atlanta, Chicago, Detroit, Boston, Baltimore, Washington, D.C., and Philadelphia (the last three are headed by black women) (American Association of School Administrators Office of Minority Affairs, 1983).

The latest figures on student enrollment in public schools show that in all of the large cities the minorities—blacks and Hispanics—are now the majority. The policymakers need to look specifically at the reasons for the changing school population of the cities. As long as those in power believe that African Americans are responsible for resegregating the cities, policies will be focused on blacks. Blaming the victim will continue to dominate the thinking of many. If it is recognized that members of the white, and increasingly black, middle class are leaving the city because of inadequate services and safety in the city, public policy will take a different direction. If city leaders want to hold middle-class whites and blacks or attract back those who have left, they must now compete with the suburbs in the services and amenities they provide. There is evidence that a few cities, such as Atlanta, Boston, and Baltimore, recognize this need. They have undertaken rebuilding programs to revitalize the downtown areas and to attract the middle class back to the cities. There is now evidence that the business communities also recognize the importance of a viable school system to maintain the health of the city and in turn their businesses. An example is the action recently taken by the Boston business community, spearheaded by the banks, to provide the opportunity for college and a job for all qualified graduates of the Boston Public high schools.

One critical fact for the cities may be the perceived quality of the school system, especially if that system is under the direction of a black American. Will it be possible for black educators (many of whom were prepared at the most prestigious white universities, so their credentials should be acceptable) to change the image of urban schools, particularly if most students are black?

The majority of students in urban schools are black because students of other races have either left the city or been enrolled in private schools. The blacks stayed, while those with whom they were being asked to integrate or racially mix left. From a black perspective, to blame the blacks who stayed for the change in the complexion of the schools is to revert to the practice of blaming the victim instead of addressing the cause. The real problem now is the assumption that when a school system enrolls a black majority, the system must deteriorate. Statistics are always reported with a tone of dismay, if not of horror, reflecting the still-prevalent belief that anything black is bad. What seems to be forgotten is that many black people did learn, and learn well, in all-black systems, even without real control of the limited resources. Perhaps the motivation was greater when the barriers to participation were so much clearer. Many black educators are trying to find ways to recapture some of that motivation for black students without returning to separate school systems:

> . . . what we must now ask ourselves is when we become equal American citizens what will be our aims and ideals and what will we have to do in selecting these aims and ideals. Are we to assume that we will simply adopt the ideals of Americans and become what they are or want to be and that we will have in the process no ideals of our own?
>
> That would mean that we would cease to be Negroes as such and become white in action if not completely in color. We would take on the culture of white Americans, doing as they do and thinking as they think.
>
> Manifestly this would not be satisfactory. Physically it would mean that we would be integrated with Americans losing, first of all, the physical evidence of color and hair and racial type. We would lose our memory of Negro history and of those racial peculiarities which have long been associated with the Negro. We would cease to acknowledge any greater tie with Africa than with England and Germany. We would not try to develop Negro music and Art and Literature as distinctive and different, but allow them to be further degraded as is the case today. We would always, if possible, marry lighter-hued people so as to have children who are not identified with the Negro race and thus solve our problem in America by committing racial suicide . . . .
>
> Any statement of our desire to develop American Negro culture, to keep up our ties with coloured people, to remember our past is being regarded as "racism." I,

for instance, who have devoted my life to efforts to break down racial barriers, am being accused of desiring to emphasize differences of race. This has a certain truth about it. As I have said before and I repeat, I am not fighting to settle the question of racial equality in America by the process of getting rid of the Negro race; getting rid of black folk, not producing black children, fogetting the slave trade and slavery, and the struggle for emancipation; of forgetting abolition and especially of ignoring the whole cultural history of Africans in the world.

No! What I have been fighting for and am still fighting for is the possibility of black folk and their cultural patterns existing in America without discrimination; and on terms of equality. If we take this attitude we have got to do so consciously and deliberately. [DuBois, 1973, pp. 149–50]

Implications for Administrator Preparation Programs

The implications listed here are limited to those that most directly relate to the black perspective I have described. Other topics, especially those related to the managerial functions of the administrator, are still essential and should be continued.

Social Sciences

In order to gain an understanding of the historical-cultural context and a perspective on the status of African Americans over the years, the preparation programs should place a greater emphasis on the social sciences. For example, attention should be given in sociology to the concept of culture. Much has been written about the "corporate culture" and the "culture of the school," and our administrators need to be familiar with this concept and their role as leaders in defining the culture of the workplace. Culture is a concept educators have borrowed from the sociologists and anthropologists. They define it as the total way of life of a people or nation (and perhaps a corporation or school) held together by bonds of kinship or common goals rooted in the traditions of the past and forming a base for the continuation of the group. Culture includes beliefs, values, skills, and the norms of conduct that guide behavior. It includes language, eating habits, religious beliefs and practices, gestures, notions of common sense, attitudes toward sex, appropriate sex roles, and even concepts of beauty and justice. The anthropologists who study cultures say that cultures can change, but the process is usually measured in generations or centuries. If external conditions do change, the cultural habits will continue to be reinforced.

When we apply this concept to the study of the status of African Americans, we can begin to appreciate how and why certain adaptive behaviors have lasted so long. Slavery lasted two hundred years and was followed by a civil war, a short period of reconstruction, and then another hundred years of legal segregation. If approximately thirty years represents a generation, then about ten generations survived under adverse conditions while fighting to gain access to the rights and privileges of the dominant society.

Another aspect of culture -suggested by the black perspective is the dilemma created by the dual acculturation process—the adaptation of black folk to the social environment of the two worlds in which the slaves were forced to live and the two worlds that continue to exist for many. The continuing implications of the badge of color and the values attributed to the color of one's skin are other areas for research.

In other social sciences—political science and economics—there are topics suggested by the black perspective important to members of the black community that may offer insights into behavior and group action. One topic that should be included would be an exploration of the relationship of the black educational leader to the local and national black community. Community studies would be one way to explore these topics.

Humanities

The black perspective calls for a greater emphasis on the arts and humanities. Such an emphasis would be profitable for all potential administrators; for is not a truly liberated person one who has developed an appreciation for the human spirit in all its dimensions? Can we perhaps learn more about human nature and the way people act and react by reading the creative works of our novelists, poets, and play writers? Is not exploration of philosophy good for the mind as well as the spirit as we struggle to define the goals for education? Or as DuBois said so eloquently,

> Life is more than living.
> We may learn how to earn a living,
> but never earn a life.

One specific literary suggestion is Ralph Ellison's *Invisible Man* (1952), a classic novel depicting many leaders that leads us to examine our values and the place of black people and black institutions as they search for an identity in this society. Another genre of literature that would assist in developing a sensitivity to another perspective is the autobiography. African Americans from many walks of life have written their stories, which provide a first-hand account of what it is like to grow up black in America. An interesting contrast could be made, for example, of men and organizations by studying the autobiographies of the leaders of two Civil Rights organizations—even the titles are provocative and tell the reader something of these leaders' philosophies and their time in history.

Examples are those by leaders of the National Association for the Advancement of Colored People (NAACP): James Weldon Johnson, *Along*

This Way (1933) and *Negro American, What Now?* (1969), Walter White, *A Man Called White*, (1969) and *How Far the Promised Land?* (1953), and Roy Wilkins, *Standing Fast* (1982).

Others are from leaders of the Student Non-Violent Coordinating Committee (SNCC); James Forman, *The Making of Black Revolutionaries* (1984); and Cleveland Sellers, *The River of No Return* (1973).

Research

A black perspective would call for a research program as part of the preparation of educational leaders that would be modeled after the practice of DuBois, the scholar-social activist who saw no separation between theory and practice. A black perspective would dictate the problems to be investigated, the way the questions would be posed "from the other side of the veil."

One example concerns reading. If our ancestors were able to teach reading to the recently emancipated slaves, who should have had negative self-concepts and certainly none of the readiness activities we now deem so essential, why cannot we use our creativity and ingenuity to take the child wherever he or she is and teach him or her to decode those printed symbols? Have we lost our belief in the stability of every child, which was the guiding faith of those early teachers? Think of the handicaps they had to overcome, yet overcome they did. Another research idea relates to the dual enculturation concept. Could it be tested? Could it be a useful starting point to generate some hypotheses, especially about communication skills considered essential for administrators? Would the fact that the kind of music valued and praised in the slave and later the black community, emphasizing improvisation, call and response, imagination and creativity, as well as how long one could keep going, suggest anything about the way in which we teach young people to decode the printed word? Contrast this kind of music with that of the Western world where what is valued and praised is how perfectly the musician can reproduce what appears on the printed musical score written by the Bachs and Beethovens.

Methods

In addition to using the methods of the social sciences more extensively with the research activities (observation, field studies, community analysis), the black perspective would call for greater use of case studies. The University Council for Educational Administration (UCEA) has conducted many case studies that focus on race-related issues within the context of administrative theory and practice. The case records now being developed by the APEX Center under the direction of Paula Silver at the University of Illinois would be another source of information to help us understand the decision-making process and would respond to the imperatives of the black perspective, which calls for reality in the preparation of administrators.

Summary

The social sciences, the humanities, research agenda, and methods have implications for the preparation of administrators from the black perspective. As the first section closed with a quotation from DuBois, this section closes with a quotation, from many years later, that expresses the same idea. Ronald W. Roskens, President of the University of Nebraska, gave the Walter Cocking Lecture at the National Conference of the Professors of Educational Administration in 1985. He ended with these words:

> Candor compels us to admit that full social integration was, at best, an elusive aspiration rather than a reality. Ethnic divisions were the rule in this nation, rather than the exception. In large part they remain so today. Demographic studies indicate that those sectors of society now considered to be minorities will, by the year 2000, become majorities in certain parts of our nation. Yet higher education is generally ill-equipped either to understand or to appreciate minority needs. More importantly, I believe that demands that these groups become acculturated to predominantly white, middle-class, Western European mores are ill-conceived and destined to fail.
>
> You must develop the willingness to celebrate differences; to fashion from respective strengths new skills and initiatives. It is not essential for Black America to become white, or Hispanics to become Anglos. Women do not need to become like men, or men like women. What is required is a sense of tolerance and appreciation. You must acknowledge with specific acts, rather than hollow words, a commitment to fairness and equality. You must evidence a willingness to forge those bonds that will allow everyone to work together for the common good. [Roskens, 1985].

References

American Association of School Administrators Office of Minority Affairs. (1983). *Perspectives on racial minority and women school administrators.* Arlington, Va: American Association of School Administrators Office of Minority Affairs.

Blassingame, J. (1972). *The slave community.* New York: Oxford University Press.

Dubois, W.E.B. (1961). *The souls of black folk.* Greenwich, Conn: Fawcett Publishing Company. (Originally published in 1903).

DuBois, W.E.B. (1973). Wither now and why. In H. Aptheker (Ed.), *The education of black people.* New York: Monthly Review Press.

Ellison, R. (1952). *Invisible man.* New York: Random House.

Forman, J. (1984). (Originally published in 1972.) *The making of black revolutionaries.* Washington, D.C.: Open Hand Publishers.

Jackson, B.L. (1981). Urban school desegregation from a black perspective. In A. Yarmolinsky, L. Liebman, and C. S. Schelling (Eds.) *Race and schooling in the city.* Cambridge, Mass.: Harvard University Press.

Johnson, J. W. (1933). *Along this way.* New York: Viking Press.

Johnson, J.W. (1969). *Negro America, What now?* New York: Viking Press.

Roskens, R.W., (1985, August). W.D. Cocking Lecture presented at the National Conference of Professors of Educational Administration, Starkville, Mississippi.

Sellers, C. (1973). *The river of no return*. New York: William Morrow and Co.

Smith, C. (1976). *Toward a theory and place for the arts and humanities in the public schools*. Unpublished doctoral dissertation, Atlanta University.

White, W. (1969). *A man called white*. New York: Viking Press.

White, W. (1953). *How far the promised land?* New York: Ams Press.

Wilkins, R. (1982). *Standing fast*. New York: Viking Press.

24

The Professoriate in Educational Administration: A Status Report

Martha M. McCarthy

The caliber of preparation programs in educational administration is a function of the kind of people we are able to recruit and retain on our educational administration faculties. To improve the preparation of educational leaders it is essential to have a solid base of knowledge about the characteristics, activities, and attitudes of professors in our field.

This paper entails a brief overview of the evolution of the professoriate, selected findings from a 1986 study of faculty in our field, and observations regarding the challenges ahead in rebuilding the professoriate in educational administration. The paper is based on the presidential address given at the Plenary Session of the University Council for Educational Administration (UCEA) in October 1986 (McCarthy, 1987). A few modifications have been made for this publication, as the speech reflected a preliminary analysis of the 1986 data.

Context

The professoriate in the United States underwent extraordinary expansion from 1950 until 1970, gaining in esteem and fiscal support (Bowen and Schuster, 1986, pp. 3–5). During this period an increasing proportion of the

317

college-age population was pursuing post-secondary education, and this population grew as the post-World War II baby boomers moved toward adulthood. With the substantial increase in college and university enrollments, programs expanded at an unprecedented pace. Ladd and Lipset (1975, p. 169) reported that "the most dramatic faculty increases occurred in the late 1960s when professorial ranks swelled by 150,000 in one five-year span. The number of new positions created and filled in this half decade equaled the *entire number* of faculty slots in 1940."

Faculties in educational administration shared the benefits of this growth period. After becoming an accepted field of graduate education at many institutions by the 1950s, educational administration programs prospered during the next two decades as the expansion of elementary and secondary school enrollments led to the need for more school administrators. By the late 1960s several hundred colleges and universities had established programs in educational administration.

However, conditions began to change for the professoriate across disciplines in the 1970s. Faculty growth started to wane in anticipation of declining student enrollments. At the state level, other needs began to take priority over higher education, and continued federal support for research and student aid became tenuous. With many institutions of higher education facing severe budgetary problems, student tuition rates climbed, outstripping inflation, and some faculty lines were eliminated. Salaries in academe, which peaked in 1972–73, declined by about 20 percent in real dollars during the next decade, the most significant decline for any nonagricultural occupational group (Schuster and Bowen, 1985, p. 14). Faculty retrenchment was accompanied by decreased mobility across institutions and reductions in clerical support and faculty development activities. It is not surprising that faculty unionism increased during this period. Despite the seeming inconsistency between unions' focus on collectivism and the historical value placed by faculty on individual autonomy (Ladd and Lipset, 1973, pp. 2–4), by the mid 1980s approximately one-fourth of the faculty in American colleges and universities was unionized.

Schools and colleges of education were particularly affected by the retrenchment activities of the 1970s, as the education profession was the first to experience the impact of changing demographic trends. Whereas traditionally one-third of all American college graduates and more than one-half of female graduates assumed teaching jobs immediately after college (Mayer, 1974, pp. 122–25), the declining school-age population led to dismal prospects for careers in education. This situation depressed college enrollments in education programs, and with reduced credit-hour production, schools and colleges of education shrank.

The period of contraction has had some positive outcomes, however, particularly in research productivity. Universities found themselves in a buyer's market, and many became selective in hiring new faculty with an interest in and a commitment to research. The strengthening of selection, promotion, and tenure standards and the "research surge" nurtured favorable conditions for knowledge production (Schuster and Bowen, 1985, p. 16). Educational administration units reflected this general trend in that fewer faculty members were hired, but a larger proportion were involved in research (McCarthy, 1986, pp. 3–11). Some institutions that had not traditionally been known for their research mission were able to hire productive researchers when filling vacancies, and research contributions were no longer confined to faculty from a few universities.

However, faculty retrenchment has had its costs in the area of program development, and preparation programs in educational administration have not been immune. Because of sharp enrollment declines and concomitant budget drawdowns, some units were threatened with losing the critical mass of faculty members necessary to offer high-quality graduate instruction in educational administration. In an effort to reverse the trend of dwindling enrollments, some programs reduced student admission standards and residency requirements, and "mail-order universities" began to offer doctoral degrees in educational administration (Willower, 1983, p. 182). Furthermore, the focus on research in the university culture and reward system engendered a benign neglect of curriculum development and program innovation.

With the aging professoriate, academe is entering a new phase. This phase will be characterized by substantial faculty turnover as the professors hired during the growth period reach retirement age. However, the ability to attract capable individuals to professorial roles is being seriously questioned (Molotsky, 1986, pp. 1, 3; Schuster and Bowen, 1985, p. 20). The number of Ph.D.'s selecting a career in academe is declining, and college freshmen indicate less interest in professorial roles than was true in the past (Schuster and Bowen, 1985, p. 20). In a 1986 publication of the American Association of University Professors that focused on higher education's "impending personnel crunch," Molotsky (1986, p. 1) asserted that it will be extremely difficult to recruit the estimated 70,000 to 130,000 new full-time faculty members that will need to be appointed every five years from now until 2009. Bowen and Schuster (1986) recently referred to American professors as "a national resource imperiled"; they contended that "the financial outlook is less promising than at any time since 1955 and the conditions and expectations of faculties are correspondingly bleak" (p. 7). There is considerable sentiment that faculty in general are demoralized and underpaid and that the pending retirement of a large portion of the professoriate constitutes a significant national problem.

The Educational Administration Professoriate in 1986

Given the mounting concern about the state of the professoriate across disciplines coupled with the fact that the last comprehensive survey of professors in educational administration was conducted in 1972 (Campbell and Newell, 1973), when I assumed the UCEA presidency I proposed that a study of professors in educational administration be undertaken. In light of UCEA's mission, it seemed long overdue to gather information on faculty in our field. L. Jackson Newell (coauthor of the 1972 study), George Kuh, and Carla Iacona joined me as members of the research team. Our purpose was to replicate the 1972 study supplemented with additional questions of current concern regarding what professors do and what they believe about their roles and preparation programs. UCEA supported the initial mailing for the study, and Indiana University and the Danforth Foundation provided support for coding and data analysis.

The population for the study was composed of educational administration faculty members employed in institutions with graduate degree programs in educational administration. To identify the institutions and faculty, we used the *Educational Administration Directory* (Lilley, 1986), the *Directory of Higher Education* (Schorr and Hoogstra, 1984), and *Peterson's Annual Guide to Graduate and Professional Programs* (Goldstein, 1986). A total of 372 U.S. and Canadian institutions with degree programs in educational administration were identified; thus, faculty at institutions that prepare administrators but do not have established degree programs were not included in the population.

Two questionnaires were used to gather data. To facilitate comparisons, the forty-five-item faculty questionnaire retained as many questions as possible from the original instrument used by Campbell and Newell in 1972. Some revisions were made, however, based on suggestions from approximately twenty experts in the field of educational administration who reviewed the instrument. The questionnaire was field tested at the University of Utah and Indiana University and then distributed to 3,087 faculty members. We sent two follow-up mailings, and of the faculty questionnaires distributed, 331 were returned as not applicable. An additional adjustment of 415 was made in the faculty population after comparing data on the number of educational administration faculty members supplied by department chairs with the number listed for those institutions in the directories. Usable questionnaires were returned by 1,307 respondents, for a response rate of 56 percent. Telephone interviews were conducted with a random sample of nonrespondents, and their characteristics did not differ substantially from those of the respondents.

In addition to the questionnaire sent to individual faculty members, a second form was distributed to 372 department chairs in educational administration to gather information on department structure, size and composition of faculties, and departmental hiring and faculty support activities. After a follow-up mailing, 297 completed forms were returned by the chairs, for an 80 percent response rate. A comparable department questionnaire was not used in the 1972 study.

The overview of the findings presented here will be limited to the data supplied by the department chairs and by 940 of the faculty respondents who identified themselves as primarily involved in K-12 educational administration. Thus, responses from those who identified their interest as higher education or community college administration are not included in this analysis.

We used the classification of institutions of higher education developed by the Carnegie Foundation for the Advancement of Teaching (1984)[1] and found that 23 percent of the responding department chairs were from research institutions (n=69), 20 percent were from other doctorate-granting institutions (n=59), and 57 percent were from other comprehensive institutions offering graduate programs in educational administration (n=169). Of the individual faculty respondents who identified their area of concentration as K-12 administration, 30 percent were from research institutions (n=283), 23 percent were from other doctorate-granting institutions (n=218), and 47 percent were from other institutions offering graduate programs in educational administration (n=439).

We have a substantial amount of data that can be analyzed from several perspectives, and complete findings from the study will be disseminated in a forthcoming book (McCarthy et al., in press). Here I will present a summary of selected data on K-12 educational administration faculty members, highlighting differences between UCEA and non-UCEA institutions and trends over time. These data on the characteristics, activities, and attitudes of professors may be useful in deliberations regarding UCEA's role in improving administrative preparation programs and implementing the recommendations of the National Commission on Excellence in Educational Administration.

---

[1] The data presented in the UCEA presidential address were based on the 1976 Carnegie classification scheme. However, the data here reflect the revised classification scheme that became available before this book went to press. According to Carnegie, designation as a "research" or other doctorate-granting institution is based on the number of Ph.D.'s awarded and the amount of federal financial support received. Institutions designated as "other comprehensive universities and colleges" lack doctoral programs or offer very limited doctoral programs. For a description of criteria used in placing institutions in various categories, see Carnegie Council on Policy Studies in Higher Education (1987).

Personal and Professional Characteristics

The typical educational administration professor in 1986 became a faculty member at age thirty-seven, currently is fifty-two, and plans to retire at age sixty-four. A white, married male, he is more likely to hold an Ed.D. than a Ph.D., probably earned his doctorate before 1975, and has held tenure for more than ten years. He likely entered the professorship primarily because of an interest in teaching, identifies teaching as his area of major strength, and considers teaching graduate students the most enjoyable aspect of his role. The aspect of the professorship that he least enjoys is committee work and faculty governance activities. He is generally satisfied with the graduate program in educational administration at his institution and probably considers the principalship or organizational theory as his area of specialization within administration. He likely received his doctorate at an institution in the Midwest, majored in educational administration, and taught at another institution of higher education before assuming his current faculty position.

Compared with the characteristics of faculty members across disciplines as depicted in data collected by the Carnegie Foundation in 1984,[2] the educational administration professoriate is older and more male-dominated, tenured, and top-heavy with full professors. However, minority representation is slightly higher in educational administration faculties than in the professoriate across fields.

Since the 1972 Campbell and Newell survey, the average age of educational administration faculty members has climbed from forty-eight to fifty-two. Also, female and minority representation has increased in educational administration units. In 1986 the department chairs reported that 12 percent of their faculty members were women (compared with 2 percent in 1972); among those hired within the past ten years, 32 percent were females. About 8 percent of the faculty members in 1986 were racial minorities (compared with 3 percent in 1972), and minority representation was substantially greater among female (17 percent) than among male (8 percent) professors. Minorities represented 14 percent of the faculty members hired within the past ten years.

Department chairs indicated that four-fifths of their educational administration faculty members in 1986 held tenure, and almost three-fifths were full professors. However, tenure status and academic rank differed substantially between male and female faculty members. Whereas less than one-

---

[2] For faculties across disciplines in 1984, the average age was forty-six; 63 percent were men; 93 percent were Caucasian; 69 percent were tenured; and 34 percent were full professors (Carnegie Foundation for the Advancement of Teaching, 1985, pp. 31–34; 1984, tables 17–20).

tenth of the males were assistant professors, almost two-fifths of the females held this rank; about two-thirds of the males were full professors compared with slightly more than one-fifth of the females.

The median number of full-time faculty members employed in educational administration programs in 1986 was 4.0, and the modal number was 2.0. Almost 40 percent of the department chairs reported a reduction in the number of faculty lines in educational administration during the past ten years; across all programs more than two faculty members had been lost for every faculty member added since 1976. Slightly over half of the individual faculty respondents indicated that they were assigned full time in educational administration, and about one-third reported that they held an administrative position in addition to their professorial role.

Compared with reports of faculty salaries across disciplines (AAUP, 1987; Bowen and Schuster, 1986, pp. 101–10), educational administration faculty members appear to be compensated above the mean. The average salary for an academic year of the 1986 faculty respondents was between $35,000 and $40,000, with 56 percent reporting salaries between $30,000 and $45,000. However, only 30 percent of the female respondents made over $35,000, while almost 70 percent of the males were compensated above that level. This finding is not surprising, given the concentration of women at lower academic ranks. Approximately 16 percent of the faculty members indicated that they received external funds or release time for research.

Activities and Attitudes

In general, educational administration professors were satisfied with their current positions; less than 10 percent indicated that they were dissatisfied. Also, under 20 percent reported that they were dissatisfied with the caliber of their graduates or the caliber of their departmental colleagues. Respondents were somewhat less satisfied with their department structure (26 percent indicated dissatisfaction) and current salary (30 percent indicted dissatisfaction). However, female respondents as a group were less satisfied with each of these items than were their male colleagues. As in the 1972 survey, the 1986 respondents overwhelmingly indicated that they would be professors of educational administration if they had the chance to make the choice again, although the percentage dropped slightly from 90 percent in 1972 to 84 percent in 1986.

Respondents were asked to rate several problems in preparation programs that have received attention in the literature. The only issues considered to be "very serious problems" by at least 20 percent of the respondents were the increase in state regulatory powers over educational administration graduate programs (24 percent) and the departmental teaching and advising load (21 percent). Many of the issues, such as placement of students upon graduation, lack of able students, poor intellectual climate in the department, lack of appropriate competency standards for students, and too much faculty time devoted to private consulting were viewed as very serious problems by less than 10 percent of the respondents. This complacency toward problems facing preparation programs was similar to the pattern found in 1972. Although more respondents in 1986 than in 1972 felt that the lack of able students and low faculty salaries were of concern, still a relatively small proportion of the faculty indicated that these issues posed very serious problems. However, female respondents in 1986 were more likely than were males to identify as very serious problems the poor intellectual climate of their departments, the lack of departmental colleagueship, the low percentage of women and minorities in the professoriate, and low faculty salaries.

Consistent with two previous surveys of educational administration faculty members (Campbell and Newell, 1973; Hills, 1965), a vast majority of the 1986 respondents (73 percent) indicated that teaching was their greatest strength. However, a comparison of these surveys indicates that there has been an increase in faculty involvement in scholarly activity. The proportion of educational administration professors involved in research has increased from under 50 percent in 1965 to almost 80 percent in 1986. Similarly, the proportion of faculty members devoting at least 10 percent of their time to research activities has increased from under one-third of the respondents in 1965 to almost half of the respondents in 1986. Despite this increase, educational administration faculty members still devote a relatively small portion of their time to research when compared to faculty across disciplines. The Carnegie Foundation (1985) reported that faculty across colleges and universities devoted an average of 18 percent of their time to research, whereas the mean for the 1986 respondents who identified K-12 administration as their area of concentration was 11 percent.

Female respondents as a group were more research oriented than were their male counterparts in that they were more likely to consider research their primary strength, to devote more time to research activities, and to believe that graduate programs should be oriented toward the preparation of professors and researchers. Female faculty members also were twice as likely as males to indicate that research was the aspect of the professorship they most enjoyed and that the AERA was their primary professional association.

Faculty perceptions of the orientation of their educational administration programs changed between 1972 and 1986. Slightly over half of the 1972 respondents indicated that their educational administration programs were oriented more toward preparing practitioners, with the remainder indicating that the programs focused on the preparation of professors or on the preparation of both professors and practitioners. In contrast, 85 percent of the 1986 respondents reported that their programs were designed to prepare practitioners.

There also was a change between the two surveys in respondents' perceptions of the most critical need facing our academic field. Whereas a more extensive knowledge base was considered the most pressing need in educational administration in 1972, the 1986 respondents perceived curriculum reform in preparation programs as the most critical need, followed by more able students. This concern for curriculum reform seems somewhat inconsistent with the 1986 respondents' assessment of the quality of their current preparation programs. Almost 85 percent rated their programs as good or excellent, and over two-thirds of the respondents indicated that their preparation programs had improved over the past ten years.

In both 1972 and 1986, faculty members were asked to respond to a series of statements about preparation programs or the field of educational administration. Responses in the two surveys were quite similar on most items. For example, in both 1972 and 1986 a majority of the respondents indicated that teaching and research are interdependent, that they would like to have more contact with professors at other institutions, and that tenure for faculty members and residency requirements for doctoral students should be retained. Also, in both surveys a majority of the respondents disagreed with the statements that scholars in a related discipline make the best educational administration professors and that standards for students in doctoral programs should be higher.

However, on one item there was a substantial change in sentiment between the two surveys. Over two-thirds of the 1972 respondents agreed with the statement that more of the literature in our field should be theory based. Only 38 percent of the 1986 respondent shared this view. An item not on the 1972 survey garnered substantial support from the 1986 respondents: over two-thirds indicated that greater attention to field studies would strengthen practice.

Given the current interest in comparative indices of program quality in academe, respondents were asked to rank the five institutions considered to have the best educational administration programs. Although the validity of reputational rankings is usually considered specious, even those who have challenged the authenticity of such rankings have had difficulty generating alternative quality indices. Composite institutional scores were compiled by assigning five points for each first-place vote, four points for each second-place vote, and so on. Ninety-five different institutions were mentioned at least once by the respondents, and seventy institutions received at least one first-place vote. The ten institutions with the highest scores were Stanford University, The Ohio State University, University of Wisconsin—Madison, University of Texas—Austin, Harvard University, Indiana University, University of Oregon, University of Chicago, Columbia University, and Michigan State University. We compared faculty members at these ten institutions with educational administration faculty elsewhere and found no significant differences in personal characteristics. However, faculty members at the ten highest-ranked institutions were substantially more research oriented, had published more articles, taught fewer hours each term, and made an average salary of $10,000 more for an academic year than did their counterparts at other institutions.

Seven of the top ten institutions in the reputational rankings also were among the ten highest producers of educational administration faculty, in that more respondents received their doctorates from these institutions. Most K-12 educational administration respondents received their doctorates from Michigan State University, The Ohio State University, Columbia University, Indiana University, University of Nebraska—Lincoln, University of Iowa, Stanford University, University of Wisconsin—Madison, Universiy of Chicago, or University of Florida. About 185 different institutions were listed as the doctorate-granting institutions of the 1986 faculty members who responded to this item, and no single institution accounted for even 4 percent of the respondents.

UCEA and Non-UCEA Institutions

We found several statistically significant differences between faculty at UCEA institutions and non-UCEA institutions. UCEA professors devoted more time to research, writing, and supervising doctoral students; published more books and articles; and were more likely to indicate that research was their area of primary strength than were their non-UCEA colleagues. Less than one-tenth of non-UCEA faculty, compared with almost one-fourth of the UCEA faculty, indicated that research and writing were the aspects of the professorship they most enjoyed. Non-UCEA faculty also were more likely to indicate that research was not emphasized in their departments and that the pressure to publish was a very serious problem. UCEA professors were more likely to indicate that more of the literature in our field should be theory based and that academic standards for the receipt of a doctorate should be higher.

Over half of the professors in non-UCEA institutions indicated that former practitioners make the best professors, while less than one-fourth of the UCEA faculty members shared this perception. More than half of the UCEA professors, compared with about one-fourth of their non-UCEA counterparts, indicated that graduate educational administration programs should be balanced between preparing practitioners and professors.

According to data supplied by department chairs, UCEA institutions tended to employ more educational administration faculty members; the median number of faculty in UCEA institutions was 8.0, compared with 4.0 in non-UCEA institutions. Almost 60 percent of the non-UCEA institutions, compared with 14 percent of the UCEA institutions, had less than five educational administration faculty members. Almost 33 percent of the UCEA programs had over ten faculty members in educational administration, compared with only 7 percent of the non-UCEA programs. However, female and minority representation was slightly lower in UCEA institutions. On the average, UCEA faculty taught fewer hours each semester, and the mean salary for an academic year was $5,000 higher among educational administration faculty in UCEA institutions. Department chairs also reported that support for faculty development and clerical services was slightly higher at UCEA institutions.

The Challenge Ahead

Given that in 1986 almost half of the educational administration faculty members were fifty-five years of age or older and the majority planned to retire by age sixty-five, we can expect substantial turnover in educational administration faculties within the next ten to fifteen years. The data suggest that our field will face even greater turnover than anticipated for academe in general. Will capable, well-trained individuals be available to assume the vacated positions? According to the faculty members surveyed in 1986, most educational administration programs are not currently emphasizing the preparation of professors, and doctoral programs have become more practitioner oriented since 1972. Furthermore, the decline in faculty compensation and the deterioration in working conditions are making it increasingly difficult to attract to academe the most able individuals, who have numerous other career options. As noted previously, interest in academic careers among young adults has declined significantly. Thus, we can anticipate less interest in the professorship among able persons at a time when there will be a large number of openings. Before we are faced with a crisis, we should mobilize our current faculty and begin preparing for the inevitable turnover in our ranks.

To capitalize on the recruitment opportunities ahead, we need to give serious attention to the types of individuals and departmental configurations that will best serve the profession. Our data suggest that professors of educational administration in general are satisfied with the status quo. Also, with a few exceptions, faculty attitudes have not changed significantly since 1972. Either we have recruited professors that "fit the mold," or the socialization process has contributed to considerable homogeneity and complacency about the professoriate and preparation programs.

Do we want to alter this image and attempt to recruit individuals with different backgrounds and fresh perspectives (perhaps to occupy new types of professorial roles)? If so, what strategies can we employ to entice talented individuals into educational administration graduate programs and to ensure that they will receive adequate support? These and related questions deserve immediate attention by the current faculty. And we need to engage in serious dialogue with individuals who can exert leverage in supporting change efforts, such as deans and other university administrators, leaders of professional associations and state educational policymakers. The UCEA has taken the first step in this direction by sponsoring the National Commission on Excellence in Educational Administration.

One promising sign is the changing male to female ratio in the professoriate in educational administration. Since almost one-third of the faculty members hired in the past ten years were women and the proportion of females in educational administration doctoral programs continues to rise, a substantial increase in female representation is likely by 1996. Female professors of educational administration as a group are more research oriented, less satisfied with the status quo, and more likely to form collegial networks beyond their own universities; thus, as female representation increases, greater diversity within the educational administration professoriate can be anticipated.

One troubling finding, however, was that department chairs reported that over one-third more women had been hired from 1976 to 1986 than were employed in their units in 1986. It is unknown whether a substantial number of these recently hired women left academe or simply moved to other institutions (thus the figure for women hired since 1976 counts some individuals two or more times). Since women as a group were more dissatisfied with their positions and the intellectual climate in their departments, the retention of women faculty in educational administration units deserve attention.

While female representation in the pool of professorial candidates is increasing, the prognosis for increasing minority representation among professors of educational administration is not as promising. The proportion of minorities in faculty positions in our field remains depressingly low, as it does in the professoriate across disciplines. We are not making sufficient progress in recruiting minorities into graduate programs, and those recruited are pursuing more lucrative positions outside academe. We need to press for governmental action to address this problem and provide incentives (such as fellowships) for talented minorities to pursue careers in educational administration.

It is disturbing that the majority of the respondents in the 1986 study perceived their preparation programs in educational administration as good or excellent. Should we be content with the quality of our preparation programs? I think not and contend that we should be held accountable for excellence—not adequacy—in our graduate programs. Practitioners increasingly are questioning the relevance of their universiy preparation, and the public is voicing dissatisfaction with the leadership in our schools. Clearly there is a gap between how those in the professoriate and consumers view administrative preparation programs.

To rejuvenate our graduate programs, a commitment of time and energy is required. While the 1986 faculty respondents perceived curriculum reform in preparation programs as the most significant need in the field, instructional innovating and clinical activities tend not to be valued in university reward systems. Morever, professors currently are not devoting their time to curriculum reform, and those entering the professoriate often are encouraged to avoid these activities so that they can devote their time to research because it "counts" toward tenure and promotion. Respondents ranked university governance activities and committee work as the least enjoyable aspect of the professoriate, and this decline in institutional commitment is bound to be manifested in some reduction in the level of commitment to the preparation program. While it would be naive to suggest that the UCEA can significantly alter university reward systems, the consortium can focus attention on the need for curriculum reform, support experimentation through its program centers, and coordinate curriculum-development projects.

The UCEA also can play a leadership role in strengthening networks for the dissemination of program innovations, and some efforts in this regard are already underway in connection with the Bitnet system. By capitalizing on the unprecedented interactive capabilities available through the merger of telecommunications and computers, we can reduce the parochial orientation that has characterized professors in our field. Collaboration across institutions is essential if significant program reform in administrative preparation is to be achieved.

Respondents in the 1986 study indicated that increased emphasis on the general practice of administration would enhance our field and that more attention should be given to practical problems and field studies. Also, almost half of the 1986 faculty indicated that former practitioners make the best professors. However, over two-thirds of the respondents did not come to their current professorial positions from a practitioner role. Thus, administrative experience is in the distant past for many educational administration professors, and some have never been practicing administrators. If we are serious about infusing preparation programs with more clinical applications, additional efforts must be made to establish partnerships with practitioners in applied research projects and to involve outstanding administrators in preparation programs as adjunct professors, clinical supervisors, or field-based mentors.

We must be cautious, however, not to exacerbate the perceived schism between research and practice or create artificial dichotomies. It was disturbing that half as many respondents in 1986 as in 1972 indicated that more of the literature in our field should be theory based. This change in sentiment could indicate that a theory-based literature has been achieved in our field. An alternative explanation is that this change in sentiment has resulted from dissatisfaction with the failure to produce unifying theory and the inadequacies of theories grounded in logical positivism to explain, predict, and influence what occurs in educational organization (Griffiths, 1988). If there is disillusionment with the search for generalizable laws, this should not negate the importance of theory development. Emerging perspectives on the nature of organizations—alternatives to the traditional positivist paradigm—have promise for enhancing our understanding of schools (Burrell and Morgan, 1980).

We should look for connections, for ways research can inform practice. This will require expanded definitions of what constitutes legitimate research in our field, with greater attention to the development of a professional knowledge base. Some movement in this direction is already evident as a cadre of educational administration researchers is focusing on the production of clinical knowledge organized around problems identified by practitioners (Silver, 1985). In addition, policy studies are gaining popularity, and such policy research has the potential to further our understanding of the impact of policy decisions on school outcomes (Bolland and Bolland, 1984; Boyan, 1981, p. 11).

We have an exciting opportunity to alter the configuration of the professoriate and the knowledge base in our field, but the current faculty members need to assume leadership. In 1985 the Carnegie Foundation declared that "rebuilding the professoriate must rank high not only on higher education's agenda, but on the nation's as well" (p. 34). It certainly should rank high on the UCEA's agenda. Never have academe in general and educational administration programs in particular been more in need of creative leadership. No longer can we afford simply to react to changing societal conditions that affect our field—*action is needed*. The consortium can play an important role in linking professors and practitioners in reform efforts. The challenge is before us, and it is up to us to act.

References

American Association of University Professors (1987). The annual report on the economic status of the profession 1986–1987, *Academe* 73(2): 3–79.

Bolland, J.W., and Bolland, K.A. (1984). Program evaluation and policy analysis: Toward a new synthesis. *Educational Evauation and Policy Analysis* 6: 333–40.

Bowen, H., and Schuster, J. (1986). *American professors: A national resource imperiled.* New York: Oxford University Press.

Boyan, N. (1981). Follow the leader: Commentary on research in educational administration. *Educational Researcher* 10(2): 6–13.

Burrell, G., and Morgan, G. (1980). *Sociological paradigms and organizational analysis.* London: Heinemann.

Campbell, R.F., and Newell, L.J. (1973). *A study of professors of educational administration.* Columbus, Ohio: University Council for Educational Administration.

Carnegie Council on Policy Studies in Higher Education (1987). *A classification of institutions of higher education*, rev. ed. Princeton, N.J.: Carnegie Foundation for the Advancement of Teaching.

Carnegie Foundation for the Advancement of Teaching. (1984). *Technical report: 1984 Carnegie Foundation national surveys of higher education.* Princeton, N.J.: Opinion Research Corp.

Carnegie Foundation for the Advancement of Teaching. (1985). The faculty: Deeply troubled. *Change* 17(4): 31–34.

Goldstein, A.J. (Ed.). (1986). *Peterson's annual guide to graduate and professional programs* Princeton, N.J.: Peterson's Annual Guides.

Griffiths, D. (1988). The professorship revisited. This volume, Chapter 21.

Hills, J. (1965). Educational administration: A field in transition. *Educational Administration Quarterly* 1: 58–66.

Ladd, E., and Lipset, S. (1973). *Professors, unions, and American higher education.* Washington, D.C.: American Enterprise Institute for Public Policy Research.

Ladd, E., and Lipset, S. (1975). *The divided academy.* New York: McGraw-Hill.

Lilley, E. (1986). *Educational administration directory, 1985–86.* Morgantown: University of West Virginia.

Mayer, M. (1974). Everything is shrinking in higher education. *Fortune* 90: 122–25.

McCarthy, M. (1986). Research in educational administration: Promising signs for the future. *Educational Administration Quarterly* 22: 3–20.

McCarthy, M. (1987). The professoriate in educational administration: Current status and challenges ahead. *UCEA Review* 28(2): 2–6.

McCarthy, M.; Kuh, G.; Newell, L.J.; and Iacona, C. (in press). *The professoriate in educational administration.* Tempe, Ariz, University Council for Educational Administration.

Molotsky, I. (1986). Help wanted: 130,000 new faculty members. *AAUP Footnotes* 4(2): 1, 3.

Schorr, M., and Hoogstra, L. (1984). *Directory of higher education: Programs and faculty,* 5th ed. Washington, D.C.: Association for the Study of Higher Education and ERIC Clearinghouse on Higher Education.

Schuster, J., and Bowen, H. (1985). The faculty at risk. *Change* 17(4): 12–21.

Silver, P. (1985). APEX center update. *UCEA Review* 26(3): 4.

Willower, D.J. (1983). Evolution of the professorship: Past, philosophy, future. *Educational Administration Quarterly* 19: 179–200.

25

A National Survey of Departmental Organization in Educational Administration

M. Scott Norton

A survey of departments of educational administration was completed in the fall of 1982. The primary purpose of the survey was to determine the organizational arrangements of such departments in major institutions nationwide.

The sixty-eight departments included in the population represented all University Council for Educational Administration (UCEA) institutions as well as twenty-five other departments in institutions of higher education. Fifty-eight departments responded, for an 85.3 percent return. States represented in the study and the number of departments or institutions that participated follow:

States	Participating Depts.	States	Participating Depts.
Alabama	1	Michigan	3
Arizona	1	Minnesota	1
Arkansas	1	Missouri	1
California	3	Nebraska	1
Colorado	1	New Mexico	1
Connecticut	1	New York	4
Delaware	1	North Carolina	1

Florida	2	Ohio	3
Georgia	2	Oklahoma	3
Hawaii	1	Pennsylvania	4
Illinois	3	South Carolina	1
Indiana	1	Tennessee	1
Iowa	1	Texas	3
Kansas	1	Utah	1
Kentucky	1	Virginia	1
Louisiana	1	Wisconsin	2
Maryland	1	Canada	1
Massachusetts	3		

Total Participating Departments = 58

General Study Summary

Summary findings pertaining to each survey question are presented in the following sections; the appendix contains information about specific departments.

"1a. What Is the Official Title of Your Department?"

As might be expected, official department titles varied considerably among participating institutions. Of the fifty-eight departments, however, eighteen had the singular title of "Educational Administration."

The title "Department of Educational Leadership" was common to six departments. Other title components coupled with the general entry of "The Department of Educational Administration and _____" included Supervision (7), Planning (4), Policy Studies (8), and Foundations (3).

Other combination titles included such components as Curriculum, Administrative Studies, Instructional Studies, Higher Education, Educational Development, Evaluation, Adult Studies, Social Policy, and Cultural Studies.

"1b. As Chairperson, to Whom Do You Report (Your Immediate Supervisor)?"

Of the fifty-eight respondents, forty-eight indicated that the dean of the college was their immediate supervisor.

In the other cases, the chair most often reported to the director of a division or to a chairperson of a division that included several departments or programs.

"2. Does Your Department Faculty Membership Consist Exclusively of Persons Prepared for and/or Representing Educational Administration Per Se?"

Nineteen of the total group answered "yes" to the above question. Each of the other thirty-nine departments had *at least one* major program component other than educational administration.

"3. What Major Educational Areas, Combinations, or Thrusts Listed Below Are Part of Your Department's Organization and College Responsibility?"

Those major areas combined with educational administration as identified in the survey were as follows:

Higher Education (30)	Multicultural Education (6)
Foundations (14)	Educational Psychology (4)
Curriculum/Instruction (12)	Special Education (Adm.) (4)
Educational Technology (9)	Policy Analysis (4)
Adult Education (8)	Audio-Visual Education (4)
	Vocational/Technical Education (3)

Many other areas were listed by one or two of the respondents. These components included such areas as bilingual education, counselor education, evaluation, research and comparative education, governance, medical professional education, teaching, and organizational theory.

"4. Is Your Department Considered a Graduate Department Only or Both a Graduate and an Undergraduate Department?"

Of the fifty-eight reporting departments, forty-four were graduate only and fourteen served both graduate and undergraduate programs.

In a few instances, the graduate only departments did note that the department had one or more service courses at the undergraduate level. However, nearly 65 percent of the departments served only the graduate level.

"5. In Brief, What Factors Contributed to the Present Department Organization (such as Mergers, Extensions, Combinations)?"

Responses to this question varied considerably and, in some cases, were quite general.

  a. General responses to the question included "mergers," "reduction," or "expediency" without mention or clarification of causal factors. In some cases, program considerations were inferred but not specifically stated. (Responses = 23.)

Such comments as "mergers and voluntary association by several individuals" and "mergers, extensions, and combinations" were given as typical contributing factors that led to the current organizational arrangements.

b. A second category centered on reorganization to meet emerging educational needs or for programmatic reasons. This category of responses also included the reason "growth needs." (Responses = 11.)

Contributing factors were identified by such comments as "educational administration and higher education merger sought for programmatic reasons; the addition of special education was both programmatic and the result of other reorganization"; and "proliferation of small doctoral programs led to a need for some consolidation. We now share a core curriculum across administration, adult, and higher education."

c. Tradition or continuation of the original organization arrangement was a third category of response. (Responses = 8.)

Brief comments such as, "history/tradition," "Hasn't changed in twenty years," and "long history of thirty years," were typical comments for contributing factors in this area.

d. General reorganization of the college due to such factors as decline, fiscal crises, economy, or the need to reduce the number of programs or departments. This category of responses included the reason of "pressure to do so." (Responses = 8.)

Contributing factors that led to the current reorganization in this area were explained by such comments as, "Enrollment decline and university pressure," "Complete reorganization of the college during a fiscal crisis," and "Decentralization of the college several years ago."

"6. How Effective Is Your Present Organizational Arrangement?"

Three response choices were provided: (1) highly effective, (2) workable, and (3) presents several problems.

While participants apparently had no serious problems choosing among the three choices provided, a few respondents marked one of the first two choices (highly effective, workable) and then made a notation that the organization "presented several problems" as well.

In any case, the effectiveness of existing organizational arrangements was rated by participants as follows:

a. Highly effective (30)
b. Workable (23)
c. Presents several problems (5)

An attempt was made to evaluate the effectiveness ratings relative to certain considerations such as the type of organization and reasons for the type of organization. While this analysis was limited, the following findings may be of interest.

Of the five departments responding that the present organizational arrangement "presents several problems," two were part of a divisional organization arrangement, one had been relegated to a small program unit as part of a department that was formerly a division, one had an unusually large number of program components, and one had been merged with higher, adult, and continuing education.

In the five instances where the effectiveness rating was noted as having several problems, the department chairs reported to the dean in three cases and in the other two cases they reported to a divisional director.

Of the twenty "educational administration only" departments, eleven judged their effectiveness as highly effective, seven judged it as workable, and only one respondent indicated that it presented several problems. In the latter instance, the problems were related to a divisional structure, and budget control was outside the department. Also, this respondent noted a loss of access to the dean.

Of the departments that were *not* educational administration (EDA) only, twenty judged the organization as highly effective, sixteen judged it as workable, and three indicated that it has several problems.

Of departments that noted that the present organization was merely merger or some measure of economy, effectiveness ratings were as follows:

a. Highly Effective (16)
b. Workable (15)
c. Several Problems (4)

In instances where organization seemingly was based on a programmatic rationale, effectiveness was assessed as follows:

a. Highly Effective (3)
b. Workable (8)
c. Several Problems (0)

And finally, in departments that had a long history of the present organizational arrangement, effectiveness was judged as follows:

a. Highly Effective (5)
b. Workable (1)
c. Several Problems (0)

"7. What Major Problems and/or Strengths Does Your Organizational Plan Provide (Your Opinion)?"

As might be expected, strengths and problems were viewed in various ways. An effort was made to analyze the strengths and problems associated with those departments organized as EDA only and those that were not EDA only. Comments concerning pluses and minuses of each arrangement follow:

Educational Administration Only

A. Strengths
   (1) Have specialists in each area
   (2) Good advisor-student capacity for doctorate—major doctoral degree institution in educational administration
   (3) Clear-cut mission, agreement on goals, cohesiveness
   (4) Small size and focus
   (5) Able to concentrate on educational administration only
   (6) Clear-cut lines of authority and communication
   (7) Logic and tradition

B. Weaknesses
   (1) Small size, low enrollment
   (2) Fragmentation (for example, a division of higher education exists)
   (3) Basic courses such as research taught by other departments
   (4) Loss of fiscal control, communication, and identity (in those instances when educational administration is placed in a division arrangement)
   (5) Some chance of becoming "insular"
   (6) Educational administration is too narrowly focused
   (7) Increased tendency to function as a totally independent unit under conditions where demands exceed resources

Not Educational Administration Only

A. Strengths
   (1) Reduces "turf" problems
   (2) Provides opportunity for new program thrusts
   (3) Excellent faculty working in a loosely coupled organization
   (4) Better use of resources
   (5) Scheduling/coordination
   (6) Logical combination of all school-related administration programs
   (7) Integration of several disciplines, mixing of personalities, new program areas
   (8) Defining common goals and programs
   (9) Cluster groups of special interests
   (10) Reduces the number of department chairs
   (11) More diverse faculty
   (12) Cross fertilization of related interests
   (13) Reduction of course proliferation
   (14) Enhancement of faculty deployment and assignments

(15) Improved services to students and schools
(16) More diverse faculty facilities collaboration across a broader spectrum of college's faculty

B. Weaknesses
  (1) Some areas in the organizational arrangement are not really congruent with EDA
  (2) Adds to the problems of planning, coordination, and focus of thrusts
  (3) Numbers involved
  (4) Bureaucratic levels, curriculum change, and the like
  (5) Lack of resources
  (6) Combination of programs of predominantly Ed.D. students (administration) and Ph.D. students (other components) makes research courses difficult
  (7) Larger unit increases complexity, and communication problems are created due to the diminution of their former department by being merged with larger unit
  (8) Determination of avenues to maximize staff utilization—common interests, development of a generic approach to leadership studies
  (9) Inequity of demand—educational administration tends to carry the loads regarding students and program
  (10) Coordination, sharing a common mission

"8. Please Provide Additional Comments Which Might Serve to Clarify and Extend the Information Concerning Your Department Organization"

Selected comments provided by respondents follow:

  a. What really makes this work is the fact that we have a good staff who work together cooperatively. After all, it's the people who get the job done, not the plan or organization.
  b. As the budget crunch progresses, we may find ourselves regressing back to a more centralized stance—elemination by reorganization of one or more dependents.
  c. Have expanded from a department of ten to thirty-one. Alignment will promote a more effective use of faculty in program development and implementation.
  d. We are such a polyglot unit that only a lengthy response could provide an adequate description.
  e. We have been asked to consider merging again with the departments we split away from some twenty years ago (for economy of size reasons).
  f. Organization without a concept of mission—better ideas about training will not prove to be educationally substantive.

g. Departments were abolished four to five years ago. Several programs were grouped into three to four larger divisions. New organization has several problems.

h. In all probability the department will be merged into a leadership program in the near future. My best guess is that we will merge with our current foundations and urban education departments.

i. We have split away from a department containing higher and adult education and foundations.

j. In 1966, we moved from a large general department to seven more specific groups.

k. The Department of Education split into three departments—Human Development, Curriculum and Instruction, and Administration and Foundational Services.

Summary of General Comments

In addition to comments regarding factors that contributed to the present organizational plan and those related to identified strengths and problems, respondents were provided an opportunity to comment generally. These comments served three purposes for the respondents: (1) to clarify and to extend the explanation of present organizational structure, (2) to project possible reorganization plans that were expected but not certain to date, and (3) to reflect on the present plan additionally.

In regard to the first of the above purposes, the respondents made such statements as:

a. Departments were abolished four to five years ago. Several programs were grouped into three to four larger divisions. Shrinking size of school was a major factor.

b. The department is composed of four somewhat independent programs: educational administration, higher education, educational sociology, and interdepartmental research studies.

c. The department uses three standing committees: program, admissions, and staff personnel.

d. Individual faculty members have responsibility for the coordination of areas of specialization within educational administration.

In relation to the second purpose of projecting possible future plans, the following kinds of comments were provided:

a. We expect to merge with higher education and drop the division structure this year.

b. We are (presently) engaged in merger discussions with three other programs: higher education, international education, and foundations of education. Some type of merger will evolve.

In relation to the respondents' reflections on the current organizational structure, the following comments were provided:

a. The organizational management is new this year. It is somewhat early to assess its effectiveness.
b. This is a fairly loose organization with a number of area coordinators. Each academic discipline has a great deal of autonomy.

Appendix: Department Organization Report

Institution	Department Title	Immediate Supervisor	EDA Only	Organizational Components	Grad or G/UG
University of Alabama	Administration and Educational Leadership	Dean	No	Higher Education/ Curriculum and Supervision	G
University of Arizona	Educational Foundations and Administration	Dean	No	Foundations, Multicultural Education, Bilingual Education, Educational Technology	G/UG
University of Arkansas	Educational Administration Program Area	To an Area Coordinator, one of five in the college	Yes	None	G
Stanford University		Dean	No	Higher Education. We have a core of 36 credits - 12 decision analysis, 12 administration	G
University of California	Educational Administration and Evaluation	Chairman, School of Education	No	Policy Planning and Analysis	G

Institution	Department Title	Immediate Supervisor	EDA Only	Organizational Components	Grad or G/UG
University of Southern California	Department of Educational Policy, Planning and Administration	Dean	No	Foundations	G/UG
University of Colorado	Curriculum, Administration and Supervision	Dean	No	Higher Education, Curriculum	G
University of Connecticut	Department of Educational Administration	Dean	Yes	None	G
University of Delaware	Department of Educational Development	Dean	No	Multicultural Education, Bilingual Education, Educational Technology, Curriculum and Development, General Elementary Education (math, science, social studies, and so on)	G/UG
University of Florida	Educational Administration and Supervision	Dean	Yes, with special areas	Higher Education; Special areas: Educational Finance, Educational Business Mgt., Community Education, Ed. Leadership	G

Institution	Department Title	Immediate Supervisor	EDA Only	Organizational Components	Grad or G/UG
Florida State University	Educational Leadership	Dean	No	Higher Education, Adult Education, Vocational Education, Policy Administration and Planning	G
University of Georgia	Bureau of Educational Studies and Field Services	Dean	Yes	None	G
Georgia State University	Department of Educational Administration	Dean	No	Higher Education, Educational Psychology, Educational Technology	G
University of Hawaii-Manoa	Department of Educational Administration	Dean	Yes	None	G
Illinois State University	Educational Administration and Foundations	Dean	No	Higher Education, Foundations, Special Education (adm.)	G/UG
Northern Illinois University	Leadership and Educational Policy Studies	Department Chairman	No	Higher Education, Foundations, Educational Technology, Counselor Education, Audio-Visual Education	G/UG

Institution	Department Title	Immediate Supervisor	EDA Only	Organizational Components	Grad or G/UG
University of Illinois	Department of Administration, Higher and Continuing Education	Dean	No	Higher Education, Adult and Continuing Education	G
Indiana University	Department of Administrative Studies	Dean	No	Higher Education, Adult Education, College Student Personnel	G/UG
University of Iowa	Educational Administration	Dean	Yes	None	G
University of Kansas	Educational Policy and Administration	Dean	No	Higher Education, Foundations	G
University of Kentucky	Administration and Supervision	Dean	Yes	None	G
Louisiana State University	Administrative and Foundational Services	Dean	No	Foundations, Educational Measurements and Statistics, Educational Technology, Counselor Education, Audio-Visual Education, Library Science (UG)	G/UG
University of Maryland	Department of Educational Policy, Planning, and	Dean	No	Higher Education, Foundations, Educational	G

Institution	Department Title	Immediate Supervisor	EDA Only	Organizational Components	Grad or G/UG
	Administration			Technology, Audio-Visual Education, Educational Policy, Curriculum Theory and Development, Comparative Education	
Harvard University	Administration, Planning, and Social Policy	Dean	No	Higher Education, Sociology of Education, Policy Analysis and Evaluation, Organizational Studies	G
Northeastern University— Boston	Department of Educational Administration	Dean, College of Human Development Professions	Yes	None	G
Boston University	Educational Leadership	A Division Director	No	Higher Education, Educational Psychology (Measurements), Curriculum	G
Michigan State University	Administration and Curriculum	Dean	No	Higher Education, Foundations, Multicultural Education, Classroom Learning and Guidance,	G

Institution	Department Title	Immediate Supervisor	EDA Only	Organizational Components	Grad or G/UG
				Adult and Continuing Education, Curriculum Specialties, Generic Curriculum	
Wayne State University (Michigan)	Administrative and Organizational Studies	Division Head	No	Higher Education, Instructional Technology	G
University of Michigan— Ann Arbor	Educational Policy, Planning, and Administration	Dean and Executive Committee of the School of Education	No	Foundations, Educational Psychology	G/UG
University of Minnesota	Educational Policy and Administration	Dean	No	Higher Education, Foundations, Special Education (administration)	G
University of Missouri	Department of Educational Administration	Dean	Yes	None	G, do have 2 required courses in educational administration for teacher education majors.
University of Nebraska— Lincoln	Educational Administration	Dean	No	Higher Education, Audio-Visual Education	G

Institution	Department Title	Immediate Supervisor	EDA Only	Organizational Components	Grad or G/UG
University of New Mexico	Department of Educational Administration	Dean	Yes	However, department faculty have developed expertise in such areas as multicultural education, higher education, curriculum and instruction, and others	G
State University of New York— Buffalo	Educational Organization, Administration, and Policy	Dean	No	Higher Education, Foundations, Occupations/ Vocational Education, in part (multicultural Education and Educational Technology)	G/UG but primarily G
New York University	Organizational and Administrative Studies	Vice-Dean	No	Higher Education, Social Foundations, Special Education Administration, all school-required doctoral research courses	G

Institution	Department Title	Immediate Supervisor	EDA Only	Organizational Components	Grad or G/UG
Syracuse University	Area of Administrative and Adult Studies	Director, Division of Educational Development, Counseling, Administrative and Adult Studies	No	Higher Education, Adult Education	G
St. John's University New York	Division of Administrative and Instructional Leadership	Dean	No	Curriculum, Teaching, Instructional Leadership	G/UG
University of N. Carolina	Organizational Development and Instructional Studies	Dean	No	Higher Education, Foundation, Adult Education	G
Ohio State University	Education Policy Leadership (Tentative)	Dean	No	Foundations, Adult and Vocational/ Technical Education; Curriculum/ Instructional/ Development; Student Personnel Administration	G/UG
University of Toledo	Administration and Supervision	Director, Division of Educational Leadership Development	Yes	NA	

Institution	Department Title	Immediate Supervisor	EDA Only	Organizational Components	Grad or G/UG
Bowling Green State University	The Department of Educational Administration and Supervision	Dean	Yes	Administration of Higher Education	G/UG
University of Tulsa	Division of Professional Studies	Chairperson, Division of Professional Studies	No	Educational Psychology, Counselor Education	G
University of Oklahoma	Educational Administration	Dean	Yes	None	G
Oklahoma State	Educational Administration and Higher Education	Dean	No	Higher Education, Law	G
University of Pennsylvania	Educational Leadership Division	Dean	No	Higher Education, Teacher Education, Curriculum and Supervision, Human Sexuality, Medical Profession Education	G
Penn. State University	Program in Educational Administration	Division Head, Division of Educational Policy Studies	Yes	Division faculty includes foundations, higher education, and adult education	G

Institution	Department Title	Immediate Supervisor	EDA Only	Organizational Components	Grad or G/UG
University of Pittsburgh	Educational Administration	Dean	Yes	None	G
Temple University	Department of Educational Administration	Dean	Yes	None	G
University of South Carolina	Educational Leadership	Dean	No	Higher Education, Foundations, Curriculum	G/UG
University of Tennessee	Educational Administration and Supervision	Dean	No	Higher Education, Foundations (philosophical), Multicultural Education, Education, Educational Technology	G
University of Texas—Austin	Educational Administration	Dean	Yes	Higher Education, (included also in Community College Leadership)	G
University of Houston	Educational Leadership and Cultural Studies	Dean	No	Higher Education, Foundations, Multicultural Education, Program Evaluation	G
Texas A & M University	Department of Educational Administration	Dean	Yes	None	G

Institution	Department Title	Immediate Supervisor	EDA Only	Organizational Components	Grad or G/UG
University of Utah	Department of Educational Administration	Dean	No	Higher Education	G
University of Virginia	Department of Administration and Supervision	Dean	No	Multicultural Education, Supervision, Community Education	
University of Wisconsin— Milwaukee	Administrative Leadership	Dean	No	Adult Education	G
University of Wisconsin— Madison	Department of Educational Administration	Dean	No	Higher Education, Special Education (administration), Vocational/ Technical Education Administration	G
University of Alberta— Canada	Department of Educational Administration	Dean	Yes (some apply even with "Yes")	Higher Education, Educational Technology	G

26

Doctoral Studies of Students in Educational Administration Programs in UCEA-Member Institutions*

M. Scott Norton and Frederick D. Levan

One of the initial activities of the UCEA Program Center for Preparation Programs was to determine the perceived value of certain kinds of preparation program information. Faculty members in UCEA-member institutions listed *curriculum* information as having the highest interest and benefit for them and their departments' preparation programs. As a result of this interest, the study of curriculum became a high-priority activity of the Program Center.

The feasibility of completing a study of the curricula of preparation programs in educational administration was discussed at length by the advisory committee of the Program Center in a one-day meeting in Tempe, Arizona. Questions of importance were: (1) Could such a study accurately determine the course work, practicum, and research activity experienced by students in their preparation? (2) What degree programs should be included in the study? (3) Should only UCEA-member institutions be included in the study? and (4) To what extent would it be possible or necessary to determine actual course content?

---

* Reprinted with permission from *Educational Considerations*, No. 1 (Winter, 1987), 21–24. © 1987 by *Educational Considerations*.

The student's official program of study was selected as the primary data document because it appeared to provide the most reliable indication of the actual courses, practica, and research activities of students in preparation programs. Since the student's program of study for the doctorate in almost all instances reflects course work completed for the master's degree and administrative certification, the Ed.D. and Ph.D. degree programs were selected for study. In addition, study of these doctoral degree programs provided some opportunity to compare differences among degrees. It was further decided to limit the study to a random sample of UCEA-member institutions.

A primary concern, and a limitation of this study, was the inability to ascertain actual course content as well as the specific nature of program practica. Any attempt to determine the actual subject matter of courses presented major problems. However, it was the consensus of the Program Center's advisory committee that such a determination was not essential. For example, it was the committee's view that it would be valuable to learn the extent to which students had been exposed to various areas of study (such as theory, policy, research), even though the specific course content might vary among institutions.

Pilot Study Activities

The feasibility of the study was examined through two pilot studies. The first pilot effort encompassed the examination of thirty-six Ed.D. programs of study at Arizona State University. Data were recorded for the following eight categories: (1) courses completed in educational administration, (2) courses completed outside the field of educational administration, (3) total number of courses completed and total credit hours, (4) practica completed, (5) research and statistics courses completed, (6) dissertation credits, (7) language requirements, and (8) residency requirements.

A second pilot study surveyed twenty-nine UCEA-member institutions. One program of study for each doctoral degree offered was examined. An analysis of students' programs was completed in the same manner as in the first pilot study. Several problems were encountered in the second effort, however. It was not always clear, for example, whether courses were indeed offered within or outside the department of educational administration. Dissertation credit was difficult to identify and in some cases was nonexistent, even though the institution did require a dissertation. Such information as requirements for residency and foreign language were not determinable by an examination of students' programs.

With the above experiences in mind, the major study of the doctoral programs of students in educational administration was initiated and is reported in the sections that follow.

The Study Sample

The following were selected in a random sample of twenty-seven UCEA-member institutions:

Arizona State University	University of Kansas
Fordham University	University of Kentucky
Illinois State University	University of Minnesota
Kansas State University	University of Missouri
New Mexico State University	University of Nebraska
New York University	University of Oklahoma
Oklahoma State University	University of Oregon
Penn State University	University of Toledo
State University of New York at	University of Tennessee
Buffalo	University of Texas
Temple University	University of Utah
Texas A & M University	University of Virginia
University of Connecticut	University of Wisconsin—Madison
University of Florida	Washington State University

Each institution was asked to send two student programs of study for each of the doctoral degrees offered. The programs were to be randomly selected and were to have been developed within the last three years. Responses were received from all of the institutions except Fordham University and Penn State University. In all, seventy-eight programs of study were received: thirty-nine for the Ed.D degree and an equal number for the Ph.D. degree.

The Study Results

Each of the seventy-eight programs of study was analyzed and each course or experience recorded under one of the following seven categories: (1) courses in educational administration, (2) research and statistics courses, (3) foundations courses, (4) seminars/workshops, (5) cognate courses, (6) field experience, and (7) dissertation. Each of these categories is discussed in the following sections.

Courses in Educational Administration

All courses in educational administration were recorded under one of fourteen course areas. For example, the course area Organization and Administration included all courses that were concerned with how schools and school systems are organized and how they are administered. Thus, such courses as Educational Administration, Introduction to Administration, Organization and Administration, and Problems in Educational Ad-

Table 26–1
Courses in Educational Administration

Course	Ph.D.	Percentage of Educational Administration Course Work	Ed.D.	Percentage of Educational Administration Course Work
Organization and Administration	104	32	88	28
Personnel	43	13	27	8
Law	27	8	35	10
Finance	23	7	26	8
Human and Community Relations and Societal Factors	21	6	28	8
Management	17	5	12	4
Theory	15	5	18	5
Principalship	15	5	20	6
Policy	15	5	8	2
Supervision	14	4	19	6
Facilities	14	4	25	8
Politics	9	3	9	3
Leadership	9	3	13	4
Superintendency	2	1	3	1

ministration were recorded under Organization and Administration. Similarly, such courses as Organizational Theory, Theory, Theory and Application, The Theory of Educational Administration, and Advanced Theory were recorded under the course area of Theory.

Table 26–1 reveals the fourteen course areas in educational administration for the Ph.D. and Ed. D. degree programs. Data do not include educational administration seminars, field experiences, research courses offered in educational administration, or credits for dissertation.

The 324 educational administration courses for the Ph.D. degree represented 39 percent of the total course work. The 331 courses in the Ed.D. degree program represented 39 percent of the total doctoral course work as well.

As indicated by the data, Ph.D. degree students completed 32 percent of the course work in educational administration, with the exceptions previously noted, in courses in the area of organization and administration. Courses in personnel, law, and finance constituted 29 percent of the course work in administration.. Thus, 60 percent of the educational administration courses was in the area of organization and administration, personnel, law, and finance. All other course areas included only 40 percent of the course work in the field of administration. As indicated in Table 26–1, courses in theory, policy, and leadership constituted only 11 percent of the Ph.D. students' course work.

Similar results are noted for Ed.D. degree students. The four course areas, — organization and administration, law, personnel, and finance — constituted 53 percent of the educational administration course work. However, Ed.D. degree programs of study contained considerably less course work in organization and administration and personnel than did Ph.D. programs. Ed.D. degree programs revealed a somewhat higher degree of course work in areas such as facilities and law.

Research and Statistics

Courses in research methods and statistics represented 16 percent and 13 precent of the total work for the Ph.D. and Ed.D. programs of study, respectively. The nine courses in research and statistics were recorded, as shown in Table 26–2.

Elementary Statistics and Intermediate Statistics dominated the course work for Ed.D. students, and Introduction to Research clearly was the primary research methods course on Ed.D. degree programs of study. Ed.D. degree programs contained more courses in statistics than did Ph.D. programs of study. For the Ed.D. degree programs, work in statistics constituted 7 percent of the total course work, while it represented 6 percent of total course work for Ph.D. students. However, Ph.D. course work in research methods clearly surpassed that in Ed.D. degree programs. Research courses in Ph.D. and Ed.D. programs represented 10 percent and 6 percent of the total course work, respectively.

Foundations

Foundations encompassed a wide variety of course work in the areas of psychology, guidance and counseling, human resources development, special education, curriculum and instruction, history and philosophy of education, and other courses related to education. In view of the generally accepted definition of foundations (that is, history, philosophy, psychology, and sociology), the area of general education might have been a more appropriate title for this classification.

Course work in the foundations area constituted 26 percent and 24 percent of the total course work for Ph.D. and Ed.D. students, respectively. These percentages were second only to the course work taken specifically in

Table 26–2
Research and Statistics Courses

Courses		Number of Courses Ph.D.	Ed.D.
Statistics			
Tests and Measurements		12	8
Elementary Statistics		23	29
Intermediate Statistics (Inferential)		16	20
Advanced Statistics (Multivariate)		2	3
	Total	53	60
Research Methods			
Introduction to Research		35	32
Quantitative Research		14	1
Advanced Research Methods		21	7
Qualitative Research		6	8
Computer (Research)		7	0
	Total	83	48

educational administration. It should be emphasized once again that the foundations area included virtually all course work in education taken outside departments of educational administration except cognate work (business, liberal arts, music, and the like) and research, statistics, and seminar courses.

In total, 219 of the Ph.D. 841 courses and 207 of the Ed. D. 844 courses were classified as foundations. It is significant to note that of the 219 Ph.D. foundations courses, only five courses were reported on at least five students' programs of study. The variability of such courses on doctoral programs appeared obvious. For example, only the courses of Philosophy of Education, Directed Reading, Sociology of Education, Advanced Educational Psychology, and Secondary School Curriculum appeared on at least five Ph.D. programs of study. The mode for the number of times a course appeared as a foundations course was one.

Similarly, only five foundations courses were common to as many as five students' programs in the Ed.D. degree. Philosophy of Education, History of Education, Advanced Educational Psychology, Psychology of Exceptional Children, and Practicum in Counseling appeared on five student programs of study. One hundred six of the 207 Ed.D. foundations courses were listed on only one program of study.

Cognate Course Work

Cognate work included courses in liberal arts, fine arts, business administration, religion, and computer applications. Cognate work constituted 7 percent of the Ph.D. and 9 percent of the Ed.D. course work. Such work had no program commonality. Virtually every cognate entry was singular. Of the 841 total Ph.D. and 844 total Ed.D. courses, 60 and 72 were cognate courses, respectively.

Seminars and Workshops

Seminars and workshops included courses both inside and outside departments of educational administration. Twenty-eight of the 43 Ph.D. seminars/workshops and 31 of the 62 Ed.D. seminars/workshops were related to educational administration. Seminar/workshop titles included School Administration, Educational Management, Fundamentals of School Administration, Policy, Secondary School Curriculum, Audiovisual Materials, and various others.

Seminars/workshops constituted 5 percent and 7 percent of the total course work in Ph.D. and Ed.D. programs, respectively. No patterns or commonalities were found among the seminar/workshop courses on the programs of study examined.

Field Experiences

Field experiences included internships, independent study, field work, and practica. Of the 33 field experience entries for Ph.D. degree programs, 26 were exclusively in educational administration. Of the 41 Ed.D. entries, 31 were in the area of educational administration. The Ph.D. and Ed.D. experiences in educational administration are categorized in Table 26–3.

As noted previously, other field experiences outside the field of educational administration were included in degree programs. Such experiences were quite limited, however.

Total Program Summary

Table 26–4 indicates the total data for each of the major areas of study·for the Ph.D. and Ed.D. degree programs.

As the data indicate, no area of study for the Ph.D. and Ed.D. degrees varies more than 3 percent. While Ph.D. programs of study did contain 3 percent more courses in research and statistics, Ed.D. degree programs contained more work in statistics than did PH.D. programs. The difference is accounted for by the greater emphasis on research methods in Ph.D. degree

Table 26–3
Field Experiences in Educational Administration

Field Experience	Number of Courses Ph.D.	Ed.D.
Internship	13	15
Independent Study	7	11
Field Experience/Application	6	5
Total	26	31

Table 26–4
Total Data for Areas of Doctoral Study

Area of Study	Ph.D. Number of Courses	Percentage of Total Work	Ed.D. Number of Courses	Percentage of Total Work
Educational Administration Course Work	324	39	331	39
Research and Statistics	136	16	108	13
Foundations	219	26	207	24
Cognates	60	7	72	9
Seminars/Workshops	43	5	62	7
Field Experiences	33	4	41	5
Dissertation*	26	3	23	3
Total	184		844	

*Represents number of listings and not credit hours.

programs. The results for the dissertation are questionable. Since dissertation credit was not clear in all cases, dissertation was recorded as only a single entry for each student's program. Credit hours completed were not considered. In any case, these data led to an obvious conclusion that differences between Ed.D. and Ph.D. degree programs in UCEA-member institutions are indistinguishable.

Summary

The data gathered from student programs of study in UCEA-member institutions supported the following conclusions:

1. Ph.D. and Ed.D. degree programs in educational administration are virtually identical pursuits in UCEA-member institutions. The amount and kind of course work completed in the field of educational administration are the same for the two doctoral programs.

2. Students pursuing either the Ph.D. or Ed.D. degree program in UCEA-member institutions could expect to complete at least 60 percent of their total doctoral work in the course areas of organization and administration, personnel, finance, law, and human and community relations and social factors.

3. Research and statistical course requirements for the Ed.D. and Ph.D. degrees differed only slightly, except for a somewhat higher expectation of research methods course work in Ph.D. programs.

4. Foundations course work for both the Ph.D. and Ed.D. programs constituted approximately 25 percent of the students' programs of study. Foundations encompassed a broad area of course work and included virtually all general education course work taken outside the field of educational administration.

5. Field experiences and workshops for doctoral students constituted a relatively small percentage of the student's program of study. A student could expect no more than 5 percent of the total doctoral program to be devoted to field experiences.

6. Cognate work, courses in disciplines outside the field of education, also represented a relatively small percentage of doctoral programs. Such course work almost always was brought to the doctoral program as previous credit earned during the master's program.

7. Course work in theory, policy, the principalship, supervision, facilities, politics, leadership, and the superintendency, when considered individually, would be expected to constitute 5 percent or less of the doctoral student's program of study.

27

Clinical Education for School Superintendents and Principals: The Missing Link

John B. Peper

Introduction

School administration as practiced by superintendents and principals bears little resemblance to school administration as taught in graduate schools of education (Pitner, 1982; Peterson and Finn, 1985). Graduate schools tend to emphasize didactic lectures to which students listen passively. At best, student administrators serve as "worker bees" in professor-directed research projects. Graduate schools often structure their degree requirements around state certification standards, and they also grant credit for loosely directed internships. From these certification or graduate programs, prospective administrators are expected to enter a world of decision and activity that requires them both to take charge of a group of other professional educators who teach in a multi-cultural milieu and to constantly interact with the community.

One should not be surprised to hear principals and superintendents sincerely question the relevance of their formal preparation in the university. To their credit, universities often do an excellent job of selecting and screening intellectual talent. In the better UCEA- member schools, administrator candidates are generally selected from applicants who meet graduate school standards on one or more basic entrance examinations. Applicants for educational administration degrees also tend to have above-average undergraduate grade-point averages. With respect to the intellectual content and types of courses required for administrative certification and in degree programs, I believe that serious candidates receive a comprehensive grounding in theoretical and intellectual information. Where then does the discrepancy between formal education and the demands of practice develop? Few, if any, university programs in school administration offer a thorough clinical experience for future school administrators to balance their fine academic and research programs. In the remainder of this paper, I will sketch what I think should be the minimum components of a clinical program in school administration. It is my assumption that universities could and should take primary leadership for resolving the discrepancy between their excellent academic preparation of administrators and the mediocre to poor clinical experiences in those same programs.

Why the universities? Significant literature addresses utopian notions of emergent partnerships rising magically among state departments, universities, school districts, business organizations, professional associations, and community groups to cooperate in providing the balance between academic preparation and clinical education for school administrators. The literature fails to acknowledge basic accountability principles, and in my opinion it provides all members of the partnership with reasons to shirk responsibility when cooperation fails. Interinstitutional cooperation in the clinical education of administrators is desirable. But responsibility for coordination of planned clinical education must be assigned, and resources must be adequate to the task if new developments are to take place as envisioned by the National Commission on Excellence in Educational Administration. Since universities are currently recognized as primary providers of administrative education, metamorphosis could occur naturally by building on present systems rather than wildly hoping that new structures will occur through transformative change. One could, however, imagine legislators being persuaded to establish new structures around state departments or professional organizations if universities ignore the pressing need for improved clinical education.

I will set aside in this discussion any major recommendations on academic content, though I do have strong thoughts about the academic side of the equation, in order to focus on the clinical education of administrators. A well-designed and executed clinical education for prospective school administrators would be one that is well grounded in a matrix of academic course preparation and rigorous research on administrative practice and policy development. Therefore, a one-sided discussion of clinical experience absent the accompanying academic coursework leaves me less than satisfied, much as the stage performer laments the applause of one-handed listeners. Ultimately a matrix of academic preparation and clinical experience must conjoin in a single developmental lattice of sequenced intersections.

What is clinical education? Clinical education is the coordinated teaching and learning of skills that are based on an established philosophy of pedagogy and predetermined learning theory and are correlated with an assessment of job-related requirements. In general, university graduate schools tend to place less value on clinical education than they place on the generation and dissemination of knowledge. Exceptions are recognized professional schools: law schools, medical schools, and business schools seem to have little difficulty rewarding their clinical faculty in the same kinds of ways that they reward their academic and research faculty. Graduate schools of education, like other professional schools, need to balance their academic teaching faculty with a skilled clinical faculty if the paradigm of university-directed clinical education is to succeed.

Clinical Education for Administrators

How does skill development occur? Bloom (1982), in his analysis of the educational patterns of concert pianists and olympic swimmers, suggests that skill development occurs in three distinct stages. First there is a period of exploration that takes place with a nurturant, generalist teacher who encourages horizontal and vertical exploration. Second there is a period of instruction under the guidance of a specialized skill instructor. The skill instructor teaches and analyzes technique. Only a few good swimmers become olympic-class swimmers, and their development takes place under the tutelage of just a few experienced coaches. Those final-stage coaches teach the artistic elements of polished success.

Joyce and Weil (1986) describe a model of acquiring teaching skills that also applies in some ways to the acquisition of school administration. One might liken skill development in administration to skill development in skiing. The novice skier would do well to seek instruction. So would the prospective administrator. Ski instructors start by outfitting potential students with safe equipment, and they explain the theoretical basis for their lessons. For example, if the graduated-length method is used, the instructor explains this theoretical approach to skiing. Then the instructor demonstrates a desired basic skill. Students are given opportunities to practice the skill first in a low-risk, success-prone environment. Moving from simple to complex tasks, from basic to artistic maneuvers, the budding skier progresses from directed to independent practice. As the novice skier gains experience, the instructor becomes an observer-analyzer and provides very little demonstration in the latter stages. In the advanced stages of development, the instructor's use of feedback and evaluation becomes more significant because performance focuses more on fine motor development and the nuances of artistic expression than on new basic skills.

I propose that clinical education for administrators must be structured in a similar fashion. Perhaps skills could be broken into eight to twelve categories, and the early levels of skill attainment could be embedded in courses and laboratory assignments to accompany academic course preparation at the university. Advanced stages of skill development would occur as explained in the next section. I suggest the following minimum skill categories for clinical education. I then suggest approaches to the attainment of those skills in a sequential model.

Minimum Skill Categories for Clinical Education

I. Communication Skills

    A. Careful analytical listening
    B. Formal and informal speaking
    C. Writing
        1. Letters and directives
        2. Agendas and menus
        3. Analytic policy studies
        4. Evaluation of program and individual performance
        5. Quantitative studies
    D. Speaking
        1. Informal
            a. Informational
            b. Humor
            c. Counseling
            d. Warmups
        2. Formal
            a. Group participant
            b. Group chairperson
            c. Evaluation conference
            d. Public speech
    E. Nonverbal messages
        1. Reading
        2. Sending

II. Analytic skills

    A. The language of inquiry
    B. Formal analyses

         1. Quantitative
         2. Logico-deductive
         3. Research based
         4. Philosophical reasoning

III. Mediation skills

    A. Conflict mediation/resolution
    B. Bargaining

IV. Facilitative skills

    A. Environmental arrangements
    B. Advising
    C. Counseling
    D. Consulting
    E. Interviewing

V. Motivational skills

    A. Incentives inventory
    B. Needs analyses (psychological)
    C. Direct motivators
    D. Indirect motivator
    E. Cultural norming

VI. Decision-making skills

    A. Creating alternate perceptions
    B. Understanding and using feelings
    C. Information gathering
    D. Analyzing perceptions, feelings, and information
    E. Synthesizing through patterns, perceptions, feelings, and information
    F. Conducting impact or consequence analysis
    G. Selecting and promulgating the decision

VII. Power and authority skills

    A. Direction and control (transactional language)
    B. Policymaking

VIII. Procedural skills

    A. Filing
    B. Scheduling
    C. Organizing
    D. Planning
    E. Accounting
    F. Investing
    G. Building
    H. Transporting
    I. Feeding
    J. Housing
    K. Budgeting
    L. Calculation skills
        1. Adding
        2. Subtracting
        3. Multiplying
        4. Dividing

Stages of Development

How would a university proceed in the development of skill categories through sequential steps? I suggest that the skill categories become a part of the administration curriculum as follows:

Level I. *Awareness and exploration* of skills would become an integral component of the didactic program. In each course the professor would make conscientious efforts to acquaint students with the theoretical underpinnings for different skills categories and levels as well as acquisition techniques.

Level II. Reports of *onsight observations* of illustrative skill users would be required. Here is where businesses, state departments, school districts, and citizen groups could play a major role without creating infeasible burdens or costs.

Level III. *Demonstration laboratories* should be provided at universities with prepared cases and practice techniques for students to begin low-risk/success-prone early experiences. These laboratories could be established with computers and video feedback materials along with examples for student use.

Level IV. *The structured internship* would be offered to all candidates under an accomplished adjunct clinical professor, principal, or other administrator. Here the skill professor would expect student administrators to undertake projects, and the clinical experience would be directed toward advanced skill attainment in a number of categories.

Level V. *Consultation in the art of practice* should be provided to principals or superintendents by one or more university-based clinical professors during a period of probation. Consultants, along with district administrators, would counsel the new appointee on the development of the polish needed to gain full professional status.

If this or a similar clinical curriculum were adopted by a graduate school, the university would need to allocate to its members responsibilities for each stage of clinical development. Members would also need to structure programs that emphasize balanced academic and clinical experiences. Laboratory space would need to be allocated, prepared, and equipped to support the clinical education programs. Since a fair amount of time would be spent coordinating activities with other institutions, sufficient staff would need to be assigned to ensure its feasibility and success.

All who dream need to recognize reality. Clinical education cannot be bootstrapped or shoehorned successfully. Clinical experiences as envisioned here will have expenses that require funding. This gives an added responsibility to state legislators, professional organizations, and university-level administrators, but the payoff is improved leadership of American schools and school systems.

References

Bloom, B. (1982). The master teachers. *Phi Delta Kappan* 63 (10).

Joyce, B., and Weil, M. (1986). *Models of teaching.* 3rd ed. Englewood Cliffs, N. J.: Prentice-Hall.

Peterson, K. D., and Finn, C. E., Jr. (1985). Principals, superintendents, and the administrator's art. *The Public Interest*, no. 79.

Pitner, N. (1982). Training of the school administrator: State of the art. Eugene, Ore.: Center for Educational Policy and Management.

28

School Administrator Preparation: The State of the Art

Nancy J. Pitner

Introduction

This paper examines the state of the art of administrator preparation. We review several major studies of administrator training that focus on the modal characteristics of the students and programs, perceived trends and needs in the preparatory programs, and the discrepancy that exists between training needs and training opportunities (Culbertson, et al., 1969; Farquhar and Piele, 1972; Silver and Spuck, 1978). The researchers drew their data from the opinions and perceptions of people personally involved in the study and practice of school administration, from literature reviews, and from questionnaire surveys of scholars, practitioners, professors, and recently graduated students of educational administration. Our review of these studies serves as a foundation for the attempt to provide a current picture of the field of school administrator training.

To this end, the paper is organized into four sections. The first section addresses the question, What do administrators do and what are the effects? We raise this question because much criticism of graduate programs rests on

Revised by the author and reprinted with permission from *Preparing Principals for School Improvement: In An International Perspective,* © 1987 Croom-Helm, Great Britain.

alleged discrepancies among administrator training, administrator work, and administrator effectiveness. The second section examines university programs for the graduate training of school administrators, as well as the purported breakdown of that training. In the third section, we consider efforts to bridge the gap between graduate training and the realities of school administration; these efforts include clinical training models and in-service training. The fourth section is devoted to proposed changes in administrator training. We identify provocative themes in the preceding sections, propose a new direction based upon these themes, and describe a structure to facilitate making the needed changes in administrator preparation.

What Administrators Do and the Effects

It is difficult to ignore the testimony of school administrators that their training programs are far from adequate in preparing them to resolve the problems they face. Since administrators claim they are unprepared for the realities of managerial work, it behooves us to examine what that work entails and its impact on the school organization.

What do we know about school administrators? In a review of the research on school administrators, Bridges (1982) notes eight perspectives that serve as the focal points of his study: expectations, power, sentiments, effectiveness, impact, traits, behavior, and work activity. This section concerns itself with only administrator effectiveness, impact, behavior, and work activity in order to consider what is or should be the relationship between administrator work and training.

Administrator Work Activity

What do educational administrators do? Several observational studies of superintendents (Campbell and Cunningham, 1959; Duignan, 1980; Mintzberg, 1973; Pitner, 1979, 1981a), principals, and assistant principals (Crowson and Porter-Gehrie, 1980; Morris, 1981; Peterson, 1978; and Wolcott, 1973) provide descriptions of the structure and content of school administrators' everyday work. The structure of administrative work is characterized by (1) a low degree of self-initiated tasks, (2) many activities of short duration, (3) discontinuity caused by interruptions, (4) the superseding of prior plans by the needs of others in the organization, (5) face-to-face verbal contacts with one other person, (6) variability of tasks, (7) an extensive network of individuals and groups both internal and external to the school or district, (8) a hectic and unpredictable flow of work, (9) numerous unimportant decisions and trivial agendas, (10) few attempts at written communication, (11) events occurring in or near the administrator's office, (12) interactions predominantly with subordinates, and (13) a preference for problems and information that are specific (rather than general), concrete, solvable, and currently pressing (Pitner, 1981b). The aforementioned studies are fairly consistent in their findings about the structure of work for line administrators in educational organizations. However, the content of administrative work varies with the organizational level of the administrative position and, therefore, we will consider separately the content of principals' and of superintendents' work.

According to the descriptive studies, principals spend most of their time working with students who are discipline problems and with teachers who have noninstructional needs (Peterson, 1978); attending to logistics, external requirements, and social pleasantries (Sproull, 1979); and overseeing organizational maintenance, pupil control, and extracurricular activities (Martin, 1980). Principals engage predominantly in service, advisory, and auditing relationships; they neither become directly involved in the work flow at the classroom level nor seek change or improvement through innovative or stabilizing relationships (Peterson, 1978).[1]

This is in contrast to the fundamental tenet of the job, that the site-level administrator in education should be the "instructional leader" of the school (Jacobson, Logsdon, and Wiegman, 1973; Lipham and Hoeh, 1974; Roe and Drake, 1980). Indeed, instructional leadership, theoretically involving such activities as classroom observation, curriculum development, and staff development, is not the central focus for most individuals occupying the position. This finding is confirmed for a wide variety of institutional settings (Morris, 1981), although Gross and Herriott (1965) note that women principals are more likely to function as instructional leaders, and Salley and others (1978) conclude that the way in which principals describe their jobs is related to the type and size of school they administer. The general conclusion is, nonetheless, that principals do not get involved with the technical core issues of schools.

---

[1] Peterson relies on a typology for analyzing the behavior of managers in organizations developed by Leonard Sayles. Sayles suggests seven types of relationships through which a manager interacts with others in the organization. These relationships are (1) *trading* (stages of the work and tactics are established), (2) *work flow* (the manager relates to activities that must be performed by different people in a relatively fixed sequence), (3) *service* (manager assists other units of the organization to minimize friction and increase regularity), (4) *advisory* (manager gives counsel, advice, and specialized information to other units), (5) *auditing* (manager monitors and evaluates the way units are following schedules, budgets, standards, rules, and organizational requirements), (6) *stabilization* (manager gives approval to other units prior to the initiation of changes in work flow or structure), (7) *innovation* (manager works to promote new developments or encourage research into new processes or new products).

Superintendents spend the majority of their time giving and receiving information (primarily about noninstructional issues), responding to requests for action, and attending to logistics and ceremonial activities (Larson, Bussom, and Vicars, 1981; Pitner, 1978). Less time is spent in decision-making activities (that is, strategy and negotiation). The dominant characteristic of superintendents' activities is constant communication (Pitner and Ogawa, 1981).

Not unlike the study of principals by Gross and Herriott, Pitner (1981a) notes differences in work between male and female superintendents. While females are inclined to articulate the specific ideology and activities that dominate each district's curricular program, men speak of aspects of organizational structure, such as the construction of a new school building, the approval of a tax levy, or the graduation of the senior class.

A consistent observation made by all of these studies is that administrators spend little time with their superiors. Levels within the organization—technical, managerial, and institutional—are only loosely connected. Relatively few of the administrator's workday activities respond to the coordination and control functions of others lower in the hierarchy. The superintendent spends little time with the school board; principals spend little time with superintendents; and teachers spend little time with principals. The activities of management seem to be only marginally related to the production activities, that is, student learning, of schools (Hannaway and Sproull, 1978-79).

It has not been the purpose of any of the descriptive studies of school administrators' work either to construct linkages between the work activities of administrators and measures of school effectiveness (student achievement in reading and math) or to evaluate the performance of administrators. While the question of the administrator's impact on a school's effectiveness is an important one, it remains largely unanswered; this represents a major gap in our knowledge about school administrators (Bridges, 1982; Duckworth, 1981; Pitner, 1981b, 1982; Rowan, Dwyer, and Bossert, 1982). Despite the potential influence that superintendents have on education and society, Bridges found in his study that "less than a handful of studies . . . investigated the impact of the chief executive officer." He goes on to assert, "This topic merits both reflection and empirical examination since nothing of consequence is known about the impact of the occupants of this role" (1982, p. 26).

Bridges concludes that technical, political, and intellectual difficulties account for the paucity of research and deter members of the educational administration research community from addressing this important question. However, to elucidate the problematic relationships among administrator work, administrator effectiveness, and administrator training, we report below the findings from existing studies.

Administrator Impact, Effectiveness, and Behavior

Numerous criteria have been used to assess the impact of the school administrator on the school organization, most specifically on teacher morale, teacher productivity, and student achievement. The administrator is treated as the independent variable in most of these studies, which have been conducted at the school site rather than at the district level (Bridges, 1982).

While most research focuses on administrators' sentiments and attributes, several studies indicate that the administrative behavior of school principals has an impact on teacher morale (Duckworth, 1981; Smith, 1976). Kalis (1980) concludes that teacher morale is related to the consideration dimension of administrative behavior, as measured by the Leadership Behavior Description Questionnaire (LBDQ).[2] In particular, personal interaction and encouragement by principals has an impact on teachers. The perceptions teachers hold that the principal works closely with teachers on instruction correlates positively with teacher job satisfaction and positive attitudes (Cohen et al., 1977). Similar conclusions have been drawn by Holdaway (1978), who advocates that the administrative functions most relevant to job satisfaction include the provision of encouragement and support, the removal or reduction of irritants, and the granting of reasonable requests. While this research indicates that administrators do have an impact on teacher morale and satisfaction, other factors such as staff cohesiveness and personal challenge may have a greater effect on morale (Brady, 1976). Several studies, however, have found that supportive leadership has no relationship to performance ratings, productivity, or the motivation of subordinates.

In addition to the consideration dimension, structure also seems to be related to satisfaction. Hoy, Newland, and Blazousky (1977) found that teachers generally desire and react favorably to administrative structure. Teachers desire definite rules and regulations, but it must also be noted that excessive supervision and tight enforcement of rules produce teacher resentment and dissatisfaction. Lortie (1975) found that teachers wanted principals to use their authority to facilitate teacher work. In the teachers' words, this meant that they wanted principals to "support them."

Cohen and Miller (1980) also found that coordination was important in school settings. Effective principals were found to coordinate, discuss, and

---

[2] "Initiating structure" refers to the leader's behavior in delineating the relationship between himself or herself and members of the work group, and in endeavoring to establish well-defined patterns of organization, channels of communication, and methods of procedure. "Consideration" refers to the behavior indicative of friendship, mutual trust, respect, and warmth in the relationship between leaders and members of their staffs. See John K. Hemphill, "Administration as Problem Solving," *Administrative Theory in Education,* ed. Andrew W. Halpin (Chicago: Midwest Administration Center, University of Chicago, 1958), pp. 89–118.

advise on instruction, while ineffective principals did none of these. Teachers judged that the ineffective administrator made poor decisions.

In their study of suburban superintendents, Campbell and Cunningham (1959) used the LBDQ dimensions to observe the behavior of the superintendents and to provide a scheme for a post-hoc analysis of the incidents recorded during observations. They found that three-fourths of the superintendents' interactions were unclassifiable into the consideration-initiating structural framework, with a range of 50 to 90 percent of behavioral incidents from which neither of the dimensions could be inferred. Another "startling finding was the paucity (less than 4 percent) of incidents from which the dimension of initiating structure could be inferred" (p. 48). These findings prompted them to stress that no claims were made by Hemphill as to the "breadth" of the LBDQ as a scheme for classifying behavior incidents. While extensive research has been conducted using the LBDQ, much remains to be learned about leadership. Still, it is already clear that the traditional assumption—that school administrators exhibit supportive (or unsupportive) leadership behavior a priori and then certain attitudes and behaviors in teachers or principals result—is an oversimplified one (Filley et al., 1976).

The means of coordinating and controlling may not take place in a highly structured environment. Duckworth (1981) notes that the means for coordination and control in schools is found in the informal interactions between administrators and teachers. Occasional observations in the classroom, conversations with teachers, discussion during committee and faculty meetings, and reports from students, parents, and administrators make it possible for administrators to collect "secrets" about teachers (Burlingame, 1978). Administrators use these secrets to manipulate or persuade. In addition, the isolation of classroom teachers from their colleagues appears to make them very receptive to personal interaction with and encouragement by administrators regarding their work. Cohen and others (1977) found that effective principals offer rewards, resources, and personal interaction with teachers in exchange for compliance and acceptance of joint responsibility for instructional outcomes. In short, this personal interaction is perceived as being supportive and informal, rather than evaluative and formal.

Numerous studies stress that effective administrators are instructional leaders who direct the activities of a group toward goal attainment (Brookover and Lezotte, 1979; Edmonds, 1979; Rutter et al., 1979; Weber, 1971). Cotton and Savard (1980) found that specific leadership behaviors appeared to promote student achievement. These behaviors include frequently observing or participating in classroom instruction, communicating expectations clearly to staff, making decisions about the instructional program, coordinating the instructional program, and having and communicating high standards of expectations for the instructional program. Cotton and Savard emphasize that in every case where effective *instructional* leadership was noted, the administrator under observation also demonstrated technical expertise in the areas of finance and facilities.

In summary, student achievement seems to be related to certain administrative behaviors. Those exhibiting these behaviors share the belief with teachers that all students can master the basic objectives in mathematics and reading, and they assume responsibility for the quality of teaching in reading and mathematics, are assertive in their institutional leadership roles, are concerned about discipline, and assume responsibility for the evaluation of the achievement of basic objectives (Brookover and Lezotte, 1979).

It should be noted that most studies linking administrative characteristics with student achievement have been carried out at the elementary level using the school site, rather than the district, as the unit of analysis. High student achievement appears to be found in schools where principals and teachers share a common "pedagogical orientation" (Bossert et al., 1981, p. 5). Student achievement is likely to be higher in schools where teachers and principals share the following: a high academic focus across all classrooms (that is, in reading and mathematics), high expectations for all students, and a system for monitoring student progress (Brookover and Lezotte, 1979; and Rutter et al., 1979). Rutter and others found in a sample of high schools in London, England, that student achievement is related to common standards and policies in discipline, homework, and staff punctuality. The administrators in these effective schools were aware of these priorities and checked to make sure that the policies and standards were maintained. The studies also conclude that the effective school principal is an instructional leader, though they appear to contradict the findings of many of the descriptive studies of administrative work. This apparent contrast, however, may be the result of the ambiguous definition of "instructional leader." It is difficult to get administrators to agree on what the concept of instructional leader means and what behavior counts as instructional leadership behavior. The interpretation of the role differs at the elementary and secondary levels and often between male and female administrators, as well.

Thus, we do not have much conclusive evidence about the relationship among administrator training, work, and effectiveness. Cuban (1976, p. 14) has remarked, "while we know to the penny what salaries administrators received, what degrees they earned, and where they were born, we know very little about what they, as executives, actually do each day" (p. iv). The paucity of research on the subject of what school administrators actually do prompted the interest in the work activity studies. We would like to add that while we know to the minutest detail the length of every phone call made and meetings attended by the administrator, the people with whom he or she interacted, and the locations of these encounters, we know very little about what impact these activities have on the school organization and, specifically, on student achievement. In the following section we consider the

training of school administrators and the possible relationship between the
training administrators receive and the work they do.

The Preparation of School Administrators

Preservice and in-service programs for training school administrators have
both formal and informal components. All preservice education is exclusively
the province of universities, while other agencies, including school districts,
professional associations, and state departments of education, as well as
universities, provide in-service education for school administrators. Although most scholarly study of administrator preparation is directed toward
doctoral degree programs, there are actually three levels of school administrator graduate training. Programs are offered at the master's, intermediate
(educational specialist degree and state certification), and doctoral degree
levels. This first section focuses on the preparation of school administrators
in formal graduate programs and on the critical evaluation of these graduate
programs by practitioners and scholars.

Academic Programs

The content of administrator preparation is frequently discussed and
debated in the literature in an effort to identify the chief components of
"comprehensive," "basic," or "essential" preparation. Gregg (1969) has
noted that there is no general agreement on these elements. Griffiths reports
that the status quo program at the doctoral level includes course work in
educational organization and administration, curriculum, supervision,
finance, school law, research, educational psychology, history and philosophy of education, the school plant, and personnel (1966, p. 53). This
information is presented through formal instruction, which is characterized
by much discussion, some simulation and case study, and limited field
experience. The doctoral programs follow a traditional preparation structure
including a core of basic courses, a specified number of hours of required
course work in educational administration, written and oral examinations to
ensure competency, the possibility of an internship, a formal dissertation,
and, often, a residency requirement (Farquhar, 1977).

The early 1960s witnessed a growing interest in the contribution of the
social sciences to educational administration. Doctoral programs during this
era, according to Goldhammer and others (1967), required cognate work in
the behavioral sciences. This idea of drawing from the social sciences for
administrator preparation was vigorously contested (Cunningham, Downey,
and Goldhammer, 1963; Cunningham and Nystrand, 1969; and Miklos,
1969), as were attempts to use materials from the humanities (Farquhar,
1968).

Farquhar (1977) reviews developments from 1954 to 1974 in the training of school administrators and concludes that change has occurred in four areas. First, the focus of training has moved from delivering information about administrative tasks and processes to an emphasis on preparing practitioners to deal with major problems they may be expected to confront (p. 345). At the same time, the content of learning experiences has been affected by the change from reliance on the insights of educational professionals to the incorporation of materials from a wide variety of disciplines. Second, the traditional lecture format has been displaced by "reality-oriented instructional methods," including workshops, seminars, computer programs, and more sophisticated supplementary field experiences. Third, students are more involved in determining what they will learn, and the characteristics of students have changed as women and racial minorities have been encouraged to seek admission to administrator graduate programs. Fourth, the staffing of departments of educational administration has altered. Professors training school administrators are "younger, better educated . . . , more liberal, less experienced (in terms of administrative practice), more diverse, . . . and better accepted by academic colleagues. . ." (p. 346). Farquhar also asserts that by 1974 students in many institutions were free to build or negotiate almost their entire program, which helped make the preparation experince as appropriate as possible to particular students' unique needs and aspirations.

On the other hand, a survey of faculty and doctoral students in sixty educational administration programs conducted in 1975 and reported in 1978 by Nagel and Nagel indicates that few if any programs appear to have achieved the kind of "flexibility and individualization" described by Farquhar. Nagel and Nagel found that

The kind of broadening of purpose and focus in preparatory programs in educational administration described by Farquhar does not seem to characterize the programs represented in this survey, for the orientation of the programs in this study was toward traditional, line administrative programs in public K-12 education and toward developing general rather than highly specialized knowledge and skills relevant to educational administration. [P. 118]

Thus, there is disagreement about whether or not changes have occurred in the structure and content of administrator training programs. Further, after a study of the three levels of graduate programs, Silver and Spuck (1978) report that programs are virtually indistinguishable in terms of methods of instruction, types of learning activities, and content of instruction (including administrative theory, leadership, school law, and decision-making). Graduate programs are also parochial; they attract students from within their community, focus on local or state concerns, and place five-sixths of their graduates within one hundred miles of the university. This localism is most prevalent in master's degree programs. Most master's students attend college part time and work full time as teachers in public schools.

Silver and Spuck (1978) suggests that school administrator preparation programs appear to be developmental in nature; each successive program builds on and extends the content of the earlier program. Boyan (1968) concluded earlier that "curriculum development in educational administration today looks very much like the conventional local school system approach. It is disparate, fragmented, uneven, scattered, and mainly non-cumulative" (p. 34). Whether or not the improvements alleged by Farquhar have occurred, we do not know that the trend has been for practice-based content to be replaced by discipline-based content and, more currently, characterized by a quest for balance (Farquhar, 1977; Griffiths, 1975). However, the essential question about administrator training remains: Does administrator training prepare administrators for their work?

The Inadequacies of Administrator Training

Lacking substantial research to verify the effectiveness of various programs (Culbertson et al., 1969), we must rely on the sentiments of practitioners and the observations of scholars to evaluate them. Complaints about formal graduate studies in educational administration are legion among school administrators (Wolcott, 1973). Wolcott observes that principals appear to be unable to bring any special body of knowledge or set of unique skills to the position; they believe they perform adequately, but they wish to perform exceedingly well. As a group, educational administrators disparage the utility of university training for preparing graduates to face the problems of practitioners (Ourth, 1979). In a survey of five hundred districts, school administrators ranked the usefulness of college and university training low. Over half said they preferred the services of the state education agency for assistance in professional development. Fewer than 2 percent of elementary school principals credit their success as school administrators to their graduate course work (National Education Association, Department of Elementary School Principals, 1968).

Several researchers have speculated on the source of administrators' discontent with their graduate training. From a comparison of the work of graduate students with the work of practitioners, Bridges (1977) concludes that graduate training is dysfunctional in the preparation of school administrators. The manager's work day is characterized by a continuous series of brief, disjointed, verbal encounters with a variety of people seeking solutions or responses to a multitude of contingencies. School administrators are frequently interrupted and often face situations demanding quick decisions. Academic programs, on the other hand, require aspiring administrators to spend long hours alone reading, writing, and contemplating potential solutions to problems.

A second major problem with academic training, relating to conflict management, results from the student's transition from a subservient position in the university hierarchy to a superordinate position in the public school hierarchy. Managers' reactions to conflict are important in determining relationships with employees. A collaborative style of conflict resolution is likely to foster a more productive relationship (Burke, 1970). Students, however, apparently learn to rely on avoidance to resolve conflicts in the student-teacher relationship (Bridges, 1977, p. 215).

A third area of concern is communication styles. Administrators typically depend on face-to-face communication to accomplish their work. They gain valuable information through the nonverbal cues present in interpersonal communication (Bridges, 1977, p. 218). Students, however, are trained in an atmosphere that emphasizes written communication. Students both send and receive significant amounts of written information. Often a student's success is determined, at least in part, by his or her writing ability.

A final area of discrepancy deals with the emotional content of the workplace. Feelings are largely irrelevant in a graduate program setting, which stresses the value of ideas and rationality. School administrators often perform in a less temperate climate. Angry parents, excited students, and aroused employees may combine to overload administrators with emotional barrages. Periods of calm may be interrupted by emotional outbursts that are not amenable to rational disposition. Yet administrators are expected to remain calm and rational. Bridges concludes that it is unlikely that graduate training prepares students to cope effectively with the realities of managerial work and even suggests that the result of doctoral programs is "trained incapacity."

While Bridges is quick to point out the discrepancies between graduate training and administrator work, he fails to recognize important similarities. Students are trained in an environment of ambiguity and uncertainty over which they feel they have little control. Most tasks are initiated by others. Students often receive little systematic feedback and evaluation of their work except at times of important transitions. They are told when they make "wrong moves" but not what the "right ones" are. Bridges alludes to the isolation of the graduate student, but fails to recognize the "lonely-at-the-top" phenomenon and the isolated feeling of the superintendent who has no occupational peer in the entire community. While these elements are not the explicit content of graduate training, they appear to be a hidden curriculum.

Zeigler and others (1981) report that superintendents "perceive a low level of disagreement in their school districts" (p. 5). They suggest that "superintendents minimize the importance of those constituents who disagree among themselves, believing instead that the majority of the public are in silent concurrence with the existing district policies" (p. 5). In his classic study, Coleman (1957) noted the consequences of unresponsiveness to pressures from the community. Zeigler (1981) concludes that "superintendents avoid conflict management in favor of more technically treatable tasks" (p. 31). Similarly, Erickson, Hills, and Robinson (1970) uncovered an inverse relationship between the instructional flexibility of elementary schools and the extent of the principal's preparation in educational administration. The less flexible schools were managed by principals with more graduate training. Perhaps this finding ought to be reevaluated. The effective schooling studies suggest that concerted action and a common goal, or focus, are necessary ingredients for improving student achievement. From Koberg (1981), we conclude that flexibility is devalued in favor of greater control as the environment becomes increasingly uncertain, unpredictable, and uncontrollable.

In general, the complaints of practitioners are that graduate faculty have not had experience as line administrators in public schools, that university programs do not provide the opportunity for applying theoretical knowledge to actual situations, that the theory itself is too often irrelevant or tangential to real-world needs, and that practitioners are not used in teaching and course development. Thus, practitioners are critical consumers, and scholars are critical observers of university training in educational administration.

The denigration of professional training by practitioners is by no means confined to the field of school administration. Dr. G. Thomas Shires, president of the American College of Surgeons, declared that about 20,000 U.S. surgeons—nearly two in seven—are insufficiently trained and would not meet current competency requirements (*Eugene Register-Guard*, 18 October 1981). Medical schools have also come under fire for their student selection policies and curricular trends. Procedures for selecting candidates in the intense competition for medical school entrance have been shown to predict first-year student success, but to be questionably related to predicting effectiveness in practice. Faculty members of prominent medical schools have been accused of using their university positions to further their own specialized interests rather than to help students become effective practitioners. In a similar view, business schools offering the Master's of Business Administration (MBA) degree are often staffed by academics with no business experience. Graduate MBAs are said to be proficient at writing reports and performing analyses but no better prepared for top management than many engineers who work their way up through the ranks. Further, chief executives in the private sector are more likely to have liberal arts degrees than MBAs. Finally, law schools are criticized for focusing on abstract concepts of legal doctrine irrelevant to all but a few highly specialized attorneys. Essential practical skills, such as successful negotiation with other attorneys, are rarely discussed, and practitioners often must learn them through trial and error on the job (Hacker, 1981).

Argyris and Schön have similarly considered a broad range of professions and have identified two important issues (1978, p. 144). First they ask, Are professionals competent? Argyris and Schön suggest the abstract and irrelevant quality of graduate school curricula is a concern that reaches across all fields of professional training. Related to this problem is the charge that professional training fails to prepare practitioners for potential, radical changes brought about by technological advances. One observer argues that the professions must bear responsibility for this technological change and therefore are confronted with an unprecedented requirement for versatility and adaptability.

Second, Argyris and Schön ask, Are practitioners influenced by cummulative learning? They point out that professionals often do not test their own theories of what constitutes good practice or communicate these theories to others in their field. This failure to test their theories or communicate with peers may mean that professionals function without benefiting from past experience.

We know that school administrators are not alone in their discontent with professional prepration. Thus, universities could be expected to act on these complaints to improve their programs. James March (1974) recognizes the need for reform in administrator training and suggests how to proceed. He observes that:

> One of the persistent difficulties with programs for reform in the training of administrators is the tendency to try to improve managerial behavior in ways that are far removed from the ordinary organization of managerial life. Unless we start from an awareness of what administrators do and some idea of why they organize their lives in the way that they do, we are likely to generate recommendations that are naive. [P. 56]

To follow this recommendation we must ask, What knowledge, skills, and abilities do administrative jobs require? With the growing collection of studies on of work activity, we can begin to formulate a response.

On the one hand, we can infer that the job requires substantial cognitive ability. The discontinuity and variety of tasks and the decision-making under conditions of uncertainty, plus the pace of the work, seem to suggest that a school administrator must have a highly developed repertoire of critical-thinking skills. Administrators face an unending stream of activities, people, and problems; the work demands that administrators be able to quickly shift mental and emotional gears. This interpretation of the job suggests analytical skills that might be taught. March identifies five critical analytical skills that are central to the job of most high-level administrators: the analysis of expertise, the analysis of coalitions, the analysis of ambiguity, the analysis of time, and the analysis of information. Each of these skills is linked closely to the everyday requirements of managerial life. On the other hand, the job can also be regarded as demanding less mental discipline and more nervous energy. Some important administrative tasks have relatively small intellectual components. Perhaps training in these areas is not best served in the academic environment.

Returning to the characteristics of administrative work, we can see that the structure and content of administrative work has substantial implications for the structure and content of both university-based preservice preparation and in-service training. First, the verbal mode, the task variety, the absence of task self-initiation, and the pace of managerial work all suggest that administrators must be able to think and speak "on their feet." The suggestion is not to eliminate writing from university courses but to provide more opportunities for oral expression, perhaps by using a Socratic method to elicit clear, articulate discussion. (Unfortunately, some content is more amenable than others to this teaching method.) Hectic pace, task variety, and lack of self-initiation of tasks suggest that we should scramble the work, make assignments at the last minute with short completion times, and vary the learning episodes by using case studies and simulation materials. Adult learning theory points to the use of clinical training strategies, such as experiential learning, to help students apply theory to practice.

Hills (1975) suggests that preparation programs should include a heavy component of educational knowledge, place emphasis on the development of critical-analytical and problem-solving skills, concentrate on process, involve an internship, and lead students to develop a relatively consistent administrative philosophy. The purpose of a program is to produce people who will act, not merely think. Both intellectual and clinical elements must be blended in such a way that each student administrator has an internalized set of guides to action. Griffiths (1977) adds that more time should be devoted to the study of research findings, whether or not they are related to theory. He concludes that the study of theory is of major value to researchers rather than administrators.

Hodgkinson (1978) goes even further in asserting that the central problems of administration are philosophical and, therefore, not solvable by rational scientific inquiry alone. Being an administrator is more than being a technician and politician. He distinguishes between management and administration. Administration deals more with the "formulation of purpose, the value-laden issues, and the human component of organization," whereas management deals with the "aspects that are more routine, definitive, programmatic, and susceptible to quantitative methods" (p. 5). After reviewing the bodies of knowledge in organizational theory, decision-making, and policymaking leadership, he concludes that the graduate training for school administrators must include the study of philosophy. For policymaking can become almost literally a translation of philosophy. Administrators are quintessential philosophers in action: Certain components of philosophy have significance for the administrator. Hodgkinson identifies these components more specifically as

1. a concern for language and meaning, since the administrative universe is semantic;
2. some of the disciplines of formal logic, since the administrative universe is increasingly technological;
3. general critical skills, since the administrative universe is increasingly fallacy-ridden; and
4. a major concern with value. [Pp. 196–97]

While the administrator may come to these "acquisitions" informally, Hodgkinson believes that they should be a recognized condition for professional status, that is, included in the graduate program.

The primary consideration of each of these recommendations is to more adequately prepare student administrators for the central problems they will face as administrators. The mainstream of school administrator preparation continues to take place in universities, as practitioners continue to seek advanced degrees.

Bridging the Gap

As mentioned previously, practioners are often critical of the utility of graduate programs for preparing them to deal with the problems they confront. They report they are unprepared for the realities of managerial work. From our review of the studies of the work activities of administrators we concluded that, while the work requires a highly developed repertoire of critical thinking skills, some important tasks have relatively small intellectual components. Griffiths (1977) sees two issues in the preparation of school administrators: Should administrators be trained solely in bona fide universities? and Should preparation programs be shaped in the competency mode? We recognize that the interest in alternative training programs at the pre- and in-service level is increasing. This interest is the result of a desire to bridge the gap between the knowledge and skills that practitioners possess and those they are thought to need. Administrators learn by trial and error, rely on one another for coaching, and participate in in-service education workshops and programs. In this section we examine clinical training strategies in graduate programs as well as in-service training in industrial and school organizations. These programs are designed to augment or replace traditional graduate training.

Nonresidential Graduate Programs

The nonresidential universities that offer doctoral (Ed.D.) programs in educational administration, such as Nova University, claim to emphasize experience-based learning. They appear to have widespread appeal for practitioners, but they are not highly regarded by the academic community. These programs are obviously different from university doctoral programs: they have no faculty in residence, no research libraries, and no campuses. The candidates can earn a doctorate in their own living rooms with the minor inconvenience of attending classes for two weeks at Nova Univerity in Florida and meeting monthy with small groups of administrators in their areas to work on their practica. Leaders in the field of school administrator training remain skeptical of the ability of such programs to produce graduates of a caliber equal to traditional training methods (Griffiths, 1977).

Clinical Training Strategies

Clinical training strategies are proposed as more relevant alternatives to traditional academic training. Although the term "clinical training" is ambiguous, clinical training strategies emphasize, first, the diagnosis of problems in the operational areas of administrator responsibility (school-community relations, curriculum and instruction, pupil personnel, staff personnel, physical facilities, and finance and business management) and, second, the establishment of specific objectives in response to this problem analysis. These training activities often are performed in field settings.

Perhaps the most widely recognized clinical strategy is competency-based training. Competency has been described as "the presence of characteristics or the absence of disabilities which render a person fit, or qualified, to perform a specified task or to assume a definite role" (McCleary, n.d., p. 2). Competency-based education has been similarly described as a move from the traditional "ability to demonstrate knowledge" to an emphasis on "the ability to do" (Houston and Howsam, 1972, p. 2).

Determining the nature of the appropriate tasks of school administration and the proper setting for developing requisite skills remains the subject of considerable disagreement among clinical training advocates. The typical procedure has been to take operational areas of administration—that is, the existing course and content of a graduate program—and to specify objectives in the "ability to do " language without reconceptualizing what the whole administrator training program ought to include. In other words, we have proceeded along the naive path that March warned us of. (It is interesting to note that the major proponent of the competency-based education is affiliated with a university that remains unaffected by the competency-based training movement, with the exception of the proponent's own courses. It is difficult to say whether this is a reflection more on the competency-based training perspective or on the nature of professors and university-based programs.)

Licata (1980–81), evaluating an in-servicee clinical training program, observes that school administrators approve of training models based on their problems and tasks they face. Specifically, school leaders perceive school problem-solving as central to their role in the educational organization. They perceive clinical training alternatives as being more relevant to school problem-solving than is traditional academic training. Licata concludes that, overall, administrators tend to perceive training programs as being at least as relevant as traditional academic training programs to the performance of the school administrator role. However, the evaluation "at least as relevant" is hardly an overwhelming affirmation of the ability of clinical approaches to prepare students and practitioners for the realities of school administrator work.

Nonetheless, we need to consider the complaints of practitioners that faculty members do not have line administrator experience and that too little use is made of actual practitioners in teaching and in course development. Reflecting on the preparation of administrators, March (1974) expresses the viewpoint that "the advantage of the university in the training of administrators is primarily in the intellective domain" (p. 26). Nonuniversity individuals and agencies might more appropriately train administrators in the less cognitive, but still essential, skills. March's statement is important for at least two reasons. First, it suggests that some training may be carried out in nonuniversity settings and by people other than professors. Second, it describes the response of practitioners to their perceived gap in knowledge and skills, or what they term "being unprepared [to meet] the growing challenges of their profession."

In-service Education in School Organizations

The theme of lack of preparation is expressed repeatedly by administrators at many of their professional meetings and workshops: "We never seem to have enough time. We are not doing what we should be doing. What should we be doing?" There appears to be an eternal quest for a clearer understanding of what the job entails and of how to go about doing the job more effectively. Compounding this feeling is an administrative ideology that suggests that if there is a problem, there is a solution and that the administrator is responsible for finding the solution (March, 1974). This quest is manifested in school administrators' participation in professional development and training programs beyond what is officially required.

In-service opportunities for school administrators are available from many different sources and are organized in a variety of ways. Among the most commonly used types of in-service training are the following: university course, workshops, seminars, professional conferences, study councils, retreats, and school visits, as well as consulting services from universities, private foundations, and state departments of education. The professional organizations and their local affiliates—the American Association of School Administrators (AASA), the National Association of Secondary School Principals, the National Assocition of Elementary School Principals, the National School Public Relations Association, and the Association for Supervision and Curriculum Development—play a key role in sponsoring a variety of programs.

The Educational Research Service (ERS) conducted a survey to determine the types of in-service training programs being offered to administrators, the amount of time and money devoted to such programs, the variety of techniques used to evaluate the programs, and the source of responsibility for planning and directing administrator in-service training at the school district level (Educational Research Service, 1974). Approximately two-thirds of the 598 school districts responding to the ERS survey provided in-service training for administrators. Administrators in responding districts were most likely to participate in programs run completely by their own school district. Lower levels of participation were reported for programs directed by the district, but sponsored by professional organizations, commercial firms, private consultants, or university-based programs. The four most widely used types of program organization were conferences, seminars, visitations to other school districts, and training sessions by professional organizations. Simulation games were reported least often. Almost two-thirds of the responding school districts did not provide salary or academic credit for participation in in-service programs, but nine out of ten offered training during regular working hours for a median number of five days per year per individual administrator.

Participating administrators appear to play an important role in planning in-service programs, whereas university personnel have a minor part in planning district-directed in-service programs. In-service programs are usually directed toward increasing administrators' knowledge and skills in human relations and management, but Louis Zeyen (1981) of AASA announced that curriculum would be a primary focus in the 1981–82 in-service season. Many of the in-service programs emphasize "how to do it," though some deal with the study of administrative theory.

We feel reluctant to review the "babble of the literature" concerning educational administration training programs and models. Instead we present model programs, which are intended to be illustrative and typical of the present training of school administrators. We will give only cursory attention to the theoretical underpinnings, execution, and results of each of the seven model programs discussed. Our purpose is to attempt to show the consistency of pattern (or syndrome) across different programs.

The seven training models we shall examine are representative of the major training variations that have evolved in recent years. They include the Assessment Center, the National Academy of School Executives, the Bush Public Schools Executive Fellows Program, the Florida Academy for School Administrators, the Results-Oriented Management in Education project. and two programs that rely on networking—Project Leadership and the Research-Based Training for School Administrators project.

Assessment Centers. Assessment centers, such as the National Association of Secondary School Principals (NASSP) Assessment Center, are designed to aid in recruiting, promoting, and training school administrators. The concept is based on intensive assessment of an individual's ability, using a variety of sources of information. Using these information sources, assessors develop profiles of the individual's strengths and weaknesses for performing the role of school administrator. This profile may be used to plan for future in-service training or to make decisions regarding future employment.

Assessment centers typically involve simulation of the tasks or problems common to school administrators. Small groups of participants are exposed to these situations or tasks through a variety of exercises, including role playing, group exercises, and paper-and-pencil tests. A skilled evaluation team observes performances, scores tests, and prepares individualized assessment profiles for use by the participant or his or her employing agency.

The results of the assessment center experience are to be realized in the practitioner's greater awareness of his or her deficiencies and strengths. Agencies and individuals are provided with rational, impartial data to help them plan for future training or employment. Good practice by school administrators is expected to influence school climate and productivity and to contribute generally to the improvement of schools.

National Academy of School Executives. The National Academy of School Executives (NASE) is exclusively an in-service program; only practicing and certified administrators are allowed to participate. NASE is strongly oriented toward practical problems faced by school administrators. The Academy curriculum is based on the belief that practicing administrators can benefit from short, intensive training and discussion of the problems facing practitioners and their potential solutions.

The NASE program consists of three separate approaches. First, short (one to four weeks), intensive in-service sessions that focus on current administrator concerns are presented at various regional centers. Second, longer (three to nine months) residential sessions are held at a central academy site. While attendance at the short in-service sessions is open, the residential academy program is invitational and is reserved for the top two hundred to three hundred school administrators nationwide. Finally, the academy supports a "think tank" of people who are noted primarily for advancing solutions to school adminstration problems or who have distinguished themselves as outstanding practitioners.

Like the assessment centers, the Academy believes that improved functioning of school administrators will result in improved schools. Academy participants are expected to improve their practice through the implementation of the ideas and research findings presented in the Academy setting.

The Bush Public Schools Executive Fellows Program. The Bush Executive Fellows Program is based on the idea that administrator practice can be improved by training participants in knowledge, skills, and attitudes in selected areas that include school-community relations, managerial accounting and finance, and conflict management.

The applicants selected are highly motivated, mid-career school administrators. Participant groups (limited to twenty-five members) are selected to incorporate a broad range of backgrounds and experience. Participants engage in thirty-five days of instruction over a period of eighteen months. In addition, they are expected to use the skills learned in the program to complete a self-selected project aimed at solving a problem in their school district. The educational techniques used include small-group problem analysis, individual preparation, and class discussion. The case method of instruction and other participative processes are used extensively. Teaching methods and topics are borrowed from both prominent graduate schools of business administration and schools of management.

The Bush Executive Fellows Program, like the National Academy and the NASSP Center, operates on the belief that improved administrative practice will, in turn, result in improved schools. Further, it is expected that private-sector management techniques are applicable to the school situation, that private-sector managers are better managers, and that school administrators trained in private-sector techniques will be more capable problem solvers.

*The Florida Academy for School Administrators.*The Florida Academy for School Administrators (FASA) is organized around the assumption that there is a set of school administrator behaviors important in promoting school effectiveness. The Florida State Department of Education is sponsoring an ethnographic study of administrators in schools where pupil achievement is high. The curriculum for the Florida Academy will be based on summary descriptions of those behaviors common to the subjects of the study. These behaviors will be taught to academy participants.[3]

---

[3] "Management Training Act and the Florida Council on Educational Management," Status report to the Florida House Education Committee (October 27, 1981), pp. 5–12.

The FASA is still being conceptualized. However, it will consist of educational experiences of substantive length rather than of one- or two-day workshops. Training will be provided by practitioners and academics who have demonstrated expertise in the behaviors identified for inclusion in the curriculum.

The Florida Academy is part of a comprehensive state program designed to improve administrative practice that is based on both preservice and in-service training in the exemplary behaviors. The goal is to raise the achievement test scores of Florida pupils to the upper national percentiles by improving schools, a process that begins with improving administrators.

Project Results-Oriented Management in Education. The Results-Oriented Management in Education (ROME) project is based on the belief that there is a set of competencies associated with good administrative practice that can be taught to practitioners in a clinical setting. Diagnosis of deficiencies plays a key role in the training provided by this project, which is designed to remedy the identified deficiencies.

Project ROME first uses the Georgia Principals Assessment System (GPAS) to identify practitioners' deficiencies both in functional areas of responsibility (such as curriculum and instruction) and in administrative processes (such as decision making, evaluation, and communication). The second step in project ROME uses the Field-Oriented Competency Utilization System (FOCUS). FOCUS entails training school administrators through field-based seminars and using supervisors to monitor participants' progress toward observable achievements that remedy the deficiencies identified by the GPAS.

Project ROME aims to identify and correct school administrators' personal deficiencies in core areas of leadership skills; it assumes that improved administrator practice will result in improved schools and greater student productivity. Evaluation of the project indicates that both field-based and competency-based instruction are positively and significantly correlated with the ability to solve school problems (Ellet, 1978).

Project Leadership. Project Leadership, a program developed by the Association of California School Administrators ten years ago, builds on networking, professional development, and skill development. Project Leadership is based on anthropological evidence that school administrators carry with them an oral tradition of training one another. The belief is that providing principals with regular opportunities for oral exchange in a collegial atmosphere of trust will allow them to gain information and ideas that will improve practice.

Participants come together in two large statewide meetings and in four to five regional satellite meetings during the school year. The training sequence is displayed in Figure 28–1.

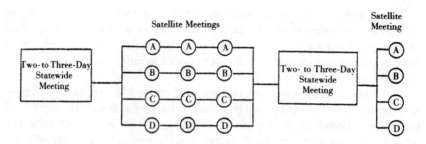

Figure 28–1
Training Sequence of Project Leadership

An experienced administrator, called the "liaison administrator," is assigned to each satellite meeting. Liaison administrators plan the statewide meetings, assist participants with their professional development plans, set agendas for the satellite meetings, and coach participants. The satellite meetings give participants an opportunity to focus on the development and implementation of personal and professional goals within small groups of ten to twenty-five administrators. Using scripted workshop materials called presenter's guides, administrators work in dyads to develop competency in one knowledge or technical skill area. Over thirty scripted workshop packages, many developed by practitioners, are available. Participants are expected to share in their schools the information they learn in the statewide and satellite meetings. The program is geared primarily for building-level administrators, although some central-office administrators also participate.

Research-Based Training for School Administrators. Research-Based Training for School Administrators (RBTSA), a project of the Center for Educational Policy and Management at the University of Oregon and funded by the National Institute of Education, is designed to overcome the often-noted problem of school administrators' difficulty in obtaining and implementing current research findings in education. Building on the peer network and workshop format of Project Leadership, RBTSA seeks to disseminate current research and improve school administrator practice. The structure of RBTSA is consistent with the ethnographic finding, mentioned above, that administrators rely on an oral tradition to train one another.

The scripted workshop format of Project Leadership is used to present research findings and state-of-the-art literature. The relevant research is interpreted and presented in conjunction with specific administrator tasks or problems identified by practitioners. Training guides are then used in workshop settings at statewide administrator conferences and at local administrator meetings. Local meetings are designed to develop peer networks for discussing information in the training guides and providing peer support for improvement in individual practice through implementation of the research findings. RBTSA expects to enhance practitioners' knowledge of relevant research through the assimilation and dissemination of research findings.

In-service Training in Industry

In-service education is not unique to the field of education and school administrators. Most successful businesses and industries that employ many workers have long-term, well-developed managerial and technological on-site and off-site training programs. The need for corporate education and training arises from the need to accommodate turnover and personnel growth, changes in knowledge and skills, the lack of turnover of certain positions, and the necessity to improve skills and performance. Lusterman (1977) notes that corporate education and training systems appear to connect with a number of education-related social and economic problems: the transition of youth from school to work, low-productivity trends, the imbalance between job skills and market needs, lack of opportunities for women and minorities, occupational obsolescence, and career changes. Most employer-sponsored education stems from business needs and is only incidentally supportive of the job and career aspirations of participating employees.

The corporate educational system has three characteristics that set it apart from university programs. First, participants are highly motivated. The rewards for success and the penalties for failure are perceived to be high, affecting present and future earnings as well as prestige, self-esteem, and the realization of career goals. Second, the workplace is the setting for both learning and doing. This learning has both visible and invisible elements, including private instruction and coaching by supervisors and peers, observation, problem solving, and learning by trial and error. Work experience is integrated with classroom instruction in a planned and serialized sequence of theory and practice. Third, the orientation of the instruction is pragmatic; it is an instrument for achieving other goals, such as business profit and growth.

In his study of education in industry, Lusterman identified four training-program charcteristics: (1) line managers are taught to distinguish training needs from motivational or organizational sources of performance problems, to conduct certain necessary training, and to guide employees to appropriate training resources; (2) a cadre of specialists assists line managers with this responsibility and provides in-house programs; (3) in-house programs are flexible enough to meet carefully analyzed and changing needs; and (4) the companies have effective mechanisms for feedback on and evaluation and improvement of both internal and external programs.

Summary

While the mainstream of administrator preparation continues to be carried out in graduate programs in universities, a considerable amount of training occurs after student administrators have left these programs and entered the workplace. We reviewed a few of these in-service programs. From this review we can construct a list of common elements.

The programs appear to be related to the specific content of the job. The curriculum is characterized by short, intensive, and fragmented sessions on topics that are often identical to the names of courses in graduate programs, such as school-community relations, finance, or personnel evaluation. The content is divided into small pieces of information that are relatively isolated from one another. There does not appear to be an accumulation of knowledge or skills. Some programs rely on traditional instructional methods, while others employ discovery learning techniques.

In-service workshops provide opportunities for people with problems (administrators) to locate people with solutions (often other administrators). Workshops typically respond to currently pressing needs as perceived by administrators. The learning activities deal with the mundane aspects of running a bureaucracy, and are far removed from the grand conceptions of educational leadership; they provide quick answers to problems that might arise in the daily lives of administrators.

Peer communication plays an important role in many of these training programs. This communication ranges from informal conversation to organized discussions about a specific problem and uses administrators as coaches, or trainers, of other administrators. Ideally, these conversations give administrators an opportunity to evaluate their experiences and convert those experiences into more-intelligent behavior. The approach to training is highly rationalized. A medical model that concentrates on diagnosing deficiencies and providing a remedy (training) guides much of its structure.

While this presentation of training models is not exhaustive, it does give us an idea of what the field of administrator in-service training looks like. In the next section we shall draw on several of the themes in the previous three sections for the purpose of recommending a future direction for administrator preparation.

Changing Administrator Preparation

Papers discussing school administrator preparation usually offer recommendations for improvement. Some of these recommendations include *providing internships* (longer internships, shorter internships, internships for experienced administrators), *focusing on skills* (analytical, problem solving, report writing), *using different instructional methods for the same content* (case study, simulation, competency based), *including different content* (behavioral sciences, humanities, philosophy, less theory, more theory, more specialized and differentiated), and *changing the structure of or responsibility for preparation* (universities should do what they do best, practitioners should be involved). In following this tradition, we reconsider and identify provocative themes in the training of school administrators. These themes will be covered under two headings: "Administrative Work" and "University Programs." Recommendations are offered for improving administrator preparation.

Administrative Work

The literature generally yields two images of administrators. On the one hand, the descriptive studies point out that administrators engage in mundane and rather trivial work. They must learn to do little things well. On the other hand, the administrator is portrayed in heroic terms.

In the first image the administrator is just another cog in the machine, whose absence would not cause the machine to shut down. The work activities identified in the descriptive studies suggest that the school administrator is really a manager by Hodgkinson's definition.[4] Viewed in this light, school administrators are ordinary men and women, rather than supermen. The descriptive studies of administrator work activities lead us to only one conclusion: most administrators are indeed made of clay, or are at least mortal.

At the same time, the rational, professional concept of authority, as identified by Weber (1971), is attacked by teachers who do not view the principal as an expert in the instructional process. At the very least teachers view themselves as the equal of principals in matters of instruction. This demythologizing of the principal is complemented by a collection of studies suggesting that administrators spend a lot of time talking with insiders about minor things, making trivial decisions, and holding meetings on unimportant agendas (March, 1978). This literature supports some teachers' beliefs that the administrator is unnecessary; teachers could do a better job running the school under a committee of teachers or through some form of industrial democracy.

Administrators like to believe, however, that their work, while not glamorous, is necessary. This administrative position is tenuous in view of our observations, and it is further undermined by the antiauthoritarian mood in our present-day culture, which affects the possibilities of administrative action. Nevertheless, we see portraits of administrators, most often superin-

---

[4] We question Hodgkinson's assertion that Mintzberg was actually studying administrative behavior.

tendents, as heroes who have taken charge of unruly forces. "Leadership is described in lofty rhetoric; the anguish, perils, and difficulties of being a leader are generally obscured by the extended portrayals of its pleasure-giving possibilities. The leader is viewed as a potent force for good in the organization; his task is to use the influence of his office to bind the wills of his subordinates in accomplishing purpose beyond their own self-serving ends" (Bridges, 1977, p. 204). Bridges charges that this attitudinal socialization of administrators inevitably leads to disappointment because such goals are unrealistic and rarely achieved.

The effective-schooling studies appear at first glance to add confusion to this debate. These studies suggest that strong administrative leadership is an important condition associated with high student achievement scores in reading and math. This interpretation is convoluted for many reasons.The scope of this paper does not permit a lengthy examination of the problems regarding the attempt to relate student achievement to instructional leadership, but several conclusions can be drawn.

First, the majority of the studies on effective schooling were conducted at the elementary school level. It is well documented that elementary school teachers have different attitudes than do high school teachers toward the authority of principals vis-à-vis their work (Lortie, 1975, p. 199). Yet, the findings of the schooling effectiveness studies are being generalized across grades.

Second, the inference that the principal is an important variable is based on teachers' perceptions that school success is caused by effective administrators who are committed to a specific course of action. This interpretation is suspect for several reasons. Research indicates that strong leaders are perceived to be consistent. Most administrators try to avoid the appearance of vacillation so that their constituents can have faith in a program, policy, or philosophy of management, and can understand the direction in which the organization is going. Moreover, attribution theory research suggests that administrators may not deserve all the blame or credit they get for an organization's fortunes. If things are going well, one tends to take the credit, but if things are going poorly, one blames others or environmental forces for the misfortune (Staw and Ross, 1978).

Third, the conclusion that effective schools are run by effective administrators appears to be a tautology accomplished by definitional fiat. Effective schooling, defined as high student achievement scores in reading and math, is stipulative and restricts the scope of further study. Because the definition is too restrictive, effective schooling ceases to lend itself to empirical investigation. Most people mean something more than test scores when they talk about effective schooling. Schools exist for more than learning how to read and how to compute. (Perhaps this definition merely reflects the back-to-basics movement.)

Finally, the relationship between effective schools and effective principals is problematic because of the uncollected data. Rutter and others (1979) state:

> Obviously the influence of the head teacher is very considerable. We did not look in any detail at the styles of management and leadership which worked best; this is an issue which is now important to investigate. Our informal observations indicated that no one style was associated with better outcomes. Indeed it was noticeable that the heads of the more successful schools took widely differing approaches. Nevertheless, it was likely that these had essential elements in common and it is important to determine what these might be. [Pp.203–04]

Here we see the belief that leadership makes a difference regardless of the situation. Kerr (1976) has reframed the question of the influence of the leader. He asks, Under what conditions does leadership make a difference?

March and March (1977) claim that differences in career outcomes do not reflect proportional differences in behavior or performance.

> . . . Most superindentents are organizationally nearly indistinguishable in their behaviors, performances, abilities, and values. This is partly a consequence of the filters by which they come to the role, partly a consequence of the ambiguity of inference in educational settings, partly a consequence of the long-run stability of educational activities and organization, partly a consequence of a lifetime spent in educational institutions. [Pp. 405–06]

Thus, if individuals in school administration are nearly indistinguishable from one another, it is premature, if not dangerous, to suggest a causal relationship between administrative behavior and school effectiveness.

Personal and social characterictics of superintendents have been relatively uniform, so far as we can determine, over the last hundred years and have probably been crucial determinants in the selection and performance of superintendents (Tyack and Cummings, 1977). Assuming this is the case, what impact might training have on school administrators?

University Programs

Tyack and Cummings (1977) note that under certain conditions special-ized training might have considerable impact on the subsequent careers of graduates. These conditions include the transmission of particuar skills and knowledge needed in a distinct occupation; rationed entry with restrictive admission and limited output; and intense socialization to the distinct norms of the group. Tyack and Cummings note, however, that graduate training for school administrators fits none of these criteria very well: the programs are not selective, the professional community intensely argues about the essential content of the training, and students pursue training sporadically (p. 58). Carlson (1972) also casts severe doubt on the importance of professional training for school administrators. In fact, we would argue that the norms of teaching are carried over into the administrative career and become dysfunctional in the enactment of the school administrator role. In view of the homogeneity of the population of school administrators, it is no small task to assess the importance of graduate training in their careers.

As we noted, there is little distinction between the master's, intermediate, and doctoral programs. What effect might this have on students of educational administration? First, it probably serves to freeze the semantic environment of administrators. Managerial talk carves up the work of organizations in a particular way. It isolates certain phenomena and has specific implications. Everyday labels get in the way of restructuring the content of training. They partition and warp reality in certain patterned ways, generating a system of blind spots and distortions. Evidence of this can be found in the fact that the titles of in-service seminars are often the same as the titles of graduate courses. These categories govern the needs assessment studies on which programs are based. By way of example, the administrator association sends needs assessment surveys to their membership who are directed to rank a list of thirty topics for in-service training. Since time management always appears on the list, it is always ranked. If a content or skill does not fall into a category, administrators do not know how to label it. If administrators cannot identify what is "ailing them," in-service training on their ailments will not be available.

Further, the lack of difference among programs leads to little accumulation of knowledge or increased proficiency in specified skills. We cannot say with certainly that an administrator with a doctorate is better than an administrator with only state certification. This lack of a distinction reinforces the attitude that completing a doctorate is "paying one's dues." By surmounting this barrier, the candidate may then apply for positions that carry the qualification, "must possess a doctorate in educational administration." The program is viewed as a ceremony and a minor barrier in his or her administrative career.

That there is little distinction among program levels is complicated by the fragmented and disparate character of individual courses that are loosely coupled with one another. The courses are presented as pieces. Recommendations for change are presented as pieces that reflect the recommender's biases. We really have not considered what the total program should include, and until we do, we cannot devise one.

We do not intend to criticize the various recommendations, for they seem to be well conceived but, unfortunately, conceived in isolation from one another. While administration is a rational pursuit, its rational boundaries are heavily circumscribed. Administrators are specialists in generalism (Hodgkinson, 1978).

In developing a curriculum, it is important to acknowledge the differences between "knowing that" and "knowing how" to do a certain thing. This distinction is between knowledge and acquisition of a skill. The first is cognitive; the other is active or dispositional. Grand generalizations about the learning that occurs in competency-based programs or through internships should be viewed with suspicion. The problem is to identify which information, skills, habits, concepts, or explanations should be learned in one setting over another. This brings us to March's (1974) recommendation that universities should do what they do best. He states:

> Universities do as good a job as anyone at most aspects of management training. They do better at providing the basic knowledge, at identifying general problems, at isolating and providing broad experience in the necessary and intellectual skills, at discussing value issues, at encouraging risk-taking and initiative, at building social and personal sensitivity, at exposure to conflicting ideas and sentiments, and at building a sense of self-esteem. . . . The university has a special domain of competence: The domain of the intellect. What the university does best, relative to other institutions, is to develop new knowledge and its implications. It is an intellectual institution. . . . It may be considerably more vital that the administrator be strong, or loving, or energetic, or sensitive, or charismatic, or a member of a particular social, ethnic, or sexual group. We can recognize the importance of such tasks and the legitimacy and value of such attributes without accepting the proposition that the university should provide either the training or the certification for them. [Pp. 24–26]

While it is possible to treat graduate training as an analytical problem, this training has very important political overtones. Several professional associations for administrators are vying for the legitimate authority to offer workshops for credit that can be applied to recertification. While they currently operate along the graduate preparation (preservice–in-service boundary, it will not be long before they convince licensing commissions and legislative bodies that graduate training at universities is unnecessary. After all, the association can provide a more meaningful apprenticeship at a reduced cost to the taxpayer. The question then becomes one of resource allocation. Does the legislature allocate monies for management training to school districts or to universities? If the question is framed as a political one—who gets what, when, and how—we can begin to construct a new training model.

Facilitating Structures

After pondering the state of the art of administrator training and searching for evidence on what administrator preparation should entail, we can put forward eight statements to guide the development of our proposal. These statements are based on our observation about school administrator work and training.

1. Administrative work requires energy, cognitive and managerial skills, philosophical understandings, and a knowledge base in organizational theory, decision making, leadership, and policymaking.
2. Administrator training should be tied to the requirements of the job.
3. School administrators claim they are unprepared for the realities of managerial work.
4. School administrators prefer to be trained by other administrators.
5. Informal verbal interaction among administrators socializes new administrators and reinforces their shared perceptions about their work.
6. University training programs are not selective and students pursue training sporadically.
7. Characteristics of adult learning point to learning laboratories for applying theory to practice.
8. The university is best suited for training administrators in the intellective domain. Less cognitive—but still essential—knowledge is more appropriately the domain of nonuniversity agencies.

These statements are not new. Yet knowledge of their validity has led to no significant alterations in training programs.

We title this section "Facilitating Structures" because instead of resolving the debate on the necessary content of administrator training, we suggest a *structure* within which to resolve it. We also suggest a structure for providing the administrator training once the content is specified.

The structure for the resolution of the debate has three parts. First, the content of administrator training needs to be reexamined. We need to collocate the information we now have on administrator work—to collect and compare it carefully and critically and to integrate it (without using the everyday labels for describing administrative work)—and then to identify the knowledge, skills, abilities, and attitudes that should be learned.

Second, the scope and sequence for administrator training should be specified. We need to decide not only in what order the content should be presented but also at what time—before the administrative career begins, during the initial years in the role, during an activity of disengagement (such as a doctoral program or retreat), or during career transitions (for example, promotions or retirements). Curriculum mapping—a strategy used in developing curriculum scope and sequence in lower schools—could be used to accomplish this task.

Third, the proper domain for each segment of the content must be determined. We must decide who should have responsibility for teaching the content—university professors without administrative experience, professors with administrative experience, or practicing administrators—and also how it should be delivered—in formal courses, workshops, simulations, or competency-based courses. In a previous paper Pitner (1981b) suggested that a group of faculty members in educational administration meet with representatives of professional associations, including the American Assocation for School Administrators, the National Association of Secondary School Principals, and the National Association of Elementary School Principals, to jointly work on this task in a colloquium that would be staged by the University of Oregon. We advocate this three-part structure to resolve the debate over the content of administrative training programs.

Assuming that this debate is resolved, another structure is needed to facilitate the collaboration of universities with nonuniversity agencies in the delivery of training, to involve administrators in the training of other administrators, and to provide a conscious articulation of the relationship between course work and real-life situations and problems. We propose that a new concept for administrator training build on the strengths of the institutions currently involved in the training of administrators. This facilitating structure was identified in our previous discussion about trends in administrator in-service training. The Research-Based Training for School Administrators project at the University of Oregon is a venture in which the university and three administrator associations are working collaboratively to improve administrator training (see page 388).

Through a graduate program and Project Leadership, a university could collaborate with the professional association in a particular state or region to offer a program that would fit the content, domain, and sequence of administrator training identified by the proposed University of Oregon colloquium. Thus, a student might spend the summer at the university taking administration courses in the intellective domain but during the school year participate in simulations that link theory and practice, or attend workshops that train administrators in less cognitive, skill-oriented material relevant to the position for which certification is desired. Graduate credit would be earned in all cases.

This plan calls for careful integration of efforts. It does not mean the abandonment of the university's responsibility, nor does it suggest that the university will no longer play a role in the training of administrators. It does not mean that the professional training program would provide only those opportunities for intellectual growth that are tied to immediately usable administrative skills. It would mean, however, that the university would support the concept of practicing administrators teaching other administrators in a specified area within a planned framework. Administrators training one another would become an essential component to the program of studies. However, courses would be clearly designated as taught by the university or by the administrator association. The school law course would not be occasionally taught by a superintendent instead of the faculty member with formal legal preparation, and administrators would not act as guest lecturers in university classes. Within this kind of framework it would be possible to attend to the shortcomings of administrator preparation.

Summary

The purpose of this paper was to examine the state of the art of the training of school administrators. Our review of studies on administrator training and the observations of scholars and practitioners led us to conclude that improvement in training is sorely needed. We suggested a structure for ascertaining what the total program for administrators should include, who should be involved in the training, and what the sequence of training should be. We recommended a program structure that calls for the careful integration of efforts among the university, school districts, and administrator associations. This program structure—Project Leadership—is currently being tested as a dissemination vehicle in the Research-Based Training for School Administrators project at the Center for Educational Policy and Management at the University of Oregon.

References

Argyris, C., and Schön, D. (1978). *Theory in practice: Increasing professional effectiveness.* San Francisco: Jossey-Bass.

Bossert, S. T., et al. (1981). "Instructional Management Program." Mimeographed. San Francisco: Far West Laboratory.

Boyan, N. (1968). "Problems and issues of knowlege production and utilization." In *Knowledge production and utilization in educational administration,* T. Eidell and J. Kitanel (Eds.), p. 34. Eugene: Center for Advanced Study of Educational Administration, University of Oregon.

Brady, J. (1976, May) "A pilot study of teacher morale in three secondary schools in the north of England." *The Journal of Educational Administration* 14: 94–105.

Bridges, E. M. (1977). "The nature of leadership." In *Educational leadership: The developing decades,* L. L. Cunningham, W. G. Hack, and R. O. Nystrand (Eds.). Berkeley, Calif.: McCutchan Publishing Corp.

Bridges, E. (1982, Summer). "Research on the school adminstrator: The state of the art, 1967–1980." *Educational Administration Quarterly* 18 (3): 12–33.

Brookover, W. B., and Lezotte, L.W. (1979). *Changes in school characteristics coincident with changes in student achievement.* East Lansing: Michigan State University, College of Urban Development.

Burke, R. J., (1970). "Methods of resolving superior-subordinate conflict: The constructive use of subordinate differences and disagreements." *Organizational Behavior and Human Performance* 5: 393–411.

Burlingame, M. (1978). "Coordination, control and facilitation of instruction within schools." Paper presented at the NIE Conference on School Organizations and Effects in 1978, San Diego, California. Mimeographed.

Campbell, R., and Cunningham, L. (1959). "Observations of administrator behavior." Chicago: Midwest Administration Center, University of Chicago.

Carlson, R. (1972) *School superintendents' careers and performance*. Columbus, Ohio: Charles E. Merrill.

Cohen, E., and Miller, R. H. (1980, October). "Coordination and control of instruction in schools." *Pacific Sociological Review* 23: 446–73.

Cohen, E. G.; Miller, R.; Bredo, A.; and Duckworth, K. (1977). "Principal role and teacher morale under varying organizational conditions." Mimeographed. Stanford, Calif.: Stanford Center for Research and Development in Teaching.

Coleman, J. S.; Campbell, E. Q.; Hobron, C. J.; McPartland, J.; Mood, A. M.; Weinfeld, F. D.; and York, R. L. (1966). *Equality of educational opportunity*. Washington, D. C.: U. S. Office of Education.

Cotton, K., and Savard, W. G. (1980, December). "The principal as instructional leader." A report on effective schooling presented to the Honorable Jay S. Hammond, Governor of Alaska.

Crowson, R., and Porter-Gehrie, C. (1980). "The discretionary behavior of principals in large city schools." *Educational Administration Quarterly* 16 (1): 45–69.

Cuban, L. *Urban school chiefs under fire*. (1976). Chicago: University of Chicago Press.

Culbertson, J.; Farquhar, R.; Gaynor, A.; and Shibles, M. (1969). *Preparing educational leaders for the seventies*. Washington, D. C.: U. S. Department of Health, Eduation, and Welfare.

Cunningham, L. L., and Nystrand, R. O. (1969, Winter). "Toward greater relevance in preparation programs for urban school administrators." *Educational Administration Quarterly* 5 (1): 16–17.

Cunningham, L. L.; Downey, L. W.; and Goldhammer, K. (1963). "Implications for administrator training programs." In *The social sciences and educational administration*, L. W. Downey and F. Enns (Eds.). Edmonton: University of Alberta.

Duckworth, K. (1981). "Linking educational policy and management with student achievement." Mimeographed. Eugene: Center for Educational Policy and Management, University of Oregon.

Duignan, P. (1980). "Administrative behavior of school superintendents: A descriptive study." *The Journal of Educational Administration* 1: 5–26.

Edmonds, R. (1979, October). "Effective schools for the urban poor." *Educational Leadership* 37: 15–24.

Educational Research Service. (1974). *Inservice programs for educational administrators and supervisors*. Arlington, Va.: Educational Research Service.

Ellet, C. D. (1978, February). "Understanding and using the Georgia principal assessment system." *CCBC Notebook* 7 (21): 2.

Erickson, D; Hills, R.; and Robinson, N. (1970). *Educational flexibility in an urban school district*. Vancouver, British Columbia: Educational Research Institute of British Columbia.

Eugene (Ore.) *Register-Guard*. 18 October 1981, sec. A, p. 7.

Farquhar, R. H. (1968, October). "The humanities and educational administration: Rationales and recommendations." *The Journal of Educational Administration* 6 (2): 100–05.

Farquhar, R. H. (1977) "Preparatory programs in educational administration." In *Educational administration: The developing decades*, L. L. Cunningham, W. G. Hack, and R. O. Nystrand (Eds.), pp. 339–40. Berkeley, Calif.: McCutchan Publishing Corp.

Farquhar, R. H., and Piele, P. K. (1972). *Preparing educational leaders*. ERIC/CEM UCEA Series on Administrator Preparation. Danville, Ill.: Interstate Printers and Publishers.

Filley, Alan C.; House, Robert J.; and Kerr, Steven. (1976). *Managerial process and organizational behavior*. Glenview, Ill.: Scott, Foresman.

Goldhammer, K.; Suttle, J. E.; Aldridge, W. D.; and Becker, G. L. (1967). *Issues and problems in contemporary educational administration*. Eugene: Center for the Advanced Study of Educational Administration, University of Oregon.

Gregg, R. (1969). "Preparation of administrators." in *Encyclopedia of educational research* (4th ed.).

Griffiths, D. (1966). *The school superintendent*. New York: The Center for Applied Research in Education.

Griffiths, D. (1975, November) "Some thoughts about theory in educational administration—1975." *UCEA Review*.

Griffiths, D. (1977). "Preparation programs for administrators." In *Educational administration: The developing decades*, L. L. Cunningham, W. G. Hack, and R. O. Nystrand (Eds.), pp. 401–37. Berkeley, Calif.: McCutchan Publishing Corp.

Gross, N., and Herriott, R. (1965). *Staff leadership in public schools*. New York: John Wiley.

Hacker, A. (1981, October). "The shame of professional schools." *Harper's* 43: 22–28.

Hannaway, J., and Sproull, L. S. (1978–79). "Who's running the show? Coordination and control in educational organizations." *Administrator's Notebook* 27 (9): 1–4.

Hills, J. (1975). "Preparation for the principalship: Some recommendations for the field." *Administrator's Notebook* 23 (9).

Hodgkinson, C. (1978). *Toward a philosophy of administration*. New York: St. Martin's Press.

Holdaway, E. A. (1978, Winter). "Facet and overall satisfaction of teachers." *Educational Administration Quarterly* 14: 30–47.

Houston, W. R., and Howsam, R. B., (Eds.). (1972). *Competency-based teacher education: Progress, problems, and prospects*. Chicago: Science Research Associates.

Hoy, W. K.; Newland, W.; and Blazousky, R. (1977, Winter). "Subordinate loyalty to superior, esprit, and aspects of bureaucratic structure." *Educational Administration Quarterly* 13:71-85.

Jacobson, P.; Logsdon, J.; and Wiegman, R. (1973). *The principalship: New perspectives*. Englewood Cliffs, N. J.: Prentice-Hall.

Kalis, M. C. (1980, April). "Teaching experience: Its effect on school climate, teacher morale." *NASSP Bulletin:* 89-102.

Kerr, S. M. (1976). Substitutes for leadership: Their meaning and measurement. In *American Institute of Decision Sciences proceedings*, H. E. Schneider (Ed.).

Koberg, C. S. (1981) "A multi-level study of relations among organizational contingencies, adaptations, and performance." Ph.D. dissertation, University of Oregon.

Larson, L; Bussom, R.; and Vicars, W. (1981). *The nature of a school superintendent's work*. Carbondale: Southern Illinois University.

Licata, J. W. (1980-81). "Learner perceptions of a clinical training component for school administrators." *Journal of Educational Technology Systems* 9 (1): 56.

Lipham, J., and Hoeh, J. (1974). *The principalship: Foundations and functions.* New York: Harper and Row.

Lortie, D. C. (1975). *Schoolteacher.* Chicago: The University of Chicago Press.

Lusterman, S. (1977). "Education in industry." A research report from the Conference Board's Public Affairs Research Division. New York: Conference Board.

March, J. G. (1974) "Analytical skills and the university training of administrators." *The Journal of Educational Administration* (1) 8: 30–54.

March, J. G. (1978, February). "American public school administration: A short analysis." *School Review,* 217–50.

March, J. C., and March, J. G. (1977, September). "Almost random careers: The wisconsin school superintendency, 1940–1972." *Administrative Science Quarterly* 22: 405–06.

Martin, W. (1980). "The managerial behavior of high school principals." Ph.D. dissertation, The Pennsylvania State University.

McCleary, L. E. (n.d.) "Competency based educational administration and applications to related fields." Mimeographed. Salt Lake City: University of Utah.

Miklos, E. R. (1969). "The behavioral and educational administration: Some reconsiderations." In *Educational administration: International perspectives,* G. Baron, D. Cooper, and W. Walker (Eds.). New York: Rand McNally.

Mintzberg, H. (1973). *The nature of managerial work.* New York: Harper and Row.

Morris, VanCleve, et al. (1981). *The urban principal: Discretionary decision making in a large educational organization.* Chicago: University of Illinois.

Nagel, J. M., and Nagel, E. E. (1978). "Doctoral programs in educational administration." In *Preparatory programs for educational administrators in the United States,* P. F. Silver and D. W. Spuck (Eds.). Columbus: University Council for Educational Administration.

National Education Association, Department of Elementary School Principals. (1968). *The elementary school principalship in 1968,* p. 28. Washington, D.C.: National Education Association.

Ourth, J. (1979, March) "Have the universities failed us?" *National Elementary Principal* 59 (3): 80.

Peterson, K. (1978) "The principal's task." *Administrator's Notebook* 26 (8): 1–4.

Pitner, N. J. (1978) "Descriptive study of the everyday activities of suburban school superintendents: The management of information." Ph.D. dissertation, The Ohio State University.

Pitner, N. J. (1979). "So go the days of their lives: A descriptive study of the superintendency." *OSSC Bulletin* 22 (5). Eugene: Oregon School Study Council.

Pitner, N. J. (1981a) "Hormones and harems: Are the activities of superintendents different for a woman?" In *Educational policy and management: Sex differentials,* P. A. Schmuck, W. W. Charters, Jr., and R. O. Carlson, (Eds.), pp. 273–95. New York: Academic Press.

Pitner, N. J. (1981b, April). "Administrator training: What relation to administrator work?" Paper presented at the annual meeting of the American Educational Research Association, Los Angeles, California.

Pitner, N. J. (1981c). "Research-based training for school administrators: An executive summary." Mimeographed. Eugene: Center for Educational Policy and Management, University of Oregon.

Pitner, N. J. (1982, March). "The Mintzberg method: What have we really learned?" Paper presented at the annual meeting of the American Educational Research Association, New York.

Pitner, N. J., and Ogawa, R. (1981, Spring). "Organizational leadership: The case of the school superintendent." *Educational Administration Quarterly* 17 (2): 45–66.

Roe, W., and Drake, T. (1980). *The principalship.* New York: Macmillan.

Rowan, B.; Dwyer, D.; and Bossert, S. (1982, March). "Methodological considerations in studies of effective principals." Paper presented at the annual meeting of the American Educational Research Association in New York.

Rutter, M.; Maughan, B.; Mortimore, P.; and Ouston, J. (1979) *Fifteen thousand hours: Secondary schools and their effects on children.* Cambridge, Mass.: Harvard University Press.

Salley, C.; McPherson, B.; and Baehr, M. (1978). "What principals do: A preliminary occupational analysis." In T. Reller (Ed.), *The principal in metropolitan schools* Berkeley, Calif.: McCutchan Publishing Corp.

Silver, P. F. and Spuck, D. W., (Eds.). (1978). *Preparation programs for educational administrators in the United States.* Columbus, Ohio: University Council for Educational Administration.

Smith, K. R. (1976, May). "Morale: A refinement of Stogdill's model." *The Journal of Educational Administration* 14: 87–93.

Sproull, L. (1979). "Managing education programs: A micro-behavioral analysis." Unpublished paper.

Staw, B. M., and Ross, J. (1978, March). "Commitment to a policy decision: A multi-theoretical perspective." *Administrative Science Quarterly* 23: 40–64.

Tyack, D. B., and Cummings, R. (1977). "Leadership in American public schools before 1954: Historical configurations and conjectures." In *Educational leadership: The developing decades,* L. L. Cunningham, W. G. Hack, and R. O. Nystrand, (Eds.). Berkeley, Calif.: McCutchan Publishing Corp.

Weber, G. (1971). *Inner city children can be taught to read: Four successful schools.* Occasional Paper No. 18. Washington, D.C.: Council for Basic Education.

Weick, K. (1976, March). "Educational organizations as loosely coupled systems." *Administrative Science Quarterly* 21 (1): 1–19.

Wolcott, H. (1973). *The man in the principal's office: An ethnography.* New York: Holt, Rinehart and Winston.

Zeigler, L. H. (1981) "Conflict management." *The school administrator* (February 1981) Arlington, Va.: The American Association of School Administrators.

Zeigler, L. H.; Kehoe, E.; Reisman, J.; and Polito, J. (1981). *A comparison of the source and substance of conflict in educational and municipal governance.* Eugene: Center for Educational Policy and Management, University of Oregon.

Zeyen, L. (1981, October 30). UCEA Plenary Session Meeting in Columbus, Ohio.

29

Women in Educational Administration: Implications for Training

Charol Shakeshaft

It is old hat to point out that the world of teaching has primarily been a female one, while the world of administration has almost always been populated by men. There have always been women school administrators, but men have dominated the field. Many speculate that this imbalance will come to an end in the next decade as more women assume formal educational leadership positions. Currently, the number of women in administrative training programs nearly equals the number of men in those programs.

Research on women administrators uncovers differences between the ways men and women approach the tasks of administration. These differences have implications for administrative training programs, which were developed by men primarily for men.

Although there are similarities in male and female managers' backgrounds and experiences, they also vary in important ways. The profiles and history of women administrators are not the same as the profiles and history of men in administration. Further, the legacy of discrimination and exclusion has shaped a world in which women's experiences and behaviors are often

Revised by the author and reprinted with permission from *The Journal of Educational Equity and Leadership*, (Spring, 1987), pp. 4–20. © 1987 by the University Council for Educational Administration.

unlike those of men. This women's world has important implications for theory and practice in a field. To be useful, theory and practice need to take into account the experiences of all the players. Unfortunately, the field of educational administration, not unlike most other fields and disciplines, has not seen the world from a female perspective and, thus, presents only a partial picture.

The Female World of Schools

A number of writers (Bernard, 1981; Ferguson, 1984; Gilligan, 1982; Lenz and Meyerhoff, 1985; Lyons, 1983, 1985; Noddings, 1984) have written about a female culture and a female world. For instance, Bernard (1981) writes that not only do women and men experience "the world differently but also . . . the world women experience is demonstrably different from the world men experience" (p. 3). Gilligan (1982) elaborates:

. . . in the transition from adolescence to adulthood, the dilemma itself is the same for both sexes, a conflict between integrity and care. But approached from a different perspective, this dilemma generates the recognition of opposite truths. These different perspectives are reflected in two different moral ideologies, since separation is justified by an ethic of rights while attachment is supported by an ethic of care. "[P. 164]

Studies of women administrators tend to confirm the view that women occupy a world, in addition to the one in which white males live, that provides them with experiences and approaches to life that are different from those of men. The research on male and female administrators and women administrators' responses in interviews lead me to believe that although both male and female administrators use a range of behaviors in their work, the patterns of use are different. Women administrators more often are guided by what Gilligan describes as "an injunction to care, a responsibility to discern and alleviate the 'real and recognizable trouble' of this world," while male administrators are informed by "an injunction to respect the rights of others and thus to protect from interference the rights to life and self-fulfillment" (p. 100).

This female world exists in schools and is reflected in the ways women work in schools. Based on what is currently known of female work behavior in schools, this female world might be conceptualized in the following ways.

1. *Relationships with others are central to all actions of women administrators.*
   Women spend more time with people, communicate more, care more
   about individual differences, are concerned more with teachers and
   marginal students, and motivate more. Not surprisingly, staffs of
   women administrators rate women higher, are more productive, and
   have higher morale. Also, students in schools with women principals

have higher morale and are more involved in student affairs. Further, parents of children in schools and districts run by women view the schools favorably and, thus, are more involved in school life than are parents of children in schools and districts run by men. This focus on relationships and connections echoes Gilligan's (1982) ethic of care.

2. *Teaching and learning is the major focus of women administrators.* Women administrators are more instrumental in instructional learning than are men, and they exhibit greater knowledge of teaching methods and techniques. Women administrators not only emphasize achievement, they coordinate instructional programs and evaluate student progress. In these schools and districts, women administrators know their teachers and they know the academic progress of their students. Women are more likely to help new teachers and to directly supervise all teachers. Women also create a school climate more conducive to learning, one that is more orderly, safer, and quieter. Not surprisingly, academic achievement is higher in schools and districts in which women are administrators.

3. *Building community is an essential part of a woman administrator's style.* From speech patterns to decision-making styles, women exhibit a more democratic, participatory style that encourages inclusiveness rather than exclusiveness in schools. Women involve themselves more with staff and students, ask for and get higher participation, and maintain more closely knit organizations. Staffs of women principals have higher job satisfaction and are more engaged in their work than are staffs of male administrators. These staffs are also more aware of and committed to the goals of learning, and the members of the staffs have more shared professional goals. These are schools and districts in which teachers receive a great deal of support from their female administrators. They are also districts and schools where achievement is emphasized. Greenberg (1985) describes this female school world: "whatever its failures, it is more cooperative than competetive, it is more experiential than abstract, it takes a broad view of the curriculum and has always addressed 'the whole child'" (p. 4).

4. *Marginality overlays the daily worklife of women administrators.* Token status and sexist attitudes toward women combine to create a world in which the woman administrator is always on display and always vulnerable to attack. Whether the assault actually occurs is less important than the knowledge that it is always possible. Women perceive their token status and realize that their actions reflect on all women. Bernard, in the *The Female World* (1981), writes of this undercurrent of danger for women: "I take the misogyny of the male world as a given, as part of the environment of the female world. It has to be recognized and dealt

with" (p. 31). This misogyny of the male world make women's lives in administration different from men's.

Administration and the Female World

What if the study of school administration took into account this female world? What would theory and practice look like? It is clear from an examination of the research and theory in educational administration that the female world of administrators has not been incorporated into the body of work in the field. Nor are women's experiences carried into the literature on practice. Prescriptions for practice in educational administration are primarily found in textbooks, in books and journal articles by practitioners, and in the conversations or lore shared within the field. A number of studies of the journals and textbooks of the field (addressed to both theory and practice) have documented that women are not a subject of these works (Nagle, et al., 1982; Schmuck, Butman, and Person, 1982; Shakeshaft and Hanson, 1986; Tietze, Shakeshaft, and Davis, 1981).

Whereas "absent" describes the status of women in the traditional educational administration literature, "imitation" is the theme in books and articles for women managers, many of which have been described as survival manuals for women in bureaucracies. Books like *Games Mother Never Taught You* (Harragan, 1977) and *The Managerial Woman* (Hennig and Jardim, 1977) "take existing institutional arrangements for granted and seek strategies to integrate women into these arrangements" (Ferguson, 1984, p. 183). These approaches have studied males and then have advised women to imitate men. Women have been told to "act like a man," "not cry," and "dress for success." What these books fail to examine are the ways in which acting like a man may not be the best strategy for a woman and, worse, may interfere with the goals of schooling.

For instance, the female world is very similar to the world of effective schools. Traditional female approaches to schooling look like the prescriptions for administrative behavior in effective schools. In a recent synthesis of studies on effective leadership behavior (Sweeney, 1982), six themes emerged as behaviors that were consistently associated with well-managed schools in which student achievement is high. According to the research, principals of such schools:

1. *Emphasize achievement.* They give high priority to activities, instruction, and materials that foster academic success. Effective principals are visible and involved in what goes on in the school and its classrooms. They convey to teachers their commitment to achievement.
2. *Set instructional strategies.* They take part in instructional decision making and accept responsibility for decisions about methods, materials, and evaluation

procedures. They develop plans for solving students' learning problems.

3. *Provide an orderly atmosphere.* They do what is necessary to ensure that the school's climate is conducive to learning: it is quiet, pleasant, and well maintained.

4. *Frequently evaluate student progress.* They monitor student achievement on a regular basis. Principals set expectations for the entire school and check to make sure those expectations are being met. They know how well their students are performing as compared to students in other schools.

5. *Coordinate instructional programs.* They interrelate course content, sequences of objectives, and materials in all grades. They see that what goes on in the classroom has bearing on the overall goals and program of the school.

6. *Support teachers.* Effective principals communicate with teachers about goals and procedures. They support teachers' attendance at professional meetings and workshops, and provide inservice that promotes improved teaching. [P. 349]

Similarly, Rutherford's (1985) five-year study of school principals found that effective principals:

(1) have clear, informed visions of what they want their schools to become—visions that focus on students and their needs; (2) translate these visions into goals for their schools and expectations for the teachers, students, and administrators; (3) establish school climates that support progress toward these goals and expectations; (4) continuously monitor progress; and (5) intervene in a supportive or corrective manner, when this seems necessary. [P. 32]

It is interesting to compare these two descriptions of effective administrators with the portrait of the female administrative world. The similarities are striking, and the implications of a female world for effective schooling are dramatic. It appears that for a number of reasons women possess characteristics conducive to good schooling. Women enter teaching with clear educational goals, supported by a value system that stresses service, caring, and relationships. Women focus on instructional and educational issues and have demonstrated that, when in charge, they are likely to build a school community that stresses achievement within a supportive atmosphere. Women's communication and decision-making styles encourage cooperation and help to translate their educational visions into actions. Women monitor and intervene more than men, they evaluate student progress more often, and they manage more-orderly schools. Women demonstrate, more often than men do, the kinds of behavior that promote achievement and learning as well as high morale and commitment by staffs. Analyzing female approaches to administration might help to isolate particular strategies and behaviors that promote effective schooling, which can be used by all administrators. Bach (1976) summarizes much of what is good for schools in women's culture and styles: "The ideal principal must now cultivate all the virtues that have always been expected of the ideal woman. Women have finally lucked out by having several thousand years to train for jobs where muscles are out and persuasion is in!" (p.465). Thus, to counsel women to act like men may not be in the best interests of either women or schooling.

While we do not really know what we would see if we reshaped the school world around female culture and experience, we do have enough information about the female world to allow us to speculate on some issues of practice. The following section addresses issues of practice, keeping gender in mind, in an attempt to begin to think about the ways gender may be an important variable for understanding effective administrative practices. Imbedded in this discussion is the notion that these issues must be confronted by the entire field: researchers need to redirect their inquiries not only to include women but also to see the world through female eyes;and the courses in administrative training programs must incorporate this literature so that both men and women can begin to understand how gender affects their administrative style.

Taking the world of women into account in research and practice means a complete reshaping of the field. What, who, and how we study organizations will change. If we were to include the perspective of women, administrative training programs would need to be completely restructured—the content of every course would be forced to change dramatically. The following issues are presented only as ways we might think about gender and administration, offering some preliminary questions to begin to move the field toward a reconceptualization of theory and practice that includes both males and females.

Supervision

Little has been written on the impact of gender on successful supervision. This issue seems particularly salient, given the structuring in schools, which results in an organization in which males most often supervise females. Research tells us that the sex of participants affects what is communicated and how it is communicated. A male supervisor's words have different meanings to male and female teachers. Conversely, an interaction between a female principal and a male teacher is not the same as an exchange between a female principal and a female teacher. What impact might our understanding of gender issues have on supervision?

We know that men and women communicate differently and that they listen for different information. It may be that in a supervisory conference in which a principal is discussing an instructional issue with the teacher, the woman participant is listening for the feeling and the man for the facts. It may also be, given what we know of the values that males and females carry into their jobs in schools, that the woman is focused on an instructional issue or a matter concerning the child, while the man has chosen to discuss an administrative problem.

Further, research tells us that there may be discomfort in communicating with a member of the other sex. Certainly, we know that male teachers exhibit more hostility in dealing with female administrators than do female teachers. We also know that women administrators have to work to get male teachers to "hear" them. Whether in job interviews or in determining job performance, women are initially evaluated less favorably than equally competent men. Knowing that women are rated as less competent or less effective than men is important for developing supervisory styles (Frasher and Frasher, 1980).

Although women are often seen in a more negative light, this view is seldom directly communicated to them. Studies tell us that male administrators are less likely to be candid with a female teacher than are female administrators. When a male subordinate makes a mistake, his supervisor tends to level with him, "telling it like it is." When a female errs, she often is not informed. Instead, the mistake is corrected by others. The results are twofold. For the male, learning takes place instantly. He gets criticism and the chance to change his behavior. He learns to deal with negative opinions of his work and has the option of improving. Females often never hear anything but praise, even if their performance is known to be less than ideal. This results in the woman being denied the opporunity for immediate feedback, which would allow her to improve her performance. It also results in a woman's misconception of her abilities. If all she hears is that she is doing a good job, it comes as a shock to her when she is fired, demoted, or not promoted. Illustrative is a sex-discrimination case in California. A woman supervisor had been demoted because of poor performance, and it was clear from the record and from the woman's own accounts that she had not been an effective administrator. And yet, in all her evaluations she was rated in the highest category possible. Further, her supervisor, the assistant superintendent, revealed that he had never communicated his displeasure, but rather had "fixed her mistakes" without her knowledge. When she was demoted, she cried sex discrimination, since she had no feedback that would have given her another picture. Why had no one honestly discussed her performance with her?

Interviews with women administrators and their supervisors indicate that her case is not unusual (Shakeshaft, 1986). Women do not get corrective feedback as often as do men. In interviews with male superintendents and principals I asked why they did not confront women, and all expressed that one reason was their fear of women's tears. The threat of crying kept supervisors from giving important corrective feedback that would have allowed women to improve their performance as educators.

Does this mean that we should advise women not to cry? I think not. In reality, women administrators seldom give way to tears. Because it is the threat of crying that deters feedback, we need to demystify this emotion by teaching people mechanisms for coping with tears in the same way that we have instructed them in dealing with the traditional male response of anger.

Authority

There are a number of ways that males and females have been advised to establish their authority as leaders, but very little has been done to determine whether these approaches work for women. Are the issues surrounding authority the same for a male and a female? Do men carry with them, by the nature of their sex, legitimate authority—authority that women must earn in other ways? Is authority the same for a female supervising a female staff as for a female supervising a male staff? How does a woman become identified as "in charge" without being identified in negative ways or as unfeminine? These are issues that women administrators often discuss and that are not covered in the sections on authority in the traditional texts in administration.

In trying to command or maintain authority, women must take into account not only the people with whom they work but also how those people view women. Many women note that ways of establishing authority that work for men do not necessarily work for them. Contrary to the notion that being like a man will automatically signify authority, many women voice concern over the effectiveness of such strategies. Some women report that they try to look less authoritarian, less in charge, and less threatening in an effort to be effective. Many comment that "the less I threaten the men I work with, the more I am able to accomplish." As a result, these women administrators often downplay their power, intellect, and skill. Through language and appearance, they make themselves more tentative and less threatening. These strategies appear to work. The success these women report is supported by studies that confirm that women with male subordinates were more influential when they used a consideration style as opposed to a dominant one, while with woman subordinates both styles worked. Similarly, studies indicate that men rate women who appear less threatening higher than they rate women whom they see as more competent.

Not surprisingly, women report using strategies that subtly signal authority. For instance, a number of women have confided that they completed doctoral work so that they could carry with them the aura of legitimate authority, transmitted by the title of "Doctor." These women want to be called "Dr." not only because it confers legitimacy, but also because they are seeking ways to shed the use of "Mrs." and "Miss," titles that diminish them. When the use of Dr. is not appropriate, "Ms." has been found to be a more powerful title than either Mrs. or Miss, since it has been shown to establish authority more quickly and to elicit the image of a person in charge more often than Mrs. or Miss does (Anderson, Finn, and Leider, 1981).

Climate

The climate in which women work may have an impact on the management strategies they choose. The more male dominated an organization, the more women are conscious of their own behavior and the more they calculate each move. Being a token means that women are always on stage, a condition that adds stress to already stressful jobs. How can we diagnose the climate of a school if we fail to include in that description the ways that a particular group of people, that is, women, are treated? Climate descriptions need to incorporate the day-to-day lives of women that men seldom experience— sexual harrassment, subtle forms of discrimination, and lowered expectations.

Motivation

Studies of motivation have demonstrated that women educators are motivated differently than are men. Women also define career in ways that are foreign to men (Biklen, 1985). The implications of this research for administrators attempting to motivate staffs are crucial to the formulation of a restructuring of the profession that has been called for in recent reform reports. Women enter education to teach, to be close to children, to be able to make a difference. Offers of money or career ladders that take women away from the instructional decisions of the school may not be effective ways of motivating them. Further, continuing to structure school so that administrative jobs become more and more disassociated with the task of learning almost ensures that women will opt out of administration. Intriligator (1983) points out that women seek leadership roles in schools that don't take them away from teaching. "Women union leaders reported that they became a union leader in order to both be in the company of adults and do important things, while at the same time maintaining their satisfying professional role as teacher" (p. 11).

Structure of Schools

The structure of schooling is itself antithetical to the ways women work best. Separating teaching from administration so that the power for change is in the administrator's hands is an organizational format that women did not choose. Studies of female-defined schools indicate that they are child centered, are small, use shared decision making, and are nonhierarchical (Greenberg, 1985; Smith, 1979). In the initial organization of schools, education did not have to follow the lead of industry and separate teaching from the decision-making process. We could have selected another metaphor of organization (Hanson, 1984). Administrative paperwork and tasks could have been delegated to secretaries or clerks, while the definition of administrator might have remained as instructional leader. However, over the years, instructional leadership has been more and more replaced by a management metaphor. Some even believe that a good school administrator need never have been a teacher or, in fact, needs to know nothing of education, since schools are really big business. Interestingly, few women educators hold this view. A female-defined organizational structure probably would not have resulted in such overspecialization, in extreme forms of hierarchy, or in administrators being mere managers.

Personnel Selection

The issues of personnel selection need to be examined in light of both gender differences and discriminatory practices. Those who hire must become aware of the subtle and not-so-subtle biases that we all hold toward women. It is crucial that we examine interview and selection procedures for the presence of bias, as well as to determine ways of overcoming these biases so that the best person is hired. Until we do that, women should be instructed in the most effective ways to confront bias in personnel selection as well as be given the context in which to understand discriminatory practices directed toward them, so that they do not internalize rejection and label it their failure.

Power

Power means different things to men and women. A number of studies provide evidence that women use power to empower others. This sharing of power is based on the notion that power is not finite, but rather that it expands as it is shared. Uses of power in this way need to be further explored, and their impact on schools should be investigated.

Similarly, the team concept for women incorporates this notion of community. Women define a team player as someone who cooperates toward the achievement of group goals. Women see the "support of group action and the achievement of group satisfaction" as the primary descriptors of a team player (Gips et al., 1984). Men, on the other hand, more often define a team player as one who has a job to do and who is responsible for one piece of the action. Women stress cooperation and collaboration while men stress autonomy and individuality. Harragan (1977) offers a contrast between a female and a male team concept:

If you ask a group of women what a team is, they will usually say it means: "Everybody should cooperate to get the job done." "Everybody pitches in, doing whatever they can do to help others." "Everyone is responsible for the team result, thus, you have to cover for somebody who slacks off.". . . if you ask a ten-year-old boy what a team is, he will often respond in baseball terminology. "There's a pitcher, a catcher, a first baseman, second baseman, third baseman, fielders, and so on." Notice, there is nothing vague about that description, no generalized vagaries about a bunch of guys supporting one another. By the time they are ten, little boys know — and they don't even know they know, but they do — that a team is a very rigid structure and has a prescribed function, that each player covers his own position and nobody else's. [Pp. 17–18]

These differences can result in misunderstandings between men and women about what is a good team player. A good team player for a male might be considered a lazy deadweight by a female, whereas a female's concept of team may cause her to be judged as an interfering meddler by a male.

The collaborative approach to decision making that shares power may cause women to be initally evaluated as weak or ineffective. Women who manage from a collaborative framework do so in a system that stresses the value of competitive individualism and personal achievement at the expense of community goals. Thus, women often report that they first establish themselves and then introduce participatory styles. Those women who initiate collaborative approaches immediately generally prepare their staffs for these approaches and acknowledge that they were at first considered weak administrators. Nevertheless, the research offers overwhelming evidence that women's collaborative style works best and over the long haul is instrumental in women being rated as effective leaders.

Community Relations

Because of these collaborative strategies, women seem to have more positive interactions with community members. Just as women administrators differ from men, so too do women school board members approach their jobs with a different perspective than do their male colleagues. Women board members not only tend to "give priority to the content and quality of the education program, they perceive their roles more politically than men, answering to a constituency" (Marshall and Heller, 1983, p. 31). Men board members leave educational decisions to the administrators but gauge a superintendent's effectiveness by how administratively efficient she or he is. Women, on the other hand, emphasize superintendent and board evaluations focused on educational content. These gender differences have ramifications for a superintendent's interactions with her or his board.

Women and Educational Administration

The implications of the research on women administrators for training programs, for practice, and for theory and research in educational administration are wide ranging. If the field were to heed women's experiences, we might restructure training programs and rewrite textbooks. Theory and research would need to be reconceptualized to take women into account. Only when this is done will we be able to understand human behavior in organizations. Until then we are writing a history and practice of males in school administration. As scholarship, this is shoddy and deficient. As practice, it is useful to only some practitioners. The most immediate action that needs to be taken is to develop a research agenda that allows us to discover the factors that we must consider if we are to respond to our women students. Specifically, the following recommendations are made to those involved in training programs in administration.

1. Courses should be expanded to include women's experiences in administration. Where materials are unavailable to address these, they should be developed. The UCEA, ASCD, AASA, and other involved organizations should be requested to prepare curricular aids that incorporate the female world.
2. Case studies of women administrators should be developed and used in classes.
3. Women speakers should be brought to the classroom and to the campus to discuss the issues relevant to female students.
4. Where possible, women students should intern with women administrators.
5. Research on the styles of women administrators should be supported and encouraged.
6. Women should be added to faculties in educational administration.
7. Workshops sponsored by the UCEA might be held for administration professors in an effort to help incorporate the research on women into course materials.

References

Anderson, L.R.; Finn, M.; and Leider, S. (1981). Leadership style and leader title. *Psychology of Women Quarterly* 5(5), (Supplement): 661–69.

Bach, L. (1976). Of women, school administration, and discipline. *Phi Delta Kappan*, 57(7): 463–66.

Bernard, J. (1981). *The female world.* New York: Free Press.

Biklen, S.K. (1985, October). "Can elementary school teaching be a career? A search for new ways of understanding women's work." Paper presented at the annual meeting of the American Educational Research Special Interest Group: Research on Women in Education, Boston.

Ferguson, K.E. (1984). *The feminist case against bureaucracy.* Philadelphia: Temple University.

Frasher, J.M., and Frasher, R.S. (1980). Sex bias in the evaluation of administrators. *Journal of Educational Administration* 18(2): 245–53.

Gilligan, C. (1982). *In a different voice.* Cambridge, Mass.: Harvard University.

Gips, C.J.; Navin, S.; Branch, D.; and Nutter, N. (1984, October). *Can women bat clean-up, or must they simply do the cleaning? A look at women as organizational team players.* (ERIC Document Reproduction Service No. ED 251 975)

Greenberg, S. (1985, October). "So you want to talk theory?" Paper presented at the annual meeting of the American Educational Research Association Special Interest Group: Research on Women in Education, Boston.

Hanson, M. (1984). Exploration of mixed metaphors in educational administration research. *Issues in Education* 2(3): 167–85.

Harragan, B.L. (1977). *Games mother never taught you.* New York: Warner.

Hennig, M., and Jardim, A. (1977). *The managerial woman.* Garden City, N.Y.: Anchor/Doubleday.

Intriligator, B.A. (1983, April). "In quest of a gender-inclusive theory of leadership: Contributions from research on women leaders in school unions." Paper presented at the annual meeting of the American Educational Research Association, Montreal, Canada.

Lenz, E., and Meyerhoff, B. (1985). *The feminization of America.* Los Angeles: Jeremy P. Tarcher.

Lyons, N. (1983). Two perspectives: On self, relationships and morality. *Harvard Education Review* 53(2): 125–45.

Lyons, N. (1985, October). "Overview: Perspectives on what makes something a moral problem." Paper presented at the annual meeting of the American Educational Research Association Special Interest Group: Reseach on Women in Education, Boston.

Marshall. S.A., and Heller, M. (1983, August). A female leadership style could revolutionize school government. *The American School Board Journal,* pp. 31–32.

Nagle, L.; Gardner, D.W.; Levine, M.; and Wolf, S. (1982, March). "Sexist bias in instructional supervision textbooks." Paper presented at the annual meeting of the American Educational Research Association, New York.

Noddings, N. (1984). *Caring.* Berkeley: University of California Press.

Rutherford, W.L. (1985). School principals as effective leaders. *Phi Delta Kappan* 67(1): 31–34.

Schmuck, P.A.; Butman, L.; and Person, L.R. (1982, March). "Analyzing sex bias in *Planning and Changing.*" Paper presented at the annual meeting of the American Educational Research Association, New York.

Shakeshaft, C., (1986). *Women in Educational Administration.* Beverly Hills, Calif.: Sage Publications.

Shakeshaft, C. and Hanson, M. (1986). Androcentric bias in the *Educational Administration Quarterly. Educational Administration Quarterly* 22(1): 68–92.

Smith, J.K. (1979). *Ella Flagg Young: Portrait of a leader.* Ames, Iowa: Educational Studies Press and the Iowa State University Research Foundation.

Sweeney, J. (1982). Research synthesis on effective school leadership. *Educational Leadership* 39(5): 346–52.

Tietze, I.N.; Shakeshaft, C.; and Davis, B.N. (1981, April). "Sexism in texts in educational administration." Paper presented at the annual meeting of the American Educational Research Association, Los Angeles.

30

An Exemplary Preparation Program: The Cooperative Superintendency Program of the University of Texas at Austin

Leonard A. Valverde, Nolan Estes, Virginia Collier, and Susan Sclafani

The Cooperative Superintendency Program (CSP) was designed in 1972 by representatives of three groups: Texas Superintendents, the Texas Education Agency, and the Department of Educational Administration of the University of Texas at Austin. In the words of Dr. Lawrence D. Haskew, a professor emeritus of the University of Texas at Austin and founder of the program, its mission is "to transform already well-equipped seasoned school administrators into readiness to be superb and leaderly chief executives for public school organizations." To accomplish this mission, the program must identify appropriate candidates and prepare them academically and clinically to assume leadership roles.

Current enrollment (1986) in the program is fifteen students. Of these, fourteen are full-time students. One has obtained a position as a practicing superintendent and is working on his dissertation.

The faculty of the Department of Educational Administration at the University of Texas includes thirteen full-time professors and four part-time instructors. All of the part-time faculty members hold doctoral degrees and are experienced public school administrators with the exception of the practicing attorney, who conducts school law classes. One faculty member is currently on leave. In addition, two retired faculty members regularly come to the campus and are available to assist students.

The Management Systems Component

Instructional Capability

The instructional capability of the Department of Educational Administration is one of the major strengths of the program. In addition to their active publishing records, the professors within the department provide consultant services to the school districts, community colleges, state agencies, and regional educational service centers within the state and across the country. This consultation allows them to monitor the pulse of American education and keep their courses current and relevant. The Department augments the strength of its program by bringing in successful practitioners as visiting scholars. These practitioners spend their time with graduate students, sharing the benefits of their experiences in the field and reinforcing the significance of the content of the academic program. During the 1985–86 school year visiting scholars included Carl Candoli, superintendent of Fort Worth Independent School District (ISD); John Ellis, superintendent of Austin ISD; Walter Marks, superintendent of Lake Travis ISD; Billy Reagan, superintendent of Houston ISD: Victor Rodriquez, superintendent of San Antonio ISD; Bill Early, former superintendent of Flint, Michigan, and currently professor at Corpus Christi State University; the late Paul Salmon, former American Association of School Administrators (AASA) executive director; June Gabler, president-elect of AASA; Ruth Love, former superintendent of Chicago ISD; Norman Hall, past president of AASA; and Richard Hill of the University of North Dakota among others.

Program Design

CSP was designed to provide a balance of clinical experiences, both on and off campus, and intense intellectual development, both on the job at the Texas Education Agency (TEA) and in academic courses. Instructional situations regularly include simulations, case studies, small and large group activities, and seminar responsibilities. Opportunities to participate in simulations of future situations such as superintendent/board interviews are also provided. The program is designed to culminate in a doctorate (Ph.D.) in educational administration.

Resource Capability

The University of Texas and TEA combine to provide resources that far exceed those of the typical preparation program. The Perry Castenada Library, a research facility on the campus, is the tenth largest academic libary in the nation. In addition, the TEA provides a research staff, an educational library on key issues, and access to the ERIC data base. Computer centers for analysis of research data are provided by both institutions. An additional resource of particular importance to graduate students is the vast amount of data on school districts available through TEA's Division of Research and Development.

Program Evaluation and Assessment Capability

At the end of each cycle, participating CSP fellows are asked to respond to a questionnaire concerning the effectiveness of the program. Responses are requested in regard to management, content, and clinical components of the program. In addition, a structured evaluation of the program by practitioners and professors of education was planned after the tenth year.

This planned evaluation was conducted during 1985–86, the first year of the program for the sixth cycle, by Patrick Forsyth, executive director of the University Council for Educational Administration, and Richard Hill, a professor of educational administration at the University of South Dakota. The study focused on the perceptions of current fellows and was augmented by perceptions of a sample of past fellows. The study design required the current fellows to complete a questionnaire and participate in a group interview. The questionnaire asked the fellows to rate the quality of the preparation they were receiving in the competencies and related tasks they were likely to encounter as school superintendents. In addition, current fellows and a sample of former fellows were interviewed to determine whether certain criteria stated for the program had in fact been achieved. The conclusions derived from this study are contained in *An Evaluation of the University of Texas Cooperative Superintendency Program*, June 1986, and are available from the Department of Educational Administration, University of Texas at Austin. The report states:

> The Texas Cooperative Superintendency Program is clearly successful, since its aim is to "secure Fellows with outstanding professional readiness . . . and then outfit them for high-level leadership positions in the school systems of Texas . . . " Program records document the achievement of that goal. Fellows from the first

five cycles pursue occupations of the variety and importance envisioned; more-over, fellows in the current cycle evidence the capacity and commitment to augment the record already established. [P. 34]

The evaluators found the design of the program to be exemplary and "to be fulfilling an important public purpose in a creative and productive manner" (p. 38). Still, as in any vital program, suggestions can be and were made concerning areas where the program leaders "might do what you are trying to do better" (p. 35). Improvements in these areas are currently being planned by the department faculty and the current cycle of fellows. It is anticipated that the final result will be a program that continues to achieve its goals while better meeting the individual needs of the fellows.

Content Component

Student Programs of Study

The academic content component is well planned for each student. The Department of Educational Administration provides a broad-based curriculum with courses taught in organizational management theory, instructional leadership, staff relations and management, resource management and allocation, special needs populations, and research and analysis skills. Programs are designed to encompass appropriate offerings from the Department of Special Education, School of Business and Management, LBJ School of Public Affairs, Department of Curriculum and Instruction, as well as other departments in the university. Articulation between departments results in the inclusion of courses in collective bargaining, ethics, and productivity and efficiency that are not included in the usual educational administrative program.

CSP Fellows work with professor-mentors to plan appropriate individual study programs. In addition, group planning sessions are held to address those common goals such as earning superintendency certification and a doctorate. The major focus is to ensure a broad background based on analysis of the fellow's strengths and weaknesses. A secondary focus is the opportunity to work with a variety of faculty before choosing a research topic and committee.

Clinical Components

Planning

The CSP includes both campus-based and field-based experiences. The university professor-coordinator and members of the Advisory Council of

Superintendents plan the specific experiences for each cycle during the first year. During the second year, the fellows themselves plan for those experiences they feel will fulfill the needs of the group. They are guided and assisted by the program director.

Campus-based Experiences

Classroom. The campus-based clinical experiences include a six-hour class designed with input from the CSP Fellows. This class addresses the more practical components of the superintendency. All sessions are conducted by a combination of university professors and practicing professionals. Topics include facilities planning, politics, hiring practices, methods for facilitating change, and superintendency-school board relations. Each class session begins with a discussion of the *Wall Street Journal*, led by students who identify national issues with implications for education.

In addition, classroom experiences are enhanced by the Visiting Scholars Program maintained by the Department of Educational Administration. Professionals of note from other universities and the field are invited to spend six weeks at the university. During this time, they are available to work with students and lecture to classes. This program assures that new thoughts and ideas are constantly being presented to stimulate both the students and the faculty.

Conferences. A second campus-based experience involves the planning of at least six conferences each year. These conferences draw speakers from across the nation as well as participants from across the state. The organization and execution of these conferences by students strengthens their planning skills and provides fellows with further opportunities to interact with key professionals. Included are the Executive Development Seminar, Women School Executives Leadership Conference, Technology Conference, and Educational Facilities Conference.

Superintendency Searches and Simulations. Whenever possible, fellows are involved in superintendency searches being conducted for local districts by professors at the university. Involvement in these searches provides concrete experience in the procedures involved in obtaining a position as a school superintendent. To prepare fellows for the interview process, simulations of interviews between school boards and superintendency candidates are conducted, videotaped, and critiqued by volunteers from the superintendency and school boards.

Field Experiences

Job Related. The backbone of the field experiences in the CSP is a two-year internship at the Texas Education Agency at a salary of approximately $25,000 for each year of the two-year cycle. This paid internship affords rich opportunities to acquire advanced skills and insights. In order to assist fellows in capitalizing on work-assignment opportunities, a TEA Associate or Deputy Commissioner and a supervising professor work closely with each fellow. Internship assignments provide opportunities to do laboratory work in local school districts and education service centers as well as to assist in the development and implementation of policy at the state level. All fellows participate in state accreditation visits to local districts, which afford first-hand study of district operations. These visits involve field-based study of district operations, interviews with district staff, and concluding reports to superintendents and school boards.

Site Visits. In addition to the field experiences provided in the internship, the CSP fellows participate in site visits to dynamic school districts of varying sizes and geographic locations. Private sessions with the superintendent, key members of the central-office staff, and selected board members are combined with campus visitations and attendance at school board meetings to provide a comprehensive picture of the district being studied. Members of the Advisory Council of Superintendents also host the fellows in their school systems, serve as mentors, lecture on administrative techniques and procedures, and assist in the placement of the fellows at the end of the program.

Superintendent Mentors. Each CSP fellow is assigned a practicing superintendent as a mentor. At some point during the program, the fellow spends a day shadowing this mentor in order to gain first-hand knowledge of the job of the superintendent. This activity provides opportunities for asking questions and discussing the basis for actions observed.

Professional Meetings. Further contact with district-level administrators is facilitated through attendance at professional meetings. The educational administration department partially funds attendance at the joint meeting of the Texas Association of School Boards and the Texas Association of School Administrators and the national meeting of the American Association of School Administrators each year. Attendance at these meetings is enhanced by the hospitality suites that the educational administration department provides for the fellows. Fellows are able to meet and interact with superintendents, central-office personnel, and board members from across the state and nation while serving as hosts in the suites.

Professional and Renewal Component

Professorial Staff

The professorial staff of the Educational Administration Department is represented in the National Conference of Professors of Educational Administration, the University Council for Educational Administration, and the American Educational Research Association. In addition, one professor has a fellowship from the Kellogg Foundation to study international education in urban areas.

Students

Selection. The CSP fellows are selected through a carefully designed assessment procedure. Since the program is highly competitive, the first part of the assessment selects the best thirty candidates of the more than one hundred applicants for each two-year cycle. This is done through evaluation of candidacy portfolios containing self-presentations, transcripts, resumes, references, University of Texas graduate school admittance, and samples of papers or projects done by the candidates. The thirty finalists are invited to a two-day assessment seminar in which they participate in written exams of reasoning ability and personality, in-basket activities, leaderless group discussions, individual verbal quizzes, knowledge-seeking and personal interviews, oral presentations, and simulations of evaluation conferencing.

Assessors include representatives from school district administrators and board members, the Texas Education Agency, professional educational organizations, and the University of Texas at Austin. They analyze each candidate's performance on the skills dimensions identified by the National Association for Secondary School Principals Assessment Center. These skills include the ability to plan and organize work, work with and lead others, analyze problems and make decisions, and communicate orally and in writing. The final choice of twelve to fourteen candidates is made by representatives of the three cooperating groups: the Advisory Council of Superintendents, the Texas Education Agency, and the Department of Educational Administration.

Involvement. The CSP fellows are participating members in the American Association of School Administrators, and their attendance at the national meetings of this group is partially funded by the educational administration department each year. Individual fellows are also members of the National Association for Elementary School Principals, the National Association for Secondary School Principals, Phi Delta Kappa, and the Association for

Supervision and Curriculum Development. All of these organizations have state affiliates that the fellows are encouraged to join. The Texas Association of School Boards is very supportive of the CSP program and provides valuable opportunities for the fellows to renew professionally through attendance at meetings sponsored by the organization.

Evidence of Excellence

Student Placement

In the first five cycles of the CSP, fifty-three individuals were selected and all completed the program. Of these, forty-two completed doctorates. Fellows have assumed the following key leadership positions:

— Five of the eight largest districts in the state
— Two of the five deputy commissioner's offices in the Texas Education Agency
— Two of the four largest state professional organizations
— Thirty of the larger school districts in Texas

Superintendencies in Texas are currently held by twenty-one former fellows (two are completing the sixth cycle); eleven are assistant or deputy superintendents; nine are central-office administrators; two are educational service center directors; two are deputy commissioners in the state department of education; three are principals; three hold executive positions with state professional organizations; one is on the governor's staff; one is the head of a college department of education; one is employed by the Job Corps; and one has established a private consulting firm.

Fellows have been recognized as recipients of numerous local, regional, state, and national awards; some of the more prestigious are:

National
National Advisory Committee on the Proper Education of Athletes
Commissioner on the Education Commission of the States
Selected by the *Executive Educator* as one of the "100 Educators to Watch" in the nation — two past fellows
Given an Award of Honor by the National School Public Relations Association
Recognized for one of two outstanding dissertations in the nation by the National Conference of Professors of Educational Administration
Forrest E. Conner Scholarship for Graduate Study in School Administration
S.D.Shankland Scholar for Graduate Study in School Administration (current fellow)

State

Texas Superintendent of the Year, Regional Finalist — three past fellows

Texas State Superintendent of the Year Finalist for 1985–86

Intergovernmental Relations Commission for the State of Texas

President's Award from the Texas Association of Compensatory Educators

Governor's Advisory Committee on Education

Outstanding Service Award —Texas Association of Secondary School Principals

Chosen for the Governor's Executive Development Program

Life Memberships presented by Texas Parent-Teachers Association

Local

Honorable Mention for the Outstanding Dissertation Award in the Social Sciences Division, the University of Texas at Austin

Dean Karl Brent Award as Distinguished Alumnae of the College of Education, the University of Texas at Austin

William Spurgeon III Award for the City of San Antonio, Boy Scouts of America

Distinguished Lecture Series, University of Houston

Honorable Mention for the Outstanding Dissertation Award in the Social Science Division, the University of Texas in Austin

SECTION VI

International Perspectives

The papers in this section compare the practice of administration in the United States with that in other countries. These comparisons provoke us to ask sometimes unasked questions, two of which are: "Why is it that our practices have seemed so difficult to change when in many other countries of the world quite different practices prevail?" and, "What practices in other parts of the world appear to make more sense than those in this country?"

Judith Chapman extends the debate to a current reform in Australia, which requires school principals to broaden substantially the decision making in a school. In creating School Councils, the Australians are testing many of the implications of the Commission's recommendations.

The papers by Michael Murphy and Paul Pohland are a pair. Murphy examines administrative practice in Western Europe and finds it distinct from practice in the United States. In Western Europe he finds less central regulation of local schools, more collegiality among teachers and administrators at the school sites, and more accountability by administrators to both teachers and parents. In these countries school principals act as chairpersons or executive directors rather than as supervisors, which is a definition of U.S. principals. Murphy's descriptions of principals' work in Western Europe is similar to what has been described elsewhere in this volume as desirable for U.S. principals.

Pohland's paper is an extensive discussion of administrator preparation in the United Kingdom. Reflecting the different work roles described by Murphy, preparation programs are quite different from those in the United States. Pohland distinguishes between preparation in the United States and in the United Kingdom on several dimensions, such as program emphasis, learning and teaching modes, relationships between universities and schools, assessment of student performance, and the bases of legitimation. Preparation in the United Kingdom appears to resemble much of what is called for by the Commission.

31

A New Conception of the Principalship: Decentralization, Devolution, and the Administration of Australian Schools

Judith Chapman

Introduction

Although some United States school districts have experimented with school-site management, no American state has undertaken as broad and ambitious an initiative in the decentralization of administrative arrangements and the devolution of authority to the school level as has occurred in the state of Victoria, Australia. Indeed, the centralizing thrust of many American states' plans for excellence have actually reduced discretion at the local school level. This trend seems to disregard what has been learned about the importance of a strong sense of community and commitment among school staff members in the design and implementation of successful reform and the creation of effective schools. Given the widespread concern for school effectiveness, the Victorian venture in Australia is of particular interest because it seeks school improvement through democratic, school-based management, with extensive community and staff involvement that necessitates a revised management role for principals.

Background

The basic administrative structure of education in Victoria established under the "free, compulsory, and secular" Education Act of 1872 created a highly centralized state system in which all major functions were under the supervision of officers of the Education Department, located in Melbourne, the state capital. All major decisions, both professional and managerial, were made by senior officers of the Education Department. The Education Department prescribed curriculum, enrollment procedures, and school organization. Schools were evaluated annually by inspectors of the Department. The principal acted as an agent of the Department, implementing policies and decisions made by officials in the central office.

In the mid 1970s, recognizing that the traditional system could no longer provide effective administration for a rapidly expanding and increasingly complex system of over 2,000 schools, it became the Liberal (Conservative) government's policy to decentralize administrative arrangements. The process had two distinct dimensions. One was associated with the creating of regional directorates and the other with the granting of increased autonomy to school principals. "The central authority, the regional directors and the school principals now share the total decision-making arena, which hitherto was the sole preserve of the central authority" (Moore, 1975).

Financial responsibility was extended to principals. Principals became responsible for budgeting and accounting for equipment, furniture, and fuel. They became responsible for determining staffing needs for instruction, support services, and administration. The withdrawal of the Board of Secondary Inspectors resulted in principals' becoming responsible for the maintenance of staff discipline, reporting on unsatisfactory teachers, and establishing and maintaining school standards. The implementation of procedures for teacher assessment and promotion also became more direct tasks for the principal.

In 1976 the Education (School Councils) Act added another dimension to the principalship. The Act, which reformed the composition and function of School Councils, reflected a new direction in government policy—the devolution of authority from the bureaucracy of the Education Department to the community of the school.

The sustained evolutionary change that marked the decade of the 1970s altered considerably the principal's role; however, this role was to undergo even more significant change in the decade to follow. In May 1979 the Minister of Education announced a major review of education. In 1980 this review culminated in the publication of *White Paper on Strategies and Structures for Education in Victorian Government* Schools (1980). A management consultant firm was retained to develop a detailed plan for the implementation of the White Paper. Their report (the PA Report) provided the blueprint for the work of an Implementation Task Force.

In the remainder of 1981 and first part of 1982 there were massive structural changes at the central and regional levels of the Education Department. In the midst of these changes came a further dramatic change. In the election of 1982 the Liberal government was toppled from power after ruling Victoria for twenty-seven years. The new Labor government halted further implementation of the PA Report and undertook a Ministerial Review of Education. The results of that review were published in a series of Ministerial Papers in which the new government announced its intention to go well beyond the plan of the Liberal government to devolve authority. It established as a major objective a shift in the focus of education to the school level. Embodied in the Ministerial Papers was the principle that all sections of the school community should work as partners in the interests of school and students. Particular emphasis was placed upon:

— general devolution of authority and responsibility to the school community
— collaborative decision-making processes
— a responsive bureaucracy, with the main function of serving and assisting schools
— effectiveness of educational outcomes
— the active redress of disadvantage and discrimination

In December 1983 the State Minister of Education released a statement on the role of principals. While reiterating the central role played by principals in the life and work of the school, the statement emphasized that "this important leadership function is to be exercised in cooperation with the School Council and the staff of the school." In the same year, the Education Act was amended to provide that the "the School Council shall determine the general education policy of the school within guidelines issued by the Minister." Contemporaneously, the changes were made to the composition of School Councils to provide for a higher proportion of teacher representation. These amendments placed a new emphasis on local responsibility and shared decision making on educational policy matters.

Within each school administrative committees were established to offer advice to the principal on the implementation of the Industrial Agreement (union contract) and on general operations. While principals retained the right of veto on the administrative committees, reasons were to be given for any advice that was disregarded.

Implications of Decentralization and Devolution for the Principal's Power and Authority

In the traditional, bureaucratic system, considerable power and authority resided in the position of school principal. This legal authority and its concomitant regulatory power was considerably eroded as a result of decentralization and devolution. The most extreme response has been to interpret the decreasing importance attached to legal authority as a complete diminution of the principal's power. While clearly this is not the case, the situation for principals is a paradoxical one. Though principals have become more visible and accountable to their local community, they remain the Education Department's most senior officer in the school. This dual responsibility carries with it considerable role ambiguity.

On the issue of accountability, the more traditional principals continue to defer to the legal authority of the Department, steadfastly guarding their claim to "ultimate responsibility" in the school; others ask, Who is the master to be? The confusion of principals confronting this issue is exacerbated when they perceive their councils and members of their teaching staff as inexperienced and uninformed, and when they find the Education Department transformed by new administrative arrangements and by changed personnel who are unknown and often unable or unprepared to offer the support provided in the past. The sense of isolation engendered by this situation becomes particularly acute on legally contentious issues or on problems that may involve industrial action.

Decision Making

On the one hand, the expanded role of school councils, the establishment of administrative committees, and the general expectation that relevant interest groups will be consulted on all issues have operated to significantly limit the principals' decision-making discretion. On the other hand, principals' decision-making arena has been expanded as they are asked to make decisions in response to new questions. In answering these questions, however, principals are required to work with new groups of people, new participants in the decision-making process. Often these new decision makers have different values from those of principals and from those of people with whom principals interacted in the past. Frequently, principals find themselves implementing decisions they would not have made themselves.

Having been schooled in a tradition where principals were expected to be the prime decision makers, some principals do not possess the skills to enable them to adapt to the new management style; for many, "crisis management" is substituting for professional development. While on-site learning is appropriate for some tasks, it is not sufficient for the thorough development of an overall philosophy or approach.

Poorly prepared to facilitate participative decision making, some principals encounter problems in managing the conflict that may arise when attempts at achieving the desired consensus fail. In particular, difficulties in schools arise when those in the minority will not accept the majority decision.

Diminished authority and external support make it harder for the principal to deal with such situations. In addition, principals are often encountering difficulty in balancing collaboration with their supervisory duties.

Finally, principals are also finding that participative decision making simply takes more time. Contributing to the problem, however, is the widely held belief that consultation and discussion must take place on all matters.

On a more positive note, however, some principals do welcome collaboration, particularly the opportunity it brings for greater commitment and a reduction in the "them-us" mentality often held by administrators and staff.

Administrative Complexity

A multifaceted system of education where resources and services are allocated from either centre or region, and where authority resides with both the official offices of the Department and the community of the school offers considerable complexity for the principal.

Rather than facilitating the provision of services to schools, the restructured regions are frequently considered by principals to be impediments to effective school management—putting another bureaucratic step in the process between the school and the centre.

The lack of clarity regarding roles and responsibilities in the new structure results in principals' experiencing difficulties when seeking authoritative answers from regional personnel. The problems appear to be particularly acute when responses are sought to other than routine problems.

Frustrations associated with the lack of clarity in responsibilities are compounded when principals are requested to duplicate effort in response to similar requests from both centre and region. Adding to these competing demands are the increased demands of the community. The danger, of course, is that principals begin running to the behest of all sorts of agencies external to the school.

Internally, the plethora of committees also contributes to organizational complexity. Principals must form and liaise with consultative groups, not only attending to the interpersonal dynamics that such intense interaction produces, but also ensuring that in the overall organizational design overlapping functions are avoided and lines of communication are clear.

Teaching Personnel

Devolution, with its associated redistribution of power, would appear to have its most positive impact upon the morale of the younger and more politically active staff. These staff report that they are increasingly more interested and centered on the school and more committed to its success; more active and positive in their attitudes to the broadened range of professional experiences now available; more confident in their ability to exercise influence in the school through general consultation and through the official bodies of the school council and the administrative committee.

Some teachers, however, find the additional responsibilities associated with decentralization and devolution a heavy burden. The additional workload has meant that teachers must spend many more hours in work-related activities, and much of this work is done after school hours. This would appear to be a significant problem, particularly given the additional demands placed on them during the day. Teachers seem especially frustrated when coping with fragmented, nonteaching duties, especially the amount of clerical and general organizational work involved.

Some principals are now encountering some difficulty in getting people to join committees because many teachers are overloaded with committee responsibilities. In these instances, the less able are perceived as obtaining committee membership by default.

Perhaps even more dangerous to the long-term success of school-site management, however, is the cynicism that excessive work demands can create. In such an environment the principal must sustain morale across all levels of staff, maintaining consultation but at the same time ensuring that staff are not overburdened by administrative concerns.

The Instructional Program

Aside from the issues of staff management noted previously, perhaps the major problem posed for the principal by decentralization and devolution is its tendency to divert human resources from the main aim of the school—the teaching and learning process—to administration. While committee work may offer an escape route for people who do not actually want to be in the classroom, for many dedicated teachers these additional responsibilities are a disruption to what they see as their major professional task.

The difficulty for the principal is that while on the one hand devolution diminishes the teaching resource of the school, on the other hand it makes the principal and the school more accountable to a local community, which will judge the school by the quality of its educational product.

It remains to be seen whether the disruptions to teaching can be effectively counterbalanced by the improvement in educational quality that the policymakers, as part of their rationale for decentralization and devolution, argued would result.

School Councils

As a result of devolution, parent members of the councils report that schools are becoming broader in their thinking, more open and responsive to parents, and more in touch with community concerns. The increased voluntary workload associated with being a school councillor is, however, a frequent cause for concern. As parent councillors normally have other work commitments, the principal is often left with assuming responsibility for what is rightfully within the council's domain.

Although as yet untested, there is a fear among some of the more progressive principals that the expanded role of the council in the development of educational policy will, in fact, be a force for conservatism in the curriculum.

Much, however, depends on the nature of the school community. Possession of "expert" knowledge, access to information about the school and the functioning of the Education Department, confidence in meeting procedures, and fluency in the English language are clearly among the most powerful bases for influence on council. Regrettably, these sources of influence are not equally distributed among council members or across councils.

Lack of expertise among some parents contributes to their feeling of being overwhelmed by the "expert" knowledge of the professional educators. The increase in the proportion of teacher representatives on the councils and the tendency for teachers to gain council membership because they are also parents increases the problem.

Different Nature of Professional Life

Decentralization and devolution have dramatically altered the nature of the principal's professional life. Principals must spend more time out of the school attending regional meetings and sitting on consultative committees.

Principals, too, are now forced to assume a more public role, interacting with people in the wider community and forging links between the school and its environments.

While such activities contribute to a more varied and fragmented professional life than experienced by principals in the past, it may also be that they are contributing to a greater incidence of stress.

Discussion

The problems encountered by principals in Victoria as a result of increased school-site management have in large measure a historical basis. For one hundred years the Victorian Education Department operated strictly on the principles of a centralized bureaucracy. Principals had been schooled in this tradition; they had undertaken their initial teacher training and received their early professional experience within this context.

The decade of the 1970s heralded the first major shift to a more decentralized system. With virtually no additional preparation or training, principals were directed to "run their own schools." Heavily reliant on Departmental support, principals came to expect to be the prime decision makers and ultimate sources of authority in schools. With varying degrees of success they adjusted to this new role.

The years 1981 through 1984 saw two successive governments conduct major reassessments of the educational system. Poised to implement its policy of decentralization and devolution at the school level and having already effected changes at the centre and region, the Liberal Party was ousted after twenty-seven years of state government. Principals, many of whom had been actively involved in discussions that had contributed to the Liberal government's proposals, were confronted with a new Labor government that held vastly different values from those of its predecessor.

In trying to overcome what one high-level departmental administrator has called "over one hundred years of the colonial management mentality of the British Empire and East India Company," the Labor government faced the problem that there was no strongly articulated majority sentiment for sweeping devolution. Instead, support came mainly from Labor Party intellectuals and state-level teachers' union and leaders of parents' organizations. At the grass roots, both teachers and parents seemed either ambivalent or only mildly supportive. Of course, an enormous amount of momentum is needed to change any system of more than 2,000 schools and 40,000 teachers. Changed administrative arrangements require that an entirely new communication network be established. The new "appropriate" people must be identified, and working relationships must be built up. New values require that the heritage, the folklore, the "understandings" of people in the system be reassessed; this within a context in which many people are experiencing personal and professional threat and insecurity.

Notwithstanding the history of Victorian education and the problems associated with the implementation of any systemwide change, much of the confusion and anxiety associated with decentralization and devolution in Victoria must be directly attributed to the nature of the implementation process.

First, the implementation of the plan suffered from a gross neglect of the need for retraining and in-service activities designed to foster the learning of the new attitudes and roles that were fundamental to the new style of management that was mandated. Second, there was insufficient provision of financial support. If you want something to be cost effective you centralize, you do not decentralize. Third, the entire process took place with considerable haste. Moreover, sources of power and resources that had been evident under the traditional bureaucratic arrangements were not precisely transformed or delegated. Principals could no longer act with the same certainty as they had in the past. Finally, the advantages of devolution were at no time communicated to principals in sufficient detail to enable them to fully understand and accept the policy. Principals' fear of the new and unexplored were never significantly allayed.

Conclusion

Those who have studied administrative reorganizations agree that such efforts rarely achieve the usual goals of increased efficiency, effectiveness, or responsiveness (Kaufman, 1977; March and Olsen, 1983; Rourke, 1984). Herbert Kaufman (1977), one of the most astute students of bureaucracy, provides perhaps a more realistic standard against which to judge the success of reorganization ventures: "The consequences of reorganization are frequently profound. But the profound determinable consequences do not lie in the engineering realm of efficiency, simplicity, size, and cost of government. Rather the real payoffs are measured in terms of influence, policy, and communication" (pp. 403, 405–06).

It is clear that substantial change in influence has occurred in Victoria. Many relationships have been altered and many people have been forced to play new roles. This is no more evident than in the new conception of the principalship.

Within a context of economic restraint and fewer resources, the principal must work with new values, new decision makers, and a new set of management decisions and responsibilities. Viewing oneself as the authority figure, supported and at times protected by departmental rules and regulations, is no longer the prerogative of the principal. Instead, the principal must be a coordinator of a number of people who represent different interest groups among the school community; together with the principal these representatives will determine the direction the school is to follow.

Regarding the redistribution of power in Victoria, there are also discernible shifts in policy in the directions favored by the reorganization designers. Consistent with the thrust of the Ministerial Papers (1983), people are being forced to think about the nature of the educational program at the school level. As members of the school community are encouraged to pay more attention to curriculum and instruction, the government's goal of school improvement stands a better chance of being achieved.

Reorganization also provides the opportunity for governments to communicate and advance their priorities and values. Indeed, it has been argued that reorganizations often are long-run successes, even if short-term failures, precisely because of the power of their rhetoric and symbols to change the climate of opinion over time. Already there has been tremendous change in the content and semantics of discourse about educational administration and school-community relations in Victoria. It is in this respect that the chief legacy of the Victorian venture is likely to be found. By changing language and thinking about administration and participation in government schools, devolution may in time produce significant change in practice.

While the Victorian experience shows, once again, that one cannot mandate new approaches, provide little by way of training and support, and expect to achieve quick results, it nevertheless suggests the extent to which thinking and ultimately practice can be redirected by the rhetoric and symbols of forceful leadership.

References

Kaufman, H. (1977). Reflections on administrative reorganization. In Joseph A. Pechamn (Ed.), *Setting national priorities: The 1978 budget*. Washington, D.C.: The Brookings Institution.

March, J.E., and Olsen, J.P. (1983, June). Organizing political life: What administrative re-organization tell us about government. *American Political Science Review* 22: 281–96.

Ministerial Paper No. 1. (1983). *Decision making in Victorian education*. Issued by the Minister of Education, Melbourne, Victoria.

Moore, T.J. (1975). Administration in the late 1970's. Proceedings of a seminar for principal and senior teachers. Continuing Education Centre, Wangaratta, Victoria, Australia, Series 3, No. 1, *Educational Administrator*, p. 26.

Rourke, F.E. (1984). *Bureacracy, politics and public policy*, 3rd ed. Boston: Little, Brown and Company.

White paper on strategies and structures for education in Victorian Government Schools. (1980). Melbourne: F.D. Atkinson, Government Printer.

32

Alternatives for Educational Administration: Lessons from Abroad

Michael J. Murphy

As the global village shrinks and markets become more international, nations' planners look to their schools as a vehicle to enhance their country's competitive position. In a recent report the Carnegie Forum on Education and the Economy made it clear that education may be the field in which the economic game is won or lost.

Students from American schools do not seem to fare well in comparisons of educational attainment among developed nations. Recently it has been shown that Japanese and Taiwanese students outperform their American counterparts in science and mathematics. And in most subjects, European students also outperform American students.

These comparisons have led to a number of papers on educational methods in European and Far Eastern nations. Attempts have been made to uncover the secret of Japanese (or Swedish or Swiss or . . .) education so that adjustments might be made in American schooling. Although these analyses address, with varying degrees of sophistication, issues of schooling practices, very little attention has been given to the role of school administrators. Nations differ markedly in how school administrators are trained and selected and in the nature of their work within the school. If administrators are at all instrumental to school performance, and there is reason to believe they are, then it is prudent to inspect the way European schools organize administrative functions and define administrative roles.

European and Far Eastern administrative arrangements in schools offer a series of natural experiments to examine. If these natural experiments show that certain arrangements relate to school performance, our choices will be better informed. If administrative arrangements have no apparent meaning to school outcomes, we can direct our energies to other aspects of schooling.

In this paper, I will highlight some of the looming forces for change in administrative roles. I will contrast school administrative arrangements in the United States with some of the European models that I know best, and try to organize the options for clarity and criticism. Finally, I will relate European models to reform efforts in the United States. This analysis will be brief and, unfortunately, incomplete. Perhaps it will serve to introduce a new element in the debate and spur interest in examining more closely other nations' natural experiments in school administration.

Views of School Administration in the United States

In recent years there has been considerable interest in describing what administrators do (Mintzburg, 1973; March, 1974). These studies have shed light on the priorities and activities in the daily work of school managers and have led us to rethink some of our training priorities and methods. This research has shown that much of administrators' work is routine; interactions are brief and time spent on any topic is very limited. School principals appear to spend much of their time attending to non-instruction-related duties. Work days are long and hectic. A large portion of the day is spent in meetings called by others. Such descriptions of administrators' work all portray how a person might behave in a job that has certain characteristics. For example, jobs in school administration are hierarchical, and the work of administrators is to make a bureaucracy work (March, 1978)

But this pattern of organization masks other alternatives, other ways that school administrators might organize their work, and their jobs. It may be that we have been seduced by the recent descriptions to think that we know not only what administrators do, but what they must do. We attack the training design question accordingly. March, Mintzburg, and others have been captives of this parochial thinking about administration in schools, that is, what it is it must be.

Forces for Change in School Administrative Practice

Yet there are reasons to think that administrative jobs in education may change in the next decade. Training designs we proffer now will affect programs in the next decade, and if we model training after an obsolete job, the training we offer will be irrelevant or contradictory.

We should ask: Is what we expect administrators to do appropriate? and, Have we got the job right? These are crucial questions, for the most elegant, complete training program designed to meet the wrong ends is frivolous—it is a waste of talent and doomed to failure.

I submit that the following are reasons to expect that administrative work in schools will change during the next ten to fifteen years.

1. *Lack of confidence in schools.* The National Commission on Excellence in Education charged that American schools are mediocre and endanger the nation's future, a view apparently widely shared. Unless they can deflect blame, administrators will inevitably be characterized as managers of mediocrity, and changes will be demanded.

2. *Teachers as a policy force.* Education policymakers are beginning to listen to teachers and to respond to the problems they describe.[1] In these interactions teachers usually do not speak favorably about school administrators. Frequently they complain about administrative overburdens, lack of administrative support, and decisional deprivation.

3. *Changing views of teaching work.* There is much talk now about empowering teachers. The Commons Commission in California, the Carnegie Forum on Education and the Economy, the Holmes Group, and the National Governors' Association have all called for the professionalization of teaching. Professionalization, if pursued, will inevitably alter administrative roles (Mitchell and Kerchner, 1983).

4. *Trend toward school autonomy.* Paralleling the call for professionalization are recommendations for deregulation and increased school autonomy. Under these recommendations American schools would be freed of much state and district regulation and empowered to determine program and instructional approaches.

5. *Awareness of European and Far Eastern models.* School administrators in other nations' schools appear to function quite differently from American school administrators. As these differences are examined, policymakers may well become convinced that there are other workable administrative systems that may be applied in U.S. schools.

Alternative Models of Administrative Work

— Suppose principals could be appointed only with the advice and consent of teachers—or suppose principals were elected by their staff for a fixed term, say four years.

---

[1] The "Talks with Teachers" program created by the Educational Commission of the States and already implemented in a half dozen states is an example. In "Talks with Teachers" governors meet for an extended period with a group of representative teachers to listen to their descriptions of their work and problems. Administrators are excluded from these conversations.

— Suppose that principals were required to teach—part time at least.
— Suppose that to become a principal, one had to work up through a series of competitive promotional teaching ranks, where each promotion resulted in increased responsibility for school quality.
— Suppose schools became more autonomous—site budgeting became a reality, school councils became a real force in school governance.
— Suppose that district administrators were restricted in their ability to schedule meetings with principals during the school day or that they lost the right to decide staff salaries, assignments, or curriculum.

Sound far fetched? Not really. Many teachers and administrators already work in schools with these characteristics. These schools are not in the United States but in western European nations, and are thought by many to be equal to those in the United States, and by some to be superior.

School policy and organization in Austria, Great Britain, Holland, Spain, or Switzerland is important for two reasons. First, as the economic interdependence of nations increases, all sorts of governmental practices will be noticed by people who transfer among multinational workplaces. Sony, Volkswagen, and Philips engineers and managers will send children to American schools and make their comparisons with homeland schools known to neighbors and friends here and abroad. The National Commission on Excellence in Education buttressed its call for a longer instructional year with reference to European and Japanese school years, not to examples in the United States, where school calendars vary little across states. It is likely that we will soon compare educational organization and practice across nations just as we now compare schools in California and New York. For example, when the Utah State Office of Education wanted background on career ladders, they sent a study team to Britain.

A second reason that school policy and organization in other industrialized nations may be important is that comparisons will reveal options we have not seriously considered. For instance, many believe schools must have a strong, full-time manager to be effective. Yet schools in Switzerland and Spain operate effectively with elected leaders who undertake administrative duties in addition to regular teaching duties.

The alternative administrative models have several things in common. One, they demonstrate that a variety of approaches can work. Schools can function quite effectively with vastly different management schemes. Schools can operate without a strong full-time manager. To be sure, adjustments are required to assure quality, but these systems seem to demonstrate that those adjustments can be made, and schools can be operated at a reasonable cost even under a system of compulsory school attendance.

Second, the European approaches all reduce drastically the amount of time administrators spend making a bureaucracy work. Administrators spend far less time in meetings called by someone else, and less time doing routine, often redundant tasks. Schools can be more creative and individual in their decisions about curriculum and instruction. Teachers are more involved in making decisions about teaching, whether it be what textbooks to use or when children are in school.

Third, they alter training demands. It is more difficult to imagine an institutionalized training program for principals who are elected for a fixed term. Like deans and department chairpersons in higher education, little training for the position is sought or received. Principals who arrive at their job successively demonstrating their abilities in a series of in-school leadership posts likewise have different training demands.

Comparative Dimensions of School Administration

Analysis of school administrative practice in Austria, Great Britain, Spain, Switzerland, and the United States suggests that several important differences in schools' contexts are associated with different types of administration. One of these is accountability. In some countries, most notably the United States, school principals are accountable primarily to superintendents and school boards. This is an upward, hierarchical accountability, which may be labeled "bureaucratic." In other nations school principals are most accountable to school patrons or teachers. In these cases principals may be elected by teachers or appointed by a local board of school governors. Parent choice may play a role either as a market reality or through representation in selection processes. It is a constituency accountability, and principals must satisfy local constituents in order to be elected and to remain in office. This form of accountability is here labeled "political market."

Another important dimension appears to lie in the degree to which school decisions are constrained by outside agencies. In some nations governments or local education authorities prescribe syllabi, courses of study, or textbooks. Schools are bound by these requirements, and it may be said that they are externally regulated. In other countries a minimum of directives is given to schools. Staffs are left free to choose curriculum, instructional approaches, staffing patterns, and the like. Schools in these countries may be described as being largely unregulated.

Obviously, schools in all nations are regulated to some extent and they are left considerable discretion in some areas. In reality, there is a continuum from completely regulated to completely unregulated. No nation's schools are at either extreme, but some tend to be more regulated than others. For simplicity of argument, however, the continuum is reduced to two ideal types, regulated and unregulated.

ACCOUNTABILITY

Bureaucratic   Political Market

		Bureaucratic	Political Market
SCHOOL DECISION ENVIRONMENT	Regulated	USA	Austria Switzerland Spain
	Unregulated		Britain*

---

* British secondary schools may be indirectly regulated by the national examinations taken at ages sixteen and eighteen. Popularly referred to as "O" Levels and "A" Levels, these examinations, along with GSE examinations, are taken by about 2/3 of the students completing British secondary schools. They are instrumental to job and college entrance and each examination subject has a prescribed syllabus.

Figure 32–1
Accountability and Decision Regulation in Selected Nations

Schools may be classified according to their type of accountability and decision environment. This classification is shown in Figure 32–1.

Accountability provisions and school decision environment seem to be related to the type of school-site leadership. In countries where bureaucratic accountability is the rule and schools are regulated, administrators inspect teachers' work, implement and enforce regulations, and provide status reports to superiors. In effect, they act as a supervisor of work in the school. Clinical supervision embodies both supervisory and regulatory functions of this role.

Where schools are regulated, but administrators are largely accountable to teachers or parents, the principal's role seems to change dramatically. In these schools principals assume a spokesperson or representative role. They function as chairperson, and their roles are very much like those of the department chairperson in higher-education institutions. These principals usually maintain a teaching interest, often carrying a significant teaching load. They seem to view their primary position as that of a teacher and see their administrative responsibility as a supplementary task for which they receive small compensation. Their motivation is duty to school and colleagues, not career enhancement or monetary gain. Many express relief when they are released from the principal's assignment and allowed to devote their full attention to teaching.

ACCOUNTABILITY

		Bureaucratic	Political Market
SCHOOL	Regulated	Supervisor	Chairperson
DECISION ENVIRONMENT	Unregulated	Manager	Executive Director

Figure 32–2
Accountabilty and Decision Regulation and Site Leadership Types

In unregulated schools where administrators are accountable to parents and teachers, principals behave as executive directors. They provide significant programmatic leadership and embody many of the characteristics of an instructional leader described in the American literature on effective schools. They are like Kingdon's (1984) "policy entrepreneurs." They negotiate with parents and teachers about resources and programs. And they link problems, solutions, and their contituency's sentiments into policy packages and action plans. To be effective they must perceive opportunities and be recognized for their expertness. In Britain they are called "head teachers," and they acquire their position by successive demonstrations of instructional and curricular leadership (Murphy, 1985).

Finally, when accountability is bureaucratic and schools are unregulated, principals can be expected to behave as managers in the spirit of the new industrial management. Attention is given to outcomes rather than means. Managers help formulate school programs that produce desired outcomes. In our sample we have no countries where bureaucratic accountability and an unregulated condition occur simultaneously. It may be that we have not yet explored widely enough, or that there are reasons that this combination is unlikely.

The administrative types are shown in Figure 32–2.

The leadership type in use has obvious implications for the selection, training, and work of building administrators. In systems of bureaucratic accountability, administrators are appointed by superordinates. In systems of political/market accountability they are elected by local constituent groups—parents or teachers. The selection criteria used may well differ between the two accountability types. For instance, superordinates may want a loyal enforcer. Local constituents may want a sympathetic representative who can obtain considerations and facilitate the accomplishment of local goals.

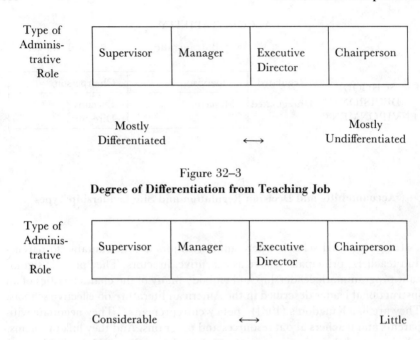

Figure 32–3
Degree of Differentiation from Teaching Job

Considerable   ⟷   Little

Figure 32–4
Specialized Training Required

The relative importance and differentiation of administrative work will vary across types. Supervisors and managers will do work quite different from teachers. Executive directors may teach, and their work, being mostly in instructional and curricular areas, will be more closely aligned with what teachers do. Chairpersons will be teachers first, and will conduct administrative business as time allows. The differentiation of administrative work from teaching work is shown in Figure 32–3.

Training needs seem to reflect both the degree to which administrative work is differentiated, the accountability type, and the decision environment of the school. When administrative work is separate and distinct, and occupies the office holders' attention most of the time, formal training is offered, and is sometimes required. In the United States a school principal must acquire a special license that certifies that he or she has received specialized training and is qualified to assume an administrative position. In Britain formal training is offered, and may help an aspirant win a headship, but it is not required. Training there is also likely to emphasize curriculum and instruction. In Austria, Switzerland, and Spain little specialized training is offered. Figure 32–4 reflects the specialized training demands of various leadership types.

Conclusions

School administration in the United States is undergoing scrutiny. The examination of models of administration in other countries enables us to enlarge our perspective. Although this analysis is an initial one, it does suggest that we might expect administrative roles to change as policy affecting schools is changed. If policymakers adopt the views of the Carnegie Forum on Education and the Economy, or of the National Governors' Association or the National Commission on Excellence in Educational Administration, and move to deregulate schools and make administrators more accountable to parent or teacher contituencies, administrative roles are likely to change. As these roles change, so will the need for training.

References

Kingdon, J.W. (1984). *Agendas, alternatives, and public policies*, pp. 188–93. Boston: Little, Brown and Company.

March, J.G. (1974). Analytical skills and the university training of educational administrators. The 1973 Walter D. Cocking Lecture in Educational Administration. In J.D. Herring and R.E. Klimes (Eds.), *Walter D. Cocking lectures: The NCPEA series of prominent papers in educational administration*, pp. 93–161. Berrien Springs, Mich.: Center for Studies and Services in Education, Andrews University.

March, J. (1978). American public school administration: A short analysis. *School Review* 86 (Feb.): 218–47.

Mintzberg, H. (1973). *The nature of managerial work*. New York: Harper and Row.

Mitchell, D.E., and Kerchner, C.T. (1983). Labor relations and teacher policy. In Lee S. Schulman and Gary Sykes (Eds.), *Handbook of teaching and policy*, pp. 214–38. New York: Longman.

Murphy, M.J. (1985). *Teacher career ladders in Britain: A study of their structure and impact*. Salt Lake City: University Council for Educational Administration, Center for Personnel Law and Employment Relations in Education.

33

The Return of the Mayflower: British Alternatives to American Practice

Paul A. Pohland

Introduction

One of the predictable manifestations of the current school reform movement is the resurgence of interest in administrator preparation programs. Such interest is signaled in "state-of-the-art" reviews, (Pitner, 1982), in scholarly attempts to predict future demands (University Council for Educational Administration, 1983–1984), in the preparation of training guidelines and proposals by professional organizations (Hoyle, 1975, 1986), in revised certification requirements, and in the search for alternatives to existing pre- and in-service training models (March, 1976). In short, the field of educational administration is once again in a state of ferment.

Ferment is not altogether a bad thing. While it may be discomfiting, it also provides a legitimate opportunity to examine alternatives. Ferment in school administrator preparation allows for exploring alternatives generated without as well as within the boundaries of the United States. Canada and Australia, for example, have well-established administrator preparation programs, and more recently rich and varied approaches have been institutionalized in most countries of Western Europe (Buckley, 1985). It is the intent of this paper to examine one of the more developed European models—the British—with the intent of determining what might be learned that could inform and enrich pre- and in-service administrator training in the United States.

At the outset, however, I will state explicitly my basic assumptions and their corollaries as they guided my inquiry. In unranked order they were:

Assumption # 1. No compelling evidence exists to support the claim of "one best way" of training school administrators.
Corollary # 1. Almost any program can be rationalized, but some rationalizations are more compelling than others.
Assumption # 2. Viable alternatives to current practices exist.
Corollary # 2. To a closed mind no alternative is viable.
Assumption # 3. Learning from one another is possible given contextual and functional similarities.
Corollary # 3. Learning is not aping. Recall the U.S. experience with the British "open classroom."
Assumption # 4. Change is threatening.
Corollary # 4. Failure to change may be more threatening.
Assumption # 5. History is both bane and blessing.
Corollary # 5. It helps to be able to tell the difference.

Finally, a few words about the genesis and structure of this paper are in order. I have been a professor of educational administration for the past sixteen years and a department chair for eight of them. During that period of time I have been involved in a variety of program design activities. Further, during the fall of 1985 I spent three months in the United Kingdom focusing to a large extent on the question, "What's the nature of school administrator training here?" I gained an initial purchase on that question by attending the annual meeting of the British Educational Management and Administration Society and subsequently through immersion in the British literature on school administration, visiting campuses, attending a variety of other meetings, and, most important, engaging in dialogue with a considerable number of faculty colleagues in the United Kingdom. From these activities partial answers to the "What's the nature of . . . ' and "What can be learned . . . ' questions were derived.

The first part of this paper briefly presents my understanding of the historic and contemporary social forces that have shaped and continue to shape the training of school administrators in the United Kingdom. The second part answers the "What's the nature of . . . " question directly but incompletely by describing selected facets of such programs. Three things should be borne in mind, however: (1) the variation in administrator training programs is extraordinarily wide and rich; (2) systematic administrator training as a recent development is marked by fluidity and "conflicting tendencies and unresolved issues" (Hughes, 1986); and (3) program characteristics presented for discussion were selected largely on the basis of their contrast with their U.S. counterparts and hence their capacity to generate alternatives. The latter issue is the focus of the third part of this paper, in which the "What can be learned . . . " question is addressed through a series of "What if . . . " questions. The paper concludes by presenting four choices available to the field of educational administration in the United States.

The Social Context of Administrator Training in the United Kingdom

The major premise of structural contingency theory is that there is no one best way of structuring an organization, but given a set of contingencies (for example, technology, history, environmental press, goals, and norms) there may be an optimal way of doing so. Minor premises include assumptions about the press for effectiveness, agreement on the dimensions and measurability of effectiveness, and the presence of sufficient organizational authority to secure coordinated, goal-oriented activity. Contingency theory, however, is not limited to organizational design: It is equally applicable to program design. This part of the paper attempts to identify those historic and contemporary contingencies that have been instrumental in shaping administrator training in the United Kingdom. Contingent similarities and differences between the United Kingdom and the United States will be described.

Similarities

An American observer of the contemporary educational scene in Great Britain is struck by a set of similarities between the countries. Headlines trumpet, for example, "Teachers' Union in New Strike Threat"; "Well-paid Staff Seen as Key to Quality in Schools as Support for Action Hardens"; and "Teacher Union will Oppose Appraisal."[1] Articles on pay disputes, curriculum reform, cuts in funding, student test performance, merit pay, the length of the school day, multicultural education, declining enrollments ("falling rolls"), white flight, and the plight of inner-city schools are part of the daily fare. Professional associations and professional politicians alike are cognizant of such issues. For example, the theme for the 1985 Annual Conference of the British Management and Administration Society was "Education and the Market Place: The Changing Roles of Resources, Producers, and Consumers," and the keynote speaker for the conference, the Rt. Hon. Neil Kinnoch, M.P., developed his remarks around the issues of parental choice (vouchers and choice of school included), curriculum reform, and standards (the decline in standardized test scores). Finally, there has been increased concern "for standards of efficiency and effectiveness" and the concomitant press for educational administrators at all institutional levels to draw on the

---

[1] *The Times Educational Supplement* is the best single source for determining the most pressing current issues.

accumulated wisdom of industrial and commercial managers (Department of Education and Science, 1985c). As Taylor (1976) wryly observes, there is a high positive correlation between the public's demand for efficiency and the fiscal resources required to support the enterprise. These issues sound all too familiar.

And Differences

Despite the above contextual similarities a set of contingencies has made the British experience in educational administration unique. Among the most significant historically have been social stratification based on birth, the headmaster tradition, and the governance structure of education. Among these three, the most powerful has been " . . . the self-conscious stratification of English society [in which] processes such as leadership, management, and decision-making can be seen more as properties of behavior of certain classes than as actions associated with the performance of particular tasks"(Hoyles, 1968).

The belief system embedded in that "self-concious stratification" gave rise to the great nineteenth century English "public" (that is, private) schools, and it was in those boarding schools that the behaviors of "certain social classes" were nurtured over extended periods of time.

Intimately related to and derived from the public schools was the headmaster tradition, the principal factor in shaping the twentieth-century "maintained" secondary school headmastership (Baron, 1956). Briefly, the early-nineteenth-century head was likely to be an Oxbridge- (Oxford-Cambridge) educated gentleman and clergyman whose essential task was to run a custodial institution (Bernbaum, 1976). Over time the definition of the role came to include: (1) a highly personal and charismatic leadership style; (2) high paternalism (the "pater pattern") (Ree, 1968); expressive rather than instrumental leadership;[2] high autonomy and autocracy;[3] and amateurism in administration. As Bernbaum (1976, p. 25) observed, "It has often been a source of pride to profess one's lack of expertise in the business of organization and administration. A concern for skill in management has been something to disown since it is felt that it affects one's profession as an educator." Further, until very recently this sentiment has been pervasive.

---

[2] The classic statement about the primacy of expressive leadership was attributed to Thomas Arnold, Headmaster at Rugby: "My object will be to form Christian men, for Christian boys I can scarcely hope to make" (cited in Peters, 1976a).

[3] The classic statement on this point is from the Headmaster of Uppenham, Dr. Thring: "I am supreme here and will brook no interference" (cited in Peters, 1976b, p. 2).

According to Taylor (1976, p. 46), "It is likely that as yet only a minority of serving heads and senior staff have had opportunities to experience any form of systematic in-service training in school administration, and fewer still have been exposed to courses that embody a thorough-going management approach."[4]

Clearly, both the historic British attitude toward management training and the consequences of that attitude are at marked variance with the American experience. At a minimum, since the days of Cubberley and scientific management, American school administrators have in the main embraced "the cult of efficiency" embodied in management training (Callahan, 1962). Further, belief in the efficacy of such training has been instrumental in formulating licensure requirements, which have ensured that only individuals managerially trained have been appointed as school administrators.

More recently, however, the British perspective on headship and thus on the training of heads has changed significantly. Major factors affecting the change have been the 1944 Education Act, school reform and reorganization during the 1960s and 1970s, national debates focusing on education, the emergent "extended professionality" of teachers combined with strong trade unionism (Hoyles, 1973), societal incursions into once sacrosanct school boundaries, and consistent pressure from the Department of Education and Science to reconceptualize headship in terms of "consultation, team-work, and participation" (Department of Education and Science, 1977). All of these have combined to produce a less Dickensian conception of headship while simultaneously legitimating the need for managerial expertise formally acquired. In the latter regard change was clearly achieved. Buckley (1985) reports that by 1980, 1,600 students were enrolled in "long award-bearing courses" offered by twenty-two universities, thirteen polytechnics, and twenty-one other colleges of higher education (p. 86). In addition, over 20,000 individuals were registered for short courses of three to five days duration in that same year (p. 87). In short, the growth rate of programs in education management in the United Kingdom has, since 1972, been nothing short of phenomenal. Some sense of that can be obtained by reviewing the developmental history of programs in educational administration at the Ulster Polytechnic:

1972 First short course in Education Management offered jointly by the Faculty of Education and Centre for Management Education.
1977 Education Management option added to the in-service B.Ed.

---

[4] The same observation could be made of European school administrators' training in general. Buckley suggests 1971 as the initiation date for France, 1972 for England, 1974 for Norway, and 1976 for Sweden and the Netherlands. See Buckley, 1985.

1978 A part-time B.A. in Public Sector Studies introduced with a specialist option in Education.

1979 A one-year, full-time diploma in Education Management introduced.

1980 Approval process begun for a M.Sc. in Education Management.(Ulster Polytechnic, 1980, p. A1).

Finally, a brief description of the educational governance system in Great Britain seems important for understanding the context of administrator training. Educational governance in England and Wales is, as the Cambridgeshire *Handbook for Governors* puts it " . . . a partnership in responsibility, locally planned and administered, but set in a national context" (p. 1). In essence, there is a three-tiered governance structure—the central government represented by a Secretary of State heading the Department of Education and Science (DES); the local education authorities (LEAs), of which there 104 in England and Wales and which operate functionally as subcommittees of the county (shire) or city councils; and the local "governing bodies," which are, in effect, individual schools' school boards. The DES establishes national priorities, allocates fiscal resources, establishes teachers' salaries and staffing formulas, and communicates its concerns to the LEAs. The LEAs, in consultation with the DES, build and equip schools, formally employ staff, and, in general have oversight over all schools within their jurisdictions, including colleges of "further and higher education" and polytechnics. Local governing bodies are charged with responding to community needs, and, in general, "with exercising the general direction of the conduct and curriculum of the school" (p. 5 of the *Handbook for Governors*).

Recent efforts to institutionalize administrator training provide a context for examining the tripartite governance arrangement. Following the debate on schools in the 1970s, Education Secretary Sir Keith Joseph announced a national initiative "to develop the [management] expertise needed to organize schools and their curriculum, and to handle resources" (Buckley, 1985). The three explicit objectives of this key 1982 initiative were: (1) to encourage the development of basic short courses (minimum twenty days) in school management on a regional basis; (2) to create a National Development Centre designed to develop a national management training capacity; and (3) to release experienced heads and senior staff on "secondments" (leave with full pay) to attend one-term training programs addressed to particular aspects of school management. In the latter case a multiplier effect was sought as trainees were expected to become trainers in their respective LEAs. Subsequently, the DES funded the initiative at six million pounds (approximately eleven million dollars). Thereafter, LEAs, singly or in consort, directly or indirectly through LEA-controlled polytechnics and colleges of further and higher education or in collaboration with non-LEA-controlled institutions (for example, universities) were charged with conducting managerial needs assessments, developing "courses" for DES approval, making funding applications, and approving secondments. Local governing bodies were held responsible for nominating heads or senior staff for secondments, securing staff replacements, identifying management issues for course inclusion, and approving the use of school facilities as training sites. In all of this the formal flow of influence was from top down, but in a historically conditioned way of heavily dependent on consultation with and receptivity to influence from below.

To summarize, it has been suggested that the contemporary British educational scene would, in many respects, appear quite familiar to an American. Appearances, however, are frequently deceptive, and close inspection would reveal some fundamental differences in attitudes toward and preparation for the role of school administrator. Ultimately such differences are rooted in social history and the evolution of social institutions. The twentieth-century conception of headship in the United Kingdom could, until fairly recently, trace its evolution through an unbroken, two-hundred-year-old, elite, clergy-dominated, private school tradition. In the United States, in contrast, the contemporary conception and practice of school administration evolved from an eighty-year-old, egalitarian, lay-oriented, public school tradition. Only recently, and largely as a function of similar economic pressures, have those two traditions begun to merge. In the United Kingdom, headship is being leavened with management, and in the United States, management with headship.[5] It is the blending of these two distinct traditions that makes mutual learning both possible and profitable.

Initial Administrator Training in the United Kingdom

Introduction

This section identifies selected features of administrator training programs in the United Kingdom that appear to have considerable potential for generating alternatives in training programs in the United States. However, in order to provide a context for comparison, a generalized thumbnail sketch of initial (M.A./M.Ed.) administrator training programs in the United States will be presented first.

---

[5] Such melding appears to be taking place independently on both sides of the Atlantic; neither side appears conscious of the other. Yet much of the best current literature on effective schools, institutional leadership, and organizational culture has much in common with the best of headship.

U.S. Programs

Students enrolled in initial (preservice) administrator training programs in the United States typically are tenured teachers who have five to ten years classroom experience but little or no administrative experience. The motivation for enrollment appears to be a combination of the desire for new challenges, professional advancement (out of the classroom and into the office!), and salary advancement. Part-time study is the norm, with students enrolled at their own expense for a course or so per semester over a period of three to five years.

Programs of study tend to consist of ten to fifteen loosely linked three-hour courses, to be sensitive to state certification requirements, and to be distributed (unevenly) over intellectual and clinical training. Taught syllabuses and instrumental learning are the norm, and considerable choice exists vis-à-vis electives. Independent study tends to be minimized, and the thesis as the culminating experience for the master's degree is becoming increasingly rare.

Programs are typically under the jurisdiction of university graduate schools and are offered by departments of educational administration or larger units under which educational administration is subsumed. Programs are typically developed and taught by faculty largely independent of LEA input, and approved via internal university processes; external approval is secured, if at all, for state or regional accreditation purposes. University policies govern most administrative processes connected with the program, and processes such as semi-annual admissions tend to become highly routinized. Given these characteristics of U.S. administrator training programs, British alternatives can be examined.

1. In-service/Professional Development Emphasis

In part, the in-service professional development emphasis is a function of: (1) the British assumption that heads need teaching experience before moving into administrative roles; (2) the headmaster tradition; (3) the absence of unique administrator certification requirements; (4) school reform and reorganization, which created new organizational leadership demands; and (5) a pervasive sense of urgency to respond to societal demands for increased school efficiency and effectiveness. Clearly it was the latter factor that impelled the 1982 DES initiative. More recently that same sense of urgency within the context of fiscal austerity has been articulated by the DES in its expressed preference for LEA-sponsored "short and sharply focussed" non-award-bearing courses (Department of Education and Science, 1985a). Such courses, in contrast to long, generalized award-bearing courses, are perceived by the DES "to represent good value for [the] money" (Department of Education and Science, 1985a) in addition to being "more effective for many purposes." (Department of Education and Science, 1985b, p. 53) In order to implement this policy preference, the DES has also shifted to direct block grant funding to LEAs for in-service purposes. LEAs are nominally free to allocate funds as they see fit, but are equally constrained by DES "guidelines of priorities." All of this is to say that in Great Britain the in-service and professional development of school administrators is a matter of national import. It is clearly reflected in, for example, the "Rationale for the Diploma in Professional Studies in Education" offered by the Oxford Polytechnic (1984, p. 6):

> Proposals for the Diploma arose from the growing recognition of the need to provide those members of schools and colleges who exercise responsibility beyond that of the normal teaching function with the skill necessary to meet the organizational and administrative demands of a complex and dynamic institution.

Given the in-service and professional development focus, the target population is also specified as at the Ulster Polytechnic (1980, p. A7):

> The course [M.Sc. in Education Management] is intended especially for principals and senior staff in schools and colleges.

Even more specifically:

> It is hoped that participants [in the 22-Day Management Course for Secondary Headteachers, 1986] will have had at least five years experience as a headteacher . . . [Mid-Kent College of Higher and Further Education, 1986, p. 1.]

There is ample evidence to suggest that the target audience has been reached. The University of Birmingham reports, for example, that the 1985–86 School Organization and Management Course counted among its members one head, three deputy heads, one acting head, four department heads, two heads of year, three teachers, and one assistant teacher. Equally, the Scottish Centre for Studies in School Administration reported that sixty-four head teachers, sixty-nine deputy heads, fifty assistant head teachers, and nine principal teachers attended twelve courses offered under its auspices in 1984–85 (The Scottish Centre for Studies in School Administration, 1984/85). Finally, Hughes, Carter, and Fidler report that 53 percent of the non-award-bearing primary management courses and 39 percent of the secondary management courses provided by LEAs were for heads only or for heads and senior staff (Hughes, Carter, and Fidler, 1981). Other indicators of the in-service and professional development focus are present. The Open University, for example, markets its programs as "Professional Development in Education."

A second indicator of the in-service emphasis is the delivery of off-campus services. A publication of the Cambridge Institute of Education (CIE), for example, reads in part, "In addition to courses currently running in Bedford,

Colchester, and Ipswich, new part-time courses will start in September in Cambridge, Kings Lynn, and Letchworth (Cambridge Institute of Education, 1985, p. 2). A third indicator, as implied in the above, is recognition of the full-time role of the professional in organizing part-time programs. As a matter of fact, full-time-only programs are relatively rare, with part-time programs or parallel part-time and full-time programs the norm. Such part-time programs may be variously organized—as "part-time day release," as "block release," as evenings only, as weekends only, or in some combination of part-time and full-time study. A fourth indicator is that "course providers" are likely to identify themselves institutionally with in-service functions. The CIE, for example, defines itself as ". . . a centre for in-service education of teachers and research in education (Cambridge Institute of Education, 1985, p. 2). Further, the director of the CIE spoke of its ethos as "consciously parochial," that is, officially and in practice attendant to the particular needs of educators in its East Anglia service area.

Parochialism is strongly associated with a fifth indicator of an in-service emphasis—strong LEA linkages. In part, such linkages are a function of the governance structure of higher education, which places colleges of further and higher education and the polytechnics under the jurisdiction of the LEAs. Those legally binding linkages are maintained through such administrative devices as LEA-sanctioned "secondments" and institutional requirements for "professional references" as part of the matriculation process. But in much larger part, the course provider-consumer linkage is a function of institutional commitment to in-service and professional development programs and a shared mission.

2. Diploma Emphasis

Closely related to the in-service emphasis is the award-bearing diploma emphasis. It is far more likely that persons currently enrolled in "long, award-bearing" courses in the United Kingdom will be working toward completion of a professional diploma equivalent to the Education Specialist or Certificate of Advanced Study than a graduate degree.[6] In part this is accounted for by the location of diploma programs in the structure of higher education. On this point the *Prospectus 1986–87* of the Institute of Education, University of London, reads: "In the Institutes 'progression of qualifications' diploma courses stand midway between initial training 'certificate courses' and the taught Master's courses and research degrees in education" (Institute of Education, 1986, p. 91). Several explanatory comments may be in

---

[6] It is expected, however, that as the cadre of B.Ed.persons increases, the shift will be away from the diploma and toward the M.A. This trend is already in evidence at, for example, the London Institute of Education.

order. First, the "progression of qualification" refers to the degree or program sequence, that is, certificate, bachelor's degree, diploma, master's degree, doctorate. Note that the diploma precedes rather than follows the master's degree. This is crucial, as will be pointed out shortly. Second, the reference to "initial training 'certificate' courses" must be understood in relation to entry into teaching in the United Kingdom. There are three basic modes of entry: (1) via a three-year certificate program (the historic norm); (2) via completion of a four-year combined B.Ed. *and* professional training program (rare, but possible in selected fields at, for example, the West London Institute of Education and Brunel University), and (3) via a baccalaurate degree other than the B.Ed. *plus* a 1-year Post-graduate Certificate in Education (PGCE). Third, and more relevant to understanding the emphasis on diploma rather than degree programs, the pattern of options for entry into teaching is also operative for admission to diploma and certificate programs. For example, and to draw again upon the University of London's Institute of Education to illustrate, six options are available for admission to the diploma program, only one of which requires the baccalaureate. Similarly, three options are available for entry to the master's program, including (roughly speaking) (1) a B.Ed. with honors, (2) a first degree plus an approved teaching qualification, and (3) an approved non-graduate certificate in Education plus a Diploma in Education. In short, the diploma program provides a mechanism for non-degree-holding teachers (the majority) to engage in advanced study at a professional level. Further, it may be used as a screening mechanism for the master's program. In, for example, the M.Sc. *or* Diploma in Education Management ("linked scheme") offered by the Crewe and Alsager College of Higher Education, admission to the M.Sc. is contingent on obtaining the "necessary standard" in the diploma portion of the program.

Four other factors help explain the popularity of diploma courses. First, the diploma as an academic award in its own right carries considerable status. As the London Institute's *Prospectus* observes, ". . . a diploma qualification is of considerable standing in its own right and certifies that the student has undergone a course which requires advanced and specialist study . . . recognized by the Department of Education and Science . . ." (Institute of Education, 1986, p. 91). Second, it may well be that the instrumental training needs of school administrators are more effectively satisfied through the course structure of diploma programs than the research structure of graduate programs. Third, the context of training may provide a bias toward the *practice* rather than the *study* of administration. Most administrator training programs are conducted under the auspices of LEA-controlled polytechnics and of further and higher education colleges rather than the universities. Even in the latter case, LEA linkages may be very tight. Insofar as LEAs are likely to have a pragmatic orientation, the practice-oriented diploma intuitively fits better than the theoretically oriented graduate degree. Fourth, the magnitude of the training task and the "progression of qualifications" in British universities conspire to emphasize the diploma courses. This condition is likely to prevail in the foreseeable future.

3. Experiental Learning

Closely related conceptually to in-service training and professional development is experiential learning. As used here, experiential learning is an umbrella term encompassing three kinds of learning—instrumental, dialogic, and self-reflective (Mezirow, 1985). Instrumental learning is essentially task focused, prescriptive, and based on models of technical learning rooted in the "empirical sciences" (Marsick and Watkins, 1986). Dialogic learning takes a more qualitative, conventionalist stance in its focus on apprehension of the meaning framework of organizational participants. Self-reflective learning focuses on personal change, and essentially involves a process of "perspective transformation" through "critical reflectivity," that is, "the bringing of one's assumptions, premises, criteria, and schemata into consciousness and vigorously critiquing them" (Mezirow, 1985).

The argument for incorporating large portions of experiential learning into administrator training programs has been made by Dennison (1985). In brief, he argues that management is a skill-centered rather than a knowledge-based undertaking, and hence experiential learning is the preferred instructional mode. In U.S. programs, such learning is largely evidenced in the "clinical" portions of preparation programs, such as internships, and is largely limited to instrumental learning.

A somewhat different approach to experiential learning exists in certain programs in the United Kingdom. At Ulster Polytechnic, for example, experiential learning is at the heart of the M.Sc. in Education Management. In developing its 1980 Proposal to the Council for National Academic Awards, the Planning Team took the position that "the professional experience of the participants should be the proper focus of the course (Ulster Polytechnic, 1980, p. A3). Further, one of the aims of the program was to "help participants interpret their managerial experience critically through exposure to the views and experiences of others"(p. A9).Thus students "would be expected to test the theories being studied against their own experience of innovation and to examine and clarify the bases of their practice"(p. B20). Finally, the students would be assessed in part on "evidence of the development of personal understanding and the generation of new insights"(p. B31). Clearly, what was intended in the program was not instrumental but dialogic and self-reflective learning to an extraordinary degree.

4. Program Design, Content, and Assessment

An American viewing administrator training programs in the United Kingdom is struck by four design features—holism, limited flexibility, the provision for substantial independent work, and rigorous assessment. Each will be discussed in turn.

Holism has multiple facets. At its simplest it refers to the organic unity of the program. In part, that unity is communicated by a language system that speaks simply of "the course." Further, if the course is structurally subdivided, and that is not necessarily the case, the subunits are large—Parts A and B (The Open University, Sheffield City Polytechnic), Parts I and II (North East Wales Institute of Higher Education), or Stages I and II (Mid-Kent College of Higher and Further Education). Similarly, subdivisions within the parts or stages tend to be large. The North East Wales Institutes' Part I (theoretical background) has four units—The Environmental Context of School Management, The School as an Organization, Curriculum Management, and Management of Change. In short, the missed frameworks are radically different from American patterns of multiple, discrete three-hour units.

Holism is also reflected in internal program consistency or emphasis. A probable planned program for an M.A. student at Brunel University with an emphasis in school administration would be:

    Group I: Theories and Methods
            a. Methods in Social Research
            b. Social and Political Thought Underlying Social Policy
            c. The History of Social Policy and Administration
    Group II: Social Policy and Administration
    Group III: Educational Policies and Government
    Group IV: Dissertation

The policy focus throughout the course is obvious.

Implicitly embedded in the program described above is a second major design feature—*limited student choice*. Programs as a whole tend to be tightly structured; electives are reasonably rare events. This is particularly true with respect to the "taught" portion of the program, usually Part I. The operative assumption appears to be that students have exercised choice upon entry, and further individualization is accomplished through independent study.

Independent study is accorded far greater importance in U.K. than in U.S. administrator training programs. Where programs are divided into parts or stages, it is not uncommon for Part II or B to be devoted to independent study with few, if any, taught courses. For example, in the Crewe and Alsager "linked" M.Sc./Diploma in Educational Management, the M.Sc. portion has only one taught course, "Research and Evaluation Methodology," and that course "is not formally assessed"(Crewe and Alsager College of Higher Education, n.d., p. 16). Part II of the Sheffield City Polytechnic's M.Sc. in Educational Management is "The individual study program" and consists in part of an individual field project and "five assignments usually negotiated individually." Part II of the North East Wales Institute's program is a ten-thousand-word project, and in the Ulster Polytechnic program described earlier, thirty of the ninety weeks of the course are set aside for independent study. In brief, it is not unusual to find one-half to one-third of a management training program set aside for supervised independent study. Such emphasis is conceptually consistent with experiential learning.

Finally, it is appropriate to note the emphasis placed on *formal assessment of performance*. Such assessment may be formative or summative (the Cambridge Institute would rank high on the former; the London Institute high on the latter); written or oral; examination-based or project- or dissertation-based; conducted by internal or external examiners. But whatever the configuration of the above variables, assessment is taken seriously. To draw again from the Ulster Polytechnic (1980) Proposal:

> There are eight assignments throughout the course which form the assessment items. These are:
> - one assignment of 4,000 words in each of the syllabuses—Context, Decision-Making, and Innovation
> - two assignments of 4,000 words each in Organization
> - one assignment of 4,000 words in Group Studies
> - the Project (10,000 words). [P. A20]

The Proposal goes on to note that the project "will be assessed by the Internal and External Examiners, and will normally include a *viva voce* examination" (p. A21). Further, it will be assessed on the basis of five explicit criteria, including potential value to the "host organization" as well as the "potential contribution to the improvement of the participant's personal managerial capabilities" (p. B31).

Finally, it must be noted that while assessment on the basis of written papers is the norm, and indeed the London Institute of Education described the substance of its "Examination" for the diploma in terms of "four papers, two for each of the subjects taken," (p. 94), course or final examinations as we know them in the United States are not unknown. An excerpt from the *Assessment Requirements* at Brunel University makes this clear: "Students must take an advance notice examination in Group III (Special Subject). Three questions must be answered in essay form in a specified period of five weeks. They will carry 75% of the Group III marks" (Brunel University, 1986, p. 7).

5. Institutional Processes

Four institutional processes round out the description of administrator training programs—legitimation, admissions, staffing, and scheduling. Each will be considered briefly.

Legitimation. Legitimation refers to the process of securing both internal and external program approval. The internal processes are not substantially different from those in the United States, but the legitimation process becomes more complex and tedious, as approval must also be secured from either the Council for National Academic Awards or one of the royally chartered, degree-granting universities. While the combination of internal and external reviews presumably increases quality control, the external review by a national body also reflects the tripartite system of governance, particularly with respect to the funding implications of new programs.

Admissions. Admissions processes in the United States and the United Kingdom are, with two exceptions, quite similar. The first exception is that ordinarily students are admitted annually only. This is consistent with the highly structured nature of most programs, particularly with respect to the "taught syllabuses," and the administrative constraints associated with "secondments." The second exception strictly speaking refers more to program options than admissions per se. It is simply noted here that the range of programs to which a student might be admitted to study school administration is wider than in the United States. At the University of London Institute of Education, for example, such options include the B.Ed., the Postgraduate Certificate in Education, the Diploma in Education, the Specialist Diploma, the M.A., the M.Phil., the Ph.D., and the Associate of the Institute.

Staffing. Several dimensions of staffing need to be considered. The first identifies the academic unit or units authorized to offer the course. In the United States the authorized unit almost without exception is a department of educational administration or a somewhat larger unit of which educational administration is a part. This is not necessarily the case in the United Kingdom. Programs at the Cambridge Institute of Education, for example, are sponsored by the Institute, while the Diploma in Education Management offered by Oxford Polytechnic is jointly sponsored by the Department of Educational Development and the Department of Management and Business Studies. In brief, the training of school administrators in Great Britain tends to be a more widely shared function than in the United States.

Second, four discrete staffing patterns can be identified. From more to less similar to U.S. patterns, they are: (1) responsibility for the program divided among faculty within or outside the sponsoring department, each of whom takes individual responsibility for one or more courses; (2) team teaching, but with a designated team leader ("course convener"); (3) heavy reliance on guest lecturers drawn from the ranks of practicing administrators, but under the general supervision of an instructor of record; and (4) major if not sole responsibility assigned to a course tutor.

The tutorial system, that is, a pattern of highly individualized interaction between tutors and students, is a distinguishing feature of higher education in the United Kingdom. It is a long-standing system, closely linked to the research-based model of the ancient universities yet conceptually and operationally consistent with the emphases on professional development, independent study, dialogic and self-reflective learning, and, more generally, on learning rather than teaching. This configuration is at considerable variance with U.S. practice and belief, and its corresponding emphases on large lecture classes, "taught syllabuses," instrumental learning, and teaching. Few U.S. students have genuine tutorial experiences short of the dissertation. However, the British propensity for tutorials is also a response of necessity. Department faculties in British universities tend to be small: faculties of one are not uncommon; faculties of ten to twenty, as in the United States, are. The entire 1985 tutorial staff of the Cambridge Institute of Education, for example, numbered sixteen, including two on study leave.

Scheduling. Three features of course scheduling ("timetabling," to use the British vernacular) strike an American observer. First, scheduling tends to be long range. A two- or three-year program may be plotted out entirely in advance, including lecture dates, examination dates, specified course topics, readings, and the like. Second, few, if any, provisions are made for accomodating individual student schedules, preferences, or other contingencies. This is consistent with the general stance toward limited flexibility. Third, time frames for program completion tend to be brief and inflexible statements like, "The dissertation must be submitted by 5:00 P.M. on the last working day of January following year two of the course" (Oxford Polytechnic, 1984, p. 24). In short, the flexibility accorded most U.S. students with respect to program completion is conspicuously absent.

To summarize, the second part of this paper has described selected features of initial administrator preparation programs in the United Kingdom, many of which vary from their U.S. counterparts. These variations are summarized in Table 33–1.

Implications

In the introduction to this paper this question was posed: "What might be learned from the British experience in educational administration that could enrich and inform pre- and in-service professional training in the United States?" Subsequently, the first part sketched some contingencies that have shaped the British experience, and the second part provided data on that experience as it is reflected in administrator training programs. This third part considers the implications of that experience for U.S. practice through a series of "What if . . ." questions. The questions are illustrative of "what might be learned," and are designed primarily to provoke thought.

Table 33–1

Major Variations Between the United Kingdom and the United States in Initial Administrator Preparation Programs

Program Variables	U.K. Practice	U.S. Practice
Program emphasis	In-service/professional development	Preservice/graduate
Program intent	Enhancement of individual and group skills (multiplier effect)	Enhancement of individual skills
Field relations	Strong LEA linkages ("parochial")	Weak LEA linkages ("cosmopolitan")
Initial award granted	Diploma	M.A. or M.Ed.
Mode of learning	Major emphasis on dialogic and self-reflective learning	Major emphasis on instrumental learning
Mode of instruction	Tutorial; individual and small group	Large group lecture
Program design	Holistic/tightly linked	Fragmented/loosely linked
Degree of choice	Limited	Broad
Independent study	Strong emphasis	Weak emphasis
Assessment	Cumulative with emphasis on formal papers	Examination based
Program legitimation	Internal and external	Essentially internal only
Staffing	Heavy reliance on tutors and part-time staff	Heavy reliance on department faculty
Admissions	Annually by cadre ("members of the course")	Semi-annually and individually
Scheduling	Long term; relatively inflexible	Short term; relatively flexible

1. What if administrator training programs were oriented more toward in-service and professional development and less toward preservice and role entry preparedness?

Proponents of such a stance have a fairly strong case. If indeed there will be a 70 percent turnover in the elementary principalship within the next five years as some predict, and if the vast majority of those potential administrators have already been trained and credentialed, then it seems reasonable to begin shifting the emphasis from preservice to in-service (*Education Week*, 1986; *Wall Street Journal*, 1986). Further, one could argue that the demand for enhanced principal competencies targets individuals already in the administrative role, and to shift the training focus in that direction would indeed constitute responsiveness.

Opponents of such a shift might claim that current licensure requirements lead training institutions to emphasize pre-service. But suppose that objection could be overcome. What are some of the benefits and costs that might accrue? First, the U.K. experience would suggest that training institutions and their clients would be brought closer together. Second, it might cause trainers to become more attentive to the needs of trainees, and consequently persuade LEAs of the importance of professional development. "Secondments" need not remain a solely British institution.

Costs would also be incurred. "Conscious parochialism" is largely antithetical to "national reputation" and "cosmopolitanism." Service might have to replace research in the institutional reward structure of higher education. Narrow faculty specialization would of necessity be superseded by breadth of knowledge anchored in experience. As exemplars of costs, these are not insignificant.

2. What if administrator training emphasized experiential rather than academic learning?

Substantial ambivalence concerning experiential learning exists. A recent UCEA document entitled "Proposed Program for the Preparation of Educational Administrators" makes this quite clear. The draft criticizes contemporary programs for being too much "*about* educational administration rather than being *in* educational administration" (Hoyle, 1986, p.1) (emphasis in original), and recommends that programs should be "a blend of both intellectual and clinical training" (p. 2). However, a close reading of the document shows a decided bias toward the intellectual. Even the "clinical experiences" have a high cognitive component. The desired experience inferred in the "record of leadership" requirement for admissions is largely ignored as a learning resource.

Suppose it were otherwise. Glatter (1972, p. 4) has suggested that ". . . the main function of training is to assist administrators to structure and analyze their own and their colleagues' experience so that they may use it more effectively as their principal learning resource." Clearly, according to Glatter, the major outcome of experiential learning is learning how to learn, and the pathway to such learning is marked by dialogue and self-reflection. This is a far cry from mastering instrumental skills no matter how strongly they may be anchored in the "empirical sciences."

Shifting from instrumental to experiential learning may also produce other favorable outcomes. The emphases in training programs might shift from teaching to learning, analyses of reality might replace analyses of simulations, and in the process a library of professional case data might be developed. Perhaps, too, the perceived gap between theory and practice might be reduced through engaging in "critical reflectivity." The latter outcome of itself would be no small accomplishment.

There would, of course, be costs, many perhaps in the psychological domain. It would be no easy matter to view students (and professors!) differently or to elevate learning above teaching. Imagine the trauma involved in selecting the Learner of the Year rather than the Teacher of the Year. The status quo is not relinquished easily.

3. What if administrator training programs were to be role and organization specific?

An article of faith of twentieth-century administrative science is that administration qua administration contains a large proportion of common variance. Consequently, major program differentiation by role or organization is warranted neither theoretically nor practically. But suppose one rejected this assumption as some U.K. colleagues do, and argued that the roles of superintendent, assistant principal, clinical supervisor, business manager, and so on and organizations like schools, school districts, state departments, corporations, and so on are substantially different and thus warrant basically different programs? Hypothetically, several things might happen simultaneously: (1) the number of programs might increase but focus might sharpen; (2) enrollments might rise overall but fall in specific programs; (3) faculties in cooperation with LEAs might have to really define priorities; (4) cooperative action might increase as a means of reducing resource strain; and (5) the concept of practice might receive more than lip service in training programs. The list of possibilities is almost endless, but one certainty is that old assumptions about program content would have to be reexamined.

4. What if administrator training programs were tightened and simplified through the elimination of electives and discrete courses?

Electives are democratically conceived "good" things, equally justified on the basis of uncertainty about the future and respect for freedom of choice.

But suppose one were to argue that given the strategic importance of schooling in society and the significance of the leadership role in schooling, student freedom of choice should be limited to the matriculation decision and subsequently constrained by the professional judgment of trainers and practitioners? Surely such a stance would increase trainer accountability, a sadly missing current element.

A similar statement could be made about most discrete courses. Fragmentation, frequently discipline based, is a notable characteristic of administrator training programs in the United States. Its roots lie in the presumed preeminence and economies of specialization in an academic context, and it is manifested in catalogues of discrete course offerings. Integration is left largely to students and to chance.

The British model as illustrated in the second part of this paper is quite different and offers a more integrated alternative. Further, the current emphasis in U.S. circles on "competencies" or "functions" provides an opportunity for restructuring programs along different lines. Imagine, for example, a master's program for school principals structured around four functions—the management of curriculum, the management of human resources, operations management, and the management of the environment. Imagine also that no further course specifications were permitted, that is, that traditional course content presented under such course titles as School Law or Supervision of Instruction would have to be incorporated into the new structure or deleted from the program. Finally, imagine a program for which course hours were computed after the syllabus was developed rather than before. The effects of such a reconceptualization might be quite salutary in forcing reconsideration of content, integration, and focus.

5. What if administrator training programs were designed to maximize independent study?

Ambivalence surrounds independent study as it surrounds experiential learning. Perhaps this is because the two are closely related. Also, like experiential learning, independent study in the United States is honored more in the breach than in the main. Even doctoral programs in the United States, to say nothing about M.A. and Ed.S. programs, consist largely of "taught" courses, internships and dissertations notwithstanding.

Imagine the consequences of shifting that emphasis, at least at the advanced levels. The consequences would be profound. Program emphases would shift from teaching to learning, paralleling the shift from instrumental to self-reflective and critical learning. Admissions committees might require an applicant to submit a prospectus detailing what was to be learned and how (interning as a possibility) rather than a Miller Analogies Test score. Institutionally defined "residencies" would become irrelevant as would the accumulation of credit hours. "Teaching" would largely be replaced by "tutoring." All of these are, of course, hypothesized outcomes, but if even a fraction of them were supported, the impact on current practice would be substantial.

Conclusion

Reference was made in the introduction to this paper to the ferment that pervades the field of educational administration. What ultimately will be distilled from that fermentation is uncertain, but what is clear is that the field is now faced with making some difficult choices. It can choose from among at least four available alternatives. One, the field can blindly embrace as its own the program revisions promulgated by third parties. Such a choice is likely to be applauded publicly. It is also a choice sanctioned by history and one that entails low risk. What it also does, however, is increase the probability of "bloody-mindedness," and cloak the abandonment of professional responsibility in the garment of public responsiveness.

Two, the field can persist in its present practices, that is, turn a deaf ear to the call for reform. Such a choice entails more risk, since external bodies will then surely act to influence the form and content of administrator training programs through, for example, certification mechanisms and perhaps the identification of trainers. And there is no reason to believe that university-based departments of educational administration will be the trainer of choice.

A third choice available is to reclothe the emperor. That is to say, old designs, concepts, and structures can be repackaged, and with full fanfare paraded as revision and reform. This choice, too, entails some risk—innocence, as the emperor discovered, has a way of unmasking sophistry.

Four, the field can search out and test creative alternatives. Further, if the search extends beyond national borders, the number of alternatives available will increase measurability. Clearly, engaging in this course of action is the choice advocated here. It also entails the greatest risk: favorable outcomes cannot be guaranteed. Some alternatives chosen may well fail—perhaps disastrously so. Some may succeed beyond anyone's wildest dreams. Most will fall somewhere between dreams and realities. However, given the present opportunity and imperative to change, the fourth alternative is surely the most desirable.

References

Baron, G. (1956). Some aspects of the headmaster tradition. *Researches and Studies* 14: 7–16.

Bernbaum, G. (1976). The role of the head. In R.S. Peters (Ed.), *The role of the head.* London: Routledge and Kegan Paul.

Brunel University (1986). *Master's degree course in public and social administration: 1986 handbook*, p. 7.

Buckley, J. (1985). *The training of secondary school heads in Western Europe.* Windsor, England: The NFER-Nelson Publishing Co., Ltd.

Callahan, R.E. (1962). *Education and the cult of efficiency.* Chicago: University of Chicago Press.

Cambridge Institute of Education. (1985). Brochure, p. 2.

Cambridge Institute of Education. *Research handbook.* n.d., p. 2.

Crewe and Alsager College of Higher Education (Faculty of Education). (n.d.). *M.Sc./postgraduate diploma in educational management*, p. 16.

Dennison, W.F. (1985). Training headteachers as managers: Current trends and developments. *The Durham and Newcastle Research Review* 2: 221–24.

Department of Education and Science. (1977). *Ten good schools: A secondary school inquiry.* London: HMSO.

Department of Education and Science. (1985a). *Further education in-service provision.* London: HMSO.

Department of Education and Science. (1985b). *Better schools.* London: HMSO, p. 53.

Department of Education and Science. (1985c). *The development of higher education into the 1990's.* London: HMSO.

Education Week. (1986, February 19) Better elementary principals called for. *Education Week* 23:7.

Glatter, R. (1972). *Management development for the education profession.* London: Geo. Harrap, Ltd.

Hoyles, E. (1968). The head as innovator. In B. Allen (Ed.), *Headship in the 1970's.* London: Basil Blackwell.

Hoyles, E. (1973). Strategies of curriculum change. In R. Watkins (Ed.), *In-service training: Structure and content.* London: Ward Lock.

Hoyle, J.R. (1975). Programs in educational administration and the AASA guidelines. *Educational Administration Quarterly* 21:71–93.

Hoyle, J.R. (1986). Proposed program for the preparation of educational administrators. Draft document.

Hughes, M. (1986). *Trends and issues in educational management development in England and Wales.* Paper presented at the 1986 Annual Meeting of the American Educational Research Association, San Francisco, Calif.

Hughes, M.; Carter, J.; and Fidler, B. (1981). *Professional development provision for senior staff in schools and colleges.* University of Birmingham, Department of Social and Administrative Studies.

Institute of Education, University of London. (1986). *Prospectus 1986–87.*

March J.G. (1974). Analytical skills and the university training of educational administrators. The 1973 Walter D. Cocking Lecture in Educational Administration. In J.D. Herring and R.E. Klimes (Eds.), *Walter D. Cocking lectures: The NCPEA series of prominent papers in educational administration*, pp. 93–161. Berrien Springs, Mich.: Center for Studies and Services in Education, Andrews University.

Marsick, V., and Watkins, K. (1986). *Learning and development in the workplace.* Paper prepared for the National Conference of the American Society for Training and Development.

Mezirow, J. (1985). A critical theory of self-directed learning. In S. Brookfield (Ed.), *Self-directed learning: From theory to practice.* San Francisco: Jossey-Bass.

Mid-Kent College of Higher and Further Education. (1986). *22-day management course for secondary headteachers 1986.*

Oxford Polytechnic. (1984). Application to the Council for National Academic Awards for the Re-approval of a Two-Year, Part-time Course Leading to the Award of a Diploma in Professional Studies in Education (Educational Management).

Peters, R.F. (Ed.) (1976a). *The role of the head.* London: Routledge and Kegan Paul.

Peters, R.F. (1976b). Introduction: Contemporary problems. In R.F. Peters (Ed.), *The role of the head.* London: Routledge and Kegan Paul.

Pitner, N. (1982). *Training the school administrator: The state of the art.* Eugene: CEPM University of Oregon. Chapter 28, this volume.

Ree, H. (1968). The changed role of the head. In B. Allen (Ed.), *Headship in the 1970's.* London: Basil Blackwell.

The Scottish Centre for Studies in School Administration. (1984/85). *Annual report—1984/85,* Appen. 2.

Taylor, W. (1976). The head as manager: Some criticisms. In R.S. Peters (Ed.), *The Role of the Head.* London: Routledge and Kegan Paul.

Ulster Polytechnic. (1980, November). *Master of science degree in educational management.* Proposal to the Council for National Academic Awards.

University Council for Educational Administration. (1983–1984). *Preparing leaders to anticipate and manage the future.* A Report in Four Parts. Columbus, Ohio: University Council for Educational Administration.

Wall Street Journal. (1986, February 18). Better principals, not just teachers.